PLATO, TIME, AND EDUCATION
ESSAYS IN HONOR OF
ROBERT S. BRUMBAUGH

PLATO, TIME, AND EDUCATION
ESSAYS IN HONOR OF
ROBERT S. BRUMBAUGH

edited by

BRIAN P. HENDLEY

State University of New York Press

Published by
State University of New York Press, Albany
©1987 State University of New York
For information, address State University of New York
Press, State University Plaza, Albany, N.Y., 12246

Library of Congress Cataloging-in-Publication Data
Plato, time, and education: essays in honor of Robert S. Brumbaugh /
    edited by Brian P. Hendley.
      p. cm.
    "Bibliography of the writings of Robert S. Brumbaugh": p. 317
    ISBN 0-88706-733-6. ISBN 0-88706-734-4 (pbk.)
    1. Plato. 2. Time. 3. Education—Philosophy. 4. Philosophy-
-History 5. Brumbaugh, Robert Sherrick, 1918- . I. Brumbaugh,
Robert Sherrick, 1918- . II. Hendley, Brian Patrick, 1939-
B395.P52 1987
100—dc19   87-21161
                                        CIP

10 9 8 7 6 5 4 3 2 1

To my parents, Bruce and Wynn Hendley

CONTENTS

Robert S. Brumbaugh

PREFACE

Robert S. Brumbaugh was born on December 2, 1918 in Oregon, Illinois. He married Ada Steele in 1940 and they have three children. After his education at the University of Chicago and service in the United States Army, Brumbaugh taught philosophy at various places, most notably at Yale where he has been a Professor of Philosophy since 1961. His interests include travel and archaeology, the New York Mets, and correspondence with students and colleagues. An illness in 1946 left him with a paralyzed left side and the assurance by his doctors that he would never have any gainful employment. He is retiring at the end of 1987 after 41 years of teaching; "employment," he notes, "if only modestly gainful".

This volume is a collection of original essays by former students and colleagues that is meant to pay tribute to the man and his work by exploring topics that have interested him through a long and productive career. The essays are grouped under general headings: Plato, Time, Education, and the History of Philosophy. Seventeen authors are included from the United States, Canada and Israel. Their approaches are different; but each is well grounded in the history of Philosophy and attempts to deal with issues in new and insightful ways that seek to stimulate further philosophical thinking in the spirit of Brumbaugh himself.

The volume is unified by our common desire to do honor to the man who through his scholarship, teaching, and ongoing friendship epitomizes for us what Whitehead called the imaginative scholar, that rare individual who combines the disciplined rigor of scholarly research with the romantic excitement of intellectual adventure. We have been privileged, each in our own way, to have been partners with Brumbaugh in some of his intellectual adventures. The book concludes with a bibliography of Brumbaugh's writings from 1947 to the present, listing some 15 books and well over a hundred articles.

Brian Hendley

Waterloo, Canada

ACKNOWLEDGEMENTS

I would like to thank Robert Neville, Rulon Wells, and the late Nathaniel Lawrence, who were among the earliest supporters of this project. The contributors to the book were uniformly enthusiastic about participating and willingly acceded to my strict deadlines. Other former students and colleagues of Bob Brumbaugh were also strongly supportive and made a number of helpful suggestions. Mrs. Nathaniel Lawrence kindly granted permission to publish her husband's essay. My colleagues, Larry Haworth and Joe Novak, were of great assistance in answering questions of style and scholarship, as was David Binkley of the Arts Library. My wife Margaret made time in her own busy schedule as a professional librarian to take on the arduous task of proof-reading.

Bill Eastman of SUNY Press liked the idea of a Brumbaugh *Festschrift* and backed my efforts from the start. The University of Waterloo provided much needed financial support from the Social Sciences and Humanities General Research Grant. This enabled me to hire Brian and Virginia MacOwan who had the technical expertise to input the manuscript on the computer, assist me with the copy-editing, and produce the camera-ready copy. I appreciated their patience and hard work, as well as the advice of Bruce Uttley of the Department of Computing Services and the help with the various figures from Graphic Services.

Finally, I would like to acknowledge the co-operation of Bob Brumbaugh himself. His own work has been the model and the stimulus for the essays in this book. Having known Bob for nearly twenty-five years, I can attest to the fact that teaching need not be incompatible with friendship. It is in the spirit of friendship that we present him with this collection of original essays in his honor.

CONTRIBUTORS

GEORGE ALLAN is Professor of Philosophy and Dean of Dickinson College (Carlisle, Pennsylvania). He has published articles on philosophical and educational topics and is author of *Importances of the Past: A Meditation on the Authority of Tradition* (1986).

ROBERT ANDERSON is an Associate Professor of Philosophy at Washington College in Chestertown, Maryland. His doctoral dissertation was a co-winner of the Jacob Cooper Prize for Greek Philosophy at Yale. He is completing a book on Plato's *Theaetetus*.

PHILIP BASHOR is Professor of Philosophy at the University of Arkansas and an organizing trustee of the Association for Process Philosophy of Education. His research has been in the areas of social philosophy and philosophy of religion.

MALCOLM BROWN has taught humanities, classics, and philosophy at various liberal arts colleges, most recently at Brooklyn College where he will retire as Professor of Philosophy in 1987. Author of a number of articles on Plato and his mathematical interests, he is also the builder of a hydroelectric powerplant at Jeffersonville, New York.

ROBERT HAHN is an Associate Professor of Philosophy at Southern Illinois University at Carbondale. He has published several articles on Plato and Aristotle and is the author of a forthcoming book, *Kant's Newtonian Revolution in Philosophy*. Winner of the Mary Kady Teu Prize in Philosophy, Hahn's dissertation won the Jacob Cooper Prize for Greek Philosophy at Yale.

BRIAN HENDLEY is Chairman of the Department of Philosophy at the University of Waterloo (Ontario). He has written articles on medieval philosophy and the philosophy of education and is the author of *Dewey, Russell, Whitehead: Philosophers as Educators* (1986).

BEREL LANG is Professor of Philosophy and Humanistic Studies and Director of the Center for the Humanities at the State University of New York at Albany. His books include *Art and Inquiry* (1975), *Philosophy and the Art of Writing* (1983), and *Faces, and Other Ironies* (1983).

HELEN LANG is an Associate of Philosophy at Trinity College (Hartford). She has published a number of articles on both Greek and medieval philosophy and has lectured both in the United States and abroad.

NATHANIEL LAWRENCE died in Williamstown, Massachusetts in March, 1986, where he had taught Philosophy at Williams College since 1960. Author of *Whitehead's Philosophical Development* (1956), *Alfred North Whitehead* (1974), and (with R. Brumbaugh) *Philosophers on Education* (1963) and *Philosophical Themes in Modern Education* (1973), he was also an accomplished naturalist, a gifted and imaginative traveller, and a great teacher.

ERNEST McCLAIN is Emeritus Professor of Music at Brooklyn College of the City University of New York. His books include *The Myth of Invariance* (1976), *The Pythagorean Plato* (1978), and *Meditations Through the Quran* (1981).

ALEXANDER MOURELATOS has taught at the University of Texas at Austin since 1965, where he organized and continues to direct the Joint Classics-Philosophy Graduate Program in Ancient Philosophy. His publications have been on topics of pre-Socratic philosophy, Plato's astronomy, Aristotle's natural philosophy, and linguistics.

GEORGE KIMBALL PLOCHMANN was Professor of Philosophy at Southern Illinois University until 1982 and is editor of the Philosophical Explorations Series for Southern Illinois University Press. His most recent book is *A Friendly Companion to Plato's Gorgias* (in press).

NATHAN ROTENSTREICH is Emeritus Ahad Ha'am Professor of Philosophy at the Hebrew University of Jerusalem and Vice President of the Israel Academy of Sciences and Humanities. He is the author of many works on philosophy and the history of ideas in Hebrew, German, and English.

W. THOMAS SCHMID is an Associate Professor of Philosophy and Religion at the University of North Carolina at Wilmington. Author of several articles on Plato, his doctoral dissertation shared the Jacob Cooper Prize for Greek Philosophy at Yale.

KENNETH SEESKIN is Associate Professor and Chairman of Philosophy at Northwestern University. He has recently published a book, *Dialogue and Discovery: A Study in the Socratic Method*, and is editing a series in Jewish Philosophy for SUNY Press.

JOSIAH THOMPSON is author and editor of several books on Kierkegaard. In 1978 he resigned as Professor of Philosophy at Haverford College (Pennsylvania) to pursue work as a private detective in San Francisco. He is also the author of *Six Seconds in Dallas* (1967) and *Gumshoe* (forthcoming, 1988).

MANLEY THOMPSON is Emeritus Professor of Philosophy at the University of Chicago. His publications have been in the areas of metaphysics and epistemology, including a book on the philosophy of C.S. Peirce. His most recent work has been on the theoretical philosophy of Kant.

Part I: PLATO

SOCRATIC PIETY

W. Thomas Schmid

I

The traditional ancient Greek conception of piety (*eusebeia*) was a virtue involving proper care or attention to the Gods, in the form of both proper worship and the proper attitude.[1] The pious man, like the priest of Apollo Chryses or the loyal swineherd Eumaios, performed the ritual acts of purification, libation, sacrifice and first fruit for the God's helpful favor (*charis*) in response to his own petitionary prayers (see *Iliad* 1.33-52; *Odyssey* 14.418-455).[2] The inner essence of such piety was the feeling of religious awe, of God-fearing reverence (*sebas*).[3] More fully articulated, this attitude involved the religious consciousness counseled by Delphi: to "know thyself" (*gnothi sauton*), i.e. to recognize one's mortality and weakness compared to the Immortals and one's place in a larger order. The opposite attitude was carelessness of the Gods (*asebeia*) and foolish arrogance (*hybris*), which eventually would be punished.[4]

Piety was perhaps the most basic ancient Greek social virtue, insofar as religion was the basic means of social integration and solidarity, the "glue" which seemed to preserve the continuity of communal life (see *Euthyphro* 14B).[5] The center of the household (*oikos*) was the hearth, and participation in the family cult shaped all essential family affairs.[6] Religion also played a constitutive role in the public life of the city-state (*polis*), as the state took institutional control over religious life during the reorganization of Greek society in the 7th-5th centuries B.C.[7] The city's religious festivals ordered its time no less than the city's temples defined its space. In the practice of the oath taken before the Gods, religion, morality and the contractual life of society seemed indissoluably linked.[8] And as the city was a sacrificial community, watched over by its own protective deities, piety was naturally regarded as a civic duty. If Socrates or anyone else was thought to subvert the worship of Athena or any of the other Gods, he was also thought to subvert the state.[9]

II

By the end of the 5th century B.C., however, the foundations of the traditional religion had been shaken in Athens, partly as a result of the impact of the two other main traditions in ancient Greek religious thought – the Greek enlightment, on the one hand, and the mystic and ascetic movements associated with Eleusis, Dionysis, Orpheus and Pythagoras, on the other.[10] Both the enlightment and the mystic traditions had their own views about the true nature and value of piety.

"Greek enlightment" is of course a very loose term, and some aspects of this movement are probably better regarded as part of the ongoing development within the traditional religion. The moral criticism of Homer's depiction of the Gods, for example, is very old; more than two centuries of reflection culminate in Euripides' contention that: "If God is truly God, he is perfect, lacking nothing. All else is poets' wretched lies" (*Heracles* 1345-46).[11] Implicit in this theological insight is the notion that the emotional medium of true piety – piety evoked by a true conception of the divine – must be reverence for the divine goodness, not fear of capricious power.[12] On the other hand, philosophers like Xenophanes and Heracleitus refuted and ridiculed the idolatry of anthropomorphic Gods and questioned the value of traditional ritual.[13] This skeptical trend in Greek thought led to the rejection of piety as mere superstition by prominent sophists in favor of humanist agnosticism (Protagoras) or atheism (Critias, Diagoras). But aside from the sophists hardly any of the pre-Socratic philosophers were agnostic or atheists, and many of them, including Anaximander, Xenophanes, Heracleitus, Empedocles and Anaxagoras, contribute to the development of a wholly new form of *theologia*, of speaking about the Gods, and a wholly new conception of nature (*physis*) as a universal order (*kosmos*) structured by rational laws.[14] There is no place in that conception of the world for the Homeric Gods, but there is for "the Divine Being" (*to theion*) that is its "source" or "principle" (*arche*). Thus a second form of piety emerges in ancient Greece, not in the form of sacrifices to the Gods but of "cognitive beholding" (*theoria*): of mystic, reverent enlightment in the contemplation of the intelligible Order of Being or of the One behind the phenomena. And yet God, thus conceived, seems even more distant than Zeus; how could the Divine Being care for the individual, be a Thou to an I?[15]

The ancient Greek mystic traditions, in contrast both to the state cults and to pre-Socratic philosophy, offered their "initiates" (*mystai*) an intensely personal kind of faith.[16] This seems to have been particularly true of Orphism and Pythagoreanism, which introduced into Greek religious and intellectual life the concept of an immortal soul lodged in the mortal body, and thereby transformed utterly both the theoretical correlative and practical ideal of piety.[17] For the Orphic/Pythagorean conception of the soul overthrew the fundamental difference between man and God in Homer – mortal vs. immortal – and made man, or the soul within man, "a kind of God."[18] It followed that one's bearing toward this inner God, one's care of his soul and concern for the afterlife, was the true locus of spirituality and measure of piety. The very different religious quality which distinguished Orphism and Pythagoreanism, on the one hand, from both the conventional cult and the esoteric philosophic faith, on the other, was also due to the rigorous, puritanical moral claims the former made upon their followers. To be saved, one had to live the Orphic or Pythagorean "way of life" (*bios*), the watchword of which was piety understood as purity from all forms of defilement, i.e. all violations of the moral-religious rules of the faith which ordered even everyday life.[19] This was then a third and again radically different conception of piety in ancient Greece, oriented neither to public ritual behavior and concern for the Gods, nor to contemplative enlightenment and recognition of the Divine Order, but rather to the inner life of the soul and to the revealed absolutist laws of ethical life which the *mystes* was bound to obey. For the Orphic or Pythagorean to be pious was to leave his social identity and previous life and submit to the path set before him; but it was also to pass in faith through the gate of death into eternal life.[20]

III

It is against the background of these three sharply different religious ideals that the *Euthyphro* and *Apology* must be understood – the *Euthyphro*, Plato's critical examination of traditional piety; the *Apology*, his defense of Socrates as the embodiment of a true religious virtue, the virtue of Socratic piety.[21] For while the Socrates of the early dialogues seems in certain respects the antithesis of the pious man, i.e. of the man devoted to the ritualistic aspects and dogmas of traditional religion, he defends himself in the *Apology* as a pious man in another sense, namely as a man who reverently and obediently serves "the God" (*to theion*) through his pursuit of wisdom and exhortation to virtue (cf. esp. 20C-23C, 28E-31C). The basic definition of

this ideal had been presented in the *Euthyphro*: piety is obedience and
"a kind of [art of] service" (*hyperetike tis*) to the Gods, such as the
type servants give their masters (13D).[22] But when Socrates had
asked Euthyphro how we should do this – what "great and noble
work" (*pankalon ergon*) it is the Gods want us to bring about on earth
– Euthyphro did not know, except to insist on the traditional notion
of sacrificial service, which Socrates suggested was unsatisfactory
(14A-C).[23] It remained, then for Socrates to develop in the *Apology*
the outlines of his own conception of piety.

In the course of his self-defense in the *Apology*, while telling the
story of the Delphic oracle and explaining his way of life, Socrates
both (a) claims that he, Socrates, was called by "the God" to his life
of philosophizing and that he continued it as a form of religious
service, "in obedience to the god" (28E-29A), and (b) gives the
answer to the unanswered question of the *Euthyphro*, by noting that
his service consists in "the care of souls," i.e. that this is the work the
God(s) wants of us (cf. esp. 29E-30A). Thus the Socratic conception
of piety in the *Apology* is modeled on the traditional notion of duty
to the Higher Being(s), but this conception is decisively altered by
Socrates' Orphic/Pythagorean-like understanding of the form that
service should take and of the human subject, i.e. the soul who
performs it. Furthermore, (c) Socrates also indicates in his account of
the oracle experience that apart from his existence and goodness,
the name and precise nature of the God(s) to be served is unknown
to man (cf. esp. 23A).[24] In this regard, the Socratic conception
reflects the philosophical-religious enlightenment revelation of a
Divine Being that is radically different from the Gods of the
Homeric tradition – an Unknown God who is, however, also
conceived of as perfectly wise and good.

In short, Socrates introduces in the process of his defense in the
Apology a new, philosophical account of piety, which may be characterized as "the service of the Unknown God through the care of
souls." This account combines, in a uniquely creative synthesis, key
elements of each of the three ancient Greek religious traditions
sketched above – the traditional norm of duty to Higher Being(s);
the enlightenment vision of the goodness, but also cognitive obscurity of God; and the Orphic/Pythagorean conception of religious
conduct as taking the personal form not of specific ritual actions but
of an entire way of life. Although the account of piety as service to
the God(s) is interpreted in the *Apology* in relation to Socrates' particular mission to the Athenians, it clearly need not apply to Socrates
alone; all who seek to serve the God(s) by caring for souls through

philosophy and the exhortation to virtue are pious in the Socratic use of the term.[25]

IV

Now let us consider more carefully the two most important features of the Socratic, philosophical conception of piety, as presented in the *Apology*. First of all, there is the fact that the official charge against him was basically true; Socrates does not believe in the Gods of the Athenian state, but in another and different kind of God(s), a God at once more distant, more caring and more like the One God of the Abrahamic tradition than the Homeric Pantheon.[26] Socrates conceives of this God as a Divine Artisan(s) whose only will, so far as we know, is for man's good, and who acts providentially, through signs and prophets like Socrates himself, to bring the true human good about, i.e. the good of a life orientated toward truth, justice and the goodness of the soul, rather than toward self-aggrandizement and worldly success (cf. esp. *Apology* 28E-31C).[27] But while Socratic piety is presented as being directed specifically toward the God(s) who called Socrates to a personal service, it reflects an embracing religious sensibility of commitment on Socrates' part to the whole order of goodness in the cosmos and the destiny of his own human community.[28] Socrates presents himself in the early dialogues and in the *Apology* in particular as a new kind of religious man, one who can no longer accept the traditional mythology, but who is not purely secular in his outlook on life. Rather, he sees life as lived within a divine horizon that is formed both by the unseen personal Power(s) that calls men to moral service and acts mysteriously within life, and by the impersonal reality of goodness in our lives and in the world at large.[29] We discover this divine reality, however, primarily from within, through the path of wonder and love and devotion to truth and virtue, and this commitment in turn forms into the enduring religious identity Socrates calls the soul.[30] Socratic piety points, finally, toward the comprehensive religious-metaphysical and moral assessment of life that Plato develops in the middle dialogues, though Socrates retains a more personal conception of God than we find there.[31]

The Socratic conception of man and God involves a radical departure from the traditional interpretation of the human servant-Divine master relationship, both as to the religious self-knowledge of the servant and the idea of his rightful practice. It is naturally a part of

Socratic piety to see others as souls whom the God(s) cares for and wants to be led in the path of righteousness, the path of philosophy and virtue; and while Socrates does not commit himself in the *Apology* to belief in the immortality and reward of the good soul after death, he holds this out as a hope, i.e. he rejects the traditional view and seems to believe there is something divine and eternal in man, whether it is a substantial being that can exist in its own right or only a quality of absolute value.[32] Obviously, too, the Socratic conception of the Divine Will implies that the essence of man's relationship to the divine cannot consist in lavishing sacrifices upon the Gods for the sake of protection and favor, but consists instead in bringing others to see that the truly human life is the life devoted to truth and virtue, a life which conforms to the will of the God(s) for man, a life which is, finally, an "imitation of the God."[33] The morally rigorous consequence Socrates draws is that the truly pious man will serve truth and virtue, even if it costs him his life – he will not compromise his soul, his moral-religious integrity, for the sake of the whole world (cf. *Apology* 28E-29D, also also 35C-D).[34]

To be Socratically pious, then, is to seek to achieve within one's life a kind of moral communion with the divine. This communion is expressed both cognitively, in a sense of enlightened reverence and humility before the Unknown God(s) that seems to care for men, calling us to virtue, and behaviorally, in a life of service that takes the form of radical dedication to truth and to the moral welfare of one's neighbors. If at the core of what Maier called "the Socratic gospel" is an ethic of wonder and love, at its outer rim is the intimation of a Universal God.[35]

V

The second distinguishing aspect of Socratic piety concerns his recognition that faith in the God(s) of Wisdom and Goodness is not a matter of knowledge – that men cannot know anything about the God(s), neither as to their nature nor even as to their existence.[36] This is the aspect of Socratic piety that is at once most paradoxical, original and confusing. For Socrates stands in relation to his religious tradition not only the manner of a Jesus, calling it to a morally higher and more encompassing conception of the religious life, but also in the manner of a Buddha, calling it to tear down the walls of its dogmatic mansion and acknowledge the uncertain cognitive foundation of religious faith.[37] But this idea runs fundamentally contrary to the common understanding of faith and piety, not only among people in the Abrahamic tradition but also among Socrates' fellow countrymen.[38] It is really quite natural that so many of Socrates' admirers and critics in ancient times and since have held him to be a humanist skeptic and pure rationalist, an agnostic in the ordinary sense of the term, and have concluded that the attitude of the *homo philosophicus* is sharply opposed to that of the *homo religiosus*.[39] For the Socratic philosopher, in proclaiming his religious faith, admits in the same breath that apart from its moral core it is really only a hope, that it never escapes the shadow of doubt. Where is there piety in this? Since the answer is hardly obvious, it seems more reasonable to assume that Socrates is simply being ironical, i.e. dissembling, when he presents himself as a servant of the God.[40]

But all attempts to make a pure rationalist out of Socrates are forced into highly strained explanations or active ignorance of what he has to say about the oracle, his *daimonion*, and the nature and care of the God(s) for men (cf. esp. *Apology* 20C-23C, 28E-31D, 40A-42A).[41] The task then is to see how the religious dimension of Socrates' life and thoughts relates to the other aspects of his philosophy, not to eliminate what is evident. I would suggest that the Socratic emphasis on the epistemologically reflective character of religious faith is consistent with the account given above of his emphasis on moral conception of the divine and religious service. The Socratically pious man stands in the midst of a mystery, not a certainty about the reality of the Divine Power(s) and the destiny of his soul, and to acknowledge this is at once to deepen and alter one's notion of *eusebeia*, of "good religious awe."[42] For to assert knowledge of the God(s) would be to impiously aggrandize for man what is not his to possess, and thus to run the risk of doing what Euthyphro does – pridefully identify with the divine in a manner that is inappropriate to genuine piety and that may easily lead to injustice.[43] Socrates, by recognizing his ignorance of the God, preserves a religious sense of humility and of the transcendence of the divine. Nor is his faith in God as easily shaken, perhaps, as that of a man like Euthyphro. For one thing, the Socratic must possess the religious courage to live with the possibility that his faith is mistaken, and so he must find in the life of truth and virtue its own reward; for another, he is enlightened with the religious wisdom to know that the God(s), in his providence, is not concerned with our victories or defeats, our fortunes or misfortunes, so much as with the moral essence of our pilgrimage, and we should not impiously presume to judge the God by them. Certainly, Plato's Socrates goes to his trial and death with the inner serenity of a man borne on his journey by an extraordinary faith in the Divine Will. It is also instructive in this regard to note what the Socrates of Plato's dialogues prays for: to become "good within" rather than to gain worldly success (cf. esp. *Phaedrus* 279B-C and *Alcibiades II* 143A, which correspond to *Apology* 29D-30B).[44]

Plato's Socrates appears to recognize both (a) that his faith in the existence of the good and caring God(s) who acts on man's behalf and in the possible immortality of the human soul is based in part at least on his simply private experience of the oracle and the *daimonion*; and more fundamentally, (b) that his faith may finally not be true – there may not be such a God(s) or afterlife at all.[45] But it seems clear that even knowledge of this would not alter in any significant respect his path of life and moral philosophy.[46] Thus Socratic piety appears already in the early dialogues not to be conceived of by Plato as a rational moral virtue in the same way as are the virtues of Socratic courage, moderation, justice, and wisdom.[47] These virtues can stand as a group apart from belief in the perfect God(s) or the immortality of the human soul, though Socratic piety cannot exist apart from them.

VI

Thus far I have discussed the historical background to and basic definition of Socratic piety, and examined its two most important and distinctive features. In closing I want to consider briefly three further points bearing on this ideal: (1) its relation to the Socratic virtue of justice; (2) its relation to the Socratic virtue of wisdom; and (3) whether in fact it is a virtue.

In the *Euthyphro* Socrates introduces the idea that justice and piety are related as parts of a larger genus of "the right" and gets Euthyphro to distinguish them as follows: piety is the part of the right having to do with the service we owe to the gods, justice the part having to do with the service we owe our fellow men (12E). The puzzle, then, is how these are different, if they are different. Some scholars (e.g. Beckman, Irwin, Taylor) hold there is no difference: what we owe the Gods and other men and ourselves is all the same thing according to Plato, justice.[48] But this interpretation seems forced when examined in the context of the trial dialogues (omitting for obvious reasons the *Phaedo*), where we find Socrates examining the concept of piety in the *Euthyphro* and presenting himself explicitly as a pious man in the *Apology*, and then focussing on the justice of his actions in obedience to the laws of Athens in the *Crito*. In the former we learn that Socrates showed his obedience and supererogatory service to the God(s) in his career of philosophizing and exhorting his fellow citizens to virtue, in the latter we learn that Socratic justice requires that one never harm or do evil to others; therefore it seems it would be a direct violation of justice and the service we owe men, regardless of what piety demands, to escape from prison, but a violation of piety, not justice, for Socrates to cease philosophizing.[49]

There is also a question as to how Socratic piety can be different from wisdom. Is not wisdom, on Socrates' view, the enlightening knowledge of the Good which fuses all the virtues and makes them one? Is it not wisdom in the light of which Socrates knows that men should devote their lives to truth and virtue, not self-aggrandizement and money; wisdom by which he recognizes his fellow-citizens as souls in need of his elenctic help and moral exhortation; wisdom which moves him to offer himself as living sacrifice and servant of the eternal Goodness?[50] Here again, however, the discussion of these virtues in the early dialogues suggests as I see it the unity of interrelationship but not identity.[51] Certainly the Socratic principle of the "sovereignty of virtue" (Vlastos) is decisive for his understanding of the care of souls and his interpretation of why the God(s) set him upon the Athenians as the gadfly to the horse; and certainly also, he has by the end of his life come to value his way of life as that which "makes life worth living for a man," such that his duty to the God(s) seems now also to be a simple matter of eudaimonic self-interest (*Apology* 37E-38A). But the Socratic moral insight concerning the absolute value of human goodness and the care of the *psyche* can be and is distinguished by Socrates from his specifically religious beliefs in the Unknown God(s), his mission and the immortality of the soul, just as the fact that he had come to regard his way of life as teleologically self-fulfilling does not imply that he did not originally act at least in part out of a sense of religious awe and duty.[52] Again: Socratic piety is not separable from Socratic wisdom – neither as regards his conception of the divine nor his conception of religious service – but Socratic wisdom (and the other virtues) can be separated from Socratic piety.

VII

Finally, insofar as piety implies a belief commitment to anything whatsoever that is not open to rational questioning, it is clearly an intellectual vice, not a virtue.[53] But there is no indication that Socrates is unwilling to submit his religious beliefs and sense of mission to rational examination, though he does not do so, and we have at least his word that one should always be willing to examine his beliefs (cf. *Euthyphro* 9E, *Apology* 38A, *Crito* 46B).[54] As for his intuition concerning the necessary goodness, wisdom, etc. of the Divine Being(s), that is surely a view he might defend dialectically, though he is not inclined to discuss such matters (see *Euthyphro* 6E, *Apology* 19C-D).[55] (And is it not a principle of genuine faith, an insight of the truly religious mind?)[56] As for justifying his sense of a God-given mission and his beliefs about the care of the God(s) for men, Socrates would surely allude as mentioned above to his personal experiences, including the *daimonion*, and to his unnatural choice of poverty, which he may reasonably believe suggest, though they do not prove, the hand of Providence in his affairs (cf. *Apology* 31D, 33E, 40C, 41D).[57]

But if not an intellectual vice, is his piety a moral virtue? I have argued that already in the trial dialogues Plato recognizes that Socratic piety is not a necessary part of human excellence, but it may still be a (secondary) virtue, if it helps him and/or his community to attain ends proper to man which they might not otherwise have attained. What seems virtuous in Socrates' piety, both for him and for his city, is not that he believes in the God or that he seeks to serve the God in his actions, but the kind of God he believes in and the kind of service that belief leads him to perform. On the latter point John Burnet showed his colors when he remarked that the Emperor Julian's words in his letter to the philosopher Themistius are "still true," namely that "... it is thanks to Socrates that all who find salvation in philosophy are being saved even now," though we may question whether salvation is to be found or wisely sought in philosophy alone.[58] Critics of Socrates ranging from Aristophanes to Hegel and Nietzsche and into the present, on the other hand, have suggested that Socrates' service may, from a communal point of view, be anything but the "great good" he claims it is (*Apology* 30A), a reactionary perspective we must oppose.[59] Howsoever much it is that inflated expectations have worked to discredit both Socrates and philosophy, the basic faith he preached abides – "the unexamined life is not worth living for a human being." So long as this is so, his practice of philosophy remains a "gift of the God" to us all.

NOTES

This essay was written in honor of Robert S. Brumbaugh, who introduced me to the spirit and study of Platonic philosophy.

1. There is to my knowledge no single study of the idea of piety in ancient Greece, though there are good specific discussions of the idea of piety and the terms to hosion and eusebeia in Walter Burkert's magesterial Greek Religion, trans. J. Raffan (Cambridge, Ma.: Harvard University, 1985), 268-275 and in Robert Parker, Miasma (Oxford: Oxford University, 1983), 328-331. See also Arthur Adkins, Merit and Responsibilty (Oxford: Oxford University, 1960), 131-138; Kenneth Dover, Greek Popular Morality in the Time of Plato and Aristotle (Berkeley, Ca.: University of California, 1974), 246-249; and Martin Nilsson, Greek Piety, trans. H. Rose (Oxford: Oxford University, 1951), 7-8. Among the good general introductions to Greek religion, see also W.K.C. Guthrie, The Greeks and their Gods (Boston: Beacon, 1950); Martin Nilsson, A History of Greek Religion, trans. F. Fielden (Oxford: Oxford University, 1925); and Clifford Moore, The Religious Thought of the Greeks (Cambridge, Ma.: Harvard, 1916).

2. See the discussion of ritual and prayer in Burkert, Greek Religion, 54-75. The emphasis on doing acts of ritual pleasing to the Gods is reflected in all of the last part of the Euthyphro 12E-15B. For religion in Homer, see in addition to the general introductions cited in footnote [1] above, Jasper Griffin, Homer on Life and Death (Oxford: Oxford University, 1980), 144-204.

3. On the notion of sebas as religious awe combining fear and reverence, see Burkert, Greek Religion, 273. Current scholarly discussion of these concepts is greatly influenced by Rudolph Otto, The Idea of the Holy (London: Oxford University, 1923), especially his discussion of the mysterium tremendum in contrast to the mysterivm auqustum, pp. 50-59. On this topic, see also G. van der Leeuw, Religion in Essence and Manifestation, trans. J. Turner (Gloucester, Ma.: Peter Smith, 1967), 1: 23-28, 180-187.

4. On Godless foolishness, see Odyssey 1.32f.; 6.120f.; 9.175f.; 13.201f.; 22.411-418; and the discussion in Burkert, Greek Religion, 246-247. This is a key point at which the traditional virtues of sophrosyne and eusebeia overlap. See Helen North, Sophrosyne (Ithaca, N.Y.: Cornell University, 1966), 10 and references on p. 387; T.G. Tuckey, Plato's Charmides (Cambridge: Cambridge University, 1951), 9-10; Nilsson, Greek Piety, 47-58; and Schmid, "Socratic Moderation and Self-Knowledge," Journal of the History of Philosophy 23, 3(July 1983): 339-348.

5. On this point, Euthyphro is simply reflecting the traditional ancient Greek conception of religion. On religion as the "glue" of public and private life, see the discussions in Burkert, Greek Religion, especially pp. 254-268; Dover, Greek Popular Morality, 246-261; Nilsson, Greek Piety, 66-69 and History of Greek Religion, 224-262; and Frederick Solmsen, Plato's Theology (Ithaca, N.Y.: Cornell University, 1942), 3-12.

6. See Burkert, Greek Religion, 60-61, 170, 255; and Martin Nilsson, Greek Folk Religion (New York: Columbia University, 1940), 65-83. Plato has Euthyphro refer to Socrates as the "hearth" (often translated somewhat appropriately "heart") of the Athenian polis at 3A. See the note to 3A7 in Ian Walker, Plato's Euthyphro (Chico, Ca.: Scholars, 1984), 47. (Socrates of course comically describes

himself as the "gadfly" to the Athenian horse in *Apology* 30E).

7. See the discussions in Burkert, *Greek Religion*, 254-260; Nilsson, *History*, 224-262; L.R. Farnell, *The Higher Aspects of Greek Religion* (Chicago: Ares, 1977), 63-91; and C.J. Herington, *Athena Parthenos and Athena Polias* (Manchester, England: University of Manchester, 1955), 43-67.

8. On the oath, see especially Burkert, *Greek Religion*, 250-254 and Dover, *Greek Popular Morality*, 248-249.

9. On the notion of piety as a duty, see especially Burkert, *Greek Religion*, 254-257, 274-275, 316-317; Nilsson, *Greek Piety*, 66-70; Solmsen, *Plato's Theology*, 3-12; and Dover, *Greek Popular Morality*, 246-250. For discussion of the prosecutions on the charge of impiety, see E.R. Dodds, *The Greeks and the Irrational* (Berkeley, Ca.: University of California, 1951), 189-190; and G.B. Kerferd, *The Sophistic Movement* (Cambridge: Cambridge University, 1981), 20-22 and references. Since Burnet there has been occasional discussion in the scholarly literature whether the charge against Socrates of *ou nomidzonta* ("not acknowledging") the Gods of the state concerned (a) his not honouring them by participation in the public cult, or (b) his not believing in them. See John Burnet's edition of Plato, *Euthyphro, Apology and Crito* (Oxford: Oxford University, 1924), 184. Probably the best comment on this point is that of Heidel: *ou nomidzonta* "not only denotes belief in the existence of the gods but also adds the idea of *nomos*, religious conformity," Walter Heidel, *Plato's Euthyphro* (New York: American, 1902), 35. Plato takes account of and defends Socrates in relation to the charge of non-belief, rather than non-conformity; Xenophon the charge of non-conformity, but not non-belief. On the validity of the charge regarding belief in the existence of the Gods of the state, see the discussion in this paper, sections IV and V; also James Beckman, *The Religious Dimension of Socrates' Thought* (Toronto: Wilfred Laurier University, 1979), 60-63; and Thomas West, *Plato's Apology of Socrates* (Ithaca, N.Y.: Cornell, 1979), 124-126.

10. Good brief introductions to the Greek enlightenment are found in George Grote, *History of Greece*, (New York: AMS, 1971), 7:1-79; Burkert, *Greek Religion*, 305-329; Moore, *Religious Thought*, 74-143. Burkert offers a good brief introduction to the mystic traditions in his *Greek Religion*, 276-304; see also Moore, *Religious Thought*, 40-73; and Nilsson, *Greek Piety*, 20-30 and *History of Greek Religion*, 180-223. On Orphism, see W.C.K. Guthrie, *Orpheus and Greek Religion* (New York: W.W. Norton, 1966). On Pythagoreanism, see Walter Burkert, *Lore and Science in Ancient Pythagoreanism*, trans. E. Minar, Jr. (Cambridge, Ma.: Harvard University, 1972); J.A. Philip, *Pythagoras and Early Pythagoreanism* (Toronto: University of Toronto, 1966); and Parker, *Miasma*, 281-307. On the Eleusinian Mysteries, see Guthrie, *Greeks and Their Gods*, 277-294 and Martin Nilsson, *Greek Folk Religion* (New York: Columbia University, 1940), 42-64. On Dionysus, see also Guthrie, *Greeks and their Gods*, 145-182 and Burkert, *Greek Religion*, 290-296.

11. For a brief history of the development of these ideas, see in particular Moore, *Religious Thought*, 74-108; and Burkert, *Greek Religion*, 246-250. For an unorthodox view that denies development, see the discussion of Zeus in Hugh Lloyd-Jones, *The Justice of Zeus* (Berkeley, Ca.: University of California, 1975), especially 155-164.

12. See below in this essay, section IV, and footnote [26] and references.

13. For the revelant fragments of Xenophanes, see G.S. Kirk and J.E. Raven, *The Presocratic Philosophers* (Cambridge: Cambridge University, 1957), 168-171; for the relevant Heracleitus fragments, 211-212.

14. On pre-Socratic theology, see especially Werner Jaeger, *Theology of the Early Greek*

Philosophers (Oxford: Oxford University, 1947); Gregory Vlastos, "Theology and Philosophy in Early Greek Thought" in *Studies in Presocratic Philosophy*, David Farley and R.E. Allen (New York: Humanities, 1970), 1:92-129; Burkert, *Greek Religion*, 305-311, 317-321; Charles Kahn, *Anaximander and the Origins of Greek Cosomology* (New York: Columbia University, 1960), 231-238; and W.K.C. Guthrie, *A History of Greek Philosophy*, (Cambridge: Cambridge University, 1962, 1965), Vol. 1 and 2.

15. This as a problem already in traditional religion in relation to Zeus, who often seems to represent not so much a Divine Person as the "Order" (*Dike*) See the discussion in Lloyd-Jones, *The Justice of Zeus*, 33, 161, 193n.34; and A. J. Festugiere, *Personal Religion among the Greeks* (Berkeley, Ca.: University of California, 1954), 19-37, 105-121.

16. See the accounts in Burkert, *Greek Religion*, 271-275, 301-304; Guthrie, *Orpheus*, 200-201, 206-207; Parker, *Miasma*, 304-305; and Nilsson, *Greek Piety*, 70-72, and the contrasts they draw between the individualism and personal quality of the "mystery" religions and "collective piety" (Nilsson) of the state cults, at least the cults of the Olympians: the cults of the heroes are another matter, cf. Guthrie, *Greeks and their Gods*, 231-253 and Burkert, *Greek Religion*, 203-215. The cult of Apollo seems also to have bridged the Homeric -mystery gulf, a fact not unimportant in relation to Socrates, who presents himself as a servant of Apollo in the *Apology*; see the accounts of the "Apolline religion" in Guthrie, *Greeks and their Gods*, 183-204; Nilsson, *History*, 180-223. See also on the personal aspect of traditional religion, Festugiere, *Personal Religion*, 1-18 and Guthrie, *Greeks and their Gods*, 27-28. On the *chthonioi* and popular "hopes and fears," see Guthrie, *Greeks and their Gods*, 217-277.

17. On the significance of this concept, see especially Guthrie, *Greeks and their Gods*, 113-116; Burkert, *Greek Religion*, 300-301 and references; and John Burnet, "The Socratic Doctrine of the Soul" in *Essays and Addresses* (London: Murray, 1929), 126-162. Compare also Griffin's account of the peculiar pathos of Homeric religion, *Homer on Life and Death*, 187-192.

18. David Claus, in his *Toward the Soul* (New Haven, Ct.: Yale University, 1981), 111-121 is skeptical of the common attribution of the concept of the immortal soul to Orphism-Pythagoreanism, but see Burkert's comment and references in *Greek Religion*, 300, 463nn.38-39.

19. On the concept of the Orphic and Pythagorean "religious way of life" or *bios* and the related notion of piety as purity, see especially Burkert, *Greek Religion*, 301-304; Guthrie, *Orpheus*, 194-207; and Parker, *Miasma*, 299-307.

20. Properly speaking, eternal life begins after passage out of the cycles of life in this world to Elysium or Heaven, but for the *mystes* it may also be said to begin when he enters onto the sacred path of the initiate. On the contrasting symbols of gate and path for the mystery religions, rather than unchanging order, see Burkert, *Greek Religion*, 275, 287 (the gate of the Mysteries), 293 (the path of the *bacchoi*); and Guthrie, *Orpheus*, 173-187 on the pure, the path of the saved in the afterlife and heaven.

21. The basic approach of my discussion in this and the following sections is set by three considerations: (1) I do not believe it is wise to attempt to identify the beliefs of the historical Socrates, so all references in this essay to "Socrates," "Socratic piety," etc. will be to the Socrates of the early dialogues; (2) I am committed to the methodological principle Versenyi has recently called that of "constructive" as opposed to "analytic" interpretation, namely a method in which particular attention is paid to the dramatic form of the dialogue, together with

the argumentative content, as a guide to the overall meaning of the work; and (3) I believe the case has been made conclusively for the view that the definition of piety given at Euthyphro 13D3-8 represents positive early Platonic, i.e. Socratic doctrine. For the reasons behind principle (1), see Gregory Vlastos, "The Paradox of Socrates" in The Philosophy of Socrates (Garden City, N.Y.: Doubleday, 1971), 1-21. For good discussions of the preferred method of reading Plato, see Robert S. Brumbaugh, "Plato's Meno as Form and as Content," Teaching Philosophy (Fall 1975), 1:107-115; Hans-Georg Gadamer, "Logos und Ergon im platonischen Lysis," Kleine Schriften (Tuebingen, W. Germany: Mohr, 1971), 3:50-63; and Versenyi, Holiness and Justice (Washington, D.C.: University Press of America, 1982), 11-22. For discussions of Socratic piety see especially Vlastos, "The Paradox," 12-15; Michael Henry, "Socratic Piety and the Power of Reason" in New Essays on Socrates, ed. Eugene Kelley (Washington, D.C.: University Press of America, 1984), 95-106 and his earlier manuscript "Socratic Piety," presented to the Vlastos 1981 N.E.H. Summer Seminar on Socrates at the University of California, Berkeley; and Mark McPherran, "Socratic Piety in the Euthyphro," Journal of the History of Philosophy, 23, 3(July 1985): 283-309.

22. For the case on behalf of Euthyphro 13D as representing Socratic piety, see now McPherran, "Socratic Piety," especially 284-297. The phrase does not necessarily imply a servile attitude. See the discussion in Burkert, Greek Religion, 189, 275; and H.W. Pleket in Faith, Hope and Worship, ed. H.S. Versnel (Leiden, 1980), 152-192. Socrates' attitude in the Apology stops short of the lowly humility and sin-consciousness called for by the later Plato in Laws 715E-716A, though Plato's conception there of piety and divine service sems very like classical Jewish, Christian and Muslim monotheistic views, with their emphasis on submission to God and His Law. See also in this context Otto, The Idea, 50-59. By comparison, Socratic piety seems to presuppose both a less clearly defined and personal relation to the God(s), and also a less pessimistic conception of the human servant, but not necessarily a less demanding or enlightened conception of the God(s) or of the pious and reverent man as His servant. Seé the discussion in sections III-IV and footnotes [23], [24] and [26] below.

23. Socrates' attitude toward traditional sacrifice is expressed by his remarking that in presenting it as piety Euthyphro has turned away from the path to the correct answer (14B), his sarcastic characterization of traditional piety as a kind of craft of "bartering" (emporike, 14E), and his observation that the latter view again is inconsistent with the notion that the Gods are perfect and need nothing from us for themselves (15A), together with the concluding rejection of this account of piety as rooting back in the notion of what is pleasing to the Gods (15B). But his comments seem to bear especially on the impious attitude of the worshipper, rather than the act itself. McPherran, "Socratic Piety," 300, 302, 305-306 discusses the role traditional ritual service might have in Socratic piety, a view rejected by Henry, "Socratic Piety," New Essays, 95-99, 102-103. However, so long as ritual sacrifice is not motivated by the desire for selfish rewards, and so long as prayer is made to the true God(s) for the right goods (cf. e.g. Phaedrus 279B-C and Alchibiades II 143A, which correspond to Apology 29D-30B), and so long, too, as it is recognized that the true God(s) need nothing from us (cf. Euthyphro 13C-D, 14E-15A), Plato's Socrates may consistently include praise and symbolic sacrifice as an appropriate if secondary part of the duties owed by men to the God(s), on the grounds that these express rightful praise toward a God(s) worthy of worship and/or praise and gratitude toward the order of goodness in the universe, an order for at least part of which the God(s) are held to be respon-

sible. (Assuming they are responsible for revelatory signs and prophets and care for good men; Plato's Socrates does not proclaim the creationist doctrine attributed by Xenophon to Socrates at *Memorabilia* 1.4:3-19.)

24. The view that Socrates presents his own account of piety in the *Apology* is traditional, though the interpretations of his account vary. See the references by McPherran, "Socratic Piety," 283. McPherran argues that Socrates does not possess "even fallible knowledge" of the *ergon* desired of men by the Gods, "Socratic Piety," 297-309, but his discussion virtually ignores the conclusive evidence of *Apology* 28A-32A as to Socrates' conception of the overall character of the God's will for man. If, as McPherran acknowledges, Socrates appears to accept the Divine Craftsman (-men) model of the God(s) introduced at *Euthyphro* 13D-E, then it is not clear that the good the God(s) desire for men is precisely the good life outlined at *Apology* 29D-30B, the life of seeking wisdom and virtue rather than wealth and prestige, and is it not then also clear that the true "service to the God(s)" is to "care for men's souls," precisely as Socrates asserts at *Apology* 29D-E? For the point, see Vlastos, "The Paradox," 14, who, however, identifies the duty as "the improvement of our souls," rather than the seeking of wisdom and care for other's souls, as would appear to be more obviously the service Socrates offers (see especially *Apology* 29D-30B and 31B). This is not to say, of course, that Socrates would claim to possess infallible, divine knowledge of the nature of the God(s) or of the service they require. For relevance of the opposition of fallible human and infallible divine knowledge, see the discussion in section VI of this essay and footnote [36] below. For the claim that the "name and precise nature of the God(s) is unknown to man," see the discussion of Socrates' notion of the cognitive obscurity of the God(s) in section V and footnotes [26] and [36] below. Socrates does not call his God "Apollo" in the *Apology*, but refers to him consistently by the neutral title-term, "the God."

25. Compare Vlastos, "The Paradox," 14; McPherran, "Soratic Piety," 306-309; also the discussion Socratic piety in of Thomas C. Brickhouse and Nicholas D. Smith, "The Origin of Socrates' Mission," *Journal of the History of Ideas* 44, 4(1983): 657-666; and the discussion of the virtue of piety in section VII, especially the Burnet quotation. A further point is that Socratic piety implies the willingness to die rather than betray his service to the God. See section IV, footnote [34] below.

26. For Socrates' conception of the God(s), see especially *Euthyphro* 6A-C: divine beings are not immoral; 13B-14B: divine beings need nothing and want to see some "great and noble work" brought about by their servants; *Apology* 21B, 23B: a divine being cannot lie and is truly wise; 28E, 33C: divine beings send commands and signs to men which they should obey; 30A-31B, 41D: divine beings care for and act on behalf of the true good of men. But the key points regarding Socrates' religious views are controversial: (1) is Socrates an agnostic, or a believer in the divine? and (2) does he hold to a personal or impersonal conception of the divine, i.e., does he conceive of the divine as = God or God(s), or as = the Good, of the Forms? For references to the scholarly debate, see McPherran, "Socratic Piety," 283-284. For recent discussions, see especially Beckman, *Religious Dimension*, 73-74, 171-181; Henry, "Socratic Piety," *New Essays*, 101-103; McPherran, "Socratic Piety," 300, 302-303; Versenyi, *Holiness*, 104-134; and West, *Plato's Apology*, 124-126, 143-150, 163-166, 194-196, 201-203. All agree that Socrates does not believe in the Gods of the Athenian state religion, but Versenyi and West regard Socrates as a thoroughgoing agnostic, while Beckman and Henry interpret Socratic piety as holding to an

impersonal, metaphysical conception of the divine = the Good. However, the Socrates of the early dialogues is not an agnostic in the ordinary sense of the term and he clearly is a believer in a personal God who displays causal powers, i.e. the God(s) who sent him on his mission and who cares for men. Socrates is an agnostic only in the sense that he realizes he lacks *knowledge* of the existence and nature of the God(s); see the discussion in section V and footnotes [36], [40] and [41] below.

27. For Socrates' conception of the human good, see *Apology* 29A-30B; *Crito* 46B-49E; also *Gorgias* 506C-508B, in contrast to 482C-486D. For discussion of Socrates' conception of the good, see Gregory Vlastos, "Happiness and Virtue in Socrates' Moral Theory," *Proceedings of the Cambridge Philological Society* 210(1984): 183-213; Ilham Dilman, *Morality and the Inner Life* (New York: Harper & Row, 1979), 39-69; Henry, "Socratic Piety," *New Essays*, 99-104; and Schmid, "Philosophy and Moral Commitment," *Ancient Philosophy* 2(1982): 134-141.

28. Thus Socrates speaks in the *Apology* of what is *themiton*, "divinely ordered," and in general conceives of human life in teleological terms, 29D-30B. See also especially *Gorgias* 506C-508B and the other citations in footnote [27] above, together with the discussion of the young Socrates' teleological theology in the autobiography in the *Phaedo* 96A-100A. Henry, in particular, has captured nicely this aspect of Socratic piety: "Socratic piety is not really directed toward the gods but toward the wisdom, truth, order and good beyond the gods, the bonds of the whole cosmos, and Socratic power is participation in the immortality and power of the whole" ("Socratic Piety," *New Essays*, 104).

29. See especially *Apology* 28E-31C. Socrates speaks quite clearly and emphatically of the God as calling him and his fellow citizens to the cause of virtue and wisdom (21B, 23A, 28E, 29D, 30A, 30D-31A, 31D, 33C, 40A-C) and of the God as acting to care for good men (41D; 30D seems more to refer to a cosmic law). His discussion of virtue and the soul also clearly has a decidedly religious tone in the *Apology*, especially insofar as the integrity of the person is guaranteed by divine ordinance (30D) and the destiny of the soul is bound up with whether or not one has lived a good life (40A f.). See [32] below.

30. Compare the interpretation of the Socratic view of the soul in Dilman, *Morality and the Inner Life*, especially 38-39, 179-186; also the stimulating account of the relationship of thinking to the formation of conscience in Socrates in Hannah Arendt, *Thinking* (New York: Harcourt Brace Javanovich 1971), 166-193.

31. This overall picture of the relationship of early Platonic, Socratic virture theory and especially Socratic existence to middle Platonic metaphysical theory I owe largely to Robert S. Brumbaugh, though he might well disagree with my formulation of it here. See the discussions of Socrates and Plato in Robert S. Brumbaugh, *The Philosophers of Greece* (New York: Crowell, 1964), 123-171, especially 141-142 on the role of Socratic idealism as a basis for the philosophical vision of the middle dialogues.

32. For Socrates' view of the soul, its welfare and primacy in human life, see *Apology* 28D-30C, *Crito* 47A-49E. The question about the immortality of the soul is left open in the *Apology*, but at *Crito* 54B-C Socrates has "the Laws" speak of the afterlife as a fact. See Vlastos' discussion of this point and the absolute value of the soul in "The Paradox," 5; and Dilman on the relation between the Socratic notions of soul and will and the concept of absolute values, *Morality and the Inner Life*, 38-39, 179-186. Of course in the *Phaedo* the soul is presented as a substantive being that survives the death of the body, but Socratic or early Platonic doctrine seems less rigid on this point. See also *Charmides* 156D-157B, which does

not imply separate existence.

33. See *Apology* 28D-30C: for Socrates the *telos* of man is to become wise and virtuous, while the God(s) is perfectly wise (23A-B) and good (21A, *Euthyphro* 6A-C, 13B-14B). Given this conception of the divine, the *telos* of man may be said to be that of striving to "imitate God" (cf. *Republic* 613A; *Theaetetus* 176B; also *Gorgias* 507E-508A) – within the context of the reflective wisdom and self-knowledge that human nature cannot possess such perfection, but only strive to achieve it (cf. *Apology* 21A-23B; *Gorgias* 507A-E; *Symposium* 208A-B).

34. On this point, see *Apology* 28E-29D, 30C-D, 35C-D and the discussion in West, *Plato's Apology*, 206 and in Schmid, "The Socratic Conception of Courage," *History of Philosophy Quarterly* 2, 2(April 1985): 113-129. The discussion at *Apology* 35C-D refers specifically to the impeity of violating oaths.

35. For discussion of "the Socratic gospel," see Heinrich Maier, *Sokrates* (Tuebingen, Germany: Mohr, 1913), 296ff. and Vlastos, "The Paradox," 4-7.

36. On Socrates' ignorance of divine things, see esp. *Euthyphro* 5A, 6B and *Apology* 19A-D, as well as the implications of 21A-23B. For the distinction between "knowledge" and "reasoned belief" and its centrality in Socratic thought, see *Apology* 21A-23B; Gregory Vlastos, "Socrates' Disavowal of Knowledge," *The Philosophical Quarterly* 35, 138(January 1985): 1-31; and Schmid, "Socratic Moderation and Self-Knowledge," cited in footnote [4] above. In the *Apology* Socrates generally uses some variant of *oiomai*, "I believe" to refer to his religious beliefs (cf. e.g. 28E, 30A, 30D); also *kinduneuei*, "it seems likely" (23A), *elpis*, "hope" (40C). This in sharp contrast both to *oida*, "I know" applied to moral principle (29B), and, in a different way, to divine wisdom (23A, also 42A). Socrates uses the term *pisteuo*, "I trust" in the *Gorgias* to speak of his "faith" in the *mythos* of a Judgement and an afterlife (524B); of course the term *pistis* is a technical term as the second level of cognition in the divided line, *Republic* 509D-511E, but it is not clear he is using it in this technical sense in the *Gorgias*. The term "faith" might be objected to on the grounds that it carries the epistemological connotation of belief in a revealed God, like the God of the Abrahamic traditions, but unlike Socrates' God(s); however, faith seems preferable to "belief" in other crucial respects, including the connotation of comprehensive outlook and significant practical consequences. See also the discussion of Socrates' use of "faith" (*pisteuo*) in the *Gorgias* in Dilman, *Morality and the Inner Life*, 170-179.

37. This is to make very loose comparisons, of course. The theme of the Buddha as a Socratic-type questioner is important in the Mahayana stream of Buddhism, especially in the Zen Buddhist tradition; and there are many dialogues in Buddhist scripture which present him in this way. See, e.g., the selection "On Theology" translated from early Buddhist scriptures in Robert Ballow, ed., *World Bible* (New York: Viking, 1944), 121-123. For an account of the Buddha's views that is in many ways similar to the Socratic stance to knowledge, see Chapter IV, "The Attitude to Authority" in K.N. Jayatilleke, *Early Buddhist Theory of Knowledge* (London: George Allen & Unwin, 1963), especially the discussion of Socratic ignorance in the Vlastos and Schmid essays cited in footnote [36] above.

38. See the discussion and references in footnote [9] concerning the prosecutions for impiety in ancient Athens. In all of the Abrahamic faiths the credal conception of religion – adherence to the basic dogmas of the faith as matters of revealed truth and religious knowledge – is predominant, though orthodoxy may be somewhat more emphasized in Christianity than in Judaism and Islam. Even theologians within the Abrahamic traditions will often hold to the view that religious knowledge is more, not less, certain than scientific knowledge (cf. e.g. Thomas

Aquinas, *Summa Theologiae* 1.1:1-3).

39. Compare the discussion in Beckman, *The Religious Dimension*, 41-44.

40. However, attempts to see in Socrates' response an attempt at "debunking" the oracle and a hubristic evaluation of himself as "the god's superior," as West, *Plato's Apology*, 107 would have it, fail to appreciate both the generally enigmatic character of the oracle's sayings and the very real quality of piety in Socrates' response: see the discussions in W.K.C. Guthrie, *Socrates* (Cambridge: Cambridge University, 1971), 87-88 and Brickhouse and Smith, "The Origin," 657-659, 663-667. Certainly, too, the most reasonable view of Socrates' relation to his *daimonion* is to acknowledge that he presents it in the *Apology* and other early dialogues as a genuinely mysterious, God-sent voice that he accepts and trusts in, which is not to say that he would obey it blindly and even let it prevent him from doing what, on reflection, he thinks is right (see the basic moral principles at *Apology* 29B and *Crito* 46B).

41. See especially 21B and 23A, where Socrates speaks clearly of his view of "the God" (*ho theos*; his obvious belief in the reality of his *daimonion*, e.g. at 31D where he calls it "something divine and spiritual" (*theon ti kai daimonion*) and 40A-C, 30D, 31A, and 41D where he speaks of the God's care for men or of "divine ordinance" (*themiton*); and 33C, where he dramatically declares his belief that he was "commanded" (*prosetaksei*)by "the God" (*ho theos*) through oracles and dreams and in every way in which any man was ever commanded by "divine allotment" (*theia moria*.

42. See Burkert's discussion of this discrimination, *Greek Religion*, 272-275. Euthyphro, in prosecuting his father, violates the most basic Apollonian principle of piety by going, from a religious basis (!), against custom; see especially on the relationship between the cult of Apollo and the morality of custom in Nilsson, *Greek Piety*, 30-52 and *History of Greek Religion*, 180-222.

43. Euthyphro's own religious stance has not always been understood by commentators. While his claims to foresee the future are extraordinary and his action in relation to his father is deeply impious by conventional standards, his definitions of piety, after the first clumsy effort, reflect traditional ways of thinking. Compare the most recent discussion, William Furley, "The Figure of Euthyphro in Plato's Dialogue," *Phronesis* 30, 2(1985): 201-208 with Richard Hoerber, "Plato's Euthyphro," *Phronesis* 3(1958): 95-107. Furley's remarks are generally sound though he underestimates the radical nature of Euthyphro's break with religious custom in prosecuting his father, p. 206, and does not discuss the important conclusion of the dialogue, 15D-16A. There Socrates emphasizes the role of caution or fear of the Gods to piety and conduct in acccordance with custom. Socrates' apparent defense of custom in the *Euthyphro* has been often misunderstood, e.g. by Peter Geach in "Plato's Euthyphro" in *Logic Matters* (Berkeley, Ca.: University of California, 1972), 31-44. But Socrates does not claim that he, Socrates, knows that what Euthyphro's father did was right, rather he seems to be engaged in his usual path of teaching humility. If you are going to violate conventional morality so radically and then brag on it, claiming wisdom, as Euthyphro does, 4B-5A, you should know what you are talking about; but as the story of the oracle indicates, Socrates found his fellow citizens who claimed such wisdom never had it. In general, Euthyphro seems to present the vice associated with piety – dogmatic fanaticism – rather than its virtue. He is a kind of sophist in relation to piety, somewhat as, e.g. Nicias is in relation to courage, or Meno in relation to virtue, though they are also the students of professional sophists, and so also represent another theme in the early dialogues,

the corrupting influence of sophistic education. But like them, he seems to lack some of the prerequisities of successful elenctic learning. See the discussion of Euthyphro in Schmid,"Socratic Moderation and Self-Knowledge," cited in footnote [4] above and the discussion of Socratic teaching in Schmid, "Socrates' Practice of *Elenchus* in the *Charmides*," *Ancient Philosophy* 1, 2(Spring 1981): 141-147.

44. See the discussion in footnote [23] above concerning Socrates' attitude toward prayer and sacrifice. As noted there, he seems to be opposed to the selfish, materialist attitude he finds in Euthyphro's understanding of sacrifice, more than the act itself. This at least is a major theme in the possibly spurious *Alcibiades* II. Consider also, in relation to the end of the *Euthyphro*, Augustine's comments on Cain's attitude toward sacrifice: "This is what is done by all those who follow their own will, and not the will of God; that is, those who live with a perverted instead of an upright heart, and yet offer a gift to God. They suppose that with this gift God is being bought over to help them, not in curing their depraved desires, but in fulfilling them. And this is the characteristic of the earthly city – to worship a god or gods so that with their assistance it may reign in the enjoyment of victories and an earthly peace, not with a loving concern for others, but with lust for domination over them. For the good make use of this world in order to enjoy God, whereas the evil want to make use of God in order to enjoy this world ..." *The City of God*, trans. H. Bettenson (New York: Penguin, 1972), 604.

45. See the emphasis in the discussion at *Apology* 28E, 29D 30A, 31B, 33C on his personal experience. It is also noteworthy that Socrates appears to be convinced at the end of the *Apology* and *Crito* of the providential quality of his experience, of the sense that God has led him not only to his mission but to the very path of his conduct at the trial and afterward, cf. *Apology* 40A-C, 41D and *Crito* 54E. As for the possibilty there may not be an afterlife, see 40C-D, but also *Crito* 54B-C and footnote [32]. The possibility that there may not be a God is implicit in his discussion of his ultimate ignorance of divine things. See the references in footnote [36] and discussion in footnote [26] above.

46. See the discussion in Vlastos, "The Paradox," 5.

47. Piety is not one of the cardinal virtues listed in *Republic* IV. However, piety or religion would appear to be a basic virtue for the craftsmen and lower guardian class, being the analogous virtue for them to wisdom in the rulers. On the role of dogmatic belief in the account of "civic courage," see *Republic* 386A-388C, 429A-430C. Compare the discussion in Averroes, *Averroes on Plato's Republic*, trans. Ralph Lerner (Ithaca, N.Y.: Cornell University, 1974), especially 9-22. For further discussion of the potential separation of piety from the other Socratic virtues, see section VI below.

48. See Beckman, *Religious Dimension*, 52-54; Irwin, *Plato's Moral Theory*, 22, 301n57; and C.C.W. Taylor, "The End of the *Euthyphro*," *Phronesis* 2(1982): 109-118. Versenyi, *Holiness*, 104-111 and his earlier *Socratic Humanism* (New Haven, Ct.: Yale University, 1963), 105-110, may also be said to hold this position, through his emphasis is on the irrelevance of the Gods to the Socratic view and on the identity of piety with wisdom, understood as knowledge of the good. For critical discussion of Versenyi's interpretation of the *Euthyphro*, see McPherran, "Socratic Piety," 287-297.

49. See *Apology* 28E-29B, 29D, 30A-B and especially 31D in contrast to 32A-D, *Crito* 49A f. on what he owes "the Laws"; also *Crito* 54B-C and *Gorgias* 507A-B on the contrast between justice and piety. See also *Apology* 32D where Socrates says he would suffer death rather than do anything "unjust" (*adikon*) or "impious" (*anho-*

sion), and then states that the government did not frighten him into doing anything "unjust" (adikon). See also, on whether or not Socrates endorses the view that piety is a part of "the right" (as suggested by Euthyphro 11E-12D), the debate between Gregory Vlastos, "The Unity of the Virtues in the Protagoras," Platonic Studies (Princeton, N.J.: Princeton University, 1973), 228 and Irwin, Plato's Moral Theory, 301n.57; McPherran, "Socratic Piety," 284-292, 297f. provides conclusive arguments in favor of Vlastos' interpretation. Overall the evidence tends to support the view that Socratic piety and justice are conceptually distinct virtues. However, insofar as Socratic piety involves the comprehensive religious sensibility and commitment to goodness discussed in section IV and footnote [28], it may also be conceived of as a fundamental virtue informing and encompassing all aspects of the Socratic way of life. Compare the discussion of Socratic courage in Schmid, "The Socratic Conception of Courage," cited in footnote [34], also footnotes [50], [51] and [55] below.

50. Compare the following from the Theologica Germanica, Chapter 10: "Where men are enlightened with the true light, they ... renounce all desire and choice, and commit and commend themselves and all things to the Eternal Goodness ... so that every enlightened man could say, 'I would fain to be to the eternal Goodness what his own hand is to a man.' ... Such men are in a state of freedom, because they have lost the fear of pain or hell, and the hope of reward or heaven, and are living in pure submission to the eternal Goodness, in the perfect freedom of fervent love." (I owe this reference and translation to Gregory Vlastos.) However, as argued in footnote [26], [28] and [29], the evidence of the early dialogues clearly testifies to Socrates' belief in the God(s) who has acted to bring about good in the world, and therefore does not support those accounts which identify the personal, if unknown God of Socratic piety and the Good or the Forms, which are the objects of metaphysical wisdom in the middle Platonic dialogues.

51. The classic statement of the interentailment theory is Gregory Vlastos, "The Unity of the Virtues," Platonic Studies, 221-265. Statements of the identity theory are found in Versenyi, Socratic Humanism, 83-110;Terry Penner, "The Unity of the Virtues in the Protagoras," Review of Metaphysics 82(1973): 35-68; and Paul Woodruff, "Socrates on the Parts of Virtue," Canadian Journal of Philosophy, 2(1976): 101-116. My own theory is presented in Schmid, "The Socratic Conception of Courage," cited in footnote [34] above.

52. On the former point, see again the discussion in section IV and Vlastos, "The Paradox," 5. For discussion of the theory that Socrates began his mission out of a sense of religious duty, see Brickhouse and Smith, "The Origin," 662-665.

53. See Richard Robinson, An Atheist's Values (Oxford: Oxford University, 1964), 113-123. Incidentally, Christians of rather different varieties are opposed to faith assents which go against one's intellectual conscience. See, for example, Thomas Aquinas' remark that it would be "wrong" even to believe in Christ if you thought it irrational, Summa Theologiae 1.2:19,5 and his discussion of rationality and faith in Summa Theologiae 2.2:2,10 ; and R.M. Hare, "The Simple Believer," in Gene Outka and John Reeder, Religion and Morality (Garden City, N.Y.: Doubleday, 1973), 393-427.

54. Thus in the Crito he does submit his views to examination, and at the end of the Apology he entertains an argument on behalf of his apparent belief in an afterlife. Unlike the religious fanatic, he has and will again examine his views rationally: compare the end of the Crito 54D-E.

55. One reason why Socrates might not feel it was generally worthwhile examining his religious views, however, is if his course of conduct no longer depends on

them; and this at the end of his life would seem to be so, for as noted earlier in relation to the potential separation of piety from the other virtues, Socrates finds his philosophical service to be intrinsically rewarding, whatever his original motivation, and his eudaimonistic arguments on behalf of philosophy and justice do not depend upon an afterlife for their validity, at least not insofar as he presents them; see especially his account of his dual reasons for philosophizing, *Apology* 37E-38A; also 40Cf. and sections IV - V, footnotes [32], [36], and [52]. So as a thoroughly practical and ethical man who claims no *knowledge* of the God(s), it might be thought Plato's Socrates would hold all beliefs about the Gods' attitudes to be superfluous, including his own (see *Apology* 19A-D, *Euthyphro* 6B). On the other hand, he does consider at the end of the *Apology*, if only for the benefit of his "true judges" and friends, the rationality of belief in an afterlife; so already in the earliest dialogues appears a Socrates who holds religious beliefs and tells myths about the human soul. Can we not imagine his examining with such friends or students as these, in a manner consistent with his philosophy and character if not with his early Platonic role as elenctic teacher, his personal religious belief in the perfect goodness and wisdom of the God(s)?

56. For discussion of the most basic divine attributes, see, e.g. Anselm, *Prosloqium* 5, 8-11, 19-21 and *Monoloqium* 15, 20-24, 31; Thomas Aquinas, *Summa Theoloqiae* 1:3-11, 21 and 24-25; also Nelson Pike, *God and Timelessness* (New York: Schoken, 1970), especially 39-52; H.A. Wolfson, "The Philonic God of Revelation," *Religious Philosophy* (Cambridge, Ma.: Harvard University, 1961), 1-26; and John Hick, "The Judeo-Christian Concept of God," *The Philosophy of Religion* (Englewood Cliffs, N.J.: Prentice-Hall, 1983), 5-14. *Euthyphro* 10A-11B concerns the ethical question of moral authoritarianism; but it also reflects one of the most basic antinomies of theological reflection, namely whether (a) the nature of God is such that He voluntarily wills what is good (or right) and thereby makes it to be good (or right), apparently implying that he can capriciously change the standard of good (or right) and/or act independent of His omniscient wisdom; or (b) God necessarily wills what is good (right) because it is good (right), apparently implying there is an independent standard of good (or right) than God's will and/or that He does not act freely. Robert Anderson has pointed out to me that Socrates does not force this "destructive insight" on Euthyphro. I am not inclined to think Socrates thought it poses an insurmountable rational obstacle to religious faith of the kind he espouses.

57. Socrates speaks at *Apology* 40C of a "great proof" (*mega tekmerion*) given to him that death is not an evil, namely that his *daimonion* would have opposed him if he were not going to something good; but he presents this as convincing evidence for himself, not necessarily for others, and he immediately then proceeds to offer in 40Cf. an argument to support the "hope" (*elpis*) that death is in general a good thing for humans, or at least for morally good people. Socrates' most pointed argument to the court on behalf of the superhuman character of his mission and the truth of his words, apart from the story of the oracle itself, is his poverty and altruism (see 31D).

58. John Burnet, "The Socratic Doctrine," *Essays and Addresses*, 127.

59. For the Aristophanic view of Socrates, see, in addition to *The Clouds*, Leo Strauss, *Socrates and Aristophanes* (New York: Basic Books, 1966), especially 3-53, 309-314. Hegel's discussion of Socrates and Athens is in his *Lectures on the History of Philosophy*, trans. E.S. Haldane and F.H. Simpson (New York: Humanities, 1952), 425-447. Nietzsche's critical view of Socrates as the degenerate and destructive spirit of rationalism is discussed in *The Birth of Tragedy*, trans. F. Golffing (Garden

City, N.Y.: Doubleday, 1956), especially 69-96. He took a more appreciative view of Socrates in later works; see Walter Kaufmann, *Nietzsche* (Princeton, N.J.: Princeton University, 1974), 391-411. Compare the views of Hegel and Nietzsche to those of Thomas West, *Plato's Apology*, 136-143, 166-178, who also sees a deep conflict between Socrates and the city.

2

MENO 86C-89A: A MATHEMATICAL IMAGE OF PHILOSOPHIC INQUIRY

Kenneth Seeskin

I

INTRODUCTION

Unlike other dialogues of search, the *Meno* has a sustained discussion of how the search is to proceed.[1] The title character argues that if we do not know what virtue is, we will not know where to look for it. Socrates responds with the theory of recollection and attempts to demonstrate its effectiveness by questioning an illiterate slave. At the end of the demonstration (86B), Meno seems persuaded by Socrates' account of the Slave's progress, and Socrates suggests that they resume their search for a definition of virtue. But Meno, recalcitrant as ever, insists that they abandon the search for a definition and return to the question of whether virtue can be taught (*didakton*).[2]

Earlier in the dialogue (70B), Socrates put off the issue of whether virtue can be taught, claiming that he could not address it until he knew what virtue is. This is his familiar point that one cannot answer the question *poion ti* (What is virtue like? i.e., What are its attendant properties?) until one has answered *ti* (What is virtue?).[3] Though Socrates agrees to go along with Meno, he insists he would rather do things his own way (86D-E): "If I governed you, Meno, and not only myself, we would not consider whether or not virtue can be taught before first inquiring into what it is. But since you don't even attempt to govern yourself, in order to remain free, but both try to govern me and succeed, I will yield to you – for what am I to do? Apparently we must consider what virtue is like without yet knowing what it is."

To get the discussion started, Socrates introduces "a method of hypothesis" borrowed from geometers. Briefly stated, the method attempts to tackle the question "Can virtue be taught?" by identifying a series of hypotheses from which an answer can be deduced.

We do not know what virtue is. But we can identify the conditions under which it will be teachable. Since knowledge is the only thing which can be taught, if virtue is a kind of knowledge, then it can be taught. It should be understood, however, that "Virtue is a kind of knowledge" is not offered as a definition of virtue. According to Socrates, it tells us what virtue is like (*poion* 87B, 97C). In any case, "Virtue is a kind of knowledge" is handled in a similar way. If virtue is good, if all good things are profitable (*ōphelimon*), and if all profitable things either depend on or include knowledge, virtue will be a kind of knowledge. It is then agreed that virtue is good (87D), from which it follows that virtue can be taught.[4] Schematically, we have

1. Virtue is good
2. Virtue is a kind of knowledge
3. Virtue can be taught.

The argument from "Virtue is good" to "Virtue is a kind of knowledge" is not very rigorous when judged by contemporary standards. Sometimes Socrates talks about knowledge (*epistēmē*) 87B), sometimes about wisdom (*phronēsis* 88C), and sometimes about good sense or intelligence (*nous* 88B). Sometimes he claims that virtue is knowledge and sometimes that it is a kind of knowledge (e.g. 87D). Even the conclusion is ambiguous: Virtue is knowledge either in whole or in part (89A4).[5] But the ambiguities of the argument do not concern me. Assume there is a good reason for thinking that "Virtue is good" implies "Virtue is a kind of knowledge." What conerns me is the method Socrates uses when he argues that one proposition is true because it follows from another.

Needless to say, this method has caused a great deal of debate. On the surface, it appears to do what Socrates had earlier said could not be done: to tell us how virtue is acquired without first answering the question of what virtue is. Has Socrates changed his mind about the priority of *ti* to *poion ti*? This seems unlikely in view of the end of the dialogue (100B), where it is restated, and in view of similar passages in the *Protagoras* (360E-361A, 361C) and *Republic* (354C). Bluck argues that the search for a definition has been abandoned and that the method of hypothesis is used to "... get over or get around the difficulty that what virtue is has not been decided."[6] But Bluck's view raises a serious question. If Socrates is still committed to the priority of *ti*, how can this difficulty ever be gotten over or gotten around? And if there is a way of getting around it, why did Socrates insist on first answering the *ti* question back at 70B?

More recently, J.T. Bedu-Addo has argued that despite appearances, the search for a definition of virtue has not been abandoned.[7]

The method of hypothesis allows Meno to attain true opinion about the nature of virtue, i.e., that it is knowledge. This state corresponds to that achieved by the slave at the end of Socrates' experiment. For Bedu-Addo, neither Socrates' reluctance to go along with Meno nor the subsequent argument to show that virtue is not knowledge are to be taken at face value. All Socrates has done is demonstrate the transitory nature of right opinion. This interpretation requires that Bedu-Addo take "Virtue is knowledge" as a satisfactory definition of virtue. We have seen, however, that the text indicates otherwise. The connection between virtue and knowledge is never formulated in a precise way and is taken by Socrates as an answer to the question *poion*. Moreover, I do not think that the argument to overturn the connection between virtue and knowledge can be written off as easily as Bedu-Addo claims. I will have more to say on this point in a later section.

What we have, then, is a difficult passage introduced by a mathematical metaphor. My translation continues (86E-87B):

> But at least relax your rule over me just a little and agree to inquire by means of hypothesis whether it can be taught, or comes to be present in some other way. By that I mean the method of inquiry geometers often use. For example, if someone asks them about a given area, whether it is possible for this area to be inscribed as a triangle in a given circle, they might reply: "I do not yet know whether the area is of this sort, but I think there is, as it were, a hypothesis to help us deal with the problem, namely: if the area is such that when applied along the line given for it, it fails short by an area similar to the one which has just been applied, I think one thing follows; but a different thing follows if it is impossible for this to be done to it. By using an hypothesis, I am willing to tell you what follows in regard to the inscription of the area in the circle, whether it is possible or not." Let us do the same with virtue. Since we know neither what it is nor what it is like, let us employ a hypothesis in the following way to decide whether or not it can be taught.

The problem with many of the existing discussions of this passage is exactly the one Robert Brumbaugh mentions in *Plato's Mathematical Imagination*.[8] They try to bypass the explanation of mathematical allusions and interpret the text without them. The most explicit example is A.E. Taylor's discussion of the *Meno* in *Plato: The Man and His Work.*[9] But Taylor is hardly alone.[10]

I hope to show that if we look closely at the mathematics of the passage, we will find that far from introducing the method of hypothesis as a model of inquiry, Socrates is holding it up to criticism. In other words, my interpretation follows Malcolm Brown's interpretation of the slave-boy passage. Brown's claim is that the introduction of a distinctively geometrical argument at 84D, as well as a *poion* statement, is an implied criticism of geometry on the grounds that it puts off fundamental questions in favor of derivative ones.[11] If I am right in suggesting that the present passage makes the same point, we have a way of accounting for the unity of the dialogue and the fact that it never achieves a satisfactory answer to how virtue is acquired. In Brown's words: "... leaving a fundamental question only hypothetically answered, like leaving it unanswered, can only lead one to a result which is not thoroughly clear." What is more, if the *Meno* is critical of the methods employed by geometers, we can see a smooth transition between it and Plato's criticism of geometry in the *Republic*.

II

THE GEOMETRY PROBLEM

The mathematical problem is difficult to interpret for several reasons. It is introduced in summary fashion, which means that Socrates is short on details. It uses technical language which differs from that of Euclid. The grammar of the passage is puzzling and has been the subject of debate. Bluck has reviewed the literature and proposed an interpretation of his own.[12]

Following Brumbaugh, we may posit three requirements for a correct interpretation.[13] (1) The passage must be "the sort of thing a geometer would say" in the sense that Socrates is here illustrating a general method in use at the end of the fifth century; (2) the problem must have intrinsic mathematical interest or be well known to someone reasonably acquainted with geometry; (3) the problem must be dramatically appropriate in the sense that Meno is capable of understanding it. The difficulty is in finding an interpretation which satisfies (2) and (3) .

Without going through each of the proposed solutions, let me summarize the results of Bluck's discussion.

1. It is all but certain that geometer has a genuine *diorismos* or

statement of the conditions both necessary and sufficient for a solution. The received interpretation of 87B-C is that "Virtue is knowledge" is a necessary and sufficient condition for "Virtue can be taught." If the geometer were not working with necessary and sufficient conditions, the analogy between the geometry problem and the ensuing dialectic would be broken. What is more, the wording of the passage "One thing follows if the area can be applied, a different thing follows if it cannot" makes necessary and sufficient conditions mandatory.

2. It is all but certain that "to fall short" (*elleipein*) is being used in a technical sense consistent with Euclid and, according to Proclus' account of Eudemus, the early Pythagoreans as well.[14] I will have more to say on the meaning of this term below.

3. It is all but certain that "it" (*autou* 87A3) refers to the area and not to the circle. Taking it to refer to the circle puts undue strain on the Greek.

4. It is natural to take "the given line" as the diameter of the circle, which is the baseline on which the inscription is performed. This is not required by the meaning of the word *gramme*, which is as general as our word "line," but some conditions have to be imposed on the given line, and this seems the simplest one.

The only interpretation which satisfies all of these points is that of Cook Wilson and later Thomas Heath.[15]

Wilson draws on the similarity between the present passage and *Euclid* VI.28, a theorem having to do with the application of areas. This procedure, spelled out in Euclid I.44-5, enabled the Greek mathematician to transform any rectilineal area into a parallelogram with a given line as base and containing a given angle. Since the simplest of all parallelograms is a rectangle, he could express any rectilineal area as the product of two numbers, the base and height of the rectangle into which the figure had been transformed. The interpretation thus runs as follows: Whether it is possible to inscribe in a given circle a triangle equal in area to a given rectilineal figure.

A fifth century mathematician would have answered as Socrates indicates: "I don't yet know whether the area is of this sort, but I think there is a hypothesis to help us deal with the problem, namely: if the area is such that when applied along the line given, it falls short by an area similar to the one which has just been applied, I think one thing follows; but a different thing follows if it is impossible for this to be done to it." To understand what he is talking

about, consider Figure 1. Let X be the area. The question asks
whether it can be inscribed as a triangle in a given circle. To begin,
asssume that the inscription is possible. Let BDE be an isosceles
triangle equal in area to X. BH is the diameter of the circle and
bisects the base of the triangle DE at right angles. Construct
rectangle ABCD on the diameter. Clearly BDE is equal in area to
ABCD so that ABCD is equal in area to X. It can be shown that BC
x CH = CD^2 If so, then BC:CD = CD:CH. Construct CDGH. Since
BC:CD = CD:CH, CDGH is similar to ABCD.[16] In other words,
ABCD falls short of BH by a rectangle similar to itself. It follows,
therefore, that if the inscription is possible, the required rectangle
can be found. Conversely, it would be easy to show that if ABCD is
equal in area to X and falls short of BH by a rectangle similar to
itself, the D lies on the circumference of the circle so that the
inscription can be done.

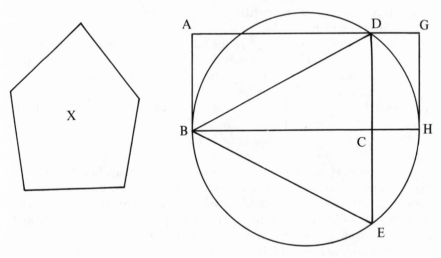

FIGURE 1

The chief advantages of the Wilson-Heath interpretation are that
it does not strain the Greek, does not require essential information
absent from the text, and alludes to an intrinsically interesting
problem. The chief disadvantage is, as Heijboer objected, and Heath
admitted, that it is equivalent to solving a biquadratic equation,
something which all parties to the debate consider beyond the capa-

bility of a fifth century mathematician.[17] There are accounts of solutions worked out before the time of Plato, but I will follow Heath, Bluck, and Heijboer in rejecting them.[18] The dramatic date of the *Meno* is 402 B.C., the actual date around 387. Why would Plato refer to a problem which was, in Heath's terms, "still awaiting a solution?" And if he did refer to this problem, which the best mathematicians of the fifth century could not solve, how could he expect an amateur like Meno to understand it? Bluck, speaking for the majority of scholars, rejects the Wilson-Heath interpretation for two reasons: (1) the solution of the problem requires mathematics too complicated for Meno to understand, and (2) Socrates' concluding remarks: "So by using a hypothesis, I am willing to tell you what follows in regard to the inscription of the area in the circle, whether it is possible or not" clearly imply that the geometer be in a position to tell whether the conditions set forth in the hypothesis can be satisfied. But since the problem could not be solved at the dramatic date of the dialogue, the geometer could not be in such a position.

III

GEOMETRY AND THE TEACHING OF VIRTUE

I wish to argue that neither of Bluck's considerations is true and that only by recognizing that the problem could not be solved by the mathematicians of the day can we see what bearing it has on the discussion of virtue. In short, what most scholars take to be the great failing of the Wilson-Heath interpretation is really another advantage.

To begin with, we must distinguish between the mathematics needed to understand what a problem is and that needed to offer a solution. The problem of quadrature, or squaring the circle, was so well known in the fifth century that Aristophanes could refer to it in a play.[19] But the mathematics needed to see that one cannot construct a square equal in area to a given circle was not developed for centuries. So it is important to separate ease of recognition from ease of resolution. In straining to find a problem whose solution lay within the powers of fifth century mathematics, Bluck and others must supply information which is not found in the text or which renders the problem uninteresting. In the second place, it is questionable whether the passage implies that the geometer must be in a position to tell whether the conditions set forth in the hypothesis can be satisfied. For purposes of illustration all that matters is that the hypothesis state conditions necessary and sufficient for a solution, not the solution itself. Suppose that we do not know whether P is true. There may be a great gain in showing that Q is itself awaiting a solution. Hippocrates of Chios made a significant discovery when he showed that the problem of doubling a cube could be reduced to that of finding two mean proportionals even though the latter problem was also "awaiting a solution."

In fact, we have trouble making sense of the rest of the dialogue if we do not keep this point in mind. As we have seen, the conclusion "Virtue can be taught" is reduced to "Virtue is a kind of knowledge" which in turn follows from "Virtue is good." How do we know that virtue is good in the sense of being profitable or beneficial? Could a person not argue that virtue brings no recognizable reward? Meno agrees that virtue is profitable but an agreement between the questioner and his respondent does not imply knowledge – anymore than agreement among the practitioners of a science on the meaning of key terms would, in Plato's view, enable them to claim knowledge. The question whether all virtuous things are profitable – whether it pays to be virtuous – was itself "awaiting a solution." It took Plato all of the *Republic* to solve it.

Here we would do well to recall the primary meaning of the word *hypothesis* in Plato. According to Robinson, a hypothesis is not a proposition put forward in a tentative way and subjected to examination; it is first and foremost a proposition put forward in order to prove something else.[20] That is, a hypothesis is normally a premise, not a demonstrand. This is certainly the meaning Plato has in mind at *Meno* 87D, when he calls the proposition "Virtue is good" a hypothesis. Nowhere in the dialogue is there a sustained discussion of whether this proposition is true. It is put forward in order to lend support to the proposition "Virtue is a kind of knowledge." Indeed, there could not be a sustained discussion of "Virtue is good" because to initiate that discussion, Socrates and Meno would have to decide what virtue is. But the question of what virtue is was put off at Meno's insistence. So everything Socrates and Meno say about the teaching of virtue is derived from an unexamined assumption.

I submit that just as the geometers of the late fifth century could not tell whether the conditions set forth in the hypothesis could be satisfied, and had to proceed in a provisional way, Socrates and Meno cannot tell whether "Virtue is good" can be satisfied either. Insisting that the geometer be able to satisfy these conditions is certain to distort one's view of the rest of the dialogue. Thus Heijboer, in discussing the application of geometrical reasoning to ethics, refers to "the simple question of how virtue can be taught."[21] Yet the dialogue reveals that it is anything but simple, for Socrates and Meno never do answer it. While use of the hypothetical method leads them to conclude that virtue can be taught, no sooner is this conclusion stated than Socrates expresses misgivings (89C). In what follows, he rejects the claim that virtue can be taught and therefore must modify the claim that virtue is a kind of knowledge (97A).

The argument for rejecting the claim that virtue can be taught has aroused controversy for it is based on the fact that there are no teachers of virtue at present. As a general rule, the absence of X-ers does not entail that something cannot be X-ed.[22] Calculus was not taught in the fifth century, but a person would have been in error to conclude that it is not teachable. I have argued elsewhere that there is no analogy between an esoteric subject like calculus and virtue.[23] No one was trying to teach calculus, but the richest and most talented families in Athens went to great lengths to have virtue taught to their sons. So while Socrates' argument does not prove that virtue cannot be taught, it does offer strong grounds for supposing it cannot. Indeed, skepticism about the teaching of virtue is one of the most persistent themes of the early dialogues.[24] I suggest, therefore, that we have every reason to take Socrates' argument about the unteachability of virtue seriously.

My purpose is not to decide Socrates' final view on this issue, only to argue, against Heijboer, that it is by no means simple. As far as the *Meno* is concerned, the method of hypothesis produces a result at variance with the available evidence. So the moral dialectic of the *Meno* does not solve the question of how virtue is acquired. It offers provisional arguments on both sides of the issue and leaves us with an *aporia*.[25]

IV

PLATO'S CRITICISM OF GEOMETRY

I conclude that the method of hypothesis is not introduced as a paradigm of philosophic reasoning or as a way of getting around the difficulty that what virtue is has not yet been decided. This does not necessarily imply that the hypotheses are untrue or that they do not entail each other in the way Socrates describes. The objection is that they follow from an unproven starting point. If this is the kind of reasoning geometers employ, then, in Plato's eyes, geometry is not a model of rigor. To test their starting points, the geometers would have to follow the advice Socrates gives at the end of the dialogue and put the search for definition first. As long as definitions are not secured, there is no way to overcome the provisional nature of what follows.

To this I should add that geometry in the late fifth century was not the streamlined science which emerged after Euclid's codification. The search for elements or starting points was therefore a real issue. The fact that people in the early Academy, most notably, Theaetetus and Eudoxus, did much to clear things up, does not show that at the time of the *Meno*, Plato was satisfied with the foundations of this science. His criticism is essentially the one voiced by Frege over two thousand years later in regard to the foundations of arithmetic: that unless we understand what we are dealing with, the rigor of the proof remains an illusion however flawless the chain of deductions.[26]

In the *Republic*, Plato's criticism is more explicit. In a well known passage (510Bff.), he complains that the geometers introduce things whose meaning or nature they take for granted, providing no further account. Later on (533B-C) he renews this attack by distinguishing dialectic, which provides an account of what each thing is, and geometry, which does not. He then concludes: "For if your premise is something you do not know, and your conclusion and the intermediate steps a tangle of things you do not know, how could any conclusion you agree to ever become knowledge?" In fact, just prior to the above conclusion, Socrates describes the geometer as being in a dream-like state, a remark which cannot fail to remind us of his description of the slave (85C). It is also noteworthy that the word for application (*parateinein*) comes in for criticism at *Republic* 527A because it suggests the geometer is involved in a process or activity.

There is nothing wrong with the methods of the geometers provided they begin their demonstrations with properly formulated definitions or *archai*. Plato's skepticism is that, left to their own devices, they will reach such definitions. As far as the *Meno* is concerned, "Virtue can be taught" is supported by a chain of provisional assertions. Robinson calls attention to the fact that the hypothetical method in the *Meno* resembles Aristotle's "syllogism from hypothesis" as outlined in *Prior Analytics* 50a16-18.[27] This technique, according to Aristotle, is an inferior mode of demonstration. If the purpose of seeking a definition of virtue is to get beyond provisionality to something known to be true, it is hard to see how Plato could be recommending the method of hypothesis as a paradigm. On the other hand, allusion to an as yet unsolved problem, where provisionality was also the order of the day, would alert the reader not to expect more from the passage than it delivers.

The question of how to get beyond provisionality raises the issue of the upward path of dialectic. Thus the words of *Republic* 511A: "It [dialectic] does not treat its hypotheses as first principles, but as hypotheses in the true sense of the word, namely as stepping stones and starting points in order to reach that which is beyond hypothesis, the first principle of everything that is." Some scholars, most notably Cornford, have interpreted Proclus as connecting the upward path of dialectic with mathematical analysis.[28] On this view, analysis asks not what a certain proposition implies, but what would imply it; in other words, analysis is a process of identifying elements or first principles. Though it begins with hypotheses, it seeks to grasp the ultimate starting point from which these hypotheses follow. Cornford is joined by Gulley in maintaining that the method of hypothesis in the *Meno* is an early description of such a procedure.[29] We begin with the hypothesis "Virtue can be taught," reduce it to a more primitive one "Virtue is a kind of knowledge," and reduce that to "Virtue is good." While the last hypothesis is not reduced to something more primitive, Socrates has provided a good idea of what such reduction would be like. All we have to do is carry the process further.

Cornford's interpretation of analysis has been disputed by Robinson.[30] According to Robinson, analysis is limited to convertible propositions. While the text indicates that "Virtue can be taught" is convertible with "Virtue is a kind of knowledge," there is nothing to indicate that the latter is convertible with "Virtue is good." So on Robinson's view, the *Meno* does not use analysis consistently. But even if Cornford is right and analysis need not be limited to convertible propositions, we must ask whether the analytic method can ever lead to a definition of virtue. Cornford himself draws a sharp distinction between dialectic as practised in the sciences and as practised in morals. The first is analytic and leads to "the existence of a One." The second leads to a definition rather than an existence claim, and according to Cornford, is not analytic but elenctic:[31]

> The objective here is a definition, not, as in the mathematical field, a primitive hypothesis or assumption of existence;

and the technique of arriving at correct definitions is not the same as that of arriving at the ultimate hypothesis of science. The mathematician exercises his analytical faculty in penetrating to a prior truth; but he will not have to "fight his way" through a series of elenchi. When he "abolishes" demonstrable hypotheses, he does so by going behind them and showing how they can be obtained by deduction and finally confirmed (*bebaioun*). But the "hypothesis" of moral dialectic is an hypothesis in the original sense – not a true and demonstrable assumption of existence, but an inadequate tentative definition, suggested by the respondent, submitted to criticism by the questioner in the elenchus, and either amended or abandoned altogether. It is transformed or destroyed by criticism, and never restored or confirmed by subsequent deduction. Such suggestions are mere stepping-stones which are kicked away in the ascent to the correct definition.

On Cornford's view, then, a hypothesis in moral dialectic is not a proposition put forward with a view to proving something else but a proposition put forward in order to be subject to examination itself.

Note that if Cornford's dual conception of dialectic is true, the dialectical method needed to reach a definition of virtue, and the notion of hypothesis which goes with it, would not be the dialectical method and accompanying notion of hypothesis discussed at *Meno* 86C-87C. Again "Virtue is good" functions as a premise not a demonstrand. It is never revised or subjected to examination. It follows that a definition of virtue can be a hypothesis but not in the sense of the term required by this passage. I think there are reasons for doubting whether Cornford's conception is in fact the correct interpretation of the *Republic*.[32] My reason for bringing Cornford into the discussion is to point out that even if the method of hypothesis in the *Meno* is an early description of geometrical analysis, it is far from clear that moral dialectic would proceed in an analytic fashion. *Republic* 534B-D, which Cornford cites, indicates that the dialectician will reach a definition of the Good by imitating the elenctic method of the early dialogues. There is no mention here of something borrowed from the mathematicians.

Cherniss has called attention to the connection between the hypothetical method of the *Meno* and the one described at *Phaedo* 100A-101E.[33] In the latter passage, Socrates claims that his procedure is to hypothesize the proposition he believes to be the strongest and lay down as true whatever is in accord with it. If the hypothesis is accepted by the respondent and has no absurd or undesirable consequences, he then looks for a more ultimate hypothesis and repeats the procedure until he reaches something satisfatory. The precise nature of this method is disputed because it is not clear whether "agreement" means consistency or deducibility.[34] More important, it is not clear whether the *Phaedo* method applies to definitions or to existence claims. What is the hypothesis (100A) with which Socrates begins – (1) Beauty is such and such, or (2) There is a form of Beauty by which beautiful things are beautiful? In the remainder of the passage, particularly 100B-101C, all of the examples Socrates gives are of the latter sort.[35] We can agree with David Gallop that definitions are not far off.[36] But it does not follow that the *Phaedo's* method is meant to disclose the essence of moral qualities, and Socrates never actually says that it is.

In short, the evidence for linking the hypothetical method of the *Meno* to methods described in the *Phaedo* or *Republic* is sketchy at best. Suffice it to say that when definitional questions are raised in dialogues like the *Republic* and *Theaetetus*, there is no indication that Plato has consciously appropriated a method borrowed from geometers. In the *Cratylus* (436D), he rejects the idea that establishing consistency between provisional claims is enough and insists that the real issue is whether the original claim has been formulated properly:

> If the giver of names began in error, he may have forced everything else into agreement with it and with himself. There would be nothing strange in this, just as there is nothing strange when diagrams have a slight and imperceptible error in the first part of the demonstration and all of the huge mass of consequences agree with one another. That is why it is to the first principle (*arché*) that every one should direct the discussion and the inquiry, whether it is laid down correctly or not. Only when that has been examined sufficiently should we consider whether the rest appear to follow.

The mention of "diagrams" is a clear reference to geometry and the sort of reasoning introduced at *Meno* 86D-E. In this respect, it is consistent with Plato's attacks on geometrical reasoning in the *Republic*. Once again, the method proposed in the *Cratylus* sounds like the elenchus of the early dialogues where a definition is proposed and examined immediately rather than a procedure where it is reached at the end of a hypothetical chain.

V

CONCLUSION

I have argued that the method of hypothesis in the *Meno* leads to an *aporia* in regard to the teaching of virtue. The feeling of puzzlement is heightened by reference to a geometry problem whose solution was beyond the capabilities of current day mathematicians. If it is asked why Plato would introduce a method in which he had little confidence, the answer is that having led us to an *aporia*, he wants us to retrace our steps and see where the crucial mistake occurred. Under the circumstances, the crucial mistake occurs when Socrates "gives in" to Meno and agrees to discuss a derivative question first. The implication is clear: putting a derivative question first is bound to cause trouble – just as it has caused trouble for the geometers.

Brumbaugh has argued that a Platonic dialogue is often shaped like a pyramid. We begin at a low level of inquiry, ascend to a peak, and descend towards the conclusion. If he is right, it is not insignificant that the passage where the hypothetical method is introduced, 86C-87C, practically bisects the dialogue. Viewed in this light, the hypothetical method is the vehicle which turns the discussion around and points it in the direction of antinomy. Following Brown's suggestion, advance warning for such a turn occurs at 84D, when the slave, also imitating the geometers, takes up a *poion* statement. In this sense, there is a close analogy between the examination of the slave and the rest of the dialogue. Eventually the dialogue comes full circle as Socrates reiterates the necessity of tackling the *ti* question first.

NOTES

1. The opinions expressed in this paper have benefitted from discussions with Reginald Allen, Henry Mendell, Ian Mueller, and Philip Ehrlich. Allen's interpretation of the mathematical problem described at 86E-87B is substantially different from my own. See R. Allen, *The Dialogues of Plato*, (New Haven: Yale University Press, 1984), 1: 144-6.
2. The word *didakton* can mean either "is taught" or "can be taught" and Socrates does not seem anxious to clear up the ambiguity. This point becomes critical at 89Dff. when Socrates argues that because there are no teachers of virtue, it cannot be *didakton*. This implies that he is using it in the sense of "is taught." But

I agree with Bluck that 93B, 93E, and 94B suggest he is using it in the other sense. See Bluck, *Plato's Meno* (Cambridge: Cambridge University Press, 1964), 199-200. More on Socrates' argument in Section III below.

3. It should be emphasized that Plato is not always consistent in the way he uses these words. But in view of the fact that he is writing dialogues rather than treatises, occasional lapses into a non-technical vocabulary are hardly surprising. In particular, the *ti* and *poion ti* locutions seem to be used interchangeably at *Euthyphro* 5C-D and *Symposium* 201E. On the other hand, the *Euthyphro* goes on to make a sharp distinction between the essence of holiness and a property which happens to be true of it at 10E-11A, while the *Symposium* passage emphasizes the need to say what Eros is before discussing his products or effects. Here I am following the basic position set forth by R. Allen in *Plato's Euthyphro and the Earlier Theory of Forms* (New York: Humanities Press, 1970), 70-9, in particular the connection between the *ti/poion ti* distinction and that between *pathos* and *ousia* as articulated at *Euthyphro* 10E-11A. Nicholas White criticized the standard interpretation of the distinction between *ti* and *poion ti* on the grounds that to be told that it is a precursor to the distinction between essential and accidental properties is not to be told very much. True, but Plato was the first one to call attention to the distinction between essence and accident so neither is it surprising that he does not provide as much detail as we would like. Relying on *Meno* 71A-B, White proposes that the distinction is really that between having firsthand knowledge of something and knowing it by report. But (1) the distinction between first and second hand knowledge is White's, the text of *Meno* 71A-B says nothing about it; and (2) once we know something first-hand, reports are superfluous, whereas the text clearly implies that *poion* statements are in some way derivative from definitions so that once the correct definition is secured, *poion* statements, rather than being superfluous, will follow as consequences. This is certainly what we would expect in regard to a definition of virtue and the question of whether it can be taught. See N. White, *Plato on Knowledge and Reality* (Indianapolis: Hackett, 1976), 35-38.

4. As I have characterized the argument, the hypotheses are: (1) Virtue is good, (2) Virtue is a kind of knowledge, and (3) Virtue can be taught. In the first edition of *Plato's Earlier Dialectic*, Robinson interpreted the main hypothesis as a conditional: *if* virtue can be taught, *then* it is a kind of knowledge. But subsequent criticisms by Friedländer in *Classical Philology* 40(1945): 255 and Cherniss in *American Journal of Philology* 68(1947): 140 convinced him to change his mind. See R. Robinson, *Plato's Earlier Dialectic*, 2nd ed. (Oxford: Clarendon, 1953), 117-8. The present formulation is also accepted by Bluck, *Plato's Meno*, 86n.4, and 325.

5. I take this to mean that all of virtue is equal to either all of knowledge or a part of knowledge. But the text could also be taken to mean that either all of virtue or a part of virtue is equal to all of knowledge. In either case, the conclusion is not very precise.

6. Bluck, *Plato's Meno*, 76.

7. J.T. Bedau-Addo, "Recollection and the Argument 'From a Hypothesis' in Plato's *Meno*," *Journal of Hellenic Studies* 104(1984): 1-14.

8. R.S. Brumbaugh, *Plato's Mathematic Imagination* (Bloomington: Indiana University Press, 1954), 3-4.

9. A.E. Taylor, *Plato: The Man and His Work*, 7th ed. (London: Methuen, 1926; rpt. 1966), 138n.3.

10. See, for example, C. Demme, *Die Hypothesis in Platons Menon* (Dresden, 1888) and Remi Brague, *Le Restant*: Supplément aux commentaires du *Ménon* de Platon (J.

Vrin, Paris: 1978), 89n.15.

11. Malcolm Brown, "Plato's Disapproves of the Slave-Boy's Answer," in *Plato's Meno*, ed. M. Brown (New York: Bobbs-Merrill, 1971), 198-242. An earlier version of this essay appeared in the *Review of Metaphysics* 20(1967): 57-93.

12. Bluck, *Plato's Meno*, Appendix.

13. Brumbaugh, *Plato's Mathematical Imagination*, 35. For an interpretation which appeared after Bluck's summary, see Sternfeld and Syskind, "Plato's Meno: 86E-87A: The Geometrical Illustration of the Argument from Hypothesis," *Phronesis* 22(1977): 206-211. These authors see, as many do not, that the geometry problem must be an example of a *poion*-type inquiry. But the resulting interpretation violates my criterion 4 below and, following Rouse, translates *hoion* (87A3) as "same" rather than "similar."

14. See Proclus' commentary on Euclid I.44. For an English translation, see Heath, *A History of Greek Mathematics*, (Oxford: Clarendon, 1921), 1:150-151.

15. Cook Wilson, "On The Geometrical Problem in Plato's *Meno*," *Journal of Philology* 28(1903): 222-240 and Heath, *History of Greek Mathematics*, 298-303.

16. This requires us to take *hoion* at 87A3 to mean "similar" as spelled out in Euclid VI, Def. I. It should be noted that Euclid's word for similarity is *homoios*. It seems to me that the words are close enough for this to be a plausible reading. For further discussion on the lack of fixidity in Plato's mathematical terminology, see Heath, *History of Greek Mathematics*, 302n.1.

17. Following Heijboer, let BC be x, CD be y, BH be m, and the area of X be p^2. Now:

$$(1)\ CD^2 = BC \times CH$$

but:

$$(2)\ BC = BH - CH.$$

Combining (1) and (2) and making the above mentioned substitutions, we get:

$$(3)\ y^2 = x(m\text{-}x).$$

If the construction is successful:

$$(4)\ xy = p^2$$

so that:

$$(5)\ y = p^2/x.$$

Substituting for y in (3) we get:

$$(6)\ p^4/x^2 = x(m\text{-}x)$$

from which it follows that:

$$(7)\ x^4 - mx^3 + p^4 = 0.$$

For Heijboer's article, see "Plato 'Meno' 86E-87A," *Mnemosyne* 8 (1955), 89-122.

18. See for example, Bluck, *Plato's Meno*, 448-9.

19. *Birds* 1005. Allen thinks that quadrature is being described in the *Meno*. See my reference in n. 1 above.

20. Robinson, *Plato's Earlier Dialectic*, 93-113.

21. Heijboer, "Plato's 'Meno' 86E-87A," 98.

22. The sharpest criticism of Socrates' argument comes from A. Koyré, *Discovering Plato*, trans. by L.C. Rosenfield (New York: Columbia University Press), 17. Cf. Terrance Irwin, *Plato's Moral Theory* (Oxford: Clarendon, 1970), 317n.22. Both claim that Plato could not take the argument seriously. But there is nothing in the dialogue to suggest he is anything but serious. Having rejected the teachability of virtue, Socrates is forced to modify the connection between virtue and knowledge; this, in turn, causes him to introduce the notion of right opinion. All

of these moves are important for the understanding of Socratic philosophy. For a more sympathetic reading, see Richard Kraut, *Socrates and the State* (Princeton: Princeton University Press, 1984), 288-94.

23. See Chapter Six of *Dialogue and Discovery*, (Albany, New York: SUNY Press, 1987).
24. See, for example, *Apology* 20A-C. 33A; *Laches* 186Aff.; *Protagornas*, 319Aff. Again, there is no reason to think Socrates is anything but serious.
25. I take the claim that virtue comes by divine dispensation without intelligence (99E) to be an admission of failure and not Socrates' real view.
26. Frege, *The Foundations of Arithmetic*, 2nd ed., trans. J.L. Austin (Oxford: Clarendon, 1959), ix.
27. Robinson, *Plato's Earlier Dialectic*, 118-9.
28. Cornford, "Mathematics and Dialectic in the *Republic* VI-VII," in *Studies in Plato's Metaphysics*, ed. R. Allen (New York: Humanities, 1965), 61-95.
29. Norman Gulley, "Greek Geometrical Analysis," *Phronesis* 3(1958): 1-14. Also see R.S. Bluck, *Plato's Meno*, 75-85, and J. Hintikka and U. Remes, *The Method of Analysis* (Dordrecht, 1974). For the Aristotelian evidence, *Nicomachean Ethics* 1112b20ff. compares geometrical analysis to deliberation (*bouleusis*), which suggests that analysis is intuitive and is not limited to convertible propositions. In *Posterior Analytics* 78a10-13, Aristotle claims that mathematics differs from dialectic in that the former deals with propositions which are more often convertible. According to Cherniss, this implies that while mathematics treats convertible propositions more often than dialectic treats them, neither is limited to convertible propositions alone. See "Plato as Mathematician," *Review of Metaphysics* 4(1950-1): 415. On the evidence from Proclus, see Heath, *History of Greek Mathematics*, 291-2.
30. Richard Robinson, "Analysis in Greek Geometry," *Mind* 45(1936): 464-73.
31. Cornford, "Mathematics and Dialectic in the *Republic* VI-VII," 86.
32. Note how much of Cornford's evidence comes from sources external to the *Republic*. Note, too, that *Republic* 534B-D does not explicitly say that a new sense of dialectic is being introduced.
33. Cherniss, "Some War-Time Publications Concerning Plato," *American Journal of Philology* 68(1947): 133-46.
34. For further discussion, see Robinson, "Mathematics and Dialectic in the *Republic* VI-VII," 123ff, Kenneth Sayre, *Plato's Analytic Method* (Chicago: University of Chicago Press, 1969), chap. 1, and David Gallop, *Plato: Phaedo* (Oxford: Clarendon Press, 1975), 179-181. I agree with Gallop that "accord" cannot be equivalent to bare logical consistency. A better relationship is Gallop's suggestion of the connection between a theory and its application.
35. Robinson, "Mathematics and Dialectic in the *Republic* VI-VII," 136-7, also argues that Socrates is not thinking about definitions in this passage. Sayre, *Plato's Analytic Method*, 28-30, suggests that *Phaedo* 101D-E is critical of the procedure followed in the *Meno*.
36. Gallop, *Plato: Phaedo*, 179-181.

3

PLATO ON DOUBLING THE CUBE: *POLITICUS* 266 AB

Malcolm Brown

I

We have a long but somewhat confused tradition to inform us about the early history of doubling the cube, and about Plato's involvement in it. Philoponus in the sixth century was already calling the story "notorious" (*poluthrullēton*). The earliest contributor to the legend from whom we have clear testimony is Eratosthenes in the third century B.C. Other echoes come from Theon of Smyrna and Plutarch, and from Eutocius the commentator on Archimedes. Still another echo, which has attracted too little scholarly notice to date, is in the pseudo-Platonic *Sisyphus*.[1] This text is quite explicit about the parallel status of square-root 2 and cube-root 2 as objects of the geometer's ignorance, and of his significant searches. Each is an unknown "*hoposos tis*" according to this text, which quotes the diagonal passage of the *Meno* verbatim.[2] It would be desirable to have a slightly longer tradition – but also a much clearer one – reaching all the way back to Plato's own texts where we could firmly anchor it. I believe that the text of *Politicus* 266 AB is a promising place to drop such an anchor.

Our ancient sources tell us about the state of cube-doubling subject before Plato took it up (some perplexed Delians), and also about its state after several solutions had been offered (a perturbed Plato, defensive about the purity of mathematics). But they say little about Plato's own intervention. One source comes near to telling us where Plato wrote explicitly about the problem. This is Diogenes Laertius, who points his finger ("Life of Archytas," 8.83) at the *Republic*. Just possibly, however, if we had a better text of D.L. himself, we might read *politikō* where we now see *politeia* The two names do not differ much in their physical (graphic) form, and their position, which is that of last word in the last paragraph of this particular *Life*, is one which is more vulnerable to physical accident, accidental emendation, than most. Or, since the *Politeia* has a well known passage devoted to the mathematics of solids (527C-528E), a helpful scribe might have made the D.L. reading easier, by substituting *politeia* for *politikō*, when relaying this work to us. A light emendation of D.L.'s text would in fact reduce a serious anomaly for commentators on the *Republic*, the one expressed by Adam on 527f: "there is at all events nothing in the *Republic* to justify the curious statement of Diogenes Laertius ...."[3] Granted, there is much more detail in the full remark of Diogenes Laertius than we have reasonable hope of anchoring anywhere in Plato's texts. He says we can find not only doubling the cube, but Plato "saying" that Archytas was the first to solve the problem. I will content myself with arguing that in *Politicius* 266 we have a genuine Platonic text which refers directly to the problem, and that later in the same dialogue there are signals of Plato's complaints about one or more of the solutions of it. D.L. can easily have been weaving together a solid attestation and some less solid material he derived from a source like Eratosthenes, who wrote a dialogue in which Plato, Archytas and Eudoxus conversed about cube-doubling. I want to argue that the immediate target of Plato's references will have been one of his own Academic companions, whom our traditions associate independently with Archytas.

II

There are clear signs in the text of *Politicus* 266 AB of its intended connection to the famous mathematical passage at *Thteaetetus* 147Bf. Commentators since Campbell have worked out the general lines of connection, through the technical notion of *dunamis* as a mathematical "raising to a power" or extracting a root (this latter is an easily derived meaning within mathematics). Myles Burnyeat has recently followed Campbell's line, and endorsed[4] the idea that "*dunamis* of two feet" and "*dunamis* of twice two feet," taken in their mathematical sense,[5] allude to the powers, or roots of the square root of 2 and the square root of 4. In order to make our *Politicus* passage fasten in a natural and consecutive way to its predecessor in *Theaetetus*, we will do much better to give up the Campbell line altogether, and give "*dunamis* of two feet" and "*dunamis* of twice two feet" the meanings cube-root 2 and cube-root 4. For these are the natural sequels to the *Theaetetus* cases. That passage had pointed forward to a further class of "such like" as quadratic *dunameis* with its final words: "*kai peri ta sterea allo toiouton*," "and another similar thing [holds] about solids." The two magnitudes cube-root 2 and cube-root 4 have a privileged position in this class, being the first examples; this was the traditional way of illustrating a mathematical property.[6] There is also the historical sense in which this pair of roots were "first." In Hippocrates of Chios' famous "reduction" of the cube-doubling problem to that of inserting a pair of means in continuous proportion between 1 and 2, that pair of means will need names very much like "power of two feet" and "power of twice two feet." Of course it would have been quite possible to devise names for them that avoided the terminology of "*dunamis*," thus requiring that the concept "*dunamis*" remain proprietary to the quadratic surds. But this would only mask over the point of similarity which is brought out in a general form in the final words of the *Theaetetus* passage, and applied to the special case of the 1 to 2 interval in the *Sisyphus* passage (admittedly, without using the *dunamis* way of speaking).[7]

There is a quite simple and functional obstacle in the way of anyone's following Campbell's line here, which requires that we take square-root 4 as a *dunamis*. If "*dunamis* of twice two feet" means raising twice two feet to the power of 2, we come out with 16. If it means extracting its square root, we come out with 2. We do not arrive at any issue of incommensurability, or any need to recall the *Thteaetetus* passage at all, still less its final words about solids. If, on the other hand, we continue down the line indicated by the *Thteaetetus* passage (a line followed by the *Sisyphus* author), we get a thoroughly Platonic sequence, beginning in *Meno*, extending through *Theaetetus* and terminating in a cube-doubling allusion in *Politicus*. The mathematics of "4 feet" offers Plato little worth commemorating in connection with the *dunamis* concept conceived by his companion Theaetetus.[8] On the other hand that value is the very same as "2 feet" (the pair of them are the joint solution) if they are the *dunamis* cube-root 2 and cube-root 4. Cube-doubling was still so vivid an issue among mathematicians that Eratosthenes caused remarks about it to be inscribed in stone.

Now this whole passage in *Politicus* is jocular in tone, and makes an explicit remark about its own suitability for comedy (266B.10). I will want to develop this non-technical side of the interpretation more fully in Sections IV and V below. But let us now keep to the mathematics and kindred sciences alluded to. The bond which links cube-root 2 to cube-root 4 and vice versa is that of proportion, or *analogia*. This is the bond to which Plato assigns the most exalted place in the cosmos, in its own forming and in its yielding knowledge (*Timaeus* 31Cff). It is correct to think of the interval between 1 and

2 as subject to a *diairesis*, one form of which will locate a "middle" or "mean" which counts as "geometrical" in the sense that it satisfies the proportion 1:X::X:2. In the language of the *Meno*, this single geometrical mean gives the answer to the *hoposos tis* question, "how many (subunits) of the side of the unit square are required to form the base of the two-unit square?" In a precisely analogous way, the interval from 1 to 2 can be bonded together out of three subintervals, demarcated by a pair of "means," so that the *diairesis* will not be dichotomous, but trichotomous. If the interval is representing a pair of *solids*, as Plato acknowledges in *Timaeus* 32AB, it is the pair of means, not the single one, that are required. Thus to bond a unit cube to a two-unit cube, the *hoposos tis* question can be answered by any consecutive pair of values in the sequence 1, X, Y, 2 forming a continuous proportion. Modern names for X and Y are "cube-root 2" and "cube-root 4." We seem to lack ancient texts in which their names would be given, unless we agree that *Politicus* is naming them, "*dunamis* of two feet" and "*dunamis* of twice two feet."

But it will be objected: does not the reference in the text of *Politicus* 266 to "the diagonal" point decidedly toward the quadratic case? No, there are reasons for holding that this points even more strongly to the solid case. For one of the surviving Academic solutions to cube-doubling not only identifies one of these roots with a diagonal, it identifies the other with the diagonal (or power) of the first one's diagonal. Here we will need to open up our text a little further, and consult an extra text in the process. The extra material is precisely the Academic solution to cube-doubling, which has been transmitted to us written by Plato. It is found in Eutocius' commentary on Archimedes.

III

The overall aim of this paper is to increase the base of Platonic text on the subject of cube-doubling. But Eutocius' reconstruction asks us to count a clearly pseudo-Platonic solution as genuine Plato, and thus creates an unwanted increase. Already in 1895 Ambros Sturm carrying out a broad review of ancient sources, pointed to a scholarly consensus about the inauthenticity[9] of this mechanical solution. It is mechanical in the literal sense: it requires notched pieces of wood, fastened together so as to allow the user to slide one piece along while rotating the whole device in its own plane. It requires further that the user make interim adjustments along the "legs" of the device to achieve an exact ratio of 1 to 2 along a pair of mutually diagonal lines. Now the tradition about this geometrical problem is uniform about one thing, and that is Plato's having disapproved of the way solutions to it by some of his friends "sullied" geometry by mixing it with mechanics. Plutarch's reports give special stress to the point.[10] It might have been evident independently from the *Republic*. No wooden device with moving parts – especially if it called for a bit of extemporaneous empirical adjusting, as this one does – would have counted as an appropriate solution, in Plato's judgement, to a problem in pure mathematics. Still less would it be right to attribute authorship of the procedure to Plato. The salient point of the geometrical argument, however, constructed by the author after the movements and adjustments are over, is the following. Just as the text of *Politicus* represents the two *dunameis* as two "diagonals," one the *dunamis* of the other, so in the author's solution we have cube-root 2 and (cube-root 2)-squared, i.e. cube-root 4 – constructed along a pair of diagonals, one diagonal to the next. Heath reviewed the diagram and the argument carefully, and quite plausibly argued that its author must have been one of the group of mathematicians close to Plato at the Academy. Bulmer-Thomas endorsed this conclusion in his Loeb edition of the text.[11]

I now propose to take a close look at the vocabulary of this proof, to reinforce the Heath attribution, from independent evidence. My text is that printed by Bulmer-Thomas. I shall be drawing upon the results of a project carried out in 1978-1980 at the City University of New York, which produced a computer concordance to the complete Heiberg-Stamatis Teubner text of Euclid's *Elements*.[12] A copy of the magnetic tape containing this information is available to the scholarly public from the Oxford Archive for machine-readable materials. Our proof uses the technical term *prokeimenon* meaning "proposition." This is very common in Aristotle's *Analytics*, but non-existent in *Elements* except for a cluster which may echo an author from the Academy. The term, along with other *prokeimai* derivatives, is used in that sense only 16 times in *Elements*, and all 16 are in Book X, where they may well echo the wordings of Theaetetus.[13] Our Academician's proof uses *"thesis"* twice, meaning "position." This term for position is unexampled in *Elements*, except in Theorem 17 of Book XII. Here too we have reliable pointers to an author from Plato's Academic circle, namely Eudoxus. This theorem serves as a sort of lemma to XII.18, which shows by exhaustion that spheres have volume ratios triplicate of their ratios of diameters. This latter proof, and the method as it now stands in *Elements*, is reliably attrib-

uted to Eudoxus by Archimedes.[14] Our Academician uses the verb
psauein twice, to mean geometrical (or mechanical) tangency. Again
Euclid is in the main unwilling to use this term, preferring *haptein*
and derivatives. Archimedes, incidentally, prefers *psauein* and derivatives in the same geometrical contexts. But the text of *Elements* has a
little lexical enclave of *psauein* words, gathered in a most interesting
stretch of theorems: they all occur in the exhaustion arguments of
Book XII. There are 9 of them there, and they are interchanged
freely with *haptein's* as if the two meant the same thing. (Elsewhere
in *Elements*, outside of the enclave, the ration of *haptein* to *psauein*
goes 82 to zero in favor of *haptein*.) Again, our Academician's phrase
en sunechēi analogiai is of great interest historically. Although it had
been common at Aristotle's time (and possibly back to to Hippocrates), it seems to have been replaced by *hexēs* by Euclid's time. So
complete was this replacement that Heath was led into the incorrect
remark (his edition, II.131): "Euclid does not use the words *diēirē-
menē* and *sunechēs* in this [sc. *analogia*] connection." In fact, as it is
easy to confirm from the computer concordance, there are 30 occur-
rences of *kata to sunechēs analogon* in *Elements*. But again there is a
curious clustering: 26 of these 30 are in Book VIII, where van der
Waerden has argued on independent grounds that the author was
Archytas. Yet this form of words alternates with the form which
seems to have been prevalent later, *hexēs*, and is outnumbered by
these. There are 26 of the seemingly older form, 52 of the newer. It
is quite different in neighboring Book IX, whose author (on the
same grounds of argument style) was probably not Archytas. In Book
IX there are 33 of the newer form, only 3 of the older. And all of
these 3 exceptions are direct quotations from Book V, Def. 10, so
are unlikely to reflect Book IX's own internal style.

So in summary, our anonymous author has lexical habits different
from those predominant in Euclid. And where he mismatches
Euclid's lexicon, he matches other pre-Euclidean authors, often such
as have been independently identified to be behind special portions
of Euclid's text. And finally, in cases where we find lexically isolated
stretches of *Elements*, and yet our author does match the language
there, we several times have independent evidence of those same
pre-Euclidean authors as responsible for the material, perhaps even
the wording. In all the cases outlined above, the stylistic differentia-
tions within *Elements* seem, on independent grounds, to be marking
out pre-Euclid style. It is clear that such style markers, in the
absence of other independent lines of evidence, will not allow us to
sub-differentiate within the pre-Euclidean group of authors. Yet we

may venture this much definiteness in our conclusion at this stage: our Academic author on cube-doubling seems to be someone, not Plato himself, close to Eudoxes and Archytas.

Let us see if the "notorious" cube-doubling story can help sharpen this conclusion. We have various sources telling us that Menaechmus and Helison of Cyzicus, both students of Eudoxus and both friends of Plato, tried their hand at this celebrated problem. Eutocius relays the actual solution of Menaechmus, and it is different from our proof, although closely similar. It cannot be ruled out that the anonymous solution was authored by Menaechmus himself, as a kind of laboratory demonstration or teaching device to illustrate his own theoretical proof. I want to propose that what we have before us in this mechanical solution is the work of Helicon of Cyzicus. He is linked by a variety of ancient evidences to Plato, Eudoxus and Archytas, and to cube-doubling. This puts him close enough to Menaechmus to have authored a kind of twin argument. And the arguments of the two solutions are in fact similar: both arrange the pair of cube-roots along mutually adjacent diagonals.

I would like to offer a speculation on an ancient mechanical device for inserting mean tones into the octave, those specific means which define the "fixed tones" of the tetrachords. The device has some mechanical similarities to the one for extracting cube roots, and has a small element of theoretical similarity also, in that as the Academic device inserts two means continuously between 1 and 2, so the music-tuning device inserts two means discontinuously in that same 1 to 2 interval (the interval between the means in the musical cases is a whole tone only, while that separating each mean from its respective extreme is two-and-one-half such units). What adds considerable interest to our reports on the musical device is that it gave a mechanical solution to problems which we know Archytas and Eudoxus worked on: determining a series of means, including those of the tetrachord and various others. Still more interesting is that the name of the instrument, "the Helicon" is reported by Ptolemy (*Elementa Harmonica* 2.2), but without any very plausible explanation of the origin of the name. Ptolemy says it had something to do with the mount of the Muses. But this is implausible since he also calls it an instrument which "theoreticians" used. Aristides Quintilianus (*De Musica* 3.3) also mentions the Helicon, but gives no guess about its name. Ptolemy reviews a variant form of the instrument which, by allowing the user to move a certain diagonal stick in it, can be altered from a one-octave-only tuning device to an any-octave device. It is a key point in this device that one diagonal be made to intersect another, and the point of intersection be allowed to vary as the hinged diagonal stick is rotated through successive positions. In general, however, this Helicon does not allow that the diagonals reach perpendicularity to each other. And its 1:2 ratio is made to lie not along a pair of diagonals, but along sides of its rectangle.

The speculation is as follows. Suppose Helicon of Cyzicus, whom we know to have been a student of Eudoxus and an associate of Archytas, has designed this "Helicon" to insert the tetrachord's means into the octave interval 1:2. The clever variation on the device, which allows one to move one of its diagonals to increase its power to select varying octaves to begin with, may also have been due to Helicon. If so, only a little further ingenuity would have induced him to see that, by locating the 1:2 interval not along the sides of the device, but rather, as in Menaechmus' solution to cube-doubling, along a pair of diagonals, the wooden device also solves the cube-doubling problem. The pair of solutions are arranged so that cube-root 2 lies along one diagonal, and cube-root 4 lies along the diagonal of this diagonal. In this case, we have complete agreement with Plato's text in *Politicus*, the reference to "*dunamis* of two feet" and "*dunamis* of twice two feet," in addition to the idea of relating them as a pair of diagonals agreeing at once with Menaechmus' solution and with Helicon's mechanical variant on it.

IV

Various ancient sources contribute to our knowledge, such as it is, of Helicon. In *De Genio Socratis* Plutarch identifies Helicon as one of the two men to whom Plato referred the cube-doubling problem. The other was Eudoxus. Epistle 13, whose authenticity Morrow defended eloquently,[15] allows us to identify Helicon as a man known person-ally to Plato, and known to be well versed in the mathematics of Eudoxus. Even if the epistle were not written by Plato, it has proved itself to be well informed. So it is likely to give reliable information about this, and about the commission which Plato gives Helicon to perform. The usual dating is 366. The mission was to escort some *pythagoreia* and *diaireseis* to the king of Syracuse. Also included was this: Helicon should be received personally as a valuable tutor to the king, in Eudoxan mathematics and other knowledge.[16] Now one possible meaning for the *pythagoreia*, perhaps more plausible that Apelt's suggestion (i.e. the *Timaeus*), would be a collection of the Academy's contributions to the cube-doubling problem. This would fit especially well with the letter's further point that Helicon and Archytas (the first to double the cube) ought to get togethe: if the occasion permitted. Naturally, the *diaireseis* would include the *Politicus*, and the *Sophist*, or perhaps drafts of these. Thus Plato would be made central to the task of cube-doubling, but not as one of those actually carrying out the mathematical work. Rather, he will have been an administrator and organizer of this work, ready to put it alongside other and more general philosophizing, and just as ready to arrange for the dissemination of the work. He will also have served as organizer of meeetings between fellow experts, Helicon (relaying ideas of Eudoxus) and Archytas in this case.

As always, Plato will have reserved the right to respond critically to solutions of problems he had had a hand in setting. Just as he might see the importance of the problem of evaluating the half-tone, but be critical of solutions that appealed to the ear; just as he might challenge astronomers to save the *phainomena* but resist someone's (Eudoxus?) carrying around a kind of visual aid hand-held model of the heavens; so he can have urged his colleagues to double the cube, yet can have recoiled from such solutions as required wooden devices, empirically manipulated. In fact this is the aspect of the traditional story that is thematic: Plato's criticism of techniques that descended from pure thought to mechanical devices and drawings.

A theme of such criticism is presented by the Stranger in *Politicus* 227C, and it sounds again in 285f. In these passages Plato's texts use just the language echoed by Plutarch when he summarizes Plato's complaints about cube-doubling solutions. These injure the good of geometry by bringing its ideas down from the a-somatic range of beings into the world of sense experience and change.[17] On my interpretation, these warnings will be intended by Plato not as cautions aimed at followers such as those of the court at Syracuse – rather cautions aimed at his own ambassadors, those teachers who intend to Platonize or Eudoxanize the court in Syracuse. Unless your pupils are entirely capable of following your reasoning (277C; cf. 286B) without such aids, you ought to avoid any appeal to illustrations or demonstrations in the physical sense.

In the next section I shall be examining the possibility that "Younger Socrates" will have been a way Plato has of designating one or another of the young teachers (Helicon seems to have been one, Philip another) representing the Academy. In the person of the Stranger, then, Plato will be able to offer a warning to such a "Younger Socrates": a solution which you young mathematicians offer to cube-doubling ought not make essential use of a wooden physial device, or the parts of such a thing. Plato allows his two characters, the Stranger and Younger Socrates, to rise up to a high plane of reflection in this passage about the "portrait" (zōon) they have just finished sketching. They reflect on the difference between a portrait which is defective, lacks parts, needs filling in, and a complete one. The meaning here is not that of a living animal (zōon), but a sketch. A mathematician's drawings, or mechanical devices, might also be thought of as mere sketches, whose filling in would be the supplying of the theoretical (purely geometrical) arguments. Thus criticisms of such devices could be met, just as Plato's characters now proceed to meet their own criticisms, by supplying the missing parts of the portrait.[18]

V

This section of my paper will deal with some proper names, such as "Younger Socrates" and some ambiguities in Plato's artful uses which I will want to make some suggestions toward clearing up: their applications to flesh and blood humans. But before launching into these logically disturbed waters, let me take bearings on some historically fixed points. It will be recalled that Theaetetus was not a creature of Plato's literary imagination. He lived and died a natural person, and left behind substantial mathematical accomplishments, of which we have more or less precise echoes in Elements, Books X and XIII.[19] Plato commemorated them, Pappus commemorated them, and recently so did Burnyeat. Theaetetus' death has been plausibly fixed to 369 B.C.

In the process of Plato's commemorative work, he does a bit of extra portrait painting. He represents some young mathematician, of the same age and schooling as Theaetetus, and skilled at dunamis theory. Very likely there existed one or more mathematicians, real persons alive in "the 360s," who could fit comfortably under this Platonic sketch. The name "Younger Socrates" will be homonymous in referring just as well to any such mathematician. Ideally, if he is to carry out the work particularly described in Theaetetus and (on any interpretation of it) Politicus, the man should contribute to the exploration of the subject bequeathed to him by Theaetetus, namely solid dunameis. This class of dunameis is well represented, for reasons already given, by its first member, cube-root 2, the construction of which amounts to the same thing as doubling the cube. Let us open up the various possibilities to which our evidences point.

Assuming that Eudemus' catalogue of geometers puts a reasonable limit upon the initial roster of candidates, we would still find an embarrassing breadth of choices: Archytas of Tarentum, Eudoxus of Cnidus, Menaechmus of Alopeconnesus and Helicon of Cyzicus, all of whom are connected by our sources to cube doubling. Archytas is only loosely connected to the Academy, and the surviving report about Eudoxus' actual solution (it erred in confounding a discrete and continuous proportion), even if it attributes something surprising to Eudoxus, does distance him also from our author. Menaechmus and Helicon are both well qualified. Both worked on cube doubling. Somewhat anomalously, Helicon is named as one of the men to whom the problem was referred by Plato; yet no solution by him seems to have survived, even in testimonies. Menaechmus, on the other hand, contributed an elegant solution based on a pair of conic sections, and a pair of lines mutually perpendicular, one diagonal to the other. Heath already noted a close similarity between Menaechmus' surviving solution and that of our nameless author.

E. Kapp did an earnest review of "Der Jüngere Sokrates" in the course of writing his *Realencycklopaedie* article on him, and published his results separately in *Philologus*.[20] He struggled to justify the biographer of Aristotle, who said there had been a "Socrates" among his, Aristotle's teachers. This "Socrates" was reported to have been a student of Plato's. Quite fitting if the name "Younger Socrates" should be Plato's way of establishing a dialogue *persona* under which one or another of his mathematically adept younger colleagues could be known in the extra-Academy public.

The role which Helicon of Cyzicus took up, probably in 366, as an ambassador and Academic teacher in the Syracusan court, gives him a special position in relation to this Platonic *persona*, Socrates the Younger. Helicon was chosen by Plato to help bring to life the ideal of the king made philosophical (and mathematical). Dionysius has the needed royalty in himself, and Helicon brings the needed *pythagoreia* and Platonic *diaireseis*. Both dialogues as we now have them have a role for "Younger Socrates" to play. It will have been a natural identification for his Syracusan hosts to make, if they received their guest and teacher as essentially the same as the character in Plato's *Politicus*, the character scheduled soon to work out a definition of the *Philosopher*.[21] That is, his public will have identifed Helicon with the character "Socrates the Younger" in the books he brought to them from the Academy in Athens.

It is appropriate to take Plato's compositions, even those we may call divisions, where the dramatic elements are minimized, as literary works to which concepts of *persona*, mask, stage name are rightly applied. In *Politicus*, and immediately following our *dunamis* passage, Plato seems to be calling attention to the comic potential of his characters' own confounding of pigs and humans. Their discussions will be noticed by "those who make it their business to get a laugh" (266B.10f). Now the sublimity of the project of leading a king to philosophy, the sublimity of conducting mathematical researches at the frontier of existing knowledge, the sublimity of exploring the philosophy of "what it is to be (the) not-being" – all these are promptly reducible to the ridiculous, if certain conditions of comic writing be satisfied. The one thing needed is some particularity to fasten onto. Helicon seems to have had the temperament to help such a shift to the comic; he is described by the author of Epistle 13 as surprisingly light-spirited and mild, considering the weight of his learning (360C.7). Arriving as he did with Platonic scripts along, he could himself have made light of the almost inevitable thrusting of himself into the role of Younger Socrates. Who else on that Syracusan scene could play so demanding a part as this successor-character to Theaetetus? Eudoxus or Menaechmus could have filled these shoes, had they come from Athens, or Archytas, had he come from Tarentum. But our evidence is that the man who in fact stepped onto the Syracusan stage, bringing with him the possibly comic role of Socrates Junior scored at the Academy, was Helicon of Cyzicus.

Let us expand a bit upon Plato's remark about comedy writers and these particulars before us. Suppose our light-spirited Helicon were so good-natured as to endorse the identity which his public in Syracuse would naturally give him, but just noted it for soberer minds present that, if ever Menaechmus were dispatched to Syracuse or Tarentum by Plato, please be so kind as to reserve to himself the name "Socrates Junior." Look at the comic potential of mistaken identity if two men with names so different as Menaechmus and Helicon got confounded under the common nickname "Socrates" (or: "Sosicles"). As much potential there as if two such similar men were both called Menaechmus![22]

VI

None of the above conjectures about comic echoes, for example in Plautus, need be true as support for the main course of my argumemt. The important thing, which is independent of these extensions, is the reconstruction of the mathematics behind *Politicus*

266AB. The piece of geometry which I have reconstructed there – more accurately it is geometrized mechanics – requires that a pair of diagonals be constructed. When the two of them intersect at right angles and cut off segments, each of the other, the two extreme lengths are middled by a pair of constructed segments. In the particular case of a ration of 1:2 taken as extremes, this results in the values of the segments being cube-root 2 and cube-root 4. Two surviving solutions to the cube-doubling problem are closely similar, those of Menaechmus and pseudo-Plato. My suggestion that we identify pseudo-Plato with Plato's friend Helicon is also inessential to the main conclusion. Both surviving solutions could have been authored by Menaechmus, and someone may have suggested (after Plato's compliants) that Menaechmus dissociate himself from the mechanical solution which was his own solution's look-alike. In any case, the essential thing is that *Politicus* is alluding to cube doubling.

Let me now conclude by piecing together my net reconstruction. When the Academy was very young the issue of quadratic surds had surfaced in Plato's writings, in his *Meno*. Only the first of this class was involved in the dialogue, square-root 2. In the *Theaetetus* the topic is treated again, and more thoroughly. This young mathematician, with friends of his own age, has now (dramatic date: 399; academic date: 369) worked out a theory which draws a clear conceptual boundary to separate all cases of quadratic surds – now called "*dunameis*" – from the balance of the numbers. Sides of these latter are simply "lengths" (*mēkē*).

Plato leaves a tantalizing final remark at the end of this passage in *Theaetetus*, which points ahead to the *Politicus* as I am here interpreting it. He has his mathematicians say that *dunameis* (or whatever other term of art one would invent) of the next higher degree, "solids," do exist and they can be sorted out similarly. Now given all this, and given also that for some time the problem of doubling the cube had been part-way solved by Hippocates of Chios in his analysis, the provocation to mathematical research on it will have been considerable. With or without added stimulus from the Delian priests, the mathematicians in Plato's vicinity at the Academy such as Eudoxus, Menaechmus and Helicon – and also Archytas in Tarentum – will have been provoked to supply solutions about cube doubling, and a total of four solutions survive, either in full textual detail or (in the case of Eudoxus) in a brief description from which one can reasonably draw some inferences. One solution is attributed, quite anomalously, to Plato. This paper's main argument is that the general compliants in *Politicus* against lowering one's aim, except for practical or pedagogial objectives, from the level of pure bodiless objects (277C; cf 286AB) are just those applied by Plato in our traditions about cube doubling. And the remarks about "*dunamis* of two feet" and "*dunamis* of twice two feet" at 266AB had alluded to just that application. The pseudo-Platonic proof will have got attributed to Plato on account of his criticism of it, perhaps elsewhere, but publicly here in *Politicus* 266 (with 286). *Politicus*, not *Politeia*, is the dialogue in which to find Plato on cube doubling.

A number of threads which we can follow more or less plausibly through the complex of persons and personages around Plato at the early Academy lead to conclusions in good agreement with this interpretation. The ancient device for defining the two standard disjunct intervals in the octave, the Helicon, is not attributed to Helicon and Cyzicus by our sources. But its name, along with our other information about Helicon, encourages a speculation that he may have invented it. Be this as it may, the pseudo-Platonic device for cube doubling is similar to the Helicon in leading into the issue common to many of Plato's remarks about pure science: drawings, physical and mechanical devices, laboratory demonstrations ought not distract the pure theoretician (except so far as he may make an allowance for his own weakness or that of his audience) in his intellectual work.

This reconstruction fits nicely with, and is corroborated by, the facts reported about Helicon's bringing "*pythagoreia* and divisions" to the court at Syracuse in 366, when he was on an educational mission there. The mission was to have the side result of getting Helicon together with Archytas if possible. Helicon, being known for his easy-going temperament, may have undergone a process of nick-naming while in Syracuse – the nickname being a natural result of Plato's calling the chief mathematician (after Theaetetus) in these division dialogues "Younger Socrates." Whether or not the Plautus play centering on the Menaechmus/Sosicles pair of twins is an echo of this Menaechmus/Socrates pair in Syracuse, it is of interest to identify a mysterious presence in Eudemus' famous "catalogue of geometers," Cyzicean Athenaeus. Helicon is our most likely identity here, as ambassador from Athens he is received as *athenaios*, and when in the Academy, he was (as Epistle 13 confirms) a "cyzicean." One of Helicon's claims to the eminence there attributed to the athenian cyzicean is exactly his contribution to cube doubling. Yet, as with other solutions to problems Plato had set, there can still remain a question as to the purity of the procedure, or lack of it. Plato will always, and did, complain about any procedure which contaminates the purity of geometry by recourse to machines, motions and gross matter. There is a natural point of contact between these warnings to Socrates in *Politicus* and the discussion about matter or absence of it, in mathematical objects. This was an issue at the Academy which outlived Plato; it found its way into Aristotle's remarks about what he had discussed with Younger Socrates.

If Diogenes Laertius, in his "Life of Archytas" meant to point to the *Politicus* rather than the *Politeia*, he will be referring cube doubling chiefly to 266AB. The essential thing is that the pair of diagonals, one representing the other's *dunamis*, is present in this Platonic text. And Plato's criticisms of it as impure geometry are expressed, although in a generalized form, later in the dialogue (286A). In this way the *Politicus*, along with some related material from its mathematical and human surroundings at Plato's Academy, provides us a place to anchor the long tradition about Plato on doubling the cube.

NOTES

I am glad to have this opportunity to thank the City University of New York Faculty Research Foundation for the grants during 1975-1979, which enabled me to carry out the project of entering and sorting the texts of Euclid and various pre-Euclidean authors of treatises in the "elements" form.

1. There can be no doubt about it: this little tract is inauthentic. But it shows a good grasp of the mathematics of square doubling and cube doubling, and also puts the two in the right relation (theory of commensurability) to link them to the "one mean for planes, two for solids" passage of *Timaeus* 32. A valuable contribution to clarifying all of these matters – from the general viewpoint of ratio theory – is now in press by D.H. Fowler (Oxford). The author of *Sisyphus*, whoever and whenever he was, took this more general point of view. The special *hoposos tis* wordings are 388e3 (square) and 388ell (cube).
2. I once shared the podium with Bob Brumbaugh at a session of the Eastern Division APA meetings given to the *Meno* as a text for contemporary educators. The discussion was later published in *Teaching Philosophy*, vol. 1. I like to think of this present article in his honor as contributing once again to Bob's kind of enterprise: scholarly research that re-enlivens Plato for contemporary educators, and acknowledges Plato's vivid mathematical imagination.
3. In his 1964 edition of Diogenes Laertius's text (Oxford Classical Texts), H.S. Long expressed doubt that *Republic* 527 is the right passage. He writes "527C?" *ad loc.*, and also cites *Sisyphus*.
4. "The Philosophical Sense of Theaetetus' Mathematics," *ISIS* (1978): 496.
5. Plato sustains a ponderous double meaning here, and has his Eleatic Stranger comment on its value as material for comic treatment (266B.10). I shall have more to say about the allusion to comic writers below, Section V.
6. Quite likely Plato's mathematical companions knew that there are infinitely many examples of solid *dunameis*. The phrase cited above, if its *toiouton* is taken comprehensively, implies that they did. D.H. Fowler's work on the *anthyphaireseis* way of expressing these magnitudes brings out the key point: first when we reach

the cubic irrationals do we encounter a special signal from this switch-back substraction algorithm: now for the first time, it fails to repeat, i.e., there is no period of recurring values, as there had been in the quadratic cases. So cube-root 2 – paired as it is with cube-root 4 – is uniquely qualified to represent all such non-repeating *anthyphaireseis* according to the reasonable rule which Aristotle attributes to the pythagoreans at *Metaphysics* A.5 (987a.22f.).

7. Paradoxically, the incommensurable values called "powers" by Plato are exactly those which numerical comparisons are "powerless" to represent. So, if Plato is saying "square-root 4" is a case of such powerlessness, he is not only wrong, but painfully forgetful of the distinction he had summarized in *Theaetetus*. It would be an error as extreme as if Aristotle, after saying that all octaves are, by their essence, expressible as the two to one ratio, offered a sample octave which that ratio was powerless to express. In both cases, our author would be in conflict both with himself, and with the truth.

8. A valiant effort to find a motivation for square-root 4 appears in Konrad Gaiser, *Platons Ungeschriebene Lehre* (Stuttgart, 1963), 129-131. He claimed to find in it "the key to the understanding of the Platonic division of ideas." (129) But I am skeptical of his result, since it requires adding and subtracting these *dunameis*, which our text is silent about. The inscription in stone is published in I. Thomas, *Greek Mathematical Works*, 1:295-297.

9. Ambros Sturm, *Das delische Problem* (Linz, 1895). He omits the traditions about the Platonic scolding of the mathematicians, however; nor does he include the *Sisyphus* in his review.

10. In a recent paper, "Menaechmus *versus* the Platonists: Two Theories of Science in the Early Academy," *Ancient Philosophy* 3(1983): 12-29, A.C. Bowen has concluded that Plutarch is not trustworthy here. He will be "retrojecting" to Plato criticisms directed against Menaechmus by Plato's disciples Speusippus and Amphinomus. I do not believe we ought to doubt Plutarch so. *Politicus* 277C and 284ff. give platonizing warnings from Plato himself of just the right type. I will review this evidence more fully in Section IV below.

11. T.L. Heath, *History of Greek Mathematics*, 1:257; cf. I. Thomas, *Greek Mathematical Works*, 1:262f.

12. I shall be drawing on concordances which I prepared both to Euclid's *Elements*, and to a variety of works of mathematics or syllogistic before Euclid's time. These early authors, other than Aristotle, are: Archytas, Hippocrates of Chios, Autolycus of Pitane, Theodosius of Bithynia and Aristoxenus. In the case of Aristotle's *Analytics*, my project at C.U.N.Y. did not enter the texts orginally; rather, we only installed the subdivision markers and produced the concordance. The Aristotle text was supplied by the Thesaurus Linguae Graecae project in Irvine, California. See further, note 23, below.

13. Aristotle uses *prokeimenon* and the related words *prothesis* and *protethen* nine times in the Analytics, all of them in *Prior Analytics*. The terms occur between 1.32 and 2.16. This means they are much less frequent than *protasis* words, which occur 285 times in *Prior Analytics* with the same meaning. In *Elements* the '*protasis*' words do not occur at all, except in a pair of summary references to material being elided, viz "and the rest of what the *protasis* states." These are isolated near the end of Book XI, and are likely due to scholiasts, abbreviating.

14. This is evidence which it would be desirable to follow up with a detailed study of style markers internal to the text of *Elements*. In fact there are a number of significant style markers upon which we may reasonably fasten our argument, if we use stylistic tools to dissect original Eudoxan material from the body of

Elements. His lexicon of proof theory, his ways of cross-referring to other theorems, his ways of shortening back-references, his choices among synonym pairs (such as *psauein/haptein*, *epei/epeidēper*), his substantially variant way of executing comparisons of sizes based on V.14. We have further, a non-standard version of all of the exhaustation arguments, preserved in a solitary MS in Bologna, in which some style points match Euclid's other manner, mismatch the chief MS (Peyrard) which Heiberg followed. Some strenuous philological work is required, but sharp tools are now at the ready, in the form of the magnetically readable texts (with all of Heiberg's appendices kept, in a separate status).

15. *Plato's Epistles*, 2nd ed. (1962), 100-109. Apelt had noted that the Thirteenth had produced among scholars "*viel Kopfzerbrechen*,": *Briefe* (Leipzig, 1921), 145. Harward suspected its authenticity, in part because of its over-concern for "good reputation." But this complaint is groundless as soon as we notice that the text's words "*kai eudoxēs*" (360E3) which on the surface are speaking of the king's building his good reputation, are no more than a pun. Helicon is bringing Eudoxus' learning, with which the king "may *eudoxize* yourself."

16. Epistle 13 anticipates that the king may have too little time to devote to Plato's offered "*pythagoreia kai diaireseis*," and advises him to delegate someone to do his listening for him (surely he will have time anon). But it seems as if this issue about the king's being short of time or being asked to follow a long road was prophetically foreseen, the fulfilment being in the "*makra ta lechthenta*" complaint registered against Platonic divisions (287A.1). "The course is too long," we might translate. Note how we might also render this into an exchange "Give me the short course, O Younger Socrates!", in the spirit of countermanding Plato's letter. And then the Stranger and Younger Socrates respond by showing that the royal road and the public road are one and the same in geometry and in philosophy. Barnes accepts the attribution of the collapsing of royal and common roads story to Menaechmus as an original. J. Barnes, ("Aristotle, Menaechmus, and Circular Proof," *Classical Quarterly* (1976). At 266C Plato is able to say that the king's road and that of his subjects is one and the same. In this too, Menaechmus and Younger Socrates are closely similar.

17. In Plutarch's terminology, the essential and pure realities are "*asōmata*." One might think this a common currency in Plato's writings. In fact, however, Plato never calls anything "asomatic" except the realities about which he is warning Younger Socrates in 286A. Brandwood's *Word Index* shows that Plutarch is citing a *hapax legomenon* in Plato.

18. Younger Socrates is to have discussed with Aristotle the relation between the make-up of a mathematical figure out of its parts and that of a "*zōon*" from its parts. This was the mathematician's suggested comparison. Here in *Politicus* we may have the other half of the intended comparison. In Plato's dialogue the "*zōon*" is the sketch, or outline, of the statesman, which now needs filling in. Aristotle's summary of the comparison by Younger Socrates is in *Metaphysics*, Z.11.

19. The computer concordance revealed a curious conflict in the spelling of the technical term "the minor" (meaning the specific irrational size). In Book X it is defined and expressed by the *koinē* spelling "*elassōn*." In Book XIII, where it is referred back to, seven of the ten times it is quoted, the spelling has altered to "*elattōn*." A likely explanation is that the special contribution of Theaetetus, the construction of the regular solids, was left as he wrote it, including his Attic spellings. The bulk of Book X, however, will have been gone over (by Hermotimus of Colophon?), and the spellings regularized, de-Atticized.

20. *Philologus* (1923), 79:225ff.

21. Already in *Politicus* we see an unusual element of the intrusion of echoes from Plato's intended audience. His Stranger is allowed to summarize complaints about the (alleged) excessive length of, or tediousness of, his divisions. And he lets his *dramatis persona* answer back to the annoyed audience: only complain, O hearer, after you have proved to me that shortening the lessons would make you a better philosopher! Possibly Plato could foresee an unacceptable increase in these intrusions upon his own mastery of his writings, were he to complete his intended trilogy, and give a still further part to Younger Socrates to play, to an audience of uncertain discipline. This would explain why Plato might prefer – and I am persuaded, with Pfleiderer that he did this – to enclose a capsule version of *Philosopher* into a safer place, internal to the edition we now have of *Republic*. It is the stretch at 474B-480A, which defines the philosopher and surprisingly countenances *koinōnia* of Forms one with another. The procedure is that of the later dialectic. The philosopher is defined by *diairesis*.

22. Do we have here the original scene behind Plautus' *Menaechmi?* Plautus' twins originally had the names "Menaechmus" and "Sosicles." Further, the two cities from the comedy of mistaken identity are Syracuse and Tarentum (Athens was in Plautus' Prologue). When one of the play's Menaechmi is trying to detect an odor and classify it in all its subtlety, he asks help from a parasite, who in turn says he must consult the *"collegium"* (line 165). Scholars have struggled to fix this meaning, without success. What about the Academy? Further: a slave is improbably named "Cylindrus." Slaves are very rarely (ever?) named after mathematical objects. Archytas used a cylinder in his doubling of the cube.

4

THE THEORY OF PERCEPTION IN PLATO'S *THEAETETUS*

Robert Anderson

I

One thing that is evident to anyone having studied with Robert S. Brumbaugh is his unique grasp of the centrality of the divided line to all of Plato's thought. That metaphor, set out in the *Republic* (509D-511E), can be seen as the most comprehensive metaphysical statement ever made by Plato. It illustrates the claim that there are four hierarchically related levels of being, each with its own respective mode of apprehension. The lower levels apparently derive their degree of reality from their imaging of the higher ones. One of the most provocative views associated with this metaphor is that the material objects that comprise the perceptual realm are worthy of being placed on only the second level, so that the mind's relation to them can be nothing more than one merely of trust (*pistis*). Immediately above these objects are the entities of mathematics on the third level, and on the fourth and highest segment are Plato's Ideas. The placing of material objects on such a low level of the line is just one example of the slight regard that Plato has for the sensible world.

Is Plato's critique of the perceptual realm a valid one? This question is not answered in the *Republic*. There the insights of the divided line remain on the metaphorical plane; no argumentation is given for them. But the topic of perception is investigated thematically in the *Theaetetus*. Is it possible that the treatment of perception in this other dialogue provides the justification that is lacking in the *Republic*? That question will be the central concern of the following investigations.

Three themes would be of special relevance in the answering of that question. The first would be a demonstration of why the mode of being of the perceptual realm is an inferior one, such that it can be an object only of trust rather than knowledge. The next would be to show that the perceptual realm is indeed dependent on the higher reality of the third level of the line, the mathematical entities, for its own existence. The final challenge would be to explain how the highest level, the Ideas, are the source of all being and knowing, including that of the inferior modes of the lower levels. The present essay will focus primarily on the first of these themes, doing so by means of an examination of Socrates' concentrated account of perception in the *Theaetetus*. Although the second theme could also be claimed to be justified in that dialogue, here it will be dealt with only tangentially, being for the most part beyond the scope of this limited investigation. The third theme is not discussed directly in the *Theaetetus* at all; its exploration would have to center on other dialogues.

II

A unique feature of Plato's theory of perception is the way he incorporates within it the doctrines of Protagoras and Heracleitus. This happens right after he has Socrates, who has just described himself as a midwife, elicit from Theaetetus the definition that knowledge is perception *(aisthesis)*.[1] Arguing from a radical interpretation of a seemingly simple example, Socrates ties all of these views together. When the same wind is blowing, one person may feel cold, another not cold. How is this difference to be understood? If knowledge and perception are the same, then neither judgment about the wind can be any more or less correct than the other. Thus Socrates maintains that Theaetetus' definition is identical to Protagoras' claim that each man is the measure of all things. But this Protagorean interpretation has even more drastic consequences. If the same wind is at the same time both cold and not cold, then it is in a strange kind of opposition with itself. Therefore, Socrates argues, the Heracleitean statement is entailed – paradoxical though it may be – that nothing is one and invariable. Finally, taking this Heracleitean doctrine as an assumption, Socrates develops two accounts of perception (153D-154B, 155E-157C). The second of these will be main focus of this essay.

Since the theory of perception is complex and full of minute details, it will be worthwhile to quote it in full before offering an interpretation.[2] Socrates begins his presentation by setting out his Heracleitean premise, positing the fundamental motions from which everything else derives:

there are two kinds of motion, each infinite in the number of its manifestations, and of these kinds one has an active, the other a passive force. From the union and friction of these two are born offspring, infinite in number, but always twins, the object of sense and the sense which is always born and brought forth together with the object of sense (156A-B).[3]

There is an unusual feature in this description. It uses a kind of reproductive imagery. The active and passive motions come together, and out of this union come offspring. The first set of motions, the active and the passive, are referred to as the parents. Later it will be asked whether this imagery can be harmonized with the midwife metaphor (whose focus on impregnation might have suggested the definition that knowledge is perception). Furthermore, it will have to be determined just what the action of the active element is. Socrates continues, describing the offspring motions.:

Now we give the senses names like these: Sight and hearing and smell, and the sense of cold and of heat, and pleasures and pains and desires and fears and so forth. Those that have names are very numerous and those that are unnamed are innumerable. Now the class of objects of sense is akin to each of these; all sorts of colours are akin to all sorts of acts of vision, and in the same way sounds to acts of hearing, and the other objects of sense spring forth akin to the other senses (156B-C).

This is an odd list of senses. Besides those which rely on bodily organs and whose objects are such familiar things as colors and sounds, Socrates has mentioned pleasures and pains, desires and fears. Do these latter "senses" have their own peculiar objects in the same manner as do the former? Eventually this particular grouping will have to be examined more closely. First, however, Socrates must be followed as he goes on to present the central portion of his theory.

After pausing to give Theaetetus a chance to respond, Socrates describes the kinds of motions more precisely:

all these things are, as we were saying, in motion, and their motion has in it either swiftness or slowness. Now the slow element keeps its motion in the same place and directed towards such things as draw near it, and indeed it is in this way that it begets. But the things begotten in this way are quicker; for they move from one place to another, and their motion is naturally from one place to another (156C-D).

At this point the description seems dangerously close to lapsing into talk of persisting things which are capable of drawing near to each other. In fact, in the example which Socrates is about to give, he will speak of an eye and a stick or a stone. How can he do this and still remain consistent with the assumption that there is nothing but motion? Before beginning to answer the questions that are accumulating, there is one remaining part of the account to quote:

> Now when the eye and some appropriate object which approaches beget whiteness and the corresponding perception – which could never have been produced by either of them going to anything else – then, while sight from the eye and whiteness from that which helps to produce the colour are moving from one to the other, the eye becomes full of sight and so begins at that moment to see, and becomes, certainly not sight, but a seeing eye, and the object which joined in begetting the colour is filled with whiteness and becomes in its turn, not whiteness but white, whether it be a stick or a stone, or whatever it be the hue of which is so coloured. And all the rest – hard and hot and so forth – must be regarded in the same way: we must assume, we said before, that nothing exists in itself, but all things of all sorts arise out of motion by intercourse with each other; for it is, as they say, impossible to form a firm conception of the active or the passive element as being anything separately; for there is no active element until there is a union with the passive element, nor is there a passive element until there is a union with the active; and that which unites with one thing is active and appears again as passive when it comes in contact with something else (156D-157A).

III

Initially this account might seem relatively straightforward. A perceiver and an object come together, and sensory perception is the result. A person looks at a stone, for example, and the sensing of whiteness and whiteness itself are produced. Yet the complexities quickly become evident. Does a color come into being only when sensed? Socrates seems to be suggesting this when he declares that whiteness is one of the offspring motions. The color itself is created simultaneously with the sensing of it and only as a result of the object's coming in contact with a perceiver. Indeed, such a view is not so implausible. A color, it could be said, arises out of the interaction of a bodily organ with some sort of emanations (particles or otherwise) coming from an object. Sensory qualities in general might admit of such an explanation.

But this leaves a problem concerning the object being perceived. If the whiteness of the stone is being produced with the perceiving, that color would not have already existed, unless it is being produced redundantly. If this were true of the other kinds of sensory qualities as well, what would be the nature of the material objects themselves? Would they not be devoid of many of the characteristics most commonly attributed to them? This seems to be an implication of the account that Socrates is giving. This account could be called a causal theory of perception.[4] Its main concern would be to explain the genesis of perceptions and perceptual qualities. It does this by describing the offspring motions as existing separately from the objects which cause them.

A causal theory would make a distinction between what might be called a sense-object and a physical object.[5] The latter is taken to be a material object as it exists in itself, and it would lack all sensory qualities. The former would be a single sensory quality, or even a collection of such, viewed as the effect of an encounter between two physical objects. One of the physical objects would be a perceiver, and in it a sensing would be produced, corresponding to the individual sense-object. An account such as this has the appearance of being what Socrates is giving in his theory of perception. The two parent motions, what are here being called physical objects, are the causes of perception. The two offspring motions, a sensing and a corresponding sense-object, would be effects.

It must be pointed out immediately, however, that such a theory, by itself, gives neither a complete nor even an accurate explanation of ordinary perceptual experience. It was imprecise to say that the term "sense-object" referred to a sensory quality. Physical objects are defined as lacking all sensory attributes; thus the sense-object which results from the causal encounter cannot be assigned to such an object at all. In this kind of theory there must be a distinct separation between the sensory effects and the objects which produce them. However, such a separation is not acknowledged in ordinary perceptual judgements. When one speaks of the color of a stone, one is treating the color just as if it were a quality of the producing thing. Thus there is a discrepancy between a causal theory and the perceptual experience that it purports to explain. Some added explanation would be needed as to how the separate sense-object is returned to the physical object as one of its qualities.

Nonetheless, a more careful examination of Socrate's account makes it clear that it cannot simply be interpreted as being a causal theory. There are too many disparities. Socrates said that sight from the eye and whiteness from the object are moving from one to the other. But if it is whiteness and sight which are being produced, how can they move before they have even come into being?[6] In a causal theory it would be more appropriate to speak of something like particles (or waves) flowing from the object and of the eye's presenting a mechanism which is capable of receiving such emanations. Furthermore, Socrates had gone on to speak of the stone's becoming white. Had he been speaking of a "physical object" as described above, he could not consistently have said that such an entity can be or become white. As has just been remarked, it is central to such an account that sensory qualities can never be attributed to its objects. Thus, unless Socrates is hopelessly confused, he cannot have a causal theory in mind.

Moreover, Socrates had gone on to state that it is impossible to conceive of either the active or the passive element separately from the union with the other. Now this might be true of the effects, the offspring motions, which must be born as twins. An act of sensing cannot exist without there being something (of some sort) sensed. But Socrates was speaking here of what would be the causes, the parent motions. Yet this could not be the case in a causal theory. In such an account the causal elements would exist prior to the perceiving process, each independent of the other.[7]

This last portion of the account, clearly out of place in a causal theory, suggests an altogether different line of interpretation. What Socrates said there is more appropriately stated of the effects than of the causes of the perceptual process. Can it be that both sets of motions, the parents as well as the offspring, are meant to be aspects of what we actually do perceive? If so, Socrates would be offering some kind of phenomenalistic account – not a causal theory at all.[8] The parent motions could then be considered to be "empirical objects." This would indicate that they are found within experience rather than being external causes of it. The stone would be some kind of collection of sense-objects, and the perceiving person would be a collection of sensings. Such an account would be more consistent with the definition of knowledge as being nothing but sensory perception. There would be no mention of presupposed causal factors, existing prior to sensory awareness and viewed as abstracted from all sensory qualities.

A phenomenalistic interpretation would account for certain aspects of Socrates' theory that are incongruous with a causal explanation of perception. Most importantly, sensory qualities would belong to material objects, as with the whiteness of the stone. But here, too, there are significant disparities. The relationship between the parent and the offspring motions would be reversed. In this type of account the "parents" are built out of collections of the "offspring." The names would no longer be meaningful. Nor would it be correct to speak of the offspring as separate from the parents. Would it not in fact be redundant to speak of two sets of motion at all? Furthermore, this theory apparently would not account for the generally accepted view that material objects and persons do combine to cause perceptual experience.[9] Since the advantages of the former interpretation would be lacking in this one, there would be a void.

Thus this phenomenalistic view is no more adequate an interpretation of Socrates' account of perception than is the causal theory. In fact, there is another problem that neither view seems able to resolve. Socrates claimed to be applying the Heracleitean doctrine that everything is in motion or change. Yet a number of different kinds of motion are described in his account, and it is not clear that they are all consistent with each other. Certain of the parent motions draw near to others, seemingly a kind of motion with respect to place. Also there is the flowing of the whiteness from the stone to the eye and that of sight from the eye to the stone. If the former of these were taken to be referring to emanating particles or waves, then, along with the motion with respect to place, it could be incorporated within a causal theory. But it is not clear that either a more literal interpretation of the flowing of the whiteness, or any of the "flowing of sight," would fit in such an account. Socrates also spoke of alteration. The stone is said to become white, and the eye becomes a seeing eye. Can this kind of change be fitted within either theory? Moreover, he also spoke of actions and passions without specifying what he meant by these. Therefore, along with all of the problems in consistently identifying the kinds of entities involved in Socrates' account, it will also be necessary to try to harmonize the various kinds of motions.

Where is one left after all of this? It is clear now that Socrates' theory cannot be interpreted either as a causal theory or as a version of phenomenalism. Comparing it to both types of account, however, has brought out apparent inconsistencies among its details. It also seems that between the two types together virtually all of these details are accounted for. One possible conclusion to be drawn is that Socrates, confusing two incompatible logical structures, was mistakenly combining aspects of each view.[10] Another possibility is that neither view is by itself adequate and that a correct explanation of perception must necessarily find some way of combining their features. The argument here will be in favor of the latter alternative. Moreover, it will be claimed that there is a common shortcoming in each of these two views, one which has been implied in the foregoing analysis. Neither of them seems capable of accounting completely for perceptual experience.

This leads to one final preliminary question. What exactly is perceptual experience? There is something odd about the history of the term "experience." Classical British Empiricism, the philosophical approach seemingly most concerned with this notion, may also have done the most to distort it. To the extent that it is influenced by Locke, this approach has been dominated by the causal theory of perception and its two main concomitant distinctions: one between qualities and ideas, and the other between primary and secondary qualities. The result of this influence, as has just been seen, is the view that the secondary or sensory qualities (or their ideas) are sundered from the objects which thereby properly manifest only primary qualities. Thus material objects, despite all appearances, could not have sensory qualities ascribed to them. It is a strange doctrine of experience, however, which has no place for the kind of object most apparently experienced.[11] In the forthcoming interpretation of Socrates' theory, therefore, special heed must be paid to the notion of perceptual experience which it involves.

IV

Clearly, after the failure to match Socrates' theory with certain traditional approaches, a new orientation is needed. One thing that has been discovered is a fundamental ambiguity in the meaning of the term "experience." It may refer either to the encountering of one entity by another, or to the resulting representation that the latter can make of the former. Both aspects seem necessarily present in perceptual experience, but any theory accounting for one must apparently exclude the other. Thus, as has been argued so far, the causal and the phenomenalistic accounts are capable of merely partial, if not distorted, explanations. Perhaps a different theory might be found which would remove all ambiguity. Another possibility, however, is that sensory perception is a human activity whose logical structure is simply not self-consistent. It is time to explore that logical structure.

It is easy to miss one of the most important details of Socrates' theory. The two off-spring motions are what are produced, according to this account. Yet their coming into being is not the only result of the perceptual process as it is here described. Another kind of change occurs – this one in the parent motions. Just as the whiteness, one of the offspring, is being born, one of the parents, the stone, becomes white. And as the sight is being born, the other parent, the eye, becomes a seeing eye. The combination of all of these happenings leads to the results that have seemed paradoxical. How can the newly born whiteness flow from the stone just as the stone is becoming white? And how can the eye come to be seeing when sight is departing from it? Each of the parent motions is giving something up, and at the same time it is gaining a quality or a function which closely resembles that which it has lost.

These questions can be answered by examining the most crucial feature of Socrates' theory, one which is so deeply imbedded in his description that it is almost unnoticeable. There are two different logical structures at work here, and each pertains to a different one of the pairs of motions. The offspring motions, related necessarily to each other as twins, exist in complete logical independence from all other pairs of offspring. They are momentary happenings, passing away almost as soon as they come into being, and they are determined solely by the peculiar encounter of their two parent motions. Since those parents are constantly subject to change, in their own makeup as well as in their relation to other objects, each instance of encounter is likely to be different from any other. But whether any of the parents change or not, new offspring are in no way determined by previously existing ones. The previous ones, also totally dependent on parents for their existence, do not according to the theory expert any reciprocal influence. Each pair of offspring, therefore, is as independent of each other pair as any atom is of all others in an atomic configuration. Thus when Socrates later in the dialogue introduces a preplexing doctrine of logical atomism (201D-202C), it may be correlated with the offspring motions in this theory.[12]

A different logical structure is manifested by the parent motions. They, however much they may be moving, are persisting subjects which possess properties. Were this not the case their peculiar kind of alteration, change with respect to quality, would not be possible. Here is what may be called a logic of predication. The basis of this logical framework is the act of attribution. Since the qualities of the things experienced are subject to change, new ones may replace the old. Direct awareness of the new qualities can occur only through sensing them. The object of sensory apprehension, though, one of the offspring motions, is an independent sense-object. How does it then come to be a property of a thing? Only when it is attributed to it as being such. What, however, are the grounds for this attribution?

At first the justification might seem obvious. Ordinary perceptual experience works in exactly this way. What is being perceived is a material object, and without its presence the color being seen would not be possible. The color is thereby said to belong to the thing. But the analysis contained in Socrates' complex theory reveals how questionable such a judgment would be. The color, regarded as an offspring, is separate from each of the parents. Furthermore, since it is dependent in part on the perceiving parents, to just that extent it is private to that perceiver. Yet the material object, equally accessible to others, must have public status. How can a private determination be predicated of a public object?

It cannot be done so consistently. As can now be seen, to do that would be to confuse two incompatible logical frameworks. Nonetheless, such attribution is regularly performed. What are the consequences of this essential aspect of sensory perception? To begin with, the distinction between the public and the private aspects of perception becomes blurred. A public object will be assigned a privately apprehended quality, and the privately oriented sense-object will be taken to belong to a public thing. Moreover, the separation of the effects from the causes of the perceptual process will be lost. The result is a confusion between the representative and the causal aspects of perception. These, of course, are some of the same problems that were found in Socrates' theory. Now, however, such inconsistencies can be seen to belong to perceptual activity itself and not just to Socrates' account of it.

V

At this point an interpretation of Socrates' theory of perception can be offered that attempts to resolve its problematic aspects. If an unjustified attribution of qualities lies at the heart of the perceptual process, a number of specific inconsistencies necessarily follow from this. Furthermore, the perceptual object will be regarded as combining aspects whose logical structures ought to prohibit such combination. Representations of material objects are formed, and a full range of sensory qualities is assigned to these things. At the same time, however, these very objects are viewed as having causal efficacy. A stone interacts somehow with a person, and from this encounter there emerges a representation of that object. Is it not the same stone which is both the cause and the object of this perception? Surely this is thought to be the case in ordinary perceptual experience, no matter how questionable the logic may be! Objects are taken to have both sensory properties and causal potency.

Thus the sense-objects are not restricted to the atomistic framework of the offspring. They are also assigned to material things as properties and, besides, are taken to have belonged to these objects all along. It is a white stone which is one of the parents of the sensed color white. The temptation will exist, following the logic of a strict causal theory, to say that particles or waves are emanating from the stone which has no color in its own right. Perhaps this is what should be said. Nonetheless the stone will be experienced as being white. This is why Socrates has the color flowing from the stone at the same time that the latter is becoming white. He is speaking metaphorically. He must speak in this manner, because there is no consistent literal meaning that could be given to these "motions." They are not locomotion, alteration, or any other of the traditional kinds. If anything, they could be called a moving from one "logical space" to another. The color begins as a property within the predicational framework, becomes an atomistic sense-object, and then is assigned back to the material thing and its framework again as a property. Clearly there is no theoretical warrant for these moves. They are pragmatic distortions, but as such they are essential to all perceptual experience.

It has thus been shown, using the causal and phenomenalistic theories as models, that the inconsistencies in Socrates' account of perception are present in the perceptual process itself. It is no wonder, then, that this mode of apprehension is placed on such a low level of the divided line. It is not yet clear, however, just what Socrates means by saying that the perceptual realm manifests a Heracleitean flux. Why does he claim that everything is in constant change, nothing being one and invariable, when there do seem to be persisting objects in his own account?[13] The answer to this question will provide further justification for Plato's denigration of the sensible world.

It is important to note that Socrates presented his account in two portions, dividing it when allowing Theaetetus a response. There is a tension between these two sections. The initial part is in one respect vague. Two sets of motions are distinguished: first the active and passive motions, then the pairs of offspring. But here Socrates says nothing as to what types of activity and passivity are involved. Instead he speaks in detail of the various kinds of sensings that comprise one of the offspring groups. It is in the second portion of the account that he is more explicit. The active motion is there described as the seeing of the eye; the passive element is the being seen of the stone.[14] The offspring that emerge are the sensing of whiteness and the corresponding color.

This is where the tension arises. The active motion as described in the second section, the seeing of the eye, is the actualizing of a potency. It thus presupposes an entity that can so function. A similar presupposition is implicit in the description of the passive motion. A stone must exist in order to be being seen. It is in this way that stable objects seem to enter the account, despite the claim that there is nothing but flux (a claim, then, that is perhaps more appropriate to the first rather than to the second section). Furthermore, a strange reversal has occurred between the two portions of the account. In the initial part it is the active and passive motions that produce the sensory realm. Yet the description in the second section, alluding to the eye and the stone, perceivable objects, now locates these motions within the very domain they supposedly give rise to. One last problem should be mentioned. Are there really two distinct sets of motions at all? What is the difference between the seeing of the eye and the sensing of the color white?

Again, there are reasons for the presence of these difficulties in Socrates' theory. The root of the problem is this. If the causes of knowledge can themselves be knowable, then just so far as they are knowable they will belong to the domain of the known. It is not surprising, therefore, that the entities believed to bring about perceptual awareness end up taking on the characteristics of perceptual objects themselves. Some such illicit transformation must attend any attempt to know what are thought to be the prior causes of knowing. And it has already been noted that the perceptual realm involves such an attempt, including or at least accommodating a causal explanation of perception itself. Socrates displays this problematic structure by first presenting the causal account separately (with the vagueness that is necessary to such an enterprise) and by then allowing it to be absorbed into the second section, which utilizes the more precise but questionable terminology.

Because of all of these problems (again problems that are characteristic of perception itself), the various motions within Socrates' theory cannot be harmonized into one self-consistent account. A difficulty occurs already in the first portion. Even the austere description of the parents simply as actions and passions, one which eschews any mention of the eye or the stone, fails to avoid the taint of stability. For if there are actions, what are the agents? If passions, what is being acted on? Nonetheless, this talk of persisting things just cannot be avoided. Ordinary language, the base from which any theory must spring, is replete with perceptual terminolgy and with the objects so prominently spoken of therein. It is hard to see how such speech could be completely eliminated.

An even greater inconsistency occurs amongst the motions of the second section. This would not be so, if the parent motions could be described by themselves. They are said to move slowly with respect to place, to actualize their potencies, and to create offspring, all of which conform to the ordinary understanding of the behavior of material objects (even if it is not made clear how the begetting occurs or whether it really is motions that are doing the moving). But it is the movements of the offspring, sight and the corresponding color, that are hard to fit with the rest.[15]

The offspring are said to move with respect to place, but to do so swiftly. Yet they are not the sorts of things that can do this in the ordinary manner. How, then, are they related to place? Sight, apprehending its objects as having locations, has its own starting point in place, the eye from which it emanates being itself visible. Moreover, sight could be said to move swiftly, as could the color, since seeing occurs almost instantaneously, even when across great distances. But why should Socrates want to speak in this way, relying so heavily on metaphor?[16] One answer might be that he does succeed, by having sight and the color moving towards each other, in expressing the fact that each exists only in relation to the other. Also, because the offspring have their unique orientation to place, Socrates distinguishes them, by calling them swift, from the things that move in the commonly understood mode, which things are said to move slowly.

By this point, however, the doctrine of motion seems utterly fragmented, its unity disintegrated into a multiplicity of kinds. Why, then, has Socrates chosen to speak in general of the Heracleitean flux? Two reasons are already evident, implicit in considerations previously set out. First, the very attempt to harmonize the various motions into one account has shown the extent to which the perceptual process is a logically inconsistent enterprise (although the source of this inconsistency will not be revealed until later in the dialogue). Second, by exhibiting all of the motions together, Socrates has made visible the division into the two logical frameworks. It is this duality which necessitates the two sets of motions. Thus, in answer to the earlier question, there is no redundancy between the seeing of the eye and the sensing of the color, or between the whiteness of the stone and the color white. On the contrary, it is the moving of the sense-object from one logical space to another, the transformation from an atomistic entity to a predicated quality, that is at the heart of the perceptual process and that constitutes the deepest meaning of the doctrine of motion.

Finally, from all of this, two conclusions emerge, manifesting the real significance of the Heracleiteanism of Socrates' account of perception. One is the fact that Socrates leaves unanswered, for now at least, a fundamental question that is implicit in his theory. It concerns the justification for the most basic of all of the motions, that between the two logical frameworks. Just how do the atomistic offspring become predicated as the properties of objects? This question, the key to understanding the labyrinthine complexities of the later parts of the Theaetetus, could not even be formulated were not the unique kind of motion it involves made identifiable in Socrates' account. The other point follows from this. For if the perceptual object is created in such a manner, depending on an act of attribution whose warrant is a dubious one, then the status of that object is itself cast into doubt. The ultimate priority, therefore, belongs to the perceptual process; the objects of perception are ontologically derivative. It is this conclusion, perhaps the most important reason for Socrates' use of the doctrine of Heracleitus, that explains why the perceptual realm is placed on a lower level of the divided line.

VI

Still, there remains the question of what, if any, actual knowledge occurs in perception. There must be some. After all, however problematic perceptual objects may be said to be, they do turn out to be remarkably stable and predictable. Our natural confidence in their recurring patterns of behavior is what enables us to deal with them prudently and advantageously. This is a far cry from the Heracleitean flux that Socrates ascribes to these entities. What is it that brings order to the supposedly chaotic realm of sensory perception? What is the basis of our trust in the reality of these objects?

These are not simple questions. Their answers range far beyond the immediate discussion, showing Socrates' theory of perception to be a mere nucleus. The widening context of complementary topics is what occupies the remainder of the *Theaetetus*. Two issues are paramount. One is the problematic, even paradoxical, relationship between the abstract concepts of the whole and the all. The other concerns the dominant role of memory in perception. These issues provide the key to an explanation of the epistemic status of the predicational framework; that in turn will reveal the source of the stability within the perceptual realm. The present discussion, focusing specifically on the account of perception, can do little more than allude to these broader themes.

Two detailed features of Socrates' account, previously noted only in passing, will help to bring these investigations to a close. First it was pointed out that the theory made use of reproductive language which might be related to the midwife metaphor. Second, the list of kinds of sensings that Socrates gave was thought to be an odd one. It included pleasures, pains, desires, and fears, as well as the more familiar examples of sight, hearing, smell, and the sensings of cold and of heat. The latter group all derive from distinct sensory organs or from specific sensitive parts of the body. The former, however, are not only more generally dispersed but also seem to be necessarily allied with one or more of the others. It is not clear that they should be called sensings in their own right.[17] Furthermore, Socrates had said that appropriate objects of sense spring forth akin to the various sensings. Seeing, hearing, and smelling have as their objects colors and shapes, sounds, and odors. To feelings of cold and hot there correspond vaguer notions of thermal properties. But what are the objects to be correlated with pleasures, desires, and their opposites?

Pleasures and pains, at least those of the body, rather than occuring in isolation tend to accompany sensings which derive from bodily organs or parts. They have no unique objects of their own. It is similar with desires and fears. Objects whose sensings usually are accompanied by pleasure are desired; painful ones are feared or avoided. Thus the list given by Socrates suggests structural interrelationships amongst various sensings, the objects being sometimes shared and sometimes distinct. Not only does this account for molecular combinations within the atomistic domain of sense-objects, but it will also point towards the source of the logic of predication. The role of desire in sensory perception provides the key.

The atomism of the sensory domain pertains strictly to the sensings and objects that arise directly from bodily organs or parts. Pleasures and pains, apparently connected with these others, do not manifest the same independence. It is with desire (and fear), however, that an even more comprehensive structure can be discerned. A desire, intending something not yet possessed, will imply a temporal duration that allows its fulfillment. Within such durations associative patterns may occur. The type of sense-object paired with a kind of tasting, for instance, will characteristically be found together with certain colors and odors. A given desire might thus anticipate, besides one specific pleasurable sense-object, a pattern of other objects which usually occur with it. The same would happen with fears. The sensory atomism, therefore, will be disposed towards familiar molecular combinations.

It is these molecular groupings that provide the raw material for the predicational framework. The faculty of memory is essential to their development. Memory, by drawing on past conjunctions, makes possible the various associations within the sensory domain. Most basic is the association (through remembrance of past connections) of the expected pleasure or pain with the motive feeling itself, and of course with whatever is being desired or feared. With respect to this last, certain clusters of sense-objects (some present, some remembered) will be grouped together, as if belonging to one and the same thing. Such combinations acquire a dispositional status. If they did not continually repeat, calculated behavior would be reduced to mere blind groping. There is thus an element of permanence. Should not these patterned combinations, all the more unified by spatial and temporal proximity, disposed to continuing identity, count as substantial objects? They need not. Collections of atoms could produce the same results. Even the molecular structuring based on desires and fears, therefore, does not by itself explain the origin of the predicational logic. But since this structuring, with memory playing the dominant role in its development, is a necessary element in the explanation of that logic, Socrates will later explore the role of memory in perception, with the aid of the two suggestive metaphors of the wax block and the aviary.

How, then, does a collection of sense-objects become transformed into a multitude of properties belonging to a single subject? The answer to this question, determined by the complex interrelationship between the whole and the all, comprises the most radical aspect of Plato's treatment of the perceptual world. Socrates, for reasons pertaining to his overall strategy in this dialogue (especially because of his concern with how the mathematical innovations of Theaetetus and Theodorus might contribute towards a justification of the relativism of Protagoras), lets that answer gradually emerge, mainly in the later parts of the conversation. It must suffice for now, therefore, to have shown how the difficulties in Socrates' account of perception lead to the formulation of that fundamental question. But there is one last feature of Socrates' account remaining to be discussed. That is its connection with the midwife metaphor.

Desire is the link between the two. Its role in the perceptual process, in creating the molecular combinations that become the properties of perceptual objects, has already been described. Desire also has a place within the midwife metaphor. Knowledge is explained there as being the product of a kind of reproduction. The soul becomes pregnant and gives birth, with the help of a midwife like Socrates (if, indeed, there could be others like him), either to genuine offspring or to windeggs. Whatever partner it might be that joins with the soul to bring about the production of knowledge, the encounter between the two would be occasioned by desire. Certainly the perceptual process could be taken to be one specific type of this reproductive activity. Moreover given the problematic nature of the perceptual object, perhaps it is best understood as being an incidental product of the bodily desires of the human organism. Thus, if perception is the result of a process whose fundamental motivation is not an epistemic one, it should be less surprising that it is so fraught with logical inconsistencies.

In conclusion, it is time to return to the other metaphor, the divided line. One of its claims can now be said to have found a justification in the *Theaetetus*. Because of the problematic logical structure of sensory perception, and because of the derivative ontological status of the perceptual object, there is good reason for Socrates to say that this mode of apprehension is a matter merely of trust rather than of knowledge. Furthermore, a second claim of the divided line could also be said to have its defence in the *Theaetetus*, even though it has only been touched on in this essay. The dialectical interaction of the whole and the all, discussed near the end of the dialogue, along with the multi-faceted relationship between the one and the many, whose extensive treatment in the *Parmenides* is alluded to in the *Theaetetus* (183E), are both themes which involve the very foundations of number. Their relevance to Socrates' theory of perception is barely sketched in this essay. But any interpretation of the later portions of the *Theaetetus* must incorporate the argumentation involved in the combination of these two themes, showing how these issues relate to the earlier account of perception. The suggestion is now being made (although its substantiation must await another occasion) that it is these arguments in the *Theaetetus* that make possible the claim of the *Republic* that whatever degree of being is possessed by the perceptual realm is derived from a higher level of the divided line, the one on which the objects of mathematics are placed.[18]

A third claim that is illustrated by the divided line, that it is participation in the Ideas that is the source of the lower levels of being, is not defended at all in the *Theaetetus*. Nonetheless, even the justification of the first two claims would be enough to show that the metaphor which is presented without argument in the *Republic* is actually the distillation of an extremely complex process of argumentation. The substantiation of the third claim, including an explanation of the role of the Ideas in the development of the perceptual object, would involve relating the theory of perception in the *Theaetetus* to a number of other dialogues that focus on related themes. Little work has been done in this area. There are many issues remaining regarding the divided line that have not been investigated sufficiently. However the challenge given by Robert S. Brumbaugh to look to that metaphor as the most fundamental interpretive principle in Platonic studies is an insight that seems likely to provide the most fruitful avenues of exploration.

NOTES

I am especially indebted to the invaluable comments of Richard I. Sugarman and W. Thomas Schmid on various drafts of this paper. Paul Schaich's critique of an early draft was extremely helpful. I am grateful to Washington College for generous support by means of a Faculty Enhancement Grant.

1. The use of the word *aisthesis* here is ambiguous. Cornford points out that "In ordinary usage *aisthesis*, translated 'perception.' has a wide range of meanings, including sensation, our awareness of outer objects or of facts, feelings, emotions, etc.." Francis M. Cornford, *Plato's Theory of Knowledge* (London, 1935). John

Cooper, in a tightly argued paper dealing primarily with later passages in the *Theaetetus*, maintains that "Plato is in effect using the notion of *aisthesis* in two ways." One refers to "the perceptual acts of the mind," the other to "the powers of the body which Plato says make these acts possible." He goes on to suggest that Plato may "assimilate or confuse with one another sensory awareness and the labelling of its objects." See John Cooper, "Plato on Sense Perception and Knowledge: *Theaetetus* 184 to 186," *Phronesis*, 15(1970): 129. It is impossible to respond adequately to Cooper's interpretations without addressing at length the passages on which he is focusing. The position that would here be defended, however, is that Socrates deliberately plays on the ambiguity in the term *aisthesis* until he completes his demonstration that Protagorean relativism takes advantage of that ambiguity; from that point on, it would be argued, Socrates follows a clear distinction between sensation and perception.

2. The question naturally arises as to whether or not this is Plato's own theory. Cornford argues plausibly that it must be: "Plato intends to refute the claim of perception (in spite of its infallibility) to be knowledge on the ground that its objects have no real being, but are always becoming and changing and therefore cannot be known. For that purpose he is bound to give us what he believes to be a true account of the nature of those objects. It would be futile to prove that what some other individual or school, perhaps wrongly, supposed to be the nature of perception was inconsistent with its claim to yield knowledge. Accordingly he states his own doctrine and takes it as established for the purposes of the whole subsequent criticism of perception." Cornford, *Plato's Theory of Knowledge*, 49.

3. Quotations are from the translation of H.N. Fowler, *Theaetetus and Sophist* (Boston: Harvard and Heinemann, 1961).

4. I.M. Crombie's brilliant analysis of Plato's theory of perception, testing it against the two models of first a causal theory and then a phenomenalistic account, contains the most perceptive critical insights ever presented on this text. I.M. Crombie, *An Examination of Plato's Doctrines* (London: Routledge and Kegan Paul, 1963), especially 2:3-33. The indebtedness of this essay to Crombie's interpretation will be obvious to anyone who has read it.

5. This terminology is suggested by Cornford in his interpretation of the example of the wind. "There are two different sense-objects, the coolness that appears to me and the warmth that appears to you. There is one physical object, 'the same wind' that is blowing." Cornford, *Plato's Theory of Knowledge*, 33.

6. Crombie argues: "But if the whiteness travels *from* the stone, why does the stone thereby become filled with whiteness? If water travels from a tap it is the bucket and not the tap that gets filled." Crombie, *Examination of Plato's Doctrine*, 2:21.

7. Crombie points this out: "According to the causal theory my glimpse of the stone, indeed, exists only in relation to me, but the stone itself exists in its own right and endures through time whether anybody is seeing it or not. It does not come into existence when it is seen; it has to be there beforehand in order to cause the seeing." Crombie, *Examination of Plato's Doctrine*, 2:19.

8. This interpretation is suggested by Crombie: "Let us then try a picture more in accordance with Phenomenalism, or Russell's Neutral Monism, than with Locke's Causal Theory. In this picture the two slow processes are not two physical objects in a state of steady physical activity, but two sets of sensory phenomena. Jones is a gradually growing biography of sense-perceptions, and the stone a gradually growing history of sense-data." Crombie, *Examination of Plato's Doctrine*, 2:22.

9. See John McDowell, *Plato Theaetetus* (Oxford: Clarendon Press, 1973), 144: "it is

hard to understand the claim that a stone, say, is partly responsible for the appearance of whiteness it presents to someone, if the stone is in fact nothing but a collection of appearances, including the whiteness."

10. This is the interpretation that Crombie finally rests with "Perhaps the following is the best account of the matter. What Plato intends to put forward is a version of the Causal Theory, but he does not fully understand the logic of the theory, which requires two sets of terms, one to stand for things as they are in themselves, the other for things as they are perceived ... It would seem therefore that the hypothesis, that Plato intended to put forward a version of of the Causal Theory, but failed to conform to the logical requirements for doing so, explains all the difficulties which we found in his account of the doctrine of the Mysteries." Crombie, *Examination of Plato's Doctrine*, 2:24-25.

11. Locke reveals his awareness of this problem when, distinguishing sensory ideas (colors, tastes, etc.) from the secondary qualities which produce them, he says of the ideas: "which *ideas*, if I speak of sometimes as in the things themselves, I would be understood to mean those qualities in the objects which produce them in us." John Locke, *An Essay concerning Human Understanding*, 2.8:8.

12. Winifred F. Hicken, following suggestions by Stenzel and Ryle, argues that the atomism could be applied to Plato's Ideas. Hicken cites the view "that the Forms of the earlier dialogues were simples of just this kind." See W.F. Hicken, "Knowledge and Forms in Plato's *Theaetetus*," *Journal of Hellenic Studies*, 77, 1(1957): 48-53. (Reprinted in R.E. Allen, *Studies in Plato's Metaphysics* (London: Routledge and Kegan Paul, 1965), 185-198). While it may be fruitful to explore such a possibility, there are strong reasons, as is here being argued, to take Socrates at face value when he refers to the atoms as *aistheta* (202B).

13. Crombie distinguishes between two versions of Heracleiteanism, a "normal" and a "rampant" interpretation. The former would say: "All properties result from change"; the latter that "All properties are subject to change." He finds a problem similar to the one here noted in the application of the doctrine to perception. "There is therefore this dilemma for the Heraclitean: – either his thesis is tenable but trivial, or he is committed to a world in which there is no such thing as a describable object ..." Crombie, *Examination of Plato's Doctrine*, 2:11.

14. This conception of the seeing of the eye as the active motion is in opposition to the more popular view that, in keeping with 159C, it is the stone that is active in perception, while the passive motion is thought to be the perceiver (See, e.g. McDowell, *Plato Theaetetus*, 137). But Cornford points out that "the subject of perception is here treated as if it were, not the mind but the sense-organ – the eye ..." (Cornford, *Plato's Theory of Knowledge*, 49-50). In the later passage Socrates describes *himself*, and not one of his senses, as the passive element.

15. Various attempts have been made to correlate the theory in the *Theaetetus* with the scientific account of perception in *Timaeus* 45B-46C, 67C-68D (See Cornford, *Plato's Theory of Knowledge*, 50n.2 Crombie, *Examination of Plato's Doctrine*, 2:1-3 McDowell, *Plato's Theaetetus*, 139-140). Crombie's remark seems apt: "Plato was well aware of the difference between a philosopher and a physiologist, and did not feel called upon to offer a physiological account of perception" Crombie, *Examination of Plato's Doctrine*, 2:1.

16. McDowell argues against any metaphorical interpretation, saying it "would be unsatisfactory, in view of the use which is made, at 181B-183B, of the distinction between motion and alteration" (McDowell, *Plato's Theaetetus*, 139-140). This argument must, of course, be dealt with when interpreting the later passage.

Nonetheless it does not seem necessary to rule out the interpretation here presented.

17. McDowell explains the presence of these odd items in Socrates' list in terms of two possibilities: "(1) He may think of pleasure, pain, desire, and fear as involving perception, by an inner sense, of one's own inner states .... (2) Alternatively, he think of them as modes of perception of outer objects. Thus, just as to see an object is, strictly speaking, to see e.g. its whiteness, ... so to fear an object is somehow to perceive its fearfulness" (McDowell, *Plato Theaetetus*, 137-138). McDowell seems to prefer the latter. Nonetheless, this explanation does not resolve the questions surrounding these items.

18. I argue these points in a forthcoming book which will present an interpretation of the dialogue as a whole.

5

KNOWLEDGE, SPECULATION, AND MYTH IN PLATO'S ACCOUNTS OF THE ORDER AND THE DISTANCES OF CELESTIAL BODIES

Alexander P.D. Mourelatos

I

INTRODUCTION

It is difficult for us to get a clear picture of Plato's doctrine concerning matters of astronomy. There is, to begin with, the *prima facie* conflict between Plato's revisionary definition in *Republic* VII of a "real astronomy" that "lets go of the heavens," i.e, of a pure science of "the solid in revolution," or of "the revolution of that which has depth"(528A, 528D, 530B), and the more familiar conception of astronomy exemplified in the passages in which Plato draws on astronomical observations and theorizes, explicitly or implicitly, about celestial phenomena.[1] Moreover, many of the latter passages are embedded in a wider context of myth, which leads one to wonder whether Plato is propounding astronomical hypotheses or constructing a vehicle for allegory. There is also the problem posed by the overlaying of a tradition of Platonist, Neoplatonist, and Pythagoreanizing interpretations on the astronomical passages. Two cases in point: The Platonists of late antiquity were confident in finding a definite scheme of celestial distances in the *Timaeus*, and this tradition of interpretation is reflected in commentaries down to our own day. But an untutored reader of the key passages of the *Timaeus* would have good reason to wonder what the scheme is, or even whether a scheme of celestial distances is implied at all. The "harmony of the spheres" (a musical scale composed by the tones generated by the celestial motions) is famously a Pythagorean concept, and it is often assumed that Plato deploys the concept in *Republic* X and in the *Timaeus*. But a careful modern reader may have difficulty finding the concept, without a commentator's prompting, in either dialogue.

My concern in this paper is to get a clear view of Plato's doctrine on just two topics: the order of the celestial bodies in the cosmos, and the distances of celestial bodies. The two topics are obviously related. If one has a doctrine of celestial distances, one has, *a fortiori*, a doctrine of order. But one can have a doctrine of the order of celestial bodies and either a purely qualitative account of the distances or no account of the distances at all. I do not intend to prejudge the question whether Plato did in fact have an established opinion on the topic of celestial distances. Indeed, my conclusions on this topic will be in large measure negative. The insights we stand to gain into Plato's accounts of order and distances will have repercussions on the larger topic of our conception of Plato's astronomy. These repercussions will be pointed out in the course of my argument and at the conclusion of the paper.

The relevant texts give us only partial indications of Plato's basis for such opinions as he held concerning order and distances. A large part of the paper will, accordingly, be devoted to answering questions such as these: (a) What empirical observations that Plato or his fourth-century contemporaries or his predecessors could have made might have had a bearing on either topic? (b) What arguments and counter-arguments developed in pre-Platonic philosophy might have provided Plato with a reasoned basis for opinion on either topic? (c) How does the approach Plato takes to these topics compare with that taken by the mathematically sophisticated astronomers of Hellenistic and later antiquity?

The term "planet" will be used throughout this paper to refer to all seven of the celestial bodies known by the ancients to move against the background of the fixed stars through the band of the zodiac in a generally Eastward direction: sun, moon, Jupiter, Mars, Mercury, Saturn, and Venus. "It was a scientific achievement not to be underrated," writes Walter Burkert, "to go against appearances, separate the five planets from the fixed stars, and classify them with the sun and moon, so that there are seven planets."[2] Plato's use of the expression *planēton* (*astron*) to refer just to the five star-like planets reflects the lingering influence of the less scientific and older (from the perspective of fifth-century science) grouping. Plato, accordingly, had to use periphrastic expressions for the full group of seven. It is more convenient, as well as true to the outlook of Plato's geocentric astronomy, to adopt the encompassing use of "planets" for the seven and to adopt the phrase "star-like planets" for the set of five.

II

ORDER OF THE PLANETS IN THE COSMOS

The texts

The earliest statements in the Greek tradition of the order of the complete series of seven planets are found in Plato, in *Republic* X.616E-617B and *Timaeus* 38D. Testimonia that we have concerning the views of pre-Socratic philosophers on this topic tend to lump the five star-like planets together. (Only Venus is specifically mentioned, in the relevant testimonia for Parmenides and Democritus.) Commentators on Plato – ancient as well as modern – have been rather rash to assume that the doctrine we find in the *Republic* and the *Timaeus* concerning the order of planets was first propounded by fifth-century Pythagoreans or even by Pythagoras.[3]

In *Republic* X.616E-617B[4] Plato does not mention the planets by name[5] – he merely speaks of the "first" or "outermost" (clearly the fixed stars), the "second," and so forth down to the "eighth" (clearly the moon). He does, however, give all the needed clues – color, brightness, "borrowed light," order of magnitude of periods – so that any reader with even an elementary knowledge of astronomical facts can ferret out the implied identities of the eight celestial bodies. Putting these clues together, the order of orbits, from outermost to innermost is: (1) fixed stars; (2) Saturn; (3) Jupiter; (4) Mars; (5) Mercury; (6) Venus; (7) sun; (8) moon.[6]

In *Timaeus* 38D the order of the four planets closest to the earth is given as follows (proceeding outwards): (1) moon; (2) sun; (3) Venus; (4) Mercury. After starting this series, Plato has Timaeus plead that to state "where the other planets have been installed [by the Demiurge] and why" would require an inappropriately long digression. But just a few lines below, at 39A, Timaeus propounds a principle that connects sidereal period with size of orbit, which I shall hereafter refer to as the Inverse Correlation principle: "[planets] that have a larger orbit revolve slower, and planets that have a smaller orbit, faster." Even if Plato and his contemporaries did not possess precise data of the sidereal periods of the planets, we can assume they had at least a qualitative sense of the order of periods. By applying Inverse Correlation, any fourth-century reader of the *Timaeus* could have understood that the series giving the order of orbits in the cosmos should be completed as follows: (5) Mars; (6) Jupiter; (7) Saturn. The only difference, then, in the statement of the spatial order of the planets in the *Republic* from that given in *Timaeus* is the trivial one, that in the latter the order is from the earth outwards. The order given at *Epinomis* 986B-987C is the same as that in *Republic* and *Timaeus*.

III

EMPIRICAL INDICATIONS OF THE ORDER OF THE SEVEN
PLANETS

The phenomenon of occultation must have been the first and obvious clue that both the fixed stars and the star-like planets move beyond the orbit of the moon.[7] Anaximander had taught that the stars (including the star-like planets) are closer to the earth than the moon and the sun (A18).[8] Had anyone objected that we never witness a transit of a star across the face of either of the two great luminaries, he would have answered, perhaps, that the sun and the moon hide any transiting star by outshining it.[9] Specifically with reference to the star-like planets, he could also have argued that their paths take them mostly slightly above or slightly below the disk of either luminary.[10] But concerning the possibility of transits across the moon, there is an obvious rejoinder: Occultations also occur at the first and last quarter of the moon's phases; but we never see a star inside the moon's horns.[11] We similarly do not see any stars transiting across the darkened moon at the time of a lunar eclipse. The view that seems most compelling to the unsophisticated observer, that the moon is the closest of the heavenly bodies, is also the view supported by searching attention to the empirical evidence.[12]

It might well seem that the sun's heat should have been an indication to the ancients that the stars and star-like planets are located beyond the sun. The glow of a fire can be seen from a considerable distance; but its heat can be felt only by those who are in the fire's immediate vicinity. Anaximenes may have used this consideration in arguing against Anaximander's thesis that the sun is the outermost of the celestial bodies (cf. *DK* 13A7[6]). It was not, however, universally assumed that the stars and star-like planets are fiery. Even for those who thought them to be so, the fire of stars may well have been assumed to be miniscule when compared to the sun's fire. So the stars might, after all, be just as close as the sun is, or even closer.

The great conceptual break-through in fifth-century Greek astronomy was, doubtless, the realization that the moon shines with "a light not its own," its bright side "always facing the light of the sun" (Parmenides B14 and B15; cf. Empedocles B43, B45, B47). With this explanation of the moon's phases, the correct explanation of lunar and solar eclipses was soon forthcoming (Empedocles B42, cf. Anaxagoras A42 [3]). Thus another view that appeals to the unsophisticated observer, that the sun's orbit lies above or beyond that of the moon, can also claim firm empirical grounding.

Another clue is provided by the phenomenon of twinkling, famously cited by Aristotle in an illustration of the syllogistic form of explanation: Objects that do not twinkle are near; the star-like planets do not twinkle; the star-like planets are near (*Posterior Analytics* I.13.78a30-b3). Since the fixed stars do twinkle we may assume that their cosmic region is well beyond that of the planets.

Naked-eye observation, without the benefit of much stronger theoretical assumptions than those required to explain such phenomena as occultations, the moon's phases, lunar and solar eclipses, and twinkling, cannot provide more than these three sign-posts: the moon closest in; the sun somewhere above the moon; the other five planets closer in than the fixed stars. This still allows for a number of alternatives to the model Plato adopts in the *Republic* and the *Timaeus*. A follower of Anaximander could still have argued that the sun lies beyond the fixed stars (transits would, as we saw, be considered undetectable), the star-like planets lying in a region between that of the fixed stars and that of the moon. Or, assuming that the fixed stars are outermost, the star-like planets could be above the sun or below the sun; or, again, some above and some below.

IV

THEORETICAL APPROACHES

Given this insufficiency of the empirical indications, it is not unreasonable of Plato to have taken to theorizing. We saw that he makes use of Inverse Correlation: "[bodies] that have a larger orbit revolve slower, and those that have a smaller orbit, faster" (*Timaeus* 39A).

"Faster" and "slower" refer here, of course, to average angular velocity, as the latter is indicated by each planet's sidereal period. It is striking that Plato applies the principle only to the motion of "the Different," i.e. to the Eastward motion of the planets. The motion of "the Same," i.e. the Westward diurnal motion of the fixed stars, is the fastest of all celestial motions, yet it involves the largest orbit. Clearly, the principle carries an unstated restriction to revolutions in the same direction. What might have been the rationale of that principle?

Aristotle makes use of the same principle in *De caelo* II.10, and explains it as follows:

> It stands to reason, after all, that the body [Saturn] that is nearest to the simple and first revolution [fixed stars] should traverse its own orbit in the greatest amount of time, whereas that which is farthest [from the fixed stars] should do so in the least amount of time .... For the one nearest [the first revolution] is maximally controlled [by it]; the one farthest away, least, because of the intervening distance. (291b3-9)[13]

The Aristotelian explanation is transparently a survival of the pre-Socratic conception of the cosmic vortex. On the pre-Socratic model, the outermost band of the vortex has the greatest speed; but a factor of drag slows down the interior bands, so that the innermost band has the slowest speed. The difference in Aristotle comes with his superimposing on the pre-Socratic model Plato's kinematic analysis of the speeds of interior bands: each band has both the motion of the outermost and a contrary motion of its own, with the result that the innermost band is conceived of as fastest, the one next to the outermost, as slowest, and *mutatis mutandis* for the other interior bands. Dynamically, Aristotle's explanation and that of the pre-Socratics are equivalent in implying a factor of inertia or resistance: Saturn "lags" only slightly behind the fixed stars, according to the pre-Socratics; or, according to Aristotle, Saturn is too close to the fixed stars to have anything but a slow contrary motion of its own.[14]

It is unlikely that such holdover of the pre-Socratic model should also be at the root of Plato's Inverse Correlation principle. For there is noticeable inconcinnity between the astronomy of the *Timaeus* and pre-Socratic cosmology: the planetary motions are imparted directly to the constitution of the world soul (*Timaeus* 35B - 36D); they depend in no way, nor are they affected by, the material properties of the planets; such factors as friction, drag, and inertia do not come into play at all. It is more likely that Plato's own rationale for Inverse Correlation would have been purely formal and *a priori* in character. We have a clue in the passage of *Laws* X that discusses the "marvels" involved in the rotation of concentric bands:

> In that rotation, motion of this sort, by carrying around simultaneously the largest and smallest circle, distributes itself in accordance with a ratio (*ana logon*) to small and to larger circles, thus (itself) being smaller and greater in accordance with a ratio (*kata logon*). For this reason it stands to be considered the source of all marvels, furnishing as it does to large and small circles tardinesses and swiftnesses that are coordinated by ratio (*homologoumena*) – a state of affairs one might well expect to be impossible. (893C-D)

In modern mechanics, the ratio referred to here is expressed in the familiar equation that connects linear velocity (v), angular velocity (a), and radius (r):

$$v = a \times r$$

Plato, clearly, has an intuitive grasp of one possible reading of the modern equation: linear velocity and radius are directly proportional, so that in the case of concentric circles that rotate with the same angular velocity, the ones of larger radius have the higher linear velocities, the ones of smaller radius, the lower. But Plato should also have had the insight that corresponds to the other possible reading of the modern equation, viz., that angular velocity and size of radius are inversely proportional, so that if several concentric circles should rotate with the same linear velocity, the ones of larger radius will have the lower angular velocities, the ones of smaller radius, the higher.

In astronomy, the first reading of the equation has applications in the study of the motion of the fixed stars – circumpolar stars and equatorial stars complete their respective circuits together. But the second reading, too, has potential astronomical bearing, if we should think of it as applying to the system of the planets. Clearly not all planets have the same angular velocity.[15] Now if the model of *Laws* X – concentric circles, all of which rotate with the same angular velocity – should have served for Plato as an ideal of balance in concentric motion,[16] an alternative – and indeed equivalent – ideal would be that of varying angular velocities with equality in linear velocities.

I am not suggesting that Plato entertained the hypothesis that the seven planets have the same linear velocity. Given that three planets (sun, Mercury, and Venus) are assumed to have roughly the same angular velocity,[17] but cannot be thought to be at the same distance from the earth, the linear velocities of at least these three must inevitably be different. Moreover, attributing the hypothesis of equal linear velocities to Plato is blocked by the astronomical passage of *Republic* X, which clearly requires eight different linear velocities for the eight celestial bodies.[18] It can, nonetheless, be said that the two alternative ideals, equality of all angular velocities and equality of all linear velocities, serve as the two outer limits that define a range of balanced distributions of angular velocities to a system of concentric circles. This point deserves elaboration, for it promises to help us better understand how the programmatic "real astronomy" of *Republic* VII is related to its homonymous inquiry that does look at the heavens – when the latter inquiry seeks to ascertain, for example, the sidereal periods of the planets.

V

THE RELEVANCE OF "REAL ASTRONOMY"

I have argued elsewhere that Plato's "real astronomy" is a general and pure kinematics.[19] It consists of geometry (plane or solid) enhanced by the postulate that figures and solids may also be formed by the translation of points, lines, or planes through space at various speeds. This wider matrix of mathematical abstraction challenges us to consider theorems and constructions connecting the composition of motions and speeds with the kinematic generation of geometric objects. It is concerned with problems of this genre: Assuming that a cylinder is rotating on its central axis at speed V_1, what is the geometry of the spiral that is inscribed in space by a point that ascends at speed V_2 from the base of the cylinder along a line parallel to the central axis? The obvious, but rather uninteresting, tie between real astronomy and ordinary astronomy is that the latter must use the former as a tool and a language in the mathematically sophisticated investigation of celestial phenomena. But there is another and more intriguing tie. It is inherent to the generative logic of mathematics that each of the mathematical sciences should select and promote certain structures as focally significant and theoretically paramount: arithmetic does this with the smaller integers and with the contrast between odd and even numbers; plane geometry, with straight lines, triangles, simple polygons, perfect arcs, and circles; solid geometry, with the sphere and the regular solids. The focal significance of these structures also makes them specially appealing to the natural philosopher or cosmologist, inasmuch as the latter seeks appropriate *explanantia* in answer to ultimate Why questions. Thus in the *Timaeus*, the ultimate question "Why are there four elements?" is given an intellectually compelling answer by having the four terrestrial elements modelled on four of the regular solids, the fifth regular solid being assigned to the cosmos as a whole.[20]

As a purely mathematical subject, real astronomy should similarly promote certain structures. What are they? The best candidate would not be composition of rectilinear motions, for in that case the familiar parallelogram of motions pretty much exhausts the possibilities of theoretical elaboration. The fullest theoretical potential of real astronomy lies, as Plato's mathematical successors discovered,[21] in the study of the composition of rotary motions. And at the heart of the subject so conceived is the structure of the concentric rotating circles with its emblematic law, $v = a \times r$. The motion of the fixed stars displays that structure under the ideal condition of equal angular velocity for all orbits, from the celestial equator to near either of the two celestial poles. It is only appropriate, then, that the planetary revolutions, which involve five different angular velocities, should display that same structure in such a way that the measures of radii and velocities fall within the limits of balanced distribution defined by the two alternative ideals: equality of all angular velocities, and equality of all linear velocities. Clearly, we could conceive of a system in which the outer circles rotate with vertiginous speed and the inner circles hardly at all. We could also conceive of a system in which not the innermost circles but rather the ones in an intermediate region have the highest angular velocity. Each of these possibilities admits of infinite variation; yet both these infinite sets of variants lie outside the range of the two ideals of equality of either angular or linear velocity. To say that the planetary motions are governed by Inverse Correlation is to say that periods and radii fall within the limits posted by the two ideals.

Before we turn to the topic of celestial distances, we should note that Inverse Correlation offers no clue as to the relative order of the three planets that are assumed to have the same angular velocity – Mercury, sun, and Venus. Unless Plato had worked out some scheme of distances, he could not have had any rational basis for the assumption he makes that the orbit of Venus lies beyond that of the sun, and the orbit of Mercury beyond that of Venus.

VI

CELESTIAL DISTANCES

Estimates in Hellenistic astronomy

Mathematically sophisticated estimates of the respective distances of the moon and of the sun from the earth were first worked out well after Plato's time: by Ptolemy's two great predecessors, Aristarchus of Samos (first half of third century B.C.), and Hipparchus of Nicaea (second century B.C). A brief overview, in this section, of the methods the great mathematical astronomers of antiquity used in estimating distances will give us a historically appropriate basis of comparison.

Aristarchus' initial approach was that of determining the ratios of the sides of the right triangle which is formed by earth, moon, and sun at the moon's first or last quarter (when the moon is "dichotomized" by the sun's rays). A more viable approach, taken in successive stages of sophistication by Aristarchus and Hipparchus, was that of the geometric and trigonometric investigation of lunar and (in Hipparchus also of) solar eclipses.[22] Adopted and developed by Ptolemy, this approach produced the measures of lunar and solar distance that remained the standard till Kepler.[23]

Crucial to the use of eclipse phenomena for determining distance is an understanding of the effect of parallax: the data of observation may need to be adjusted, to allow for lunar parallax; or lunar parallax may itself be the relevant datum. Even without the benefit of instruments of measurement, the effect of lunar parallax should be obvious to anyone who reflects on a certain striking difference between lunar and solar eclipses. Ptolemy gives a marvelously clear account of this difference:

[I]n the case of solar eclipses, which are caused by the moon passing below and blocking [the sun]...the same eclipse does not appear identical, either in size or in duration, in all places.... Whereas in the case of lunar eclipses there is no such variation due to parallax, since the observer's position is

not a contributory cause to what happens at a lunar eclipse.
(*Almagest*, IV.1, Heiberg, vol. 1, part 1, 267)[24]

The corresponding phenomenon, of occultations of stars and star-
like planets by the sun, was, however, practically unobservable for
the ancients. As for solar parallax, Ptolemy did offer calculations of
it; but he could not measure it directly. Nor did there seem to be
any possibility of detecting, let alone measuring, parallax in the case
of any of the star-like planets. Indeed, Ptolemy warns that any planetary model that places the orbits of Venus and Mercury below that
of the sun must avoid placing them so close to the orbit of the moon
as to give detectable parallax to these two planets.[25]

Without parallax for the five star-like planets, the question of
their respective distances from the earth had to be for all of antiquity one that was in principle undecidable by any method that drew
on empirical data. Ptolemy did eventually provide numerical figures
for the distances of the star-like planets, too – not in the *Almagest*
but in the *Planetary Hypotheses*. These, however, were not derived
through the application of geometry and trigonometry to empirical
data; they were simply the "speculative by-product of the first
complete system of mathematical astronomy."[26] That is, Ptolemy
made some *a priori* assumptions concerning the order of the seven
planets; he used the distances of moon and sun as his empirical base;
then, for the ratio of the two distances each of the other five planets
has from the earth at perigee and apogee, he used the numbers
required by his purely kinematic model in the *Almagest*; and he made
the further assumption that there is no gap or void in the celestial
region defined between one planet's apogee and the perigee of the
planet immediately above it.

The concept of parallax in fourth century astronomical debates

I know of no passage either in Plato – or, for that matter, in Aristotle – that suggests a grasp of the fact that such phenomena as the
moon's phases and either solar or lunar eclipses have a definite
bearing on questions concerning the distance of the two luminaries
from the earth. It is, nevertheless, tempting to suppose that the
difference between solar and lunar eclipses (see the text from
Ptolemy quoted above) should have alerted fourth-century astronomers and cosmologists to the effect of lunar parallax, and thus to the
implications which that effect has concerning the distance of the
moon from the earth.

The general concept of parallax is certainly not beyond the reach of fifth-century (let alone fourth-century) inquiry. The cognate phenomenon of perspective had been investigated by Anaxagoras and Democritus.[27] It is thus quite possible, and even likely, that effects of parallax in the viewing of ordinary objects should have attracted attention – one thinks of the familar experience of nearby objects jumping from left to right as one alternately covers the left and then the right eye, and vice versa – and that the question of similar effects of perspective in our observation of the heavens may have been raised. Indeed, once it was understood that a solar eclipse results from the moon's passing in front of, or below, the sun, would it not also have become obvious that lunar parallax is part of the explanation of a solar eclipse?

Obvious though this connection between solar eclipses and lunar parallax may seem to us, it was, in fact, missed by Aristotle. There is, remarkably, a passage in *De caelo* II.13 that shows some understanding of the general effect of parallax; but the conclusion Aristotle and others, who are referred to in this passage, seem to have drawn was that celestial bodies are so enormously distant that no effects of parallax at all are detectable. It emerges from *De caelo* II.13 that the general concept of parallax had figured in controversies concerning the heterodox astronomical scheme of the Pythagorean Philolaus. In that scheme not only the seven planets but also the earth, as well as a "counter-earth" (invisible), revolve around a central fire. Aristotle implies that advocates of the Philolaic scheme were confronted with the objection that the celestial phenomena would be quite different if the earth too revolved around a central body, along with the seven planets whose orbits lie above that of the earth. Aristotle reports the Pythagoreans' remarkable rejoinder as follows:

Since the earth is not a center point (*kentron*), rather [its inhabited surface] is distant by an entire hemisphere [from the earth's center], they hold (*oiontai*) that nothing prevents that the phenomena should appear to us in the same way they would appear if the earth were in the middle [of the universe, *epi tou mesou*], since in both cases alike (*homoiōs*) we do not inhabit the [earth's] center. For, they point out, there is also not any empirical indication, as things stand (*outhen gar oude nyn poiein epidēlon*), that we are half a diameter away [from the earth's center]. (293b26-30)[28]

In this rejoinder, the Pythagoreans begin by pointing out that the terrestrial observer is not at the middle of the cosmos on either theory, and that the displacement of the observer from the true middle by an earth radius is assumed by advocates of the geocentric view to produce no detectable parallax. On the latter assumption, which the Pythagoreans do not dispute, the distance from the earth to the locus of the phenomena is incomparably greater than the earth's radius (the earth having the ratio of a point to the sphere of the locus of the phenomena, as Aristarchus later put it). Why, then, the Pythagoreans ask, should displacement of the observer by the measure of the radius of the earth's orbit, even if that displacement should be several times the size of an earth radius, make a detectable difference? Aristotle cites this Pythagorean rejoinder with no indication that he disapproves of it.[29] It is relevant to note that when, in the chapter of *De caelo* that immediately follows, Aristotle gives for the circumference of the earth the estimate of 400,000 stades, which is considerably larger than any of those given by Hellenistic scientists (and it is nearly twice the true figure), he comments that the earth is "not big" (*De caelo* II.14.298a8). This would seem to confirm his endorsement of the Pythagorean rejoinder: the distance from the earth to the locus of celestial phenomena is so enormous that it lies outside any comparison based on terrestrial dimensions.

The difficulty posed by this passage is the one I have skirted by using the phrase "locus of celestial phenomena." Aristotle gives us no indication what the "phenomena" at issue are. The debate between the Pythagoreans and their critics may have focused strictly on the movement of the fixed stars, raising no issues at all concerning the planets. That is how Simplicius understood the passage in his commentary: he imagines the geocentricists arguing that if the earth were not at the center of the universe, the horizon would not bisect the zodiac.[30] It is quite understandable that Simplicius should give this explanation; for he knows Ptolemy, and he knows that there is both lunar and solar parallax, and possibly even some parallax of Venus and Mercury. For Simplicius it is the fixed stars (in contrast to the seven planets) that can be assumed as a class to show no parallax. In a pre-Ptolemaic context, however, it is far more likely that the critics of the Pythagoreans had referred to the movement of all celestial bodies; certainly, the global character of Aristotle's allusion to "the phenomena" strongly argues in favor of this reading.[31]

Plato's recourse to speculation

The significance of *De caelo* II.13 for our reconstruction of Plato's views concerning distance is this. The text I have discussed here places the origin of the parallax concept in the interval between Philolaus and the date of composition of Aristotle's *De caelo*. But this first intimation of the concept is embedded in an argument that brings out an assumption made by both geocentricists and Pythagoreans that no effects of parallax for any celestial phenomena can be detected. If Plato did not have the parallax concept at all he would not, of course, have had any inkling of its bearing on questions of distance. The only evidence that he might have had the concept is that of the fourth-century debate concerning Pythagorean astronomy. But in that context the bearing of considerations of parallax on questions of planetary distance is, in effect, discounted. It is, therefore, quite unlikely that Plato should have had any expectation that the distances of the sun and the moon might some day be determined through the application of geometry to empirical data. Questions of the distance of the two luminaries must have appeared to him just as undecidable on the basis of observation as questions of the distance of the star-like planets must have appeared – not just to him but to the whole of ancient astronomy.

Plato has often been berated by historians of science for offering purely speculative models of the distances of the seven planets. In fact, the speculative hints he offers are so cautious, so noncommital, so multiply hedged, and so transparently symbolic that the censure is quite unwarranted. The uncharitable assessment of Plato's forays into this subject can be blamed, in part, on overinterpretation of the relevant passages.

The qualitative model of celestial distances in Republic X

In the astronomical model of *Republic* X.616D-617B, a system of eight concentric bands or zones (actually, concentric hemispheres or shells) represents the firmament of the fixed stars and the seven planets. The relative width of the eight bands is indicated purely qualitatively, in ordinal specification, as follows:[32]

Band	Order of Width
Fixed stars	1 (widest)
Saturn	8 (narrowest)

Jupiter	7 (next to narrowest)
Mars	3
Mercury	6
Venus	2 (next to widest)
sun	5
moon	4

It is clear how the fixed stars are related to their band, which is said to be "spangled": they fill it. But how are the seven planets related to their respective bands? A plausible interpretation would be that each planet is firmly attached against the outer boundary of its zone – Saturn just inside the band of the fixed stars, Jupiter just inside the band of Saturn, and so on. But the fact that Plato does not allude to any such attachment of the planetary bodies is probably significant. Plato may well have meant to exploit the latitude – quite literally – afforded him by the image of bands. As is only proper in the context of a *mythos*, Plato is being noncommital and allusive. Within its own zone, a planet could either be assumed to occupy always the same position, as it is carried by the movement of the band; or it could have its own lateral and retrograde movements that supervene on the general movement of the band. Indeed, the former alternative may apply to some planets, the latter to others. On either of these interpretations, the ordinal specification of the widths, taken together with the indicated order of the planets, would constitute a qualitative account of interplanetary distances. The latitudinarian interpretation would, however, imply that the distance of at least some of the planets could only be thought of as an average of distances between apogee and perigee.

The widths of the bands notoriously do not correspond to any observed features of the planets. It was, however, noticed in the nineteenth century that the eight ordinal numbers group themselves in pairs each of which adds up to 9, and so as to produce the following arithmetically balanced scheme:[33]

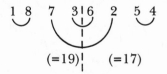

The balance is not perfect, to be sure; but it would be significantly upset if either 3 and 6, or 7 and 2, were transposed. That this scheme is deliberately encoded is shown by the fact that a similar scheme governs the (otherwise scrambled and curiously arbitrary) order in which the colors of the celestial bodies are given at 616E8 - 617A. Thus if we identify each of the eight bodies by an ordinal number representing its position in the cosmos (1 for the outermost body, the fixed stars; 8 for the innermost, the moon), the order in which the bodies are given in the list of colors (extreme left for first, extreme right for last) yields the scheme:

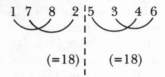

$$(=18) \quad (=18)$$

This rather playful and allusive encoding of a principle of balance makes an obvious comment on the treatment of the topic of celestial distances in the *Republic*. Plato is expressing his faith that the structure of the heavens conforms in some unspecified way to an intelligible principle; he is not propounding a hypothesis, however speculative, concerning the actual distances.

Is a doctrine of planetary distances implied in the Timaeus?

It is often thought that in the *Timaeus* Plato does offer a hypothesis concerning the distances of the planets. At 36D, we read:

> [God] left that one revolution [that of the fixed stars] undivided. The inner revolution, however, he split at six places (*hexachēi*) into seven unequal *kykloi* ["circles" or "bands"] in accordance with (*kata*) the several spans (*diastasin hekastēn*) of the double and triple intervals, there being three respectively. And he ordered that the *kykloi* should move against one another: three equal in speed, and four unequal in speed to one another and to the three, yet moving in accordance with ratio (*en logōi de pheromenous*).

The "double and triple intervals" are the two series of 2-4-8 and 3-9-27, i.e., 2 and 3 together with their respective squares and cubes. A page earlier in the dialogue (35B-36B) these two series, augmented by their common unit, the number 1, serve as the initial basis for the (much more elaborate) cutting of harmonic intervals into the quasi-mythical fabric of the world soul. Clearly, though only six cuts are made, seven numbers will be needed, either to mark the positions of the seven *kykloi* or to measure the intervals between them.

It needs to be pointed out immediately that Plato nowhere states that the seven numbers have some specifically astronomical significance. The passage translated above is the final section in Timaeus' account of the formation of the world soul. At this early stage of God's work, the celestial bodies have not been formed yet, as we are pointedly reminded at the end of 36D: "Once, then, the whole of the soul's constitution had been brought into being..., he then fashioned inside it [i.e., inside the soul] everything of corporeal nature." The division described in 36D applies in the first instance and primarily to the spiritual matrix of the world soul. Since, however, the seven planetary bodies are later described as placed "in" or "at" the seven "revolutions" of the world soul (38C), and since the allusion to seven speeds, three of which are equal and four unequal, points rather obviously to the periods of the seven planets, it is not unreasonable of interpreters to have sought an astronomical interpretation of the passage.

That Plato speaks of the division as applying to the "inner revolution" might make one suppose that the numbers apply to the speeds of the planets. Clearly, however, the numbers do not correspond to the periods of the planets.[34] Indeed, the numbers cannot be assigned to speeds in any sense (periods or linear velocities), in view of the fact that the apportionment of speeds is presented as a distinct creative act, one that follows upon God's establishing the seven *kykloi*.[35] It is also clear from the structure of the passage that the "ratio" mentioned as holding among the speeds is something quite distinct from the series of "double and triple intervals."

The text gives no hint of the order in which the seven numbers are to be taken. After starting with 1, shall we proceed in the order of magnitude, 2 - 3 - 4 - 8 - 9 - 27? Or shall we complete the series based on 2 before we start the series based on 9? Or, after 2 and 3, shall we have the powers of 2 alternate with those of 3? Or shall we take them in some quite scrambled order? Of all these possibilities, the first allows that the numbers could have cumulative significance, i.e., that they mark progressively larger segments of a single continuous quantity. On all other interpretations the numbers would have to represent distinct quantities or intervals.

The interpretation most widely favored, among both ancient and modern commentators, takes the seven numbers as indices of the respective radii of the seven planetary circles. Accordingly, the distance from earth (considered as a point and as the center of all circles) to moon would be a correlate of 1; to sun, of 2; to Saturn, of

27; and correspondingly for intermediate distances.[36] It is proper to use the cautious formulation "is a correlate of" rather than "is" since Plato's quite indefinite phrasing does not permit us to assume that the seven numbers give actual measures of the seven radii. Thus a variant tradition among ancient Platonists takes the actual distances to be cumulative multiples of the numbers in the series: the sun's distance being twice that of the moon, Venus' three times that of the sun, and so on.[37]

Another interpretation takes the seven numbers of the augmented series to be relative measures of interplanetary distances. Thus 1 would represent the spread between those two orbits that are closest together, and 27 the spread between those successive orbits that are farthest apart. It should be noted that this reading does not yield a complete model of distances. For if the numbers of the series do not correspond to radii of orbits but to interplanetary distances, there are, as we saw, no constraints on the order in which the interplanetary distances should be taken. The text could thus be made consistent even with the playfully arbitrary scheme of widths of *Republic* X – the number 1 would correspond to the distance from the orbit of Jupiter to that of Saturn, 27 the distance from the orbit of the sun to that of Venus (see above).

There is, however, a major objection that can be pressed against any interpretation that takes the seven *kykloi* produced by the six cuts to be circles of planetary orbits. In its use generally, *kyklos* can also mean "band"; and this is in fact the meaning the term has in the immediately preceding passage, 36B-C, which describes in mythical terms the formation of the two revolutions of the world soul as the joining of two bands obtained from the cutting of a single fabric into two strips. The sense of "band" for *kyklos* must almost certainly carry over into 36D. One might well suppose, then, that the seven numbers measure neither orbits nor interplanetary distances; they would seem to measure the width of certain zones of celestial motion – celestial eddies, as it were, within which and by which the planets are carried. The numbers would have some relation to a model of planetary distances; but they would not, in themselves, furnish that model.

It is tempting to find such celestial eddies implied in 38C-D, the passage that describes God's installing of the planetary bodies in their respective "revolutions":

God, having made bodies for each of them [the planets], placed [the bodies] in the revolutions (*ethēken eis tas peri-*

phoras) performed by the circular motion (*periodos*) of the Different, there being seven [revolutions], as there are seven [bodies].

This very passage, however, steers us away from too concrete an interpretation of the *kykloi*. In a pre-Socratic cosmology there would indeed have been eddies of the cosmic vortex; the celestial bodies "placed in" would be actually floating in the eddies. In the *Timaeus*, by contrast, the reference cannot be to physical eddies; it must be to revolutions in the spiritual substance of the world soul. The locative sense, accordingly, should not be pressed. It may indeed be significant that Plato does not use the more strongly locative construction of *en* + dative but the looser *eis* + accusative, which might even permit the translation "he assigned them to the revolutions." And even as we adhere to the translation "in," we ought to remind ourselves that the role the world soul has of controlling and encompassing (metaphysically, not just cognitively) all corporeal things is conveyed by speaking of the latter as being "inside the world soul" (*entos autēs*, 36D-E).

So, even though the *kykloi* of 36D are "bands" and not "circles" or "orbits," they are not band-shaped regions of cosmic space; they are zones of psychic influence and psychic activity. That was, after all, how they were introduced in Timaeus' exposition. What we have here is not speculative astronomy but symbolic psychometrics. Like the balanced ordinal numbers of *Republic* X, the seven numbers of our *Timaeus* passage constitute what Brumbaugh has very aptly called "mathematical metaphor."[38]

To determine and formulate the tenor of such metaphors lies beyond the scope of this paper. Part of that tenor, almost certainly, would be the principle that fundamental structures of the cosmos involve those very structures which the branches of pure mathematics, including real astronomy, severally promote as focally significant. But Plato's recourse to mathematical metaphor highlights, once again, the difference between "real astronomy" and cosmology. With the former we have precision – provided we let go of the heavens. When we attempt natural philosophy, we can be confident of some quite general principles – Inverse Correlation, for example. But the opacities and uncertainties that plague observation, let alone the indeterminacy inherent in a world of Becoming, give us standing notice not to expect precision, and admonish us to view details as suggestive at best. Planetary order and celestial distances are cases in point. On such matters our stance should be undogmatic, speculative in the sense of "venturesome," and even playful: "It could be like this.... It could be like so...." As Plato would have it, the appropriate vehicles in natural philosophy are indeed those of mythic statement and mathematical metaphor.

NOTES

1. I have a strong conviction that my own interpretation of Plato's "real astronomy" (see within, Section V and n. 19) was ultimately inspired by ideas Bob Brumbaugh developed in the undergraduate and graduate classes of his I attended at Yale, and by conversations he and I had at Saybrook College. I remember vividly one particular discussion in the Saybrook common room in which Bob, with his usual kindness and humor, tried to convince an incredulous and refractory Alex (who was going through a positivist phase at the time), that there is an *a priori*, and even aesthetic, component in all scientific explanation. After nearly thirty years, this *opsimathēs* is happy to acknowledge that Bob has won that argument.

2. Walter Burkert, *Lore and Science in Ancient Pythagoreanism*, trans. Edwin L. Minar, Jr. (Cambridge, Massachusetts: Harvard University Press, 1972), 310 n. 62.

3. See Burkert, *Lore and Science in Ancient Pythagoreanism*, 308-316.

4. For the generally accepted interpretation of this deliberately enigmatic passage, see James Adam, *The Republic of Plato*, 2 vols. (Cambridge, 1902), X.616E-617B and appendix 6, esp. 473-79. Cf. Robert S. Brumbaugh, *Plato's Mathematical Imagination* (Bloomington: Indiana University Press, 1954), 171-203.

5. Indeed, in the context of the Myth of Er in which the passage is embedded, it is, as Brumbaugh has pointed out *Plato's Mathematical Imagination* (179), inappropriate for Plato to make the astronomical allusions explicit. The details Plato offers make it, nonetheless, unmistakable that the "spindle of Necessity," the bob of which consists of eight concentric shells, is an allegory of the cosmos.

6. I assume, with Adam *The Republic of Plato*, 2:475-79) and Brumbaugh (*Plato's Mathematical Imagination*, 173-74, 202), the standard reading of 616E, that of the MSS, not the "older" reading reported by Proclus in his commentary.

7. Aristotle makes this inference at *De caelo* II.12.292a4-7, reporting his own observation of an occultation of Mars by the moon.

8. In references to the pre-Socratics, numbers preceded by the letter A refer to testimonia, numbers preceded by the letter B to fragments, as in Hermann Diels, *Die Fragmente der Vorsokratiker*, 6th ed., rev. W. Kranz, 3 vols. (Berlin: Weidmann, 1952). I henceforth refer to this edition by the initials *DK*.

9. Ptolemy in *Planetary Hypotheses* used this very argument to account for our failure to observe transits of Mercury and Venus across the sun, an effect that was, in fact, predictable from Ptolemy's theory: see Otto Neugebauer, *A History of Ancient Mathematical Astronomy*, (New York: Springer Verlag, 1975), 1.227-30; cf. G. J. Toomer, *Ptolemy's Almagest: Translated and Annotated* (London: Duckworth, and Berlin: Springer, 1984), 419 n. 2.

10. Ptolemy points out this obvious limitation of the argument from the absence of observed transits across the sun: "To us a judgment made on this basis has an element of uncertainty: for it is possible, to be sure, that some planets may be below [i.e., closer in than] the sun; but that does not necessarily also place them across any of the planes that run between the sun and our eye" (*Syntaxis Mathema-*

tica [= *Almagest*], IX.1, ed. J.L. Heiberg, 2 vols. (Leipzig: Teubner, 1898-1907), 1.2.207). Toomer gives an infelicitous translation of the phrase *mēketi de pantōs kai en tini...epipedōi*, rendering it "but nevertheless not always be in one of the planes...(which suggests they mostly *are* in one of those planes)? Toomer, *Ptolemy's Almagest*, 419

11. Aristotle in *De caelo* II.12.292a4-7 is careful to specify that the occultation was observed when the moon was half-full.

12. Curiously, the view that there were sublunary celestial bodies persisted into the late fifth century, notably in the cosmology of Anaxagoras (A42) and the astronomical scheme of Philolaus (*DK* 58B37, cf. *DK* 44A16, 17). These were, however, regarded as permanently invisible bodies. As Aristotle points out (*Metaphysics* I.5.986a3-12; *De caelo* II.13.293b21-25), such bodies were postulated *ad hoc*: in the case of Anaxagoras, to explain the frequency of lunar eclipses; in the case of Philolaus, in order to bring up the number of celestial bodies to the numerologically significant figure of 10.

13. Translations of all Greek texts cited are my own, unless I indicate otherwise.

14. Aristotle's explanation is, in fact, inconsistent with his own view that the celestial bodies are constituted of a fifth (or first) element, distinct from the four sublunary elements, and immune to friction: *De caelo* II.1, II.9.

15. In reference to planetary average angular velocity or average linear velocity, I omit here and henceforth the obvious qualification "average."

16. Cf. Brumbaugh, *Plato's Mathematical Imagination*, 201.

17. *Republic* X.617A-B; *Timaeus* 38D.

18. See Thomas Heath, *Aristarchus of Samos: The Ancient Copernicus: A History of Greek Astronomy to Aristarchus Together with Aristarchus's Treatise on the Sizes and Distances of the Sun and Moon, A New Greek Text with Translation and Notes* (Oxford: Clarendon Press, 1913), 157.

19. See my two articles, "Plato's 'Real Astronomy': *Republic* VII.527D-531D," in John P. Anton, ed., *Science and the Sciences in Plato* (Delmar, New York: Caravan Books, 1980), 33-73; and "Astronomy and Kinematics in Plato's Project of Rationalist Explanation," *Studies in History and Philosophy of Science*, 12(1981), 1-32. For a related view, with excellent discussion of ancient "sphaerics" as a realization of the Platonic program of "real astronomy," see Ian Mueller, "Ascending to Problems: Astronomy and Harmonics in *Republic* VII," in Anton, ed. *Science and the Sciences in Plato*, 103-21.

20. For the full argument, see Mourelatos, "Astronomy and Kinematics," 24-30.

21. See Mueller, "Ascending to Problems."

22. See Albert Van Helden, *Measuring the Universe: Cosmic Dimensions from Aristarchus to Halley* (Chicago: University of Chicago Press, 1985), 6-14; cf. Neugebauer, *A History of Ancient Mathematical Astronomy*, 2.634-43, 1.325-29.

23. See Van Helden, *Measuring the Universe*, 15-27

24. Toomer, *Ptolemy's Almagest*, 173-74. See also the relevant diagram and explanation in Van Helden, *Measuring the Universe*, 10-11.

25. *Almagest* IX.1; Heiberg, 2.207; Toomer, *Ptolemy's Almagest*, 420. Eventually, in the *Planetary Hypotheses*, Ptolemy decided that Mercury, Venus, and Mars do have some parallax; but the effects at isssue in part were, and in part were assumed to be, undetectable with the instruments available to ancient astronomers. See Van Helden, *Measuring the Universe*, 26.

26. Van Helden, *Measuring the Universe*, 15-27.

27. For Anaxagoras and Democritus, see the testimony of Vitruvius (7 praef. 11), excerpted in *DK* 59A39; for Democritus, cf. *DK* 68B15b. Burkert makes two

original observations that have relevance here: The term *ekpetasmata*, "project-ions," which served as the title of one of Democritus' books (see *DK* 68B11q), may have an astronomical sense (Burkert, *Lore and Science in Ancient Pythagore-anism*, 312); it is significant that Plato's astronomically-minded associate Philip of Opus wrote a treatise titled Optika (Burkert, *Lore and Science in Ancient Pythagore-anism*, 341f.).

28. It is important to note that the *oratio obliqua* is sustained through both sentences of the passage (*oiontai, poiein*). Aristotle has the Pythagoreans using *kentron* to speak non-committally of the earth's center, but *epi tou mesou* to refer to the geocentric middle. My translation gives good sense to "also not" of the final remark: in the Pythagoreans own scheme there is double displacement – from the earth's center as well as from the middle of the universe. These important details have been missed in the standard translations of this passage: J.L. Stocks, *The Complete Works of Aristotle: The revised Oxford translation*, ed. Jonathan Barnes, 2 vols. (Princeton: Princeton University Press, 1984), 1.483; W.K.C. Guthrie, *Aristotle On the Heavens: With an English Translation* (Cambridge, Massachusetts: Harvard University Press, 1939), 221; Paul Moraux, *Aristote Du ciel: Texte établi et traduit* (Paris: Les Belles Lettre, 1965), 87.

29. For an indication of disagreement in a passage later in the treatise, see the following note.

30. See *In Aristotelis De caelo commentaria*, vol. 7, *Commentaria in Aristotelem Graeca*, ed. I.L. Heiberg 293b16ff., 516. The issue of bisection of the zodiac was similarly raised by critics of Copernicus: see G.E.R. Lloyd, *Greek Science After Aristotle* (New York: Norton & Co., 1973), 115-16. Copernicus made use of the same rejoinder Aristotle attributes to the Pythagoreans. In *De caelo* II.14.296a35-b7 Aristotle argues that if the earth were in orbit around the world's center, the sphere of the fixed stars would appear to wobble, and the fixed stars would not have invar-iant risings and settings: see D.R. Dicks, *Early Greek Astronomy* (Ithaca, N.Y.: Cornell University Press, 1970), 196-97. In this later passage Aristotle seems to have forgotten his earlier endorsement of the Pythagorean rejoinder, which works against this argument no less effectively that it does against the argument from bisection. Curiously there is a similar inconsistency in Ptolemy, who uses the bisection argument at *Almagest* I.5, but at I.6 concedes that the earth has the ratio of a point to the sphere of the fixed starts: cf. Lloyd, *Greek Science After Aristotle*.

31. It would be gratuitous (in the absence of any evidence that Aristotle or his contemporaries and predecessors suspected lunar parallax) to suppose that the Pythagoreans' critics were aware of lunar parallax and had challenged the Pytha-goreans with the objection that lunar parallax would be even greater on the Philolaic model. Indeed, on this reading, the argument from "the phenomena" would have become pointless – since no actual measures of parallax were avail-able to either party in the controversy.

32. See Adam, *The Republic of Plato*, 2.444, 2.449-50; cf. Heath, *Aristarchus et Samos*, 157.

33. These two schemes were first noticed by W.A. Craigie, and reported by him in a note contributed to B. Jowett and Lewis Campbell, *Plato's Republic: The Greek Text Edited with Notes and Essays*, 3 vols. (Oxford: Clarendon Press, 1894), 3.475-76. Cf. J. Cook Wilson "Plato, *Republic*, 616E," *Classical Review*, 16(1902), 292-93, who pointed out that Plato is making use of a "principle of equable distribution"; and Adam, *The Republic of Plato*, 2.473-75. Craigie and Cook Wilson found schemes that involve sums of 9 and balanced distribution also in Plato's account

of the absolute angular speeds of the eight bodies. More recently, Brumbaugh has argued that there is evidence of two more "laws of nine": one applying to a celestial body's material composition (as indicated by color) taken together (as a sum) with its volume (as indicated by the distance between successive bodies), this combination referred to as "mass"; and the "final law," which applies to the combination of "mass" with absolute angular speed. See Brumbaugh, "Colors of the Hemispheres in Plato's Myth of Er (*Republic* 616 E)," *Classical Philology*, 46(1951), 173-76; Brumbaugh, "Plato's *Republic* 616E: The Final 'Law of Nines'," *Classical Philology*, 49(1954), 33-34; cf. *Plato's Mathematical Imagination*, 198-202, and Brumbaugh, "The Mathematical Imagery of Plato, *Republic* X," *Teaching Philosophy*, 7:3 (July 1984), 223-27. These additional laws are not, however, as directly suggested by Plato's text as Craigie's original two. Moreover, their formulation depends on several ancillary assumptions, including one (concerning the treatment of equal sums) that seems *ad hoc*.

34. The periods, as Plato is likely to have known them, are: moon, 27 days (sidereal month); sun, Venus, and Mercury, 365 days; Mars, 2 years; Jupiter, 12 years; Saturn, 30 years. That Plato understood the distinction between the synodic and the sidereal month is strongly suggested by *Timaeus* 39C, where the wording marks the completion of two distinct circuits: "The month is completed when the moon, having made the full round of its own proper orbit, should catch up with the sun" (*perielthousa ton heautēs kyklon hēlion epikataabēi*). For the number of days in a solar year, see *Laws* 828A-B. For the periods of Mars, Jupiter, and Saturn, see Neugebauer, *A History of Ancient Mathematical Astronomy*, 2.681, 2.688; Dicks, *Early Greek Astronomy*, 185-86.

35. The act of splitting the undivided band of the Different into seven bands is expressed by the aorist participle *schisas*, "having split"; the assignment of speeds by the aorist *prosetaxen*.

36. These two traditional interpretations, and others as well, are discussed by Heath in *Aristarchus of Samos*, 163-64, and A.E. Taylor, *A Commentary on Plato's Timaeus* (Oxford: Clarendon Press, 1928), 160-64. Brumbaugh (*Plato for the Modern Age* (New York: Crowell-Collier Press, 1962), 117) adopts the view, which is also represented in the ancient tradition, that the seven numbers of the augmented series can be used to derive (by multiplication and division) the five different planetary periods. The derivation does not, however, make significant use of all numbers in the series, and it tolerates drastic adjustments (either 27 or 32 for Saturn's period of 30 years). See also preceding note and related text, above, for a fundamental objection to this traditional view.

37. See Heath, *Aristarichus*, 164.

38. Brumbaugh, *Plato's Mathematical Imagination*, esp. p. 7, and chs. 3-4.

6

WHAT DID THALES WANT TO BE WHEN HE GREW-UP? OR, RE-APPRAISING THE ROLES OF ENGINEERING AND TECHNOLOGY ON THE ORIGIN OF EARLY GREEK PHILOSOPHY/SCIENCE

Robert Hahn

I

INTRODUCTION

In this paper, I want to re-appraise the origin of early Greek philosophy/science, by re-appraising the social and political context in which it is set. I see this enterprise as providing an argument in support of two of Robert Brumbaugh's contentions: (1) that the earliest Greek philosopher/scientists – the Ionian *phusiologoi* like Thales and Anaximander – were engineers,[1] and (2) that *techne*, tied to that engineering tradition, is more significant for an understanding of Greek philosophy and the rise of rational thinking than is ordinarily supposed.[2] This leads me to review the importance of the "technological hypothesis" for the origin of Greek philosophy/science, tied to the engineering *techne*: that although *techne* is not a sufficient condition to account for the origin of a critical and self-conscious thinking, it so happened to play a significant, decisive, and vastly underestimated role in the emergence of Greek "philosophy/science." [Henceforth, I shall tend to use "philosophy" or "science" as shorthand for this phrase, because it seems that their origins are coincidental.]

Thus, as I see it, Professor Brumbaugh has suggested two important ideas for our re-appraising what has become a commonplace of Greek philosophy: the earliest Greek philosophers were engineers, and *techne* plays a central role in an understanding of the emergence of rational and critical thinking. What Professor Brumbaugh has not provided is a fully-detailed argument in defense of his thesis; in this short space I can only hope to sketch such an argument. I first set out what strikes me as the most elegant statement of the conventional view on the origins of Greek philosophy by G.E.R. Lloyd, and then proceed to reconsider the "technological/engineering" hypothesis.

II

LLOYD ON THE ORIGIN OF GREEK PHILOSOPHY/SCIENCE

G.E.R. Lloyd, in his recent and important book, *Magic, Reason, and Experience: Studies in the Origins and Development of Greek Science*,[3] distinguishes the Greek contribution from that of its eastern predecessors, and supposes their central achievement to be:

1. The Greeks introduced and perfected a highly articulated "notion of proof" which amounts to "the notion of rigorous demonstration."[4]

2. The "scientific" inquiry for the Greeks is characterized by its success in bringing into the open and setting forth as an issue of debate "second-order questions concerning the nature of the inquiry itself." In contrast with eastern predecessors, "the investigations only acquire self-conscious methodologies for the first time with the Greeks."[5]

Thus, a peculiar kind of self-consciousness emerged in the Archaic period, developing through the Classical: investigations into nature brought with them the reflective consciousnes of the ambiguities of the inquiry itself; this self-consciousness found expression in attempts to formulate rigorous demonstrations in the effort to overcome the ambiguities of investigation.

How are we to account for the origin and development of this self-consciousness? Lloyd pursues the emergence of the self-consciousness of scientific inquiry in the context of a dawning self-consciousness in other social and political domains, envisaging the growth of scientific inquiry as a symptomatic expression of open debate in an increasingly democratic social organization. The growth of the city-state and the codification of legal codes and the subsequent proliferation of constitutional forms securing voting-rights to a vast number of citizens which underlined the importance of both freedom and free speech are central to an understanding of a "scientific" spirit of rational investigation in terms of the openness of inquiry. Thus, Lloyd embraces the suggestion of others, that models in the political and legal domains which suggest that "the world-whole is a cosmos, that natural phenomena are regular and subject to orderly determinate sequences of causes and effects" provided a context against which one might investigate the broad range of natural phenomena.[6] These sorts of claims are accommodated within the wider and more forceful thesis advanced by those like Gernet,[7] Vernant,[8] Vidal-Naquet,[9] and Detienne[10] – and embraced by Lloyd[11] – that "Greek rationality in general is the product of the city-state." In this regard, Lloyd envisages the radical examination of the "framework of political relations" and of "beliefs about natural phenomena and the world" to have emerged co-relatively; he claims that developments in the legal and political domain provided images and analogies by which the spheres of law and justice could provide important models for thinking about cosmic order.

Thus, Lloyd's hypothesis about the origins of early Greek science focuses upon an examination of why certain kinds of intellectual inquiry were initiated in ancient Greece, and explores transitions in the social and political domain for their explanatory richness. Lloyd grants – for understanding of the emergence of the Greek scientific spirit – the importance of (1) economic surplus and the use of "money" as a medium for exchange, since the setting-up and administering of a city-state would have been impossible without it. He agrees that (2) access to, and curiosity about, other societies was crucial to the broadening of mental and geographical horizons. And he concedes that (3) the advent of literacy was indispensable to the reflective spirit in the community. What Lloyd adds to these hypotheses are factors, broadly political in dimension, which he suggests are mirrored in the dawning scientific spirit. These relevant factors of a scientific mentality include:

1. "the possibility of radical innovation,"
2. "the openness of access to the forum of debate,"
3. "the habit of scrutiny,"
4. "the expectation of justification – of giving an account – and the premium set on rational methods of doing so."

Various explanatory hypotheses have been proposed to account for the origins and development of early Greek science. Lloyd sets-out four which he regards as at best necessary but not sufficient. There can be little doubt that all of the following hypotheses played a contributing role – though it is not clear that his vision of contributing factors is exhaustive; debate is largely focused upon just how considerable that contributing role was. The four hypotheses are: (1)

Farrington's technological thesis: technological mastery is a sufficient condition for the development of critical inquiry;[12] (2) an exclusively economic interpretation, mentioned by Aristotle: the availability of leisure made possible by the wealth of economic surplus is a sufficient condition for the development of speculative thinking;[13] (3) the knowledge of other belief-systems hypothesis: interacting with other social organizations possessing radically different belief systems is a sufficient condition for the growth of an open and critical attitude towards the fundamental assumptions of one's own society and world-view;[14] (4) Goody's development of literacy thesis: written records provide a sufficient condition to account for a distinct kind of critical evaluation.[15] In each of these cases, Lloyd rejects the hypothesis as sufficient, since other ancient civilizations had technological achievement, economic surplus/leisure, foreign trade and intermingling of belief-systems, and even written records, but never realized the demonstrative and self-conscious methodologies exhibited by Greek science.

The hypopthesis of technological mastery which Lloyd explores is exclusively that of Farrington. What Farrington proposed – that technological mastery was sufficient to account for the Greek scientific mentality – was rightly criticized by Lloyd as unsatisfactory since other near eastern civilizations far surpassed the technical achievements of the Greeks and yet never advanced a wide-spread social phenomenon of the Greek spirit of "critical inquiry." What is inadequate in Lloyd's treatment is that the technological hypothesis, investigated more broadly, leads directly to a deeper appreciation of just those factors which Lloyd himself regards as most significant – the social and political foundations of Greek science. For the "technological hypothesis" leads to a deeper understanding: (1) of just those contingencies which, it so happened, gave rise to an articulated vision of necessity, and (2) of the function of *techne* which underlines the very possibility of a social and political domain. To that argument I now turn.

III

RE-APPRAISING THALES AND THE ORIGIN OF GREEK SCIENCE

Greek Science Originates in the Breakdown of Aristocratic Authority Which is Penultimate to the Ultimate Development of the Polis

If the *polis* or "city-state" was ultimately the result of the breakdown of an aristocratic authority, sanctioned by a genealogical or "inheritance" model of human excellence, it nevertheless was not the penultimate result – that was the breakdown of aristocratic authority signaled by the rise of tyranny throughout Greece.[16] If the flourishing of science, whatever its ultimate character by the close of the Classical period, is inextricably connected with the institutionalization of the *polis*, the origin through the Ionians, like Thales, must be viewed in its penultimate development, and that cannot be so closely identified with the institution of the city-state, whose defining marks had not made themselves known in practice to the Milesians, Lydians, Phrygians, Kimmerians, Samians, or other Ionians contemporaneous with Thales. Nor would Thales have benefited by reflecting upon a *polis* structure which he might have discovered in travels to Egypt or elsewhere in the near-east where central palace civilizations continued to thrive. The rise of the Ionian *phusiologoi* or "nature-accounters," like Thales, is itself an expression of that penultimate result, not with the flourishing of the city-state, but with the breakdown of aristocratic authority signaled by the rise of tyranny.

The *polis* could not play the central role in the origins of early Greek science that it could and would play in its later development, and in the hypostasization of its practice. The structure of the *polis*, and specifically its legislative model, was not in place in Ionia, in Thales' time, and thereby could not play the central role often attributed to it in this opening chapter of a scientific mentality. Unlike the situation in Athens, which Solon addresses in the *Seisachtheia*, mercantile trade, and not land ownership, was the economic context in Thales' Miletus.[17] While Solon in Athens proposed a redistribution of the classes and a revision of the power structure for those who could hold office as a resolution to the apparently inescapable revolution formenting from the lower three classes, Thrasybulus was tyrant in Miletus, a man who recommended to his friend Periander, tyrant at Corinth, to follow the policy of executing any citizen who stood out from the rest, as one would cut off the tops of the tallest growing corn.[18] The social and political conditions were further removed from a developed *polis* in Miletus than they were in Athens; thus the conditions which gave rise to the origin of the scientific mentality in Miletus were also less far along.[19]

In general then, the Ionian rise of science suggests an intermediating chapter in the political developments toward the *polis*, and thus an intermediary step en route to a more open, critical, and scrutinizing social attitude recommended by the democratic conditions of the *polis*. When Aristotle, in the *Metaphysics*, declares in effect that science and philosophy emerge together for the Greeks with Thales of Miletus, at the opening of the sixth century B.C., the characteristic mark of that episode is an expression of the consciousness of an orderliness in nature which the prevailing Homeric/Heroic aristocracy denied; the point is that although Thales marks a break with the earlier ethos, he is still embedded in the social fabric of his specific historical context. The Homeric/aristocratic model is displayed by Odysseus, most clever of all the Greeks, who advised in book 18 of the Odyssey,[20] that in a world of chaos and confusion, the best strategy for mortals is to simply accept what has been given. Thus, the aristocratic mentality supposed a world in which chaos and confusion were the fundamental nature of things. The Homeric/aristocratic mentality embraces the ideology that, like the whimiscal and capricious deities who inform the ultimate context which the social organization could collectively grasp and project – as a social phenomenon – the cosmos was not an ordered whole. And even if it were, mortals were not supposed to be capable of penetrating, and so grasping, that divine organization.

Thales is supposed to have broken from this earlier tradition by exposing a mentality which recognized both an order to nature, and a human capacity to discover and articulate that order. In so discovering the idea of and internal order of nature, Thales, Anaximander, and Anaximenes, expose a peculiar self-consciousness in which the common identity of things is sought, as a universal among particulars; unlike the pursuit of the universal in Homeric religion, the pursuit for one over many is de-mythologized. Thales' speculations are thus taken to announce, however vaguely, a discovery of human potential which transforms the meaning of a traditionally accepted human project contained within an Homeric/Heroic ethos. Thales' speculations suggest that the world, and one's place in it, become questionable in a new way: and that a new candidate emerges, however vaguely stated, as an answer to that inquiry – naturalistic/rationalistic explanation, which has dispensed with the exclusively mythological constraints. This point of view had been adopted long ago. Cornford advanced the thesis that Ionian philosophy arises as a rationalization of ancient creation myths; for the Ionians, nature-speculation arises in cosmologies.[21] Robin argued, in the same vein, that the origin of Greek philosophy begins with the de-mythologizing of the Ionians; this tendency developed rational explanation.[22] Guthrie shared the same conclusion, when he insisted that the "birth of philosophy in Europe consisted in the abandonment, at the level of conscious thought, of mythological solutions to problems concerning the origin and nature of the universe and the processes that go on within it." For Guthrie, the habit of natural explanation develops the habit of generalization, and thus the consciousness of universals, while mythic explanation remains personal and particular; thus Guthrie can conclude that "Philosophy/Science begins by grasping the universal."[23] And Kirk and Raven, sympathizing with the same proclivity, declared that "Thales evidentally abandoned mythic formulations: this alone justifies the claim that he was the first philosopher, naive though his thought still was."[24] Thus the general consensus has been to agree that philosophy/science emerges with the abandonment of mytho-poetic forms of thought, of personified and anthropomorphized theistic explanation. But, what has been largely overlooked was the specific social and political context which gave rise to that new enterprise.

Who was Thales? and What could he aspire to be as a Child? – The Origins of Science in terms of Social Roles

"Ancient science failed to develop not because of its immanent shortcomings but because those who did scientific work did not see themselves, nor were they seen by others as scientists, but primarily as philosophers, medical practitioners, or astrologers."[25] So wrote an historian of science some twenty years ago. From this point of view, "philosopher" and "scientist" emerge together as new roles, in the personage of Thales. The historical fate proved to secure the role of "philosopher," through the establishment of the Platonic school in the gardens of Academe, and of an Aristotelian school in the Lyceum, among other such schools. But the role of "scientist" was never secured and thus, on this hypothesis, never developed, as it did in the seventeenth century. The Ionian origins are characterized by a kind of nature-speculation; that direction was transformed by the sophists and Socrates, who placed "nature-speculation" as secondary at best, and an investigation into the domain of "human-actions" as first and foremost. Consequently, on this hypothesis, the role of philosopher developed, but not that of scientist.

Now, if we consider that the roles of philosopher and scientist were new with Thales, that in Aristotle's terms the origins of philosophical and scientific speculation properly begin with him,[26] then with what social roles were Thales' family and friends ensconced, and against what background of social roles did Thales' enterprises represent a meaningful departure? Asked differently, to what sort of roles – current in Miletus and environs – could Thales aspire when he was a boy?

The social and political circumstances in Miletus were not identical to those in Athens and elsewhere on the mainland. By considering some of those differences, perhaps we can make some sense of the kinds of achievements with which Thales is credited. Skills in navigation would be all the more important where mercantile trade and not land-ownership became the medium of wealth, as was the case in Miletus at the end of the seventh century B.C., tied more to its port on the sea than inland connections [it was no longer on the caravan route].[27] Those economic and trade realities suggest a context for both the theoretical and practical accomplishments whereby Thales was said to have devised a way for locating the north star – crucial for navigation in the northern hemisphere – using the "Little Bear," and for determining the distance of a ship at sea. The general circumstances of trade would surely provide for a cosmopolitan social organization which leads to cultural diversity, and the mercantile success would provide a signifiant element of leisure. Efforts in prose-writing surely contributed to a self-conscious reflection upon thinking, and those like Anaximander provide written evidence for both the expression and understanding of natural processes in terms of legal and political models and analogies.[28] Thus, it was undoubtedly the experience of an intermingling of belief-systems – in a remarkably independent Miletus – which partly led to a kind of openness and critical reflection upon one's beliefs. And if Herodotus is accurate when he claims that the earliest settlers of Miletus did not bring their own wives, but married the women who were already there,[29] the social organization would have been inherently diverse, and had already resolved certain problems on the social level of seeking unity amidst diversity. On Thomson's thesis that the intellectual understanding of the Ionians was a projection of the structure of the tribe, the problem of the One over Many is a projection of the social phenomena which those like Thales envisioned as a dilemma and felt compelled to address. The

Milesian resolution to the consciousness of diversity and a search for an underlying unity, in the social domain, found expression in a search for universal features – an underlying unity – of the diverse phenomena the rich city of Miletus was able to sustain, by virtue of its mercantile success.

When we begin to list the accomplishments, real or imagined, commonly attributed to Thales, one cannot help but be struck by their technological dimension. Thales is credited with introducing geometry into Greece, and perfecting several theorems of his own; the theorems include:

(a) a circle is bisected by its diameter; (b) the angles at the base of an isosceles triangle are equal; (c) if two straight lines intersect, the opposite angles are equal; (d) the angle inscribed in a semi-circle is a right angle; (e) a triangle is determined if its base and the angles relative to the base are given.[30]

Thales evidently applied his theoretical grasp of geometrical principles in practical ways leading to: (1) a prediction of an eclipse, which stopped a war with the Lydians,[31] (2) diverting the river Halys for Croesus' army,[32] (3) measuring the height of the pyramids,[33] and (4) determining the distance of a ship at sea.[34] In addition to meteorologically predicting a bumper crop of olives and business-smart buying out the presses which he would rent out later at a high price,[35] he is also credited with the political suggestion of urging the twelve Ionian principalities to federate against the challenge from the Persians.[36] In general, these are accomplishments of a practical genius, but it is interesting to note that several of them are either in engineering or are theoretical presuppositions or consequences of it.

From what available social roles, current in seventh century Miletus, did Thales develop and sustain these interests within his own community? When Thales was a boy, to what role could he aspire within his social organization, from which he could be supposed to inaugurate a new highly self-conscious human enterprise – one which supposed that nature had an order, and could be investigated by mortals? The intellectual achievement of Thales and Anaximander was not *ex nihilo* – this was an important observation that Cornford made earlier in this century. But what has not been pursued in sufficient detail, partly because it was supposed to be impossible to get more specific information on Thales, was the question, "from what social roles did Thales' mentality have its roots?" The answer I wish to pursue is this: from the tradition of engineers working in monumental architecture. If one grants that supposed source of tutelage for Thales, then by unpacking the social roles and motivations of construction in monumental architecture, an intriguing socio-political story which is penultimate to the rise of the *polis* suggests itself. The origin of early Greek science is tied to the breakdown of aristocratic authority – not the rise of the city-state, *per se* – and is an intellectual projection of the dilemma of one over many from the social and political sphere.

IV

THALES, TECHNOLOGY, AND THE TRADITION OF ENGINEERS IN
MONUMENTAL ARCHITECTURE: THE SOCIAL AND POLITICAL
ORIGINS OF EARLY GREK SCIENCE

*Why are roles associated with Monumental Architecture likely to have
informed Thales' thinking?*

If one understands that Thales' speculations are characterized by the advent of a rational, naturalistic, and de-mythologized explanation, of an investigation aimed at disclosing an underlying unity and order among diverse and apparently unconnected things, we can wonder if the technical confirmation of such an idea was current theoretically in Miletus. It seems to me that "monumental architecture" is just such an idea-producing institution, and it was available to Thales. The persuasiveness of my case rests upon the plausibility that monumental architecture requires a theoretical plan, and the likeliness that such theoretical enterprises informed Thales' thinking about things. That theoetical plan provided an application, however crudely, of principles of geometry to practical construction. But, the case is more complex since an analysis of the motivation for monumental construction brings us back to a political story – the penultimate development *en route* to the *polis* – and thus, at once, presents us with a vision of "science" inextricably embedded within a complex web of social and political dimensions.

First of all, the following historical transitions seem clear. After the fall of Mycenae, there is no clear sign of monumental architecture in the so-called "dark-ages."[37] The resumption of monumental architecture can be placed more or less in the eighth and seventh centuries B.C. on the Peloponessus, and in Ionia – on the eastern Greek islands and the west coast of Turkey – likely connected with the resumed trade with the east and the return of metallurgical arts. In Ionia, monumental temples appear in Samos to Hera, in Ephesus to Artemis, and in Didyma under the aegis of Miletus, to Apollo. Each of these projects took many years, with many men, to complete, and at an extraordinary expense. The success at monumental construction displays a practical knowledge of the principles of geometry, the recognition of a regular and orderly structure which nature is capable of expressing, and which found expression in the efforts of the *architekton* and those directed by him.

Unlike other social projects for which technological and engineering expertise are not crucial, monumental architecture requires a theoretical plan. As Coulton so clearly put it,

> The architect [as opposed to the person modeling clay, or painting, or even sculpting marble can make changes as one proceeds, but] on the other hand must always start his buildings on the bottom, and cannot modify at all what he has built first in the light of what follows. Mistakes made at the start can therefore, not be corrected, and they will also be ruinously expensive, for a monumental building will occupy many men for many years. For these reasons an architect more than any other artist needs a technique of design, a technique which will allow him to visualize the finished building beforehand with sufficient accuracy to ensure that the lower parts of the building will suit the parts which are about to be put on them, and that the whole building is satisfactory in form, function, and structure. Design work in a rather different sense is also needed to communicate the architect's intention to the builders, for whereas a statue can in most cases be completed by one man with his own hands, this is normally impossible in architecture.[38]

Thus, the construction of monumental architecture needs a theoretical plan, integrating form, function, and structure. The theoretical plan requires a vision of a complex world of interconnected ideas: monumental architecture is a social phenomenon, an expression of a social organization, not an individual; its results are designed to impress by virtue of their dimensions which require the resolution of a host of technical problems. The response to those problems proves to be a strategy of "One over Many" in the labor force and work force, and understanding of general principles of construction – a "One over Many" – so that the building will not collapse, and a grasping of "One over Many" in the multifarious technical problems of: (a) quarrying monolithic stones, weighing as much as eighty-thousand pounds, (b) moving those stones from their quarry to building sites often very far away,[39] and (c) hoisting them in place.[40] The formal and aesthetic considerations of overall appearance, and the dressed state of the masonry, are also integral.

Important evidence of theoretical plan comes from two significant sources: (1) Haselberger's discovery that the theoretical plans for the Temple of Apollo at Didyma were etched into its own walls,[41] and (2) Kienast's discovery that the complexity of the construction of the tunnel of Eupalinos, in the north-end, could not be accounted for without supposing a theoretical plan.[42] Recently, Haselberger published his archeaological reconstructions of the Temple of Apollo at Didyma, and he proved that the Greeks indeed had employed a theoretical plan: "Actually the blueprints were under the archeologist's nose all along. I recently discovered an entire archive of construction plans still in place at the site ... [consisting in] finely etched lines on some temple walls."[43] Now, although the blue-print or theoretical plan was etched right into the temple itself, this plan belongs to a reconstruction begun in the fourth century B.C. just after the arrival of Alexander the Great.[44] Nevertheless, it encourages us to confirm the hypothesis that such a plan must have preceded any monumental construction, whether it was made on papyrus or in stone. The tunnel of Eupalinos is an earlier construction, belonging to the sixth century B.C. [circa 530 B.C.], and was built from two separate ends, not visible to each other, with entrances on either side of the hill.[45] Kienast has argued persuasively that the technique of "staking-out" the hill was employed.[46] The complexity of the construction, however, lies in the north-side. After digging a very short distance, the architect Eupalinos detected two problems: (1) the stone was too hard, unlike the softer stone at the southern end, and (2) there was too much natural ground water coming down and flooding the surface. The architect was thus forced to dig away from the straight line, and it so happened out of the hill toward the sea, in order to find softer stone and an absence of ground water running naturally through the hill. And the construction itself attests that more than one – perhaps as many as three – divergences from the straight line were necessary for the construction to continue.[47] What Kienast has shown is that without a theoretical plan, it would have been impossible for Eupalinos to determine where the north-end was to finally meet the south-end; for once the straight line is lost, the technique of "staking-out" a hill ceases to be effective. Thus, the actual success of uniting the two-sided tunnel construction in the same plane, some ten to twelve years later, some four hundred meters from the southern entrance and some six hundred meters from the northern end, which leaves a straight line several times, attests to a theoretical plan.

The evidence suggests that the idea of a complex but interconnected world is known to those who engaged in the theoretical plan and practical execution of monumental architecture. That technical enterprise, whose glorious accomplishments were present in Thales' Miletus is an achievement relative to those enterprises undertaken by communities, contemporaneous with Thales, which would come to see their technical successes as reasons for aspiration, and thereby securing those social roles. Thus Thales was nurtured in a community which achieved outstanding success in monumental architecture, with the temple of Apollo at Didyma, the road to which from Miletus, its patron city, was lined by monumental sculpture.[48] Indeed, other principalities which he recognized as Ionian – like nearby Ephesus and Samos – had competitively achieved comparable or even greater status. But even if traditions, with secured roles, like monumemtal arhitecture nurtured Thales' thinking about the One over Many, and an orderliness of nature which compelled one to discover unity amidst diversity, it still remains for us to unfold the motivation for monumental architecture in Miletus and the Ionian world in the eighth and seventh centuries B.C. All of the technical constraints for undertaking monumental architecture – from the temple construction itself and its theoretical plan, to the organization of the work force, and the mechanical difficulties of quarrying, transporting, and hoisting monolithic stones – must somehow succeed in transmitting the peculiar idea which was nothing less than the purpose of the monumental construction. What was the idea? Why build these temples anyway?

Why Monumental Architecture? Aristocracy, the Crisis of Sovereignty, and the Social Roles which contributed to the Rise of early Greek Philosophy

In the Mycenaean world, political authority was directed by the *wa-na-ka* or chieftan, who inherited his kingship. The prevailing genealogical model of human excellence granted him the right of authority on the basis of a divine connection established through lineage. The *wa-na-ka* was thus a divine descendent who made the law, interpreted it, and enforced its provisions. The fall of the Mycenaean civilization, circa 1200 B.C., was the collapse of central-palace civilization, and with it was born a new political problem: who should rule, and by virtue of what authority? This is, to use Vernant's parlance, the "crisis of sovereignty."[49]

The signs of drastic depopulation following the collapse of the central-palace system, suggests a return to small tribal organization.[50] But with the quadrupling of population in the early Archaic period, the struggle for authority was a full-formed problem. Those already in positions of authority were aristocrats, and they found themselves increasingly under pressure to relinquish authority. For after all, it became an issue to wonder why they ought to rule. And if so, by virtue of what right? The fall of the central-palace had effectively undermined the view that one individual, by virtue of divine lineage, had the right to sovereignty.[51] In many quarters of Greece, as Thucydides described it, competition for land became great, and various strategies were developed to try to retain whatever authority one had succeeded in marshalling.

Competition for land, with the increasing importance of land ownership, was a strong motivation for colonization.[52] And many young men set out for new land, in Asia Minor and southern Italy. On the mainland, as Snodgrass points out, an interesting chapter in aristocratic efforts to secure their eroding authority unfolded. With the re-introduction of metallurgical techniques, aristocrats fighting off neighboring factions heavily armed their townspeople to fight against insurgents. This was the creation of the *hoplite* or "heavily-armed foot-soldier."[53] The practice was unusual because it brought common-people into the fighting arena whereas heretofore such actions were largely restricted to the aristocracy alone. The creation of hoplites also created new problems of military strategy – leading to the formation of the *phalanx* – to direct masses of men; it also served to undermine an heroic ideal since the power of the *phalanx* depends not on individuals who step forward to face the enemy, as an Achilles, to win or die; the *phalanx* requires cooperation in which each man holds the line along with his comrades. Cooperation, and a mutually recognized equality, rather than heroic individuality, is the required virtue or human excellence.[54] All this was well and good, from the perspective of aristocratic stategy to secure authority. But, what happened when in a year of drought, with food-stuffs kept within the aristocratic fortification, fifty or sixty aristocrats found themselves with a thousand of their heavily-armed townspeople banging furiously at their doors? A new equality dawned, as the aristocrats, believing that they were securing their eroding power, found their strategies had back-fired.[55] The result was a further erosion of aristocratic authority. It is this sort of break-down of aristocratic authority which constitutes the penultimate result of social reform *en route* to the ultimate result of the rise of the city-state. The rise of early Greek sience, through the circum-stances of monumental architecture, provides a story similar in kind.

Besides the creation of hoplites, another attempt to secure authority, connected to securing land ownership, was achieved through the building of temples or cult-sanctuaries. The archaeolo-gical record supplies evidence in the 8th century B.C. of both the phenomena of the temple and the rise of cult dedications. Snodgrass claims that both suggest a move toward social integration in the securing of regularity of worship through the establishment of a central sanctuary, important land-marks toward establishing the *polis*. The social organization sought a unification of those occupying similar geographical locations; the ultimate formation of the *polis* thus represents in the socio-political sphere what later became articu-lated in the pre-Socratic philosophical sphere: the search for the One over Many.

As tribalism, traditionally connected with stock-raising, began to decline with the rise of the *polis*, we find the flourishing of graneries and agricultural interests connected with arable farming. This is important to emphasize because "... in the classical era of Greek history there is no closer link than that between citzenship in the *polis* and ownership of land."[56] Thus, as population continued to increase, there was increasing need for arable farming as opposed to the centrality of "stock-raising," to feed the bursting new population, and hence competition for land, which led in turn to increasing disputes over land-ownership.

Repeatedly, when the Greeks of the historical period engaged in land-disputes, we hear of their having recourse to the legendary past as a source for justification: if a party could claim to be linked by descent or other close associa-tion, plausibly or even implausibly, with a legendary perso-nage who had once inhabited a place, then their claim to ownership of that place was greatly enhanced ... but the trump card was the physical discovery of the legendary hero, in the form of a skeleton in a tomb.[57]

Snodgrass' assessment finds support in various stories, some from Herodotus, in which disputes over land-ownership sought resolution by one party who claimed special descent from either hero or god, in that geographical location. Spartan Lichas, for example, turned the tide in the war against Tegea when, with the help from the Dephic oracle and a garrulous Tegean blacksmith, Lichas "located" the bones of Orestes and brought them back to Sparta;[58] or when anti-Argive Kleisthenes, tyrant of Sikyon, persuaded the Thebans to exhume the bones of the hero Melanippos, deadly enemy of the Argive Adrastos, so that he could re-inter the bones at the cult-site of Adrastos and so drive out the cult.[59] Snodgrass thus leads us to see that dedications at "supposed" Mycenaean/hero graves and the rise of city-sancturies – both connected with the rise of the *polis* – are attempts to "consolidate land ownership." Thus, "... by instituting a cult of a local hero, a community could acquire a sense of security in an age of apparently fluid and unpredictable settlement."[60]

Now, in Miletus, the circumstance was not identical, for land-ownership, although important, did not play the primary role in the seventh and sixth centuries that it apparently did on the mainland. Yet, the social problems of retaining authority over land must have been significant. However commercially successful Miletus was, the more interesting it would be to nearby kingdoms which sought its riches. Herodotus, at the opening of his *Histories*, reminds us of the Lydian sucession from Gyes to Ardys to Sadyattes to Alyattes and to Croesus; the Lydians attacked Miletus again and again.[61] In order to establish a claim on their land, its seems likely that Miletus, like Ephesus and Samos, constructed monumental temples as a sign of their right to it. But who, in that social organization, patronized these exhorbitantly expensive constructions? It could be none other than the ruling aristocracies, or what amounts to the same kind of financial source, the tyrants.

As Coulton recognized, before the late Archiac and early Classical periods, public building was not sponsored by the public at large. The patrons of these great projects were by and large aristocrats. "There is, therefore, some probability that building programmes in the archaic period were organized rather differently from the later ones which we know about. The importance of aristocratic individuals and families as providers of funds, as contractors for (and so as supervisors of) whole buildings, and presumably also as instigators of building; was very much greater, and the architect must have dealt more often with the individual and family concerned that with the state."[62] This point is made all the clearer if we consider the touchiness of the Athenian assembly when Themistocles or Pericles seemed to be continuing just this aristocratic tradition.

Thus, why monumental architecture? Monumental architecture was initially an aristocratic effort to impress, and thereby safe-guard the prevailing authorities in Miletus, Ephesus, Samos, and elsewhere. Why temples and cult-sanctuaries? Because an appeal to the divinities, sung in Homeric epic, was part of the larger "argument" – if we may call it that – advanced by the aristocrats in the struggle for the right to retain authority; that right was secured by appealing to a special relation, often genealogically inherited, to the deity, whether Apollo at Didyma/Miletus, Artemis at Ephesus, or Hera at Samos. The monumental temples, instigated and inspired by the aristocracy to secure their land and authority, were a response to the crisis of sovereignty. But that effort, like heavily arming the townspeople back-fired.

Monumental temples and cult-sanctuaries were aristocratic inspirations to secure an eroding authority. The aristocrats hired architects and builders to construct monuments to their "rightful authority." In the process, however, those involved in the theoretical plan and practical construction came to grasp a highly articulate order in nature, incompatible with the very vision of chaos and confusion, sung by Odysseus, to which the buildings were testimony. Why should the aristocrats exercise authority? Why was their claim to sovereignty stronger than that of opposing forces? Because, so the Homeric argument goes, the aristocrats had descended from the divine and heroic personages – the preoccupation with the genealogical trees testifies to a model that human excellence is inherited – and in a world of chaos and confusion, the recognition of the power of the deity was the mortal's only hope for survival. The discovery that nature had an order which could be articulated by mere mortals undermined the very aristocratic world-view which motivated the monumental projects in the first place.

Thus, those who did the buildings of aristocratic patrons in monumental constructions discovered a world of relations which could not be incorporated within an epic mentality. The activities of monumental architecture provided the data which opened-up a domain of human investigations and enterprise, and devastatingly called into question a vision of human nature as both "unknowing" and "incapable of grasping." The crediting of Thales with theorems about diameters of circles, the quality of base-angles in an isosceles triangle, the equality of opposing angles which result from the intersection of two straight lines, and the inscription of a right angle in a semi-circle, are examples not only of a discovered regularity in nature – the kinds of principles indispensable for monumental architecture – but also that the formulation of the theorems is in perfect accord with Lloyd's estimate that proof or rigorous demonstration is characteristic of the special contribution which the Greeks made to the development of a scientific mentality.

The cultural connection between the rise of philosophy, on the one hand, and monumental architecture, on the other, also finds circumstantial support within another domain. It had been supposed that the origins of philosophy can be located with the first surviving prose-writing of Anaximander, in the mid-sixth century B.C. And it has been commonly supposed that prosaic writing is peculiarly characteristic of the self-consciousness which gives rise to rational or naturalistic explanation. And those same rational and naturalistic dispositions emerge quite clearly in the design and execution of monumental architecture. This case is advanced by the record of Vitruvius, in book 10 of the *Ten Books on Architecture*; for contemporaneous with Anaximander's prose-writing were prose-writings on architecture. Concurrent with the origin of philosophical prose was architectural prose, one by Theodorus on the temple of Hera at Samos and another by Chersiphron on the temple of Artemis at Ephesus – both claimed for the mid-sixth century B.C. These accounts encourage us to see a kinship between these enterprises: both are theoretical enterprises whose successes were recognized in the visible and practical domains. Thales theorized about the structure of things in geometric descriptions and in terms of some underlying unity among things. He sought to grasp and articulate something about the organization of the heavens, using geometric techniques; and he is credited with predictions, real or imagined, of the possibilities of various phenomena, be it an eclipse, a bumper crop of olives, the height of a pyramid, the distance of a ship at sea, or the diverting of a river for the army of a Lydian King. The architects, like Theodorus and Chersiphorn, writing about constructions of monumental temples, would likely have theorized about geometric principles of construction, the organization of huge work forces, and technical problems of quarrying, transporting, and hoisting into place, monolithic stones. Both are concerned to grasp unity amidst diversity, and to use "geometrical" principles to think about the unity. When Thales supposedly advances the hypothesis that "all things are made of *hydor*," of "water," he has stepped beyond the speculative domain of the architects, to be sure. But is it not likely that the kind of social roles which informed the kind of thinking in which he was engaged could be plausibly suggested to have been born in monumental architecture? And granting that his speculations concerning an underlying order undermine the ethos of an epic mentality, can we not get some glimpse of the origins of early Greek science as an unforeseeable and unanticipated consequence of a social and political tale within the crisis of sovereignty, just as the attempts of the aristocracy to secure their eroding power by heavily arming their townspeople simply back-fired?

So, what did Thales want to be when he grew-up? Of course, it is impossible to say with certainty. But it seems likely that his thinking was nurtured by a community engaged in projects of engineering, where technological expertise played a crucial role in providing the detailed theoretical data which might lead one to a vision that nature has an exquisite order and that mortals can penetrate into its mysteries. Thus, the origin, if not the development of Greek science by the Classical period, owes more to technological and engineering concerns than one might suspect from reading Lloyd's excellent work; and this is, in part, a consequence of locating the origin of Greek science, not so much in the rise of the *polis* as in the breakdown of aristocratic authority announced by the rise of tyranny. But the gist of the account remains the same: ancient Greek philosophy/science emerges from and is complexly interwoven within the social and political fabric of experience; one cannot succeed in fully extricating the "rational" investigation from the socio-political context without misrepresenting its nature and function.

NOTES

1. Robert S. Brumbaugh, *The Philosophers of Greece* (N.Y.: Thomas Crowell, 1964).
2. Robert S. Brumbaugh, "Plato's Relation to the Arts and Crafts," in *Phronesis*, 2(1976): 40-52.
3. G.E.R. Lloyd, *Magic, Reason, and Experience: Studies in the Origins and Development of Early Greek Science* (Cambridge University Press, 1979).
4. Lloyd, *Magic, Reason, and Experience*, 230.
5. Lloyd, *Magic, Reason, and Experience*, 232-233.
6. That the spheres of law and justice provide important models of cosmic order is defended by R. Hirzel, *Themis, Dike und Verwandtes* (Leipzig: 1907); H. Gomperz, "Problems and Methods of Early Greek Science," *Journal of the History of Ideas*, 4(1943): 161-176; L. Gernet, *Droit et societe dans la Grece ancienne*, 1957, and in "Les origines de la philosophie," *Bulletin de l'enseignement public du Maroc* 183(1948-9): 1-12, 1948-9. 1968; G. Vlastos, "Equality and justice in early Greek cosmologies," *Classical Philology*, 43(1947): 156-178; and again in *Plato's Universe* (Oxford: 1975); J.P. Vernant, "La formation de la pensees positive dans la Grece archaique," *Annales* 12(1957): 183-206; P. Vidal-Naquet, "La raison greque et la

cite," *Raison Presente* 2(1968): 51-61.

7. L. Gernet, *Recherches sur le development de la pensee juridique et morale en Grece* (Paris: 1917).

8. Vernant, "La formation de la pensees positive ..." and *Les origines de la pensee grecque* (Paris: 1965), esp. 285ff.

9. Vidal-Naquet, "La raison greque et la cite."

10. M. Detienne, *Les Maitres de verite dans la grece archaique*, (Paris: 1967), esp. 99ff.

11. Lloyd, *Magic, Reason, and Experience*, 246-267, esp. 246-249.

12. Lloyd, *Magic, Reason, and Experience*, 235.

13. Lloyd, *Magic, Reason and Experience*, 236.

14. Lloyd, *Magic, Reason, and Experience*, 236-239.

15. Lloyd, *Magic, Reason, and Experience*, 239-240.

16. The standard treatment of Greek tyranny can be found in A. Andrews, *The Greek Tyrants* (London: 1956).

17. This case is made by C.J. Emylyn-Jones, *The Ionians and Hellenism* (London: Routledge and Kegan Paul, 1980), 28.

18. Curiously enough, the story is told by both Herodotus and Aristotle. Herodotus [5.92.6] describes the advice as having come from Thrasybulus to Periander; Aristotle, in the *Politics* (1284a and 1311a) describes it the other way round.

19. Aristotle informs us that the rise of the tyranny was different in Miletus than elsewhere. It emerges from the prolongation of the chief magistry [= the *prytaneia*] which may have reflected the power given to the *aisymnetes* at the time of the fall of the kingship. Cf. Emylyn-Jones, *The Ionians and Hellenism*, 30.

20. Homer *Odyssey* 18.130ff.

21. F.M. Cornford, *Principium Sapientiae* (Cambridge: Cambridge University Press, 1952), esp. 186-189. Such an enterprise supposes that: (a) the world has a beginning, and (b) the formation of the world is a natural, not super-natural event. W. Jaeger's thesis in *The Theology of the Early Greek Philosophers*, trans. E.S. Robinson (Oxford: 1936), argues that the Ionian *phusiologoi* represent a transition from "mythological cosmology" to "natural theology." And in Cornford's *The Unwritten Philosophy* (Cambridge: Cambridge University Press, 1950), in the process of criticizing the marxist, technological, and general economic hypotheses of the origin of early Greek science in Ionia [specifically focussing upon both Farrington and Thomson], the insistence is again made that the "rationalization of an ancient creation myth" is the key ingredient, p. 122.

22. L. Robin, *Greek Thought and the Origins of the Scientific Spirit*, trans. M.R. Dobie (London: n.p., 1928). The de-mythologizing of the Ionians is the result of aiming one's theory immediately at action; this tendency developed rational explanation. In speculation, the Ionians discovered the secret of action (32). Thus, the moral dimension of philosophy and science is here emphasized.

23. W.K.C. Guthrie, *A History of Greek Philosophy* (Cambridge: Cambridge University Press, 1971), 1:29. Again, he says, "For religious faith, there is substituted scientific Faith ..." (40). And with particular regard to the evolutionary cosmologies of Ionia, Guthrie declares that: [God] Design was not responsible for world-order; design arose from something more basic. Nature herself has generative power, and it is [*phusis*] that out of which the world is made. Thus nature is active [*hylozoism*] and thereby capable of initiating changes to which it itself is subject. Only with the later pre-Socratics is thought separated from matter. [Cornford also takes pains to point out that "Ionian cosmologies" which suppose a beginning of the world are not subscribed to by Parmenides, Heraclitus, or for that matter Aristotle].

24. G. Kirk and J. Raven, *The Pre-Socratic Philosophers* (Cambridge: Cambridge University Press, 1957), 98. Elsewhere (72), "What gave these [Milesians] the title of philosopher was the abandonment of mythopoetic forms of thought, of personification and anthropomorphic theistic explanations, and their attempt to explain the seen world in terms of its seen constituents." And (73) "This attitude [sc. of isolating a single primary material] was clearly a development of the genetic or geneaological approach to nature exemplified in Hesiod's *Theogony*."

25. Joseph Ben-David, "The Scientific Role: The Conditions of its Establishment in Europe," in *Minerva*, Autumn 1965, 15-50; reprinted in *The Rise of Modern Science: Internal or External Factors* (Lexington, Mass.: D.C. Heath and Co., 1968), 47. The gist of his thesis is this: Ben-David views the development of science in terms of external factors. The growth of any enterprise depends upon the securing of social roles. For social development requires that activities are perceived by the social organization as valuable and worthy of aspiration. Ancient science failed to secure the role of "scientist." That role was secured in the seventeenth century.

26. Aristotle *Metaphysics* A.983b20: "Thales, the founder of this type of philosophy, says the *arche* is water ..."

27. Cf. Emylyn-Jones, *The Ionians and Hellenism*, 28 "Mainland Ionia in the early seventh century B.C. lay neither at the end of a major caravan route across Anatolia (as was at one time supposed) nor on the direct sea route from mainland Greece to the Levant." The character of Miletus is "sea-going, trading, and colonising ..." (18) According to Pliny the Elder, Miletus established no less than ninety colonies (*Natural History* 5.112), but it is more likely around forty-five, which is still rather substantial, and confirms the view that Miletus was a seafaring city interested in colonizing.

28. The earliest preserved fragment of western philosophy is generally attributed to Anaximander: *ex hon de he genesis esti tois ousi, kai ten phthoran eis tauta ginesthai kata to xreon, didonai gar auta diken kai tisin allelois tes adikias kata xronou tazin:* "And the source of coming-to-be for existing things is that into which destruction too happens, 'according to necessity; for they pay penalty and retribution to each other for their injustice according to the assessment of Time'." The fragment is preserved by Simplicius in the fifth century a.d. in his commentary on Aristotle's *Physics*.

29. Herodotus, *The Histories*, trans. Aubrey DeSelincourt (Harmondsworth, Middlesex: Penguin Books, 1954), 1.146.2-3. Emylyn-Jones points out that there were six tribes in Miletus (not four as in Attica), which lends credence to Herodotus' proclamation.

30. Theorems (a), (b), (c), and (e) come from Proclus in his commentary on Euclid, whose authority was Eudemus. Diels-Kranz in *Die Fragmente der Vorsokratiker*, (1922) lists them in A 11 and 20. Theorem (d) is quoted by Diogenes Laertius [1, 24], from a complier from the first century A.D. named Pamphila. Cf. this discussion in Guthrie, *A History of Greek Philosophy*, 53.

31. Herodotus 1.74. In Diels-Kranz, *Die Fragmente der Vorsokratiker*, A5, supposedly taking place during the war between the Lydians, led by Alyattes, and the Medes, led by Cyaxares: "When the war between them had dragged on indecisively into its sixth year, an encounter took place at which it happened that the day suddenly became night. This is the loss of daylight which Thales of Miletus predicted to the Ionians, fixing as its term the year in which it actually took place." The date has been determined to be 28 May 585 B.C., and that date has served to mark-out the origins of early Greek philosophy and science. It is,

however, highly unlikely that Thales could have achieved such a prediction, even with a knowledge of the *saros*, the cycle of 223 lunar months [= 18 years, 10 days, 8 hours] after which both lunar and solar eclipses are likely. Nonetheless, it is significant that tradition not much more than a century later held such a view.

32. Herodotus 1.75. Although Herodotus himself expresses doubts over the engineering feat; Herodotus supposes that Thales made use of existing bridges.

33. Measuring the shadows of the pyramids is credited to Thales by Diogenes Laertius (1, 27), Pliny the Elder (*Natural History* 36.82), Plutarch (*Conv.* 147A), and in Diels-Kranz, *Die Fragmente der Vorsokratiker*, A21.

34. Theorem (e): "A triangle is determined if its base and the angles relative to the base are given," is usually associated with the practical feat of measuring the distance of a ship at sea.

35. The story is told by Aristotle in the *Politics* 1.1259a.6. It has generally been supposed that Aristotle tells the story to counter-balance those who claim that, like Plato's tale of Thales in the *Theaetetus* (174A), the philosopher was rather absent-minded. In the *Theaetetus* the story goes that a servant girl laughed at Thales who, while star-gazing, fell into a well; for how was he hoping to discover something in the heavens when he could not see what was happening at his own feet.

36. Herodotus 1.170; Diogenes Laertius relates a story (1.25) that Thales persuaded Miletus not to make an alliance with Croesus.

37. J.J. Coulton, *Ancient Greek Architects at Work* (Cornell: Cornell University Press, 1977), 30: "Between about 1100 and 700 B.C. there was no truly monumental architecture in Greece."

38. Coulton, *Ancient Greek Architects at Work*, 51.

39. Cf. Lothar Haselberger, "The Construction Plans for the Temple of Apollo at Didyma," *Scientific American* (December 1985): 126-132. The distance from the quarry to the contsruction site at Didyma was about 30-35 kilometers! (p. 128) Temple construction was suspended, unfinished, after 600 years!

40. Coulton, *Ancient Greek Architects at Work*, 140-160. In chapter 7, "Aspects of Stucture and Technique," Coulton reviews various technical problems, including moving monolithic stones over great distances, by placing the stones in wooden crates, as if rectangular stones were "inscribed" in cylindrical wheels – Metagenes' method circa 550 B.C.

41. Haselberger, "The Construction Plans for the Temple of Appolo at Didyma," 126-132.

42. Herman Kienast, "Die Wasserleitung des Eupalinos auf Samos," *Proceedings of the Deutsches Archaeologisches Institut*, Athens, 1973.

43. Haselberger, "The Construction Plans for the Temple of Appolo at Didyma," 126.

44. Haselberger, "The Construction Plans for the Temple of Appolo at Didyma," 126.

45. Kienast, "Die Waserleitung des Eupalinos auf Samos."

46. The technique of staking-out a hill employs stakes of equal height and each is placed one-stake length apart. Thus, the distance of a hill is computed by adding the lengths together. So, when one is digging the tunnel, if one could be assured that the digging proceeded in a straight-line, secured by lining up three-stakes, it would be possible to know exactly where one was in the hill, and thereby how far to continue until completion. However, as was the case in the north-end, once the digging leaves the straight-line, it is impossible to tell by the method of "staking-out" one's location in the hill.

47. Kienast, "Die Waserleitung des Eupalinos auf Samos." The divergences from the straight-line are shown graphically from Kienast's drawings, reconstructing a cross-section of the hill. He makes clear the problems of both the hardness of the stone and natural ground water.

48. Emylyn-Jones, *The Ionians and Hellenism*, 18.

49. J.P. Vernant, *The Origins of Greek Thought*, (Cornell: Cornell University Press, 1982). The treatment of the Mycenaean *wa-na-ka* is presented in chapter 2, pp. 23-38; the third chapter is entitled "The Crisis of Sovereignty."

50. Anthony Snodgrass, *Archaic Greece: The Age of Experiment* (n.p.: University of California Press, 1980), 21.

51. Vernant, *Origins*, 38-48.

52. J. Boardman, *The Greeks Overseas* (London: 1964, 1980), esp. 23-34, 35-68.

53. Snodgrass, *Archaic Greece: The Age of Experiment*, 102-107. Of course, he understands that the relation between the development of the hoplite and the origins of the phalanx are controversial.

54. Snodgrass, *Archaic Greece: The Age of Experiment*. Snodgrass understands a transition was being effected in archaic Greece, "... thus the needs of the community were given preference over the those of the family, and above all the aristocratic family, which had particularly subscribed to the warrior's ethic" (99).

55. Snodgrass, *Archaic Greece: The Age of Experiment*. "This change, great in its implications, must not be regarded as revolutionary in intention: as it was defensive militarily, so it was politically neutral as a conception. By calling on others to join them on the battlefield, the aristocrats can have had little notion that they were jeopardizing the structure of society .... The military reform, as has been well observed, merely provided a means for bringing such alternatives into effect, when a hundred war-hardened aristocrats suddenly found themselves in confrontation, not only with their opposite numbers in a neighbouring state, but with a thousand well-armed commoners of their own" (107).

56. Snodgrass, *Archaic Greece: The Age of Experiment*, 37.

57. Snodgrass, *Archaic Greece: The Age of Experiment*, 38.

58. Herodotus 1.68.

59. Herodotus 5.67.2-4.

60. Snodgrass, *Archaic Greece: The Age of Experiment*, 39.

61. Herodotus, 1.14, 1.17, 1.18, 1.19, 1.20, 1.21, 1.25.

62. Coulton, *Ancient Greek Architects at Work*, 22.

7

TONAL ISOMORPHISM IN PLATO AND THE *I CHING*: BRUMBAUGH AS CULTURAL ANTHROPOLOGIST

Ernest G. McClain

I

INTRODUCTION

The publication of *Plato's Mathematical Imagination* by Robert Brumbaugh in 1954 provided conceptual tools for a new avenue of research into the "harmonic mythology" of the ancient world. The ethno-musicological studies grounded on Brumbaugh's insights[1] testify to the advantage in having a philosopher first wrest from the chaos of confusion the essential guiding principles.

To show these principles in action I summarize here a musicological treatment of their application to the "tyrant's allegory" in book 9 of *The Republic* and then shift cultural perspective to demonstrate that the *I Ching* ("Book of Changes") is musicalized by the same insight which led Socrates to his "Marvelous and baffling calculation" of the measure of a tyrant's suffering as exactly $9^3 = 729$. What is involved is an appreciation of the necessity for limitation, which in both cultures means moderation or "self-limitation," for the harmonic example was accepted, East and West, as the paradigm of a natural law applicable to the behavior of individuals and states as well as to the "community of tones" in the scale.

My two cross-cultural examples from the same time-frame (400-200 B.C.), half a world apart, probably owe no historical debts to each other and perhaps none to any common source. The possibility of a common remote Babylonian origin cannot be ruled out completely, I believe; and Joseph Needham believes that "there undoubtedly existed a trans-Asian continuity, greatly enhanced after Alexander's conquest in 320 B.C."[2] But there is growing evidence that Chinese development in acoustical science was indigenous, early, and far superior to that of Greece in applied technology. The isomorphism presented here points toward universal bio-physical constraints which any culture might discover at a certain stage of musical systematization.

II

BRUMBAUGH'S HERMENEUTIC PRINCIPLES

The following interpretive principles, conclusions from his intensive study of Plato's mathematical imagination, are gleaned from various contexts in Brumbaugh's book[3] and assembled here in a way convenient to my purpose. I contend that they constitute the sufficient and necessary hermeneutics for important advances in the cultural anthropology of the ancient world.

1. Respect ancient sources; take on yourself the burden of discovering their intentionality. "An author and his intended readers have in common certain habits of imagination and notions of pedagogy"[4] – our modern problem is to recover them. Brumbaugh emphatically declines to follow "the humanistic tendency [a plague on both Greek and Chinese scholarship] to delete or bypass mathematical passages, on the ground they they are nonfunctional or not serious."[5]

2. Respect archaic procedures. "The method by which a doctrine is constituted should be the method by which it is interpreted."[6] Brumbaugh freely employs modern mathematical concepts (matrix theory and modula residues) as a means to his own understanding; but he assumes that analysis is incomplete until it can show that ancient methods with abacus and counting board reach similar results, so that such concepts "do not really involve what seems to be an anachronism."[7]

3. Remember that in the ancient world "mathematics was not sharply separated from other branches of natural science" but was assimilated with philosophy. "Our modern view of mathematics has completely disassociated 'number' from such attributes as sex or justice, and assimilated mathematics to the purely formal study of logic, rather than to ethics, physics, or aesthetics."[8]

4. Explore the power of visual (i.e., non-verbal) schematization. "'Mathematical' passages in Plato which have seemed nonsense or riddles to previous students in fact describe diagrams which Plato had designed, and were intended to accompany and

clarify his text."[9] "Plato himself was visualizing verbal matrices," a technique "effective in dealing with factors in arithmetic, and with combinations in ratio theory."[10] [Chinese methods and materials are as graphic as the Greek.]

5. Study the circle as the primary cyclic metaphor; do not overlook the fact that it "must take account of some sort of *reciprocity*."[11]

6. Notice that in the absence of an algebraic notation "for a mathematical or logical variable," ancient mathematics was dependent on the principle of "aesthetic economy"; "the first (i.e., smallest) integers having a given property are used with the convention that these represent *any* term or number that has the same relevant property."[12]

7. "The 2:1 ratio of the concordances of the initial octave scale carries with it a cyclic or modular metaphor. (The concept of a modulus, a mathematical metaphor that is natural for reiteration, seems to have been already formulated by Plato's time.) This 'matrix of doubles' is ... extremely attractive as a starting-point."[13] [This principle, mathematical language for the musician's assumption of "octave equivalence," is the universal foundation for acoustical theory.]

8. The "proper criterion" of adequacy in our modern interpretations is whether or not our methods "illuminate the passages discussed." The "mathematical illustrations chosen" must be appropriate "to the contextual points they are intended to elucidate."[14] [Note the absence of any claim to "proof"; interpretation, which must appeal to self-evidence in the reader, can never hope for anything more than plausibility, Plato's "likely story."]

III

TONAL CONSEQUENCES

The harmonic mythology of the ancients can be studied in one model octave 2:1, "bent round into a circle," as Plato requires in *Timaeus*, to make, in effect, a circular logarithmic scale on base 2. This "modulus" (Brumbaugh) or "circular model" (Plato) makes "female" powers of 2 modular identities and turns "male" odd numbers into irreducible "modular residues." These sexual metaphors, common to Greece and China, are the consequences of what musicians call "octave equivalence," a mode of thought which has the effect of making the prime number 2 into a kind of "mother" (i.e., *matrix*, or "earth") for all harmonic theory, as numerous Chinese sources attest, and as Plato's *Timaeus* creation imagery confirms, although Brumbaugh may be the first Platonist to recognize this clearly enough to sense its general importance.

In the ancient world, tones were correlated with months of the year, with the consequence that a circle divided into seasonal parts represented both linear (i.e., arithmetic) time (the calendar) and logarithmic tone-space (the scale). Subdivisions of the model octave are obviously fractional string-lengths lying between the whole and the half. The numerosity assigned to these subdivisions – on the principle of smallest integers for a given context – is purely a function of our interests at the moment. It is a pity that the septimal-scale-bound term "octave" has become indelibly associated in our minds with the 2:1 ratio, for this interval is variously divided into 3, 5, 6, 12, 18, 24, 60, 360, etc. parts according to our concerns of the moment. It is too late historically, however, to return to the earlier Greek term for the 2:1 ratio, "*diapason*" meaning "through all the tones," and the reader must bear with current usage.

My own work is a methodical application of the Brumbaugh principles articulated above. His concept of a "modulus" and its "residues" of course sounds anachronistic although hours, days, and months have been counted as "modular residues" from time immemorial. The octave modulus 2:1 probably was also universal no matter how many tones were involved, or in what culture; but musicologists could not be certain of this in Greece until Plato's mathematical allegories were unravelled (confirming Aristoxenus' claim about his predecessors), nor certain of it in China until the 64 chime-bells of the Marquis of Zeng were unearthed in 1978 showing the same twelve engraved tone names being used repeatedly through five octaves. Brumbaugh's technical terms are quite appropriate for timekeepers and musicians, and he has given fair warning that pre-Euclidean mathematical thought was not abstracted from practical applications and from integration with philosophy.

Only one crucial idea was perhaps not fully articulated by Brumbaugh. Pythagorean ratios always had double meanings as both multiples and submultiples (of some arbitrary basic unit); this point was always assumed (hence Plato's "great and small," and Nicomachus' "perverse" insistence on symmetry), and it gave the pythagorean mathematical cosmos a perfect inverse symmetry. This ancient reciprocity is the arithmetical counterpart of modern insight that wave-length and frequency are reciprocals, so that ratios always have two tonal meanings, one in a rising progression and the other in a falling one. Such "dialectical" double meanings, emphasized in the pythagorean musicology of Sigmund Levarie and Ernest Levy[15] and Levy,[16] must be studied simultaneously (i.e., dialectically, Socrates' fundamental precept), for Plato's tonal allegories to become intelligible. (Here is the reason that purely geometrical explorations of Plato's mathematical allegories have remained essentially barren; the geometry must be applied to the string, with perfect inverse symmetry, and then "bent round" into a cyclic "modulus" which eliminates octave-redundancy and exposes its residues. Pythagorean ratio theory compels attention to these distinctions between "reality" and "appearances.") Simultaneous double meanings are implicit, of course, in the very terms "great and small"; they are hinted at in Brumbaugh's postulate that Plato's circles "take account of some sort of *reciprocity*," and they have beautiful and extensive analogies in his account of Plato's theory of vision (see Brumbaugh's matrices and four provocative diagrams concerning the reversal of images in a mirror, and the "effect of reversed intellectual vision."[17]

Acoustical arithmetic practiced with pythagorean constraints can involve dizzying transformations of numerosity according to context; one must, for the sake of sanity, hold fast to the "tonal invariances" involved. Modern tone names, because they repeat at the octave, function as a convenient algebra (not, however, for the unmusical, which platonists have allowed themselves to become). The systematic application of Brumbaugh's principles has lead to the surprising conclusion that the mathematical allegories of the *Republic, Timaeus, Critias,* and *Laws* are integral parts of one extensive "pythagorean" treatise on tuning systems. Each of four Platonic cites has its own specific model tuning system, with appropriate related arithmetic. The "tyrant's allegory" is an integral part of this sequence of "political" lessons.

IV

THE TYRANT'S NUMBER

To compress three long arguments into a short one,[18] Socrates, after an extensive prelude to prepare his auditors for what is coming, calculates "the extent of the interval between the king and the tyrant in respect of true pleasure" as $9^3 = 729$. To this argument (Socrates is recalling the conversation) Glaucon, Plato's older brother, responds:

"An overwhelming and baffling calculation," he said, "of the difference between the just and the unjust man in respect of pleasure and pain." "And what is more [Socrates' continues], it is a true number and pertinet to the lives of men if days and nights and months and years pertain to them." "They certainly do," [Glaucon] said (*Republic* 587E).

Now it is a habit of Plato to try to contrive that his mathematical allegories deliver their insights at the third (i.e., cube) dimension; "causal efficacy proceeds from a point to a solid."[19] During his clearly sophistical "preludizing" Socrates establishes 9 as the appropriate "linear" measure for the tyrant's distance from a true "philosopher king" who practices "moderation" ("the philosopher king of himself"). (Brumbaugh deduces the seven intervening characters.) Socrates then continues through the "square" dimension to the "cube."

	point	line	plane	solid	
	1	9	81	729	(Socrates' computation)
falling	D	C	Bb	Ab	"multiples" = string length
rising	D	E	F$\sharp$	G$\sharp$	"submultiples" = frequency

V

SOCRATES' INSIGHT

Socrates' numbers are the modular residues ("male," odd numbers) which define a musical tritone, the most dissonant interval, often called the "diabolus in musica." [i.e., Three consecutive wholetones of 9:8 reach $(9/8)^3 = 729/512$; in the tone-circle powers of 8 disappear as modular identities.] Dialectical implications require that this tritone be studied simultaneously rising and falling. The reciprocal meanings of 729 (i.e., as 729/512 and 512/729) are made "commensurable" (Plato's term) by squaring the fractional expression:

$$(729/512)^2 = 531,441/524,288.$$

This is the ratio of the familiar "pythagorean comma," now known as the "comma maxima" in China, normally thought of as arising at the 12th step (i.e., thirteenth tone) in the spiral of fifths. This comma is worth approximately 24 cents, about a quarter of our modern semitone, which is conceived as 100 logarithmic cents. We must either ignore this discrepancy (earlier Chinese practice, before Ching Fang in the 1st century B.C.) or eradicate it from our scale systems (modern equal temperament). Plato's solution, anticipating equal temperament by two millennia, was to deny that civic justice could be founded on the principle of giving every man [symbolized by male "modular residues"] "exactly what he is owed" (*Republic* 331E). The two values of the comma lie so close together in the "modulus" that we cannot readily distinguish them by ear in a musical context (they are easily distinguished in the laboratory); if they do intrude, they can corrupt our harmonies and lead us away from our tonic references. Since wholetones 9:8 are generated in both Greece and China as alternate tones in the spiral of fifths 3:2 [i.e., $(3/2)^2 = 9/4$, with a "residue" value of 9:8], the intruder can be expressed either as 3^{12} or as $9^6 = 531,441$, modularly reduced by the nearest power of 2, which is $2^{19} = 524,288$. The musical lesson is that either the spiral of fifths must be truncated after 12 tones, Western practice through the whole of history (that is after $3^{11} = 177,147$, the reference number used by Ching Fang in the first century B.C. in a procedure he claimed was already ancient in China), or else, as in modern equal temperament, the 3:2 ratio of the "perfect" fifth must be "tempered" by a slight contraction. Only the philosopher, "king of himself," educated in the quadrivium of "hard" sciences, can be trusted to possess this wisdom.

I submit that Socrates' numerical progression makes little sense except in acoustical theory practiced according to Brumbaugh's articulation of an "octave modulus" and its "residues." I have shown elsewhere the meticulous care Plato took to prepare his auditors for this musicological lesson. In the tone-circle of Figure 1, I merely graph the double meanings of 1, 9, 81, and 729 to achieve the visual analogue Plato himself possibly drew in the sand. Notice the slight overlap between the double meanings of 729 as Ab and as G$\#$, viewed from the center of symmetry on D, representing "the One itself."

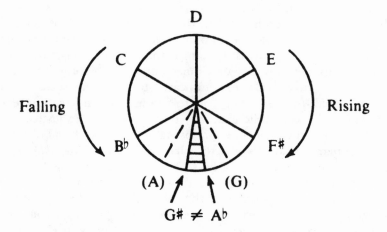

FIGURE 1: RECIPROCAL MODULAR RESIDUES OF 9, 9², AND 9³

Socrates' numbers are modular residues with the values of 9/8, 81/64, and 729/512, defining a musical "tritone" (three consecutive wholetones of 9:8). Double meanings as both multiples and submultiples make them applicable to both rising and falling tonal progressions, D E F# G# and D C Bb Ab, taking D as the center of symmetry (i.e., as $9^0 = 1$). The "dialectical" meaning of 729 (as 729/512 and 512/729) produce the pythagorean comma in the middle of the octave as an overlap between Ab and G#. The normal view of this sequence would be as six consecutive wholetones rising from Ab.

VI

PLATO'S SOURCES

We tend to forget – now that we have a standard semitone – that the ancients never had one; the oldest Greek conception of the octave was not of 12 semitones but rather of six wholetones, (see Philolaus, fragment 6), or more precisely of 5 wholetones 9:8 and 2 *leimmas*, "left-over" intervals slightly smaller than a semitone, readily observed in Figure 1. That the scale was thought of as approximately six wholetones is possible inspiration for an ancient year of six "double months." Philolaus' conception of the year as 729/2 = 364 1/2 "days and nights" makes 729 an appropriate "Socratic" calendar count for Greeks who knew no better and who trusted music to reveal divine intention.

The oldest formal treatment of the "pythagorean comma" is in the *Sectio Canonis*, proposition 9, attributed to Plato's friend Archytes, the most prominent pythagorean of their generation. "Six sesquioctavan [i.e., 9:8] intervals are greater than one double interval." The demonstrative proof consists merely of setting forth the sequence of smallest integers which illustrate the point; they lie between 8^6 = 262,144 and 9^6 = 531,441.

Since we learned to find seven numbers, each greater by an eighth than the preceding [in proposition 8], let there be found A, B, C, D, E, F, G, and let A be 262,144.

A -	262144	[=string-length value of G#]
B -	294912	[=string-length value of F#]
C -	331776	[=string-length value of E]
D -	373248	[=string-length value of D]
E -	419904	[=string-length value of C]
F -	472392	[=string-length value of B*b*]
G -	531441	[=string-length value of A*b*]

and G is greater than the double of A.[20]

Plato, I suggest, has merely taken Archytas' arithmetic, itself a formal proof for Philolaus' insight, and expressed the result as 9^3 read dialectically instead of 9^6 read directly. This "mathematical game" which he plays with his students and friends throughout his political treatises is an elegant teaching device; note the powerful reduction in numerosity, together with the need to think through opposite (i.e., perfect inverse symmetrical) potential consequences.

There is much more of interest in the tyrant's allegory – Socrates builds his "musical" case with great care, virtually all of it overlooked by unmusical translators and commentators – but I gloss over it here in order to show a Chinese correlate, that is, that a sequence of six wholetones with precisely the same values as in Greece (i.e., five consecutive ratios of 9:8), was accepted as a fundamental "law of nature" governing heaven and earth.

VII

TONAL ISOMORPHISM IN THE *I CHING* ("BOOK OF CHANGES")

Perhaps the most revered book in ancient China, the *I Ching* apparently began as a collection "of ancient peasant-omens" and grew into "a repository of concepts"; in this proess (8th-3rd c. B.C.) it became suffused with the much later *yin-yang* doctrine of "two fundamental forces," which apparently dates only from Plato's 4th century B.C.[21] During the next few centuries the *I Ching* acquired the remainder of its "ten Wings," the extensive commentaries now appended to it and which contain strong "pythagorean" elements. During the Han period (202 B.C. to 220 A.D.), when it was edited into its present form, the *I Ching* was prized as an aid both to meditation and to divination. The book is a grand paean to the endless vicissitudes ("Changes") of fortune within a reassuring cosmic continuity. The symbol for *I*, "change," is a combination of the symbols for sun and moon, natural archetypes of effortless change. Among the 64 hexagrams built from unbroken *yang* (male) lines (–) and broken *yin* (female) lines (- -), around which commentary is organized, there are twelve which the historian Pan Ku (1st c. A.D.) associated both with calendar months and with chromatic tones.[22] In Figure 2 I have merely placed Pan Ku's tonal hexagrams in juxtaposition with notation for the standard Chinese spiral of fifths (rising fifths 3:2 alternate with falling fourths 3:4) so that the eye can follow the logic involved.

The twelve tones in this generative sequence are alternately male and female, odd and even respectively. The basic Chinese pentatonic scale can be thought of as formed or "generated" by any five sucessive tones in this sequence, the "tonic" being moved according to various calendrical schemes of which Pan Ku's *I Ching* example is only one. The formula for computing string and pipe lengths for the spiral of fifths, "add or subtract one-third," attributed to Kuan-Tzu (d. 645 B.C.) is itself a striking example of "aesthetic economy." (Why Greece, which knew these pitches, loosely referred to in the West as "Pythagorean tuning," had no comparable simple formula, is a musicological question I gloss over here; it concerns "tetrachord" theory and "moveable" tones in the enharmonic mode which resulted in 24 or more microintervals in the octave.) Eleven successive operations approximate a twelve-tone equal division of the "octave modulus" (Brumbaugh's basic concept) if two sucessive additions are taken in the middle of the sequence (see G-D-A in Figure 2). This

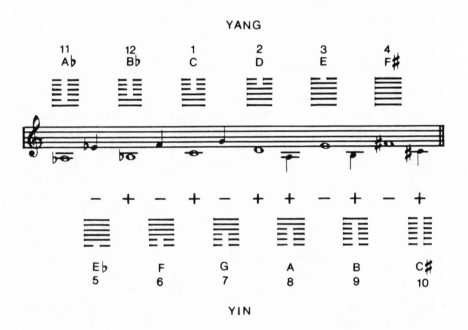

FIGURE 2: "SPIRAL FIFTHS" TUNING AND ITS I CHING CORRELATES:
MONTHS, TONES, AND HEXAGRAMS.

The tuning is generated by sucessive subtractions and additions of one-third of the string or pipe lengths. Note that the six *yang* tones form an unbroken scale of wholetones 9:8, isomorphic with Socrates' construction in Figure 1. The *yin* tones are also wholetones of 9:8 except in the middle of the sequence where two successive additions of one-third (necessary to stay within the ocatve modulus) sunder them into two groups. The historian Pan Ku ecorded these correlations between tones and hexagrams in the 1st century AD. The lines themsleves, unbroken *yang* and broken *yin*, conceived as 9's and 6's respectively, not only preserve the 3:2 ratio of the musical fifth but mirror the structure of the chromatic octave modulus.

particular "modulus" remained the foundation of Chinese music theory until it was replaced in modern times by equal-temperament.

Notice that the six *yang* (male) tones form an unbroken sequence of wholetones 9:8 which are tonally, arithmetically and geometrically isomorphic with Socrates' structure in Figure 1. They divide this circular or cyclic "modulus" into six parts, corresponding with six double-months. The standard Chinese year-count from Shang times (2nd millenium B.C.) was six cycles of 60 days each, even though the year was known to contain 365 1/4 days, and was also thought of as divided into 12 months. (Ancient Chinese thought seems remarkably rich in alternative viewpoints, often warmly disputed, but also sometimes set side by side without comment.) The hexagrams (read always from the bottom upwards) designate these six tones by 1, 2, 3, 4, 5, and 6 successive unbroken lines respectively, each line being interpreted in *I Ching* metaphor as a "nine." (Nakaseko labels the *yang* hexagrams "nine-one, nine-two, nine-three," etc.) Thus not only the end result but the succession of 9's is also analogous to Socrates' procedure. (How far this analogy is a true one is a question I defer until later.) In early times (see the list of bell names from the *Kuo Yu*), it was only these six *yang* "male" tones which carried the designation *Lü*, "a term that is generally translated 'pitch-pipe,' but the essential meaning of which is regular steps or regularity."[23] "The six *Lü* are the root stock of the myriad things" in *Shih Chi*[24] "Six governs the pitchpipes" in *Ta Tai Li Chi*.[25] We moderns have become so used to the 12-month year and 12-tone scale that we tend to overlook the fact that, like moon months, the chromatic semitones of the spiral of fifths are irregular in size; the tonal intervals resulting from the procedure in Figure 2 oscillate between undersized "diatonic semitones" (C# to D, for instance) of 90 cents and oversized "chromatic semitones" of 104 cents (C to C#, for instance). Hence in the ancient world semitones, however defined with the arithmetic materials available, could not provide any useful standard of measurement; six was thus a more logical basic division than twelve for any "yearly" cycle which mirrored tonal regularity.

It now remains to be shown how Chinese philosophical commentary on the six tones of this isomorphic construction (remember that we are looking exclusively at the 6 *yang* tones) compares with that of Socrates.

VIII

I CHING CORRELATIONS AND COMMENTARY

Yang and *yin* originally referred to the sunny and dark sides of a hill respectively, and, according to Pan Ku, in the *I Ching* the month hexagrams are associated with tones so that *yang* increases (i.e., from 1 to 6 unbroken lines, read upwards, associated with the unbroken wholetone scale on the tonic) as the sun moves from the cold winter solstice in the eleventh month towards the warm summer solstice in the fourth month. *Yin* then grows in the second half of the year while the sun recedes (from 1 to 6 broken lines, always read upwards), associated with the "broken" line of the tonal "interstitials," as the Chinese conceived these *yin* tones in figure 2, with their sequence sundered into two groups of 3. (The *yin* whole-tone C#-E♭ is diminished by a comma, thus these six tones are sundered into three's no matter how they are examined, in tuning order or in scale order.) Thus the seasonal change from *yang* to *yin* in the scale, six tones each, is correlated with the seasonal motion of the sun between its six-month solstitial limits. In the modern numbering of the hexagrams (ostensibly by King Wen, 12th century B.C., progenitor of the Chu dynasty), *Ch-ien*, "The Creative," with six unbroken lines, comes first. It is assigned to the fourth month (May-June, F# in my example) when the sun reaches its zenith, and thus it symbolizes the strongest male force, the "primal power, which is light-giving, active, strong, and of the spirit."

> Applied to the human world, these attributes show the great man the way to notable success: "Because he sees with great clarity causes and effects, he completes the six steps at the right time and mounts toward heaven on them at the right time, as though on six dragons."[26]

The tones have proceeded successfully through the octave matrix. But notice the further commentary associated with the 6th (i.e., top) line of this particular hexagram:

> "Nine at the top means: Arrogant dragon will have cause to repent." Everything that goes to extremes meets with misfortune .... This line warns against titanic aspirations that exceed one's power. A precipitous fall would follow .... Arrogance means that one knows how to press forward but not

how to draw back, that one knows existence but not annihilation, knows something about winning but nothing about losing. It is only the holy man who understands how to press forward and how to draw back, who knows existence and annihilation as well, without losing his true nature. The holy man alone can do this.[27]

Legge offers a similar translation of *I Ching* commentary on this hexagram: "In the sixth (or topmost) line, undivided, (we see its subject as) the dragon exceeding the proper limits. There will be occasion for repentence."[28]

This is precisely the moral lesson in Socrates' tyrant's allegory. The good man in both cultures, whether called philosopher-king, the great man, or holy man, or alluded to as the "dragon," understands moderation. He knows how to limit his own tendency toward arrogance and unlimited acquisition. "Wisdom" in both cultures is thus linked to the same lesson in mathematical acoustics. A "natural" acoustical law (octave identity), or, if you prefer, an irresistable mathematical "modulus," tied to the sun and to the scale, is accepted as the paradigm for moral law. Needham, a biologist, discounting the influence of acoustical science altogether, finds it a paradox "that law could be derived from where no law existed." He assumes that by "physical law" the Chinese meant only "the fixing of quantitative metrological standards by decree of positive law,"[29] missing the point that metrological standards were themselves derived from pitchpipes correlated with the calendar in extremely subtle ways.

IX

HOW VALID IS THE ANALOGY?

What right have we to believe that our apparent Greek-Chinese analogy is a true one? Chinese numerology – especially 9's and 6's, symbolized by unbroken *yang* and broken *yin* lines respectively – must first be shown to be as "musicalized" as Plato's. Sinologists make no such assumption as Brumbaugh does for Plato about the likelihood of any rational meaning. The early volumes of Needham's great and continuing work, *Science and Civilization in China*, are dominated by Marcel Granet's conviction that,

The notion of the quantitative plays practically no role in the philosophical speculations of the (ancient) Chinese .... Numbers were manipulated as if they were symbols ... [and] did not have the function of representing magnitudes.[30]

Needham actually ignores the vast amount of his own evidence to the contrary and supports Granet's general conclusion that "the Chinese notion of Order positively excluded the notion of [natural] Law."[31]

I must leave to another context a detailed refutation of these opinions and limit present argument to the minimum needed for the particular Greek-Chinese analogy presented above.

The *I Ching* itself assigns the odd numbers 1, 3, 5, 7, and 9 to "heaven" and the even numbers 2, 4, 6, 8, and 10 to "earth" (the "Great Appendix," Chapter IX, paragraph 49). More to the point of our tuning schema in Figure 2, we read that,

Anciently, when the sages made the *I*, in order to give mysterious assistance to the spiritual Intelligences, ... the number 3 was assigned to heaven, 2 to earth, and from these came the (other) numbers (Appendix V, chapter 1).

Now Legge, working within the divination context of the *I Ching*, where each line of a hexagram is laboriously chosen by three manipulations of the "yarrow sticks" or, alternatively, by a triple tossing of three coins (18 operations are required to determine a hexagram), assumes that "other numbers" refers only to 6, 7, 8, and 9 which result from this complex process, obviously designed to ensure that the hexagram selected for divination is chosen at random. It is unclear why the *yin / yang* lines were ever taken metaphorically as 6's and 9's in the first place.[32] (The numbers 8 and 7 were considered to be "young" *yin* and *yang* respectively, and to "change" into their opposites.)

If we are alert to Chinese musical habits, however, a somewhat different picture emerges in the *I Ching*. The document was heavily edited from the 5th century B.C. onwards when Chinese musical development was at its peak, when the pitchpipes (*Lü*) were taken as the highest symbol of order, and when 5-element "correlative" thinking stemming from Tsou Yen (4th century B.C.) and his school was being extended over everything imaginable. These constituted "common certain habits of imagination and notions of pedagogy" (see Brumbaugh's first principle) which literate Chinese of the classical period could take for granted. That the *I Ching* is colored by these developments we can see best from looking at Kaun Tzu's arithmetization of the pentatonic scale. He states the tuning rule ("add or subtract one-third"), points out that the computation must begin with $3^4 = 81$ ("3 taken four times"), and gives the resulting integer values necessary to avoid fractions (the "principle of aesthetic economy").

schema	do	sol	re	la	mi
	C	G	D	A	E
integers	81	108	72	96	64
procedure		+1/3	-1/3	+1/3	-1/3

Notice that this is not a monochord sequence, but an abstract one; monochord operations start with the full string length sounding the "ground" tone (i.e., lowest pitch), and it must be assigned the largest number. Later Chinese practice made the tonic (corresponding to our *do*, usually taken as C) the lowest tone in the normative mode. Here are both string-length and frequency ratios for the normative pentatonic scale together with an approximation of correct "ideal" frequencies by five of the largest Zeng bells, cast in the fifth century B.C.

schema	do	re	mi	sol	la
	C	D	E	G	A
string lengths	81	72	64	54	48
vibration ratios	64	72	81	96	108
Zeng bells (hertz)	64.8	72.6	80.1	98.4	103.2

Kuan Tzu's scale numbers appear to be the foundation for much (and perhaps most) of the numerology which sinologists today find so offensive, and assume has no physical basis. It is my theory that the ancients were mainly generalizing from the known to the unknown, that "symbolic" numbers acquired their power in cultural imagination from their logical function in acoustical theory practiced under Brumbaugh's constraints. Look at the above numbers and consider that the *I Ching* is a commentary on *64* hexagrams, and that the prestigious "Great Appendix" to it (Legge's Appendix III), consists of two large sections, the first with *81* numbered paragraphs and the second with *72*. Then recall the affirmation that all numbers are generated by *3* and *2*, "heaven" and "earth" respectively, and remember that 6 *yang* tones are the "natural" limit.

Other ancient documents,[33] establish a more general context for this emphasis on the prime matrix number 2 and the prime heavenly number 3 which generate the "modular residues" of interest to musicians. A strong undercurrent of this schematic "tonal-trinitarianism" pervades Taoism:

> The Way begot one,
> And the one, two;
> Then the two begot three
> And three, all else.
> (*Tao Te Ching*, chapter 42)

The "Way" is the way of music at the time of Lao Tzu, the putative author, two or three centuries after Kuan Tzu. This example is of particular interest because the chapters in this Taoist canon also total $3^4 = 81$, the base Kuan-Tzu necessarily used to generate five tones for the pentatonic scale, and chapter 42 which contains this formula happens to be a Taoist 2-digit approximation for the 12th tone of a scale which begins on 81.[34] Ching Fang, himself a Taoist adept, declared that the pitchpipes are "the root source of the Tao."[35] Tsou Yen, founder of the 5-element school, himself conceived China to be one 81st part of the whole world, a ninth of one of nine great continents, the whole world being measured by the 81 on Kuan Tzu's string. Ching Fang assigned his string $3^{11} = 177,147$ so that his first 12 tones involved no fractional remainders. (All Chinese tonal/calendrical associations assign the ground tone to the 11th month, perhaps for this reason?) Chinese pitchpipe calculations traditionally began with a 9-inch fundamental pipe; thus the first new tone, a perfect fifth 3:2 above, was 6 inches. Han fluency with acoustical arithmetic within some convenient "modulus of doubles" (even taking advantage of Chinese decimal notation to commence with a fundamental pipe of 8.1 inches) in the centuries immediately preceding Pan Ku's is too well-documented to need further attention here.[36] I find it intriguing that a 9-inch Han pipe (ca. 23cm.) can sound a frequency within range of the Chinese year-count (360-366 hertz), and that Han metrology was coordinated with the length and volume of this particular pipe. Twentieth century archaeologists have discovered two bronze chime sets, one of 19 bells and the other of 14, in which the "tonic" (i.e., lowest pitch, on the largest bell) also vibrates in this range, at 362 and 366 hertz respectively.[37] Chinese interest in acoustical theory was acute, and Chinese virtuosity in applied acoustical technology still awaits explanation. Let us not ignore Kuan Tzu's numbers when we meet them in ancient texts. The entire culture was musicalized – officially.

X

CONCLUSIONS

However and whenever *I Ching* numerical symbolism because established, it seems clear that by Han times musical theorists, from experience with acoustical arithmetic and its applications to strings and pipes, were fluent with "modular residues," and familiar enough with the function of "9" to read the progression of unbroken, *yang* lines in the calendar hexagrams as the "residues" associated with a wholetone scale of 9:8 ratios – and in a way quite similar to Socrates'. They would also have read the progession of 6's in the broken *yin* lines as allusions to the 3:2 ratio of the musical fifth which link these series together, 9:6 being their first embodiment on the pitch-pipes. The lack of literary documentation forbids us, however, to be dogmatic concerning exact tuning and its possible influences on the *I Ching* before the 3rd century B.C. Because multi-stringed zithers with moveable bridges are at least a thousand years older in China, musicians find it easy to suppose that tome ratios were known at a very early time, for those ratios would have been impressed not only on the ear but on the eye and the sense of touch. In this we are at odds with those sinologists who believe that "exact pitch probably did not become a dominating factor among [the Chinese] till Babylonian influence made itself felt at the beginning of the 4th century B.C."[38] Recent archaeological findings make such opinions untenable. I conclude that for at least some literate Han Chinese, the Plato/*I Ching* analogue presented here is a true one.

Modern scientists may continue to protest that Brumbaugh's "modular arithmetic" is inappropriately applied to the ancient Greeks and Chinese, who missed the full range of implication. But notice how useful hermeneutically this notion is in helping us understand the intensity of ancient "trinitarianism" and its related enthusiasm for 9's. Scholars who feel too offended by numerology to study its patterns (classicists and sinologists are alike in this respect) are denying to the ancients the only pre-euclidian language they knew, a kind of "mathological mythologizing," for encoding important elements of their rationality. Our new terminology, shorn of any subjective feelings whatever, and admittedly historically anachronistic beyond the limited sense shown here, should give us some power to understand ancient affection for an harmonics which was always bound to calendrical and tonal modules and their residues.

ADDENDUM

That Kuan Tzu's pentatonic scale was of any concern to Plato is hidden from classicists in the numerology of the *Laws*, where a strict exploration by Brumbaugh's principles has uncovered a "map" of Magnesia, shown in Figure 3, which serves also as its tonal calendar.[39] The five solid radical arms which point to Kuan Tzu's tones are Plato's five "guardians from the highest property class" (i.e., from the largest "superparticular" integer ratios possible, 3:2 and 4:3, within the octave matrix 2:1), to whom he assigns special responsibilities (as "Captain of the Guard" or "Country-Wardens"). Kuan Tzu's numbers are multiplied by 5 to make them "commensurable" with Plato's "citizens of the second class" who complete an alternate "just" chromatic tuning generated by the three prime numbes 2, 3, and 5. This enlarged "numerosity" – required to make the "leaders" generated by the prime number 3 commensurable with "citizens of the second property class" generated by the prime number 5 – adds no new tones to the five in the spiral of fifths, however, because it makes available no further integers at the ratios of 3:2 or 3:4.

Kuan Tzu	81	108	72	96	64	
x 5	405	540	360	480	320	(= 640)

And right here is where we notice a significant parting of East and West. Structural tonal isomorphism there was in full measure, and supporting the same "wisdom," but notice that Greek interest is turning toward pure number theory, concentrating on a systematic study of primes and abstracted from the string, as Socrates insisted that it must be (*Republic* 525). Chinese applied technology was destined to lead the West for most of the next 2000 years, as Needham's work has shown; Greek number theory died with Diophantus early in the Common Era and slumbered for over a thousand years until its modern reawakening to fuel a new science and a new technology, and discover new functions for "modular residues."

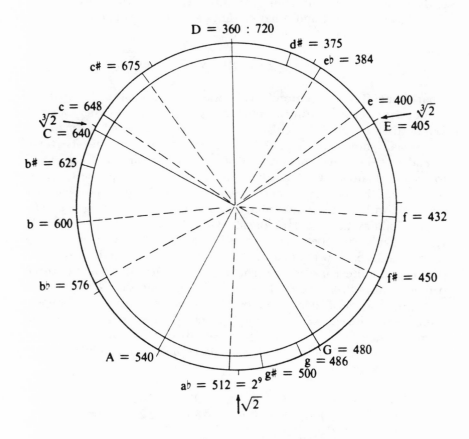

FIGURE 3: THE PENTATONIC SCALE AS PLATONIC "LEADERS."

The five tones of Kuan Tzu's pentatonic scale (generated by the prime numbers 2 and 3) are shown here as solid radial lines. Their numerosity is multiplied by 5 to make these "leaders" commensurable with "citizens of the second property class" indicated by dashed lines (generated by the primes 2, 3, and 5). Only the Greeks made this distinction between prime generators (From *The Pythagorean Plato*.)

NOTES

I have never met Robert Brumbaugh, but for 15 years I have been his grateful student. His book was a landmark not only in Platonic studies but in the history of science and in cultural anthropology. What he accomplished for classical scholarship in *Plato's Mathematical Imagination* still remains to be done for biblical scholarship and for the mathematical imagery of ancient China, India, Egypt and other cultures with ample literary records. His achievement, which owes so much to his own imagination, in a larger sense owes everything to the respect he showed his subject.

1. Cf. Ernest G. McClain, *The Myth of Invariance* (New York: Nicolas Hays Ltd., 1976), *The Pythagorean Plato* (Stony Brook: Nicolas Hays Ltd., 1978), *Meditations Through the Quran* (York Beach: Nicolas Hays Inc., 1981), and "Structure in the Ancient Wisdom Literature: the Holy Mountain," *Journal of Social and Biological Structures*, 5(1982): 233-248.

2. Ernest G. McClain, *Meditations Through the Quran* (York Beach: Nicolas Hays Inc., 1981), 59.

3. Unless otherwise cited, all quotations from Robert S. Brumbaugh are from his book, *Plato's Mathematical Imagination* (Bloomington, Indiana, 1954).

4. Brumbaugh, *Plato's Mathematical Imagination*, 11.

5. Brumbaugh, *Plato's Mathematical Imagination*, 4.

6. Brumbaugh, *Plato's Mathematical Imagination*, 148.

7. Brumbaugh, *Plato's Mathematical Imagination*, 11.

8. Brumbaugh, *Plato's Mathematical Imagination*, 5-6.

9. Brumbaugh, *Plato's Mathematical Imagination*, 3.

10. Brumbaugh, *Plato's Mathematical Imagination*, 72-73.

11. Brumbaugh, *Plato's Mathematical Imagination*, 88.

12. Brumbaugh, *Plato's Mathematical Imagination*, 257, 295.

13. Brumbaugh, *Plato's Mathematical Imagination*, 226.

14. Brumbaugh, *Plato's Mathematical Imagination*, 8.

15. Siegmund Levarie and Ernst Levy, *Tone: A Study in Musical Acoustics* (Ohio: Kent State University Press, 1968).

16. Ernest Levy, *A Theory of Harmony* (Albany: SUNY Press, 1985).

17. Brumbaugh, *Plato's Mathematical Imagination*, 233-237.

18. *Republic* 572-588; Brumbaugh, *Plato's Mathematical Imagination*, 151-160; McClain, *Meditations Through the Quran*, 33-40.

19. Brumbaugh, *Plato's Mathematical Imagination*, 66.

20. Eva Braun, "The Cutting of the Cannon," *The Collegian* (December, 1975): 1-63.

21. Joesph Needham, *Science and Civilization in China*, Vol. 2 (Cambridge: Cambridge University Press, 1956).

22. Kazu Nakaseko, "Symbolism in Ancient Chinese Music Theory," *Journal of Music Theory*, 1(1957): 147-180.

23. Joesph Needham, *Science and Civilization in China* (Cambridge: Cambridge University Press, 1962), 4:135.

24. Needham, *Science and Civilization in China*, 4:199.

25. Needham, *Science and Civilization in China*, 2.271.

26. Richard Wilhelm, *The I Ching or Book of Changes*, trans. Cary F. Baynes (Princeton: Princeton University Press, 1950).

27. Wilhelm, *The I Ching or Book of Changes*, 383.

28. James Legge, trans. *The I Ching* (New York: Dover, 1963), 58.

29. Needham, *Science and Civilization in China*, 2.550.

30. Needham, *Science and Civilization in China*, 4.288.
31. Needham, *Science and Civilization in China*, 4.572.
32. Legge, *The I Ching*, 58n.
33. Needham, *Science and Civilization in China*, 4.271.
34. Cf. Fritz Kuttner, "Prince Chu Tsai-yu's Life and Work," *Ethnomusicology*, 19 (1975): 163-204, and Ernest G. McClain, "Chinese Cyclic Tunings in Late Antiquity," *Ethnumusicology*, 23(1979): 205-224.
35. Kenneth de Woskin, *A Song for One or Two: Music and the Concept of Art in Early China* (Ann Arbor: University of Michigan, 1982).
36. Kuttner, "Prince Chu Tsai-yu's Life and Work," and Needham, *Science and Civilization in China*, Vol. 4.
37. Ernest G. McClain, "The Bronze Chime Bells of the Marquis of Zeng: Babylonian biophysics in ancient China," *Journal of Social and Biological Structures*, 8(1985): 147-173, and "Preface to an Enthnology of Ancient Techno-science," *Journal of Social and Biological Structure* (in preparation).
38. Needham, *Science and Civilization in China*, 4.160.
39. The inspiration is Brumbaugh's own "map" on page 58 of *Plato's Mathematical Imagination*.

Part II: TIME

8

TIME, HISTORY, AND ESCHATOLOGY

George Allan

I

The world for Robert Brumbaugh is always from a perspective that instantiates one of the four kinds of perspectives defined by Plato's divided line. I share this belief about beliefs, and all the methodological commitments it entails. Accordingly, if for this essay in Brumbaugh's honor I wish to undertake a critique of eschatological beliefs, I should proceed in a way that encompasses in some relevant fashion the fourfoldness of viewpoints that for Brumbaugh is the necessary condition for attaining truth.

A proper approach, it might seem, would be to begin with *eikasia* and in orderly fashion to ascend through the regions of interpretation to the level of *nous* where full understanding is at last acquired. This neo-Platonic strategy is not what Brumbaugh advocates, however, for it implies a hierarchy of adequacy whereas for him adequacy is the concomitance of all four perspectives. It does not matter where we begin, provided that all of the ways of knowing are utilized to their fullest. The divided line is not a ladder which like Wittgenstein's we are to discard once it has brought us to some lofty new vantage point. It is a foundation set on four pilings, the togetherness of which provides the stability, the truth, we seek.

For heuristic reasons, I shall begin with the third of this tetrad, proceeding thence to the second and eventually to the first. That is, from an analysis of the structure of time *á la mode Brumbaughisme*, I shall move to a discussion of historical development and from there shall come at long last to the goal of this essay, an explication of the sources of error underlying the eschatological beliefs that so bedevil our hope for personal happiness and our dream of commonweal.

II

[3]

A worldview is an abstraction, an interpretive construct from the totality of what is available from experience. It constitutes a perspective, and can reflexively be understood as doing so by those who are themselves constituted by it, even though there is no possible locus for understanding that is not in some fashion similarly constituted. The necessary condition for any worldview is that it be meaningful, that it be logically coherent and consistent, unrestrictedly adequate to experience, and valuationally tiered. A worldview, in other words, must have an ontology, an epistemology and an axiology. It must provide effective notions of necessity, possibility and existence, of subject, object, and agency, of good and evil. Most crucially, and as the key to all of these, it must sustain a systematic attitude regarding the nature of time.

In *Unreality and Time*, Brumbaugh claims that there are exactly four worldviews that satisfy these criteria: [1] classical materialism, which "treats time as consisting of successive, atomic moments which have no, or minimal, duration"; [2] process thought, in which space-time is "a locus of dynamic process" marked by "shifting directional intensity"; [3] the Aristotelian view, wherein time delineates "sequential stages of growing organization"; and [4] the Platonic tradition, in which time is "a continuous field within which such things as paths of motion can be graphically conceived, and understood by single equations of formulae."[1] I shall attempt in what follows to extend Brumbaugh's quadrivial claim about time in a way that I think will be illuminating and useful. It is not my intent in doing so to provide a clarification of Brumbaugh's position, nor even to be faithful to it. I shall, instead and more humbly, take his views as mentor and stimulus for a line of argument largely my own. I shall also make use of distinctions developed by Robert Hartman in a somewhat different context and discussed appreciatively by Brumbaugh in his book.[2]

A type of entity is anything able to satisfy the essential defining criteria for that entity. That there are four types of time-beliefs is thus to claim that integral to each of the four distinctive ways in which the criteria for worldview indicated above can be met is a distinctive understanding of temporality. The process of identifying these ways is not empirical, however. It is closer to a Kantian transcendental deduction of the various possible kinds of conditions necessary for the existence of any worldview whatsoever. Brumbaugh's quatrain of worldviews and their associated time-beliefs, in other words, is a set of something close to Weberian ideal types. If primary reality must be construed either as form or as content, and if its relata are fundamentally either internal (synthetic) or external (analytic), the result is a matrix with four realizations:[3]

	internal	external
form	4. Platonic	3. Aristotelian
content	2. Process	1. Atomism

To each of these world-creating perspectives Brumbaugh assigns a characteristic view of time, most usefully identified in terms of the verbal tense to which it gives priority:

	internal	external
form	4. present eternal	3. present progressive
content	2. future inception	1. past perfective

We can ask, however, whether this two-dimensional matrix is really sufficient to capture the essential alternatives. If internal/external relata correlate with epistemology and form/content with ontology, then an axiological dimension must be added to the typology since it provides the third of the necessary conditions for anything being a worldview. Indeed this would seem especially crucial with respect to the associated views of time, since the axiological function in a time-belief has to do with freedom and determinism, with the question of whether the time-system is open or closed.

A three-dimensional matrix of paired criteria would turn Brumbaugh's four-type arrangement into one with eight types:

	epistem	ontol	axiol	time-view
4	inter	form	closed	present eternal
3	exter	form	open	present progressive
2	inter	content	open	future inceptive
1	exter	content	closed	past perfective
5	inter	form	open	present inceptive
6	exter	form	closed	past eternal
7	inter	content	closed	present perfective
8	exter	content	open	future progressive

But the eighth worldview is a radically Heraclitean flux devoid of any principle of meaningful order, whereas the seventh is its polar opposite, a Parmenidean plenum lacking any principle of meaningful change. The fifth worldview is self-contradictory, since an unrestricted network of purely formal internal relations precludes alterations in the network. The sixth incoherently combines formal pluralism with no way for the many forms to be realized. So the logically possible alternatives derived from my expanded set of criteria reduce nonetheless to Brumbaugh's four systems.[4]

Types cannot be evaluated as better or worse. They all either meet the criteria defining the generic entity of which they are typal instances or they do not. But they can be arranged into any number of ordered sets. For instance, Brumbaugh arranges them in terms of degree of decreasing concreteness, from time as a function of fully determinate material atoms in motion to time as an absolutely formal plenum determining the boundary conditions for all realization, from maximal individuation to maximal unity, from flux to permanence.

This principle of order defining a hierarchy for the types is echoed within each type. And appropriately so, for whatever the belief regarding what is foundational with respect to generality/concreteness, one/many, flux/permanence, each time-belief must in a manner appropriate to its unique perspective take account of the whole spectrum of possibilities. If, for example, time is taken in a Platonic mode to be [4] the way in which perfection sets the conditions for whatever is not complete in itself, that viewpoint must go on to give an accounting of imperfections of all kinds, [1] multiplicity, of [2] becoming and perishing, and of [3] formal difference.

To provide this accounting systematically is to give an exposition of the type: an exposition of the ontology, epistemology and axiology that generate a view of time which has a distinctive way of understanding plurality, change, structure, and significance. Thus for the purpose of ideal-typical exposition, each type should be taken as encompassing four typal levels. By means of such an exposition the full character of the type is exhibited: not simply the evidence of its adequacy to the criteria essential for a belief to be a time-belief but in addition all of the qualities that comprise the distinctiveness of its adequacy, that display the way it is a type of time-belief different from and not reducible to the other types.

Each formal type is empirically realizable in an indefinite number of instances. Any such realization is an empirical fact, an historical event, a contingent reality in the sense that its becoming actual cannot be deduced from the formal reality of the type. Since we are dealing here with the types of worldview and their associated time-belief, a typal realization would be what we mean by a culture. For a culture is the beliefs and practices that create and sustain a multitude of human beings as a community, as a people characterized by an identifiable, distinctive way of understanding themselves, others, their environment. A culture, in other words, is an actual as opposed to an ideal-typical worldview. The empirical investigation of cultures is called ethnology; someone has proposed that the study of cultural worldviews be called, accordingly, ethnometaphysics.[5] A particular cultural totality realizing some typal worldview might well be called, therefore, an ethneme.

Ethnemes, unlike types, can be evaluated as better or worse than one another; they realize their type to varying degrees of completeness. For Leibniz the realizations of the type possible-world were infinite in number, but some of these were better than others and one of them could in principle be said to be the best. Similarly here: an ethneme may be deficient in the manner of its realizing some aspect, or even all aspects, of its proper type. Indeed it may be that all ethnemic realization is of necessity deficient, that a type includes characteristics all of which cannot be simultaneously instantiated. But whether or not this be so, the deficiencies are enumerable and as a result any set of ethnemes can be ordered from best to worst by reference to some specified characteristics, with the typal exposition of those characteristics taken as normative. Deviation need not be understood negatively, however. The importance of a ethneme may be its deviance from the standard, its idiosyncracies, its radically individuating peculiarities. We love persons and cherish objects for their unduplicated individuality, not for their replicable, generic qualities. It is insofar as we are interested in persons or things as means to our ends, as instrumentalities, that their generic features become important.

An ethneme has its exposition, too. As an instance of a type it echoes the structure of that type. [1] The time-sense of a people finds expression in their emotionally rooted assumptions about what things are transient and trivial, and about what things are tied in to the enduring importances that give them a place and purpose within the cosmos. [2] These habits of the heart find practical embodiment in the behavior patterns of a culture's populace, in its customary practices and the institutions that clothe those practices in stone and mortar. [3] Cultures need to articulate such feelings and doings in explicit propositional form, to turn awareness into self-awareness, to lift pragmatic practice to the level of a science, to oganize themselves in terms of well-established theories of nature and polity. [4] And ultimately a culture attempts critical understanding, the capacity to measure itself against its type and to reform its considered beliefs, its institutions, its commonsense certainties accordingly.

Hence an ethnemic exposition includes reference to a culture's myths, its social organization and practices, its constitutional principles and metaphysical theorizings, and its nomological ultimates. But an ethneme is still not the fully concrete reality. It is an empirical type, concretely realized only in the life of actual individuals, self-reflexive organisms that create a material and intangible world out of memory, imagination, muscle, and facticity. Here also the realizations can be ordered along a spectrum from extreme deviation to maximal conformity, from idiosyncratic individuation to replication of the average and normal. An individual can be judged by its culture as evil because deviant or as good because creatively original. But whatever the judgement, the grounds for it lie in the comparison of type with instance, in this case the empirically instantiated type but quite possibly the formal type as well – or instead.

Thus we can say that Plato wrote the dialogue *Republic* in Athens 2350 years ago as [1] an individual's act of theorizing, which act was thereby a realizing of [2] Athenian culture at the level of activity appropriate to speculative theorizing, which culture is part of the ethnemic instantiation of [3] a type-2 worldview's systemic structuring activities, which type is a kind of that thing we call [4] a worldview. Plato's theorizing effort, an instance of the third of the expositional levels of activity, is thus manifested by each aspect of the notion of worldview in a manner appropriate to that aspect, all four of which are needed to understand adequately his action.

Plato did more than [3] write dialogues, of course. He realized his culture [1] in his own uncriticized assumptions and commonsense convictions (e.g., that Socrates was wrongly put to death, that women are not capable of political activity), [2] in his practical involvements and achievements (e.g., founding the Academy, teaching Aristotle), and [4] in his character, the guiding principles that gave his life its consistency and its sense of purpose. Other people realized the Athenian ethneme differently, just as other cultures realized the Aristotelian type of worldview in other ways. (That Plato's accomplishments did not occur within the distinctive sort of worldview that bears his name provides us with an insight into both his genius and the sources of his discontent.)

The result of my structural analysis of the notion of worldview (and the associated notion of time), its types and ethnemes, can be depicted in Figure 1.

What is the value of this typologizing? Fourth of all, to understand: to attempt to know what is the case, its nature, its accomplishments, its possibilities, its worth. This is an undertaking which is its own justification, but the value of doing so is also instrumental. For, thirdly, from such understanding comes the capacity to judge adequacy, to compare a standard with the instances that claim to embody its perfection or its accuracy. Of such judgements is science composed, the laws of nature and of nations. And from these judgements flows, in the second place, actions aimed at creating new realities, reforming and transforming old. Hence the first and most concrete reason for typologizing is that it contributes importantly to the quality of human life, to the securing of existence and the pursuit of happiness.

III

[2]

If this typology has managed to provide only and all the logically possible worldviews and time-beliefs that define human understanding, the truth thereby entailed is still not known. The question remains: are there really ethnemes instantiating each one of the types? And if there are, as Brumbaugh claims, then why is this so? Why have a full range of realizations of these types arisen historically? Why in the comparatively brief period of a few millennia has a complex schema of alternative time-perspectives found itself in all its instances incarnated in the activities of the organism *homo sapiens*?

4] system	worldview/time-belief			
essence (definition)	ontol, epistem, axiol			

3] type	4:Platonic	3:Aristot	2:Process	1:Atomism
	eternal	decisional	futurist	determ
exposition	4:value 3.struc 2:purpose 1:imagin	etc.	etc.	etc.
	etc		etc	etc

2] ethneme	Athens	Sparta	Corinth	Thessaly
exposition	4:nomos 3:philos 2:insti 1:myth	etc.	etc.	etc.
		etc	etc	etc

1] individual	Socrates	Alcibiades	Pericles	Plato
exposition	4:character 3:convictions 2:role/station 1:commonsense	etc.	etc.	etc.

Brumbaugh's answer is deceptively simple: because they work.[6] The four worldview types work because each relates to a specific kind of human activity, the distinctive perspective of which is especially conducive to resolving the problems and achieving the goals it comprises:

> Pragmatically, our frameworks or systems are tools in a box, alternatives awaiting our selection. It takes only modest temerity to suggest that we will be best satisfied when we pick the tool that is best adapted to the objective structure of the problem, which is in turn a function of purpose and of subject matter.[7]

Brumbaugh identifies these frameworks as mathematics (and other purely abstract enterprises), medicine/politics (and other applied human sciences), fine arts (and other creative activities), and technology (and other applied natural sciences).[8] Since the typology at work here is generated logically, it follows that these disciplinary kinds are nonarbitary, indeed that they are necessary. The division of labor characterizing a social order is thereby given a natural base. I agree with Brumbaugh's point, although it does not follow that I nor he must go on to agree that Plato is correct when in the *Republic* he assigns responsibility for governance, security, and productivity to individuals on the basis of their inherent potentialities. Natural roles do not entail natural assignments to those roles.

Brumbaugh seems to confuse a type with the levels of its exposition, however, so I shall need to modify somewhat his equating of, for instance, the discipline of mathematics with a type-4 worldview. A society is a gathering of individuals who have organized their environment and themselves in some meaningful, effective fashion. The mode of this oganization is multiform because it works, because a division of labor permits effective problem-solving of a quality and efficiency otherwise not available. Thus each type of worldview is exposited across a range of activities both concrete and abstract. It makes sense that the differences among these activities would be a function of the differing subject matters toward which they are directed. These can be usefully distinguished into four kinds that echo the four kinds of worldview. But it would be misleading to characterize the work-kinds, as Brumbaugh does, as specific disciplines. They mark divisions of labor within a societal perspective, but are not themselves societal perspectives, even though humans have a seemingly irresistible tendency to want to identify their workview with their worldview, to turn a class ideology into a universal truth.

A first kind of societal activity has to do with the techniques for immediate problem solving, for coping with the challenges that willy-nilly impede our purposes. These are behaviors established by trial and error, reinforced by successful repetition, and secured by habit. They dominate the practical concerns of a community, its methods for producing food, shelter, and progeny, its approaches to conflict resolution.

A second kind of activity involves invention, the capacity to hypothesize, to go beyond tried and true methods for the sake of improving the effectiveness with which the ends they serve can be attained, or for the sake of altering those ends. This more speculative way of behaving is still quite concrete in its style and intent. Imagination is prized, but less for the pleasure of its novelties than for their relevance. Social stability requires changes of this sort, this capacity to conjure alternatives to the habitual, to bring them into constructive relation with what is extant, and as a result to adjust the instrumentalities of the community to ever-shifting conditions. By means of such integrative innovation are individual and collective needs most likely to be fulfilled.

Thirdly is generalized reasoning and its cultural articulation. This involves the creation and manipulation of an ordered system of abstractions capable of being elaborated independently of its applications. Included in this are the skills of leadership, of intellectual vision, political persuasion, coercive timeliness, which make use of those abstractions for the coordination of social purposes and the mediation of social conflict. Such knowledge is capable of being learned didactically, apart from first-hand experiential involvement. Formal education, utilizing anonymous texts prepared for no specific occasion, rather than apprenticeship to a specific person, becomes the vehicle for transmitting expertise. By being abstract, a web of relata derived from, relevant to, but not determined by the content they relate, the results of this kind of activity are readily generalized. They are thereby both protean and undelimitable, in this doubly important sense universal. The science of nature and the science of governance make use necessarily of such universals in their endeavor to find or create a unified subject matter and then to predict and control how it functions.

One other kind of activity, the fourth, remains: that having to do with the discovery and articulation of criteria of judgment regarding what constitutes a proper means (what is appropriate as distinct from what is effective), what the proper use is of the results of achieving the ends served by such means (what is just as distinct from what is desired), and which ends among those available for pursuit and realization are worthwhile (what is good as distinct from what is possible).

Certainly there are actual social roles and institutions – academic disciplines and guilds, castes and classes – especially focused around each of these kinds of activity. For instance, craftsmen and technicians, inventors and engineers, managers and scientists, statesmen and seers tend to be concerned respectively with *poesis*, *phronesis*, *theoria*, and *noesis*. But it is the activity, not its institutional analogue, that is primary; an individual might perform in a given period of time more than one kind of activity without this implying any change in social role. United Mine Workers officials, although managers, still carry their union cards, theoretical physicists instruct the citizenry on matters of nuclear disarmament, presidents of the United States set national agendas with one eye, sometimes two, on the implications for their reelection. The four levels of exposition of a cultural type can readily all be manifest in the beliefs and actions of a given individual, although at any given time one will predominate in virtue of the individual's societal roles and hence come to characterize who that person essentially is. Too much confusion of roles, too easy a blurring of the basic lines of responsibility, does not work. A fully functioning society engages its world tetrarchically.

Can a single one of these four expositions come to characterize the type itself? Can a workview determine a worldview such that its particularities are refracted in appropriate fashion throughout the full spectrum of that type's workviews? Can a cultural type be said, for instance, to be predominately practical in its view of things, its sense of time, in all of its characteristic activities from ethical reflection to sanitary engineering?

The answer, I would contend, is yes. If differences in the problems relevant to a society's successful adaptation to its situation result in different kinds of cultural activities, then it should be expected that some of these problems will be sufficiently important and widespread to be generic. But they will be the same for everyone in the society only as filtered through the screen of the kind of activity circumscribing each person's and each class of person's point of view. Problems that require for their solution the totality of the fourfold division of labor are *per force* societally generic. In marshalling its collective energies to address such problems, the society would take on in distinctive fashion those qualities characteristic of the kind of problem at issue. And if different societies are confronted by different sorts of generic problems, it would follow that those societies will realize predominately different types of worldview. The challenges that define workviews define worldviews as well when they are generic challenges, these worldviews in their turn defining all of the society's workviews and not just the one characteristically associated with the challenge at hand.

An interpretation of societal types in terms of problem types, of ethnemes in terms of the activities deployed for meeting effectively the challenges they confront, would be merely arbitrary if approached via the logical schema developed earlier in this essay. There would be no reason why one rather than another type of problem should be salient, hence no reason why one kind or ethneme rather than another should exist. The necessity of the quadrate exposition would be lost.

But this would be to proceed ahistorically in dealing with the history of cultures. If instead we approach our typology in a properly historical manner, the logical pattern of an exposition is transmuted into a sequential pattern. Logical differences become developmental differences, the generic becomes genetic. It is now possible to claim that the various kinds of societal challenges comprise a ordered series of stages in the durational extension of a culture, challenges appropriate to its origin, deployment, completion, and dissolution. This series is genetically necessary: it must be traversed by every society that is historically realized. The expositional levels of a worldview are, historically considered, societal stages. An ethneme instantiates a type in the sense that its history from its emergence to its perishing is the sequential articulation of all four of its typal aspects.

[1] The challenge in response to which a society is formed is one having to do with survival. The primordial motivation for social organization is Hobbesian, protection from the terrors of history through cooperation. These may be in the form of threats to accustomed food sources, the degradation of environmental supports, the intrusion of alien peoples, the collapse of internal polities. Over against this enemy, be it of natural, human, or supernatural origin, a group arises in defiance, seeking through its pooled strength the resources requisite for controlling, diverting, or eradicating the enemy's purposes. By this rejective act the many define themselves as one group, a "we" in contrast to the enemy's "them."[9] This originative mode of social existence is tribal: a *Gemeinschaft*. It authorizes as acceptable those beliefs and behaviors which effected the transition from risk to security, and repudiates as dangerous whatever deviates from their authority. The kinds of basic problems that call forth new social orders call forth as well powerful forces of conservation –

mythic beliefs, ritualized behaviors, the veneration of things past – to assure the conformity needed to secure what has been so freshly established. The terror of history begets the terrors of socialization. The fear of losing old values gives birth to new values which are sustained by a new terror directed toward whatever is not compatible with the new.

[2] But life once secured soon becomes restless out of a hope for better life. The established techniques for providing a society with the necessities for its continuance are not enough to provide the luxuries, not enough to support the shift in social emphasis from overcoming scarcity to attaining abundance. Growth requires some measure of liberation from the past, liberation from its pragmatic norms for the sake of speculative norms about future betterment. This needed breaking of the cake of custom leads to social diversification. Different individuals propose differing routes of improvement and win support from some but not all of those around them. The society, now comparatively secure, can afford to tolerate these divergences and soon benefits from the variety of realizations that result. Specialization flourishes; ends and means are judged by their ability, within the constraints of social stability, to fulfull individuated desires. Institutions arise that serve parochial or even private ends while still furthering collective ends. The State appears, among such institutions, its specialized aim being to provide for the group's security both internal and external. *Gemeinschaft* is made over into *Gesellschaft*; the mediation of differences replaces a conflation of similarities as the condition for social unity.

[3] As a society succeeds in this press toward diversification, overall unity becomes increasingly a problem. Some kind of rationalization of the plurality is needed, replacing a more personalized *ad hoc* mediation. Such a systemic approach requires a bureaucracy for its maintenance. By military force or commerce or cultural allure, the myriad components of the society are brought into an ordered whole, the system managed by people trained to place the value of the whole over those of its parts. Even external enemies are incorporated into that whole, as pacified components or as predictable, containable boundary conditions. The tribe become a state is now made over into an empire; *Gesellschaft* is transmuted into *Reich*.

This is the apotheosis of societal achievement, the summertime of collective accomplishment. But insofar as it is of necessity a partial realization of typal compossibilities, it is importantly deficient. [4] Critical self-understanding is required if the society is to survive. The limits of its strengths must be disclosed: the frictions that are wearing out the machinery of its orderliness, the spores of dissent that await the proper stimulus to explode into viral infections. But more insidious than this is the irony that a society's own success often comes to replace its enemies as enemy. It must therefore learn to ferret out all the ways by which the rationalization of successful practice dilutes the innovative vitality motivated by challenge and adventure that is the source of its success. It must be alert to all the ways by which the rationalization of belief undermines the compelling authority of belief. So self-criticism at the levels of technique, invention, and policy can eliminate some of the obvious dangers of success. But others are endemic. Social self-criticism eventually withdraws into self-understanding, into passive reflection upon the intrinsic worth of what has been and the lessons to be learned, if any, for the sake of current enlightment and the practices of whatever might succeed the eventual failing of that light. The *Reich* inexorably falls into decline, becomes more and more a part of the culturally ideal, the *Sollen* that defines the norms, positively or negatively, for new social creation. The owl of Minerva takes flight in the gathering gloom, its gray on gray a sign of the passing of the old, a promise of new achievements soon emerging.

Thus a genetic/historical reading of the typological exposition of a Brumbaughian worldview generates a philosophy of history. It is as though we were recapitulating the intellectual journey from Kant to Hegel. Or, perhaps, from Kant to Spengler and Toynbee. For one immediate question is whether the developmental sequence from a society's becoming to its perishing can be applied to history itself, whether there is a development from society to society. In other words, can the types themselves, as opposed to the expositional levels of each, be understood as a necessary sequence? Hegel's answer to this question is yes, with the fourth type being the historical realization of the ideal of a concrete universal.[10] But a Brumbaughian typology, and therefore its historical articulation, is not Hegelian because it denies the claim that the four types can be ordered valuationally, as worse or better realizations of that of which they are types. For Hegel the sequence from the Oriental to the Germanic type of culture is both historically necessary and, in terms of the development of Spirit, progressive. The Germanic world completes and fulfills the undeveloped potentialities found in the Chinese and Indian worlds. In contrast, a typal sequence such as I have been describing would traverse difference but not stages in a progression toward ideal realization. The kind of philosophy of history of which Hegel's is an example is, as I will argue in the next section, a misuse of the typology of worldviews.

Let us confine a philosophy of history, therefore, to the analysis of the rise and fall of any given society. That cycle, for both Spengler and Toynbee, is initially progressive but ultimately regressive. According to Spengler,[11] it is a movement from culture which is vital, dynamic, creative, organic to civilization which is rigid, mechanical, repetitive. According to Toynbee,[12] the phases of a society during genesis and growth are the work of a creative minority and a majority eagerly mimicking its dynamic leadership, but breakdown and disintegration overtake the society when *mimesis* is lost and creative leadership becomes mere domination.

Spengler sees the sequence of societal development as rigidly necessary. From the vitality of its cultural phases to the rigidity of its civilizational phases, every ethneme traverses a sequence that is as inexorable as the biological development of an individual. Indeed birth and death are not metaphors; they apply to societies quite literally. The trajectory followed by each ethneme is identical, but the way of that following is distinctively individuated. The Apollonian, the Magian, the Faustian, and each of the other dozen identified culture-civilizations is a unique realization of one of the typal patterns, each as varied as the flowers of the field and as serendipitous.

For Toynbee the developmental sequence is not necessary, but it is natural and therefore normal. Nor is the shift from earlier to later stages necessarily one of growth followed by decline. The challenges resulting in societal genesis set new challenges. Insofar as the response to these successive challenges is successful, they become increasingly "ethereal," resulting in greater complexity and subtlety of social order and hence profounder opportunities for human fulfillment. Nothing would prevent the sequence from culminating in a worldwide order, a truly global human community characterized by harmonies and realized potentialities commensurate with the best of the ideals of the higher religions. But Toynbee's vision is nonetheless tragically beclouded, for the responses to challenges can be inadequate and, given the sinfulness of human purpose, have so far always been thus. And so the progressive movement of a civilization eventually stumbles, usually over the level-3 problem of integrating specialized institutions into a greater totality. Coercive action is then resorted to and Toynbee's societies are transformed into Spengler's. The owl of historical resignation stirs once more.

In the sense these sketchy comments imply, I would thus claim that history is the moving image of typology, the result of mapping the logical onto the actual. To deploy an abstract structure as a hermeneutic for interpreting the flux of human events yields a developmental narrative. Logical alternatives become historical stages. The type is tensed as it is brought into the context of purposes and their realizations.

What from the perspective of formal structure is a typology is from the perspective of developmental concreteness a history. Each is what the other is but under a different perspectival interpretation. Historical content is as meaningful as typological formality. The two are differing realizations of a truth that is fully but not exclusively grasped by each.

IV

[1]

Typological structure and developmental stages are susceptible to a specific kind of error: transposing types. I mean by this the act of substituting a typal level or stage appropriate to one type for the parallel level or stage of another type. A worldview appropriate to a culture's historical situation, drawing from and anticipating other phases and fully exposited across the spectrum of its constituent activities, has meaning. That is, it satisfies the definitional criteria for a worldview: it must be coherent and consistent, adequate to experience, and valuationally ordered. Typal transposition does logical violence to these criteria, so that the result is an ersatz worldview, a conceptual illusion. The result historically is a social enormity, a distortion of the cultural fabric in ways no longer conducive to meaningful human existence.

Let me illustrate by examining briefly the notion of eschatology, the belief that history has a *telos*, that it will end in the actualization of a concrete perfected order of things, the ideal realized in history or through the overcoming of history. My purpose in what follows is to sketch the reasons why eschatological belief should be understood as an illusion and its historical realization an enormity.

The time-belief appropriate to normative reflection, i.e., to the level-4 exposition of any type, is what Brumbaugh calls, in terms of the grammatical verb tense to which it gives prominence, a "present eternal" orientation. The concerns of such a perspective have to do with conditions for judgement, especially ultimate judgements of intrinsic worth and unconditional significance, beliefs regarding the place of things within a landscape of meaning that is without horizon. In originative and expansive phases of culture, in the youth and maturity of an individual, this dimension of ultimacy is crucial. It sets present activity into a wider perspective, dampening the prideful consequences of success and providing a crucial framework of political legitimacy and personal vocation. But in the autumn of an individual's life, in the fading of a culture's viability, such reflection can come to dominate the character of the whole type. And there is a worldview, the fourth of the types identified by my Brumbaughian analysis, which takes this perspective as its essential defining characteristic, which throughout its expository range, which from origin to dissolution, gives primacy to the present eternal. This "Platonic" view of things differs from the other types not by its belief in transcendent norms, for all types give some sense to this belief, but rather by its claim that such norms are the foundation for all else, that the really real is immune to change and division, that the becoming and perishing of the many things of the world find their ground in a timeless One.

There is a worldview, in short, in which it is true to say that all things perish, that whatever comes to be must in due course cease to be, and that nonetheless the reality of those things is not exhausted by this melancholy fact. This sensibility insists that we recognize that there is an enduring significance to the real which allows us to separate the flux of these brief achievements into good ones and evil, into beautiful ones and horrible, into the sheep and the goats. From this perspective it is the instruments for such assessment, the norms that guide, that are primary whereas all else is derivative. For without a clear recognition of worth and without the assurance that such worth is immune from our desires regarding it, duty would have no meaning and suffering no justification. And hence life itself would be without significance. In this sense is it true that truth is eternal, that it only is without qualification real?

Now import this sense of things into the second type of worldview, one that gives primacy to becoming and perishing, that is tensed "future progressive" because it understands becoming as the constant transformation of possible futures into present reality, understands perishing as the condition for and ground of that transformative activity. A conceptual tension results from this importation: a belief in the primacy of the creative advance and at the same time a belief in the primacy of permanent norms. Change is thought to be fundamental but so also changelessness. The obvious way to blend this duality into a coherent utility is to give the creative advance a destination, change an endpoint, in the realization of changeless value. This miscegenated time-belief is what eschatology is all about.

From a point of view where achievement is central, timeless norms are interpreted differently than from a perspective where perfective completeness is central. They are seen as themselves achievements. They are understood to be abstractions from the prodigious creativeness of the world's entities, abstractions that capture the central tendencies in the menagerie of entrepreneurial realization that constitutes the continual advance from a settled past into an open future. Norms are summative and as such can be usefully taken as regulative for future efforts. But only as long as the violation of the norms is understood to be the life-blood of originality, of refreshment, novelty, improvement. Indeed the contrast of summative norm and individual accomplishment is what gives art its value, our experience of it the intensity we find fulfilling and liberating.

Insist, now, in contrast to this, that norms are constitutive principles for creation, that they are discovered not invented, that they are not to be transgressed, that to deviate from the norm is to go astray, to devolve. And locate these inflexible norms within the flux of things as formal necessities for realization. Creativity so canalized is turned into an instrument for the becoming of the ideal, for the historical manifestation of what is perfect, for the attainment of the concrete universal. The realm of change is not to be denigrated as such, for were it merely illusion, then its work would be of no significance. On the contrary: the work of historical change is taken to be of monumental significance for it is the bringing to be of the changeless. Utopia is not no-place but rather some place very specific; it is located at the endpoint of the process now going on, its culmination. Utopia is the place where history comes to an end and the negativities consequent upon the struggle for existence and its fragile attainments are swallowed up in ideal finality.

This combination of the primacies, of a type-4 sense of normativeness and a type-2 sense of historical transition, yields an apocalyptic eschatology. An apocalypticist believes that the historical process necessarily culminates in utopia. The process could be progressively upward and onward, the transition from imperfect to perfect smooth and predictable. Or it could be dramatic, a radical intrusion into what until the denouement could only be called a meander of achievment. The predictions of the Biblical *Book of Daniel* are an instance of the latter; Joachim of Flora's three ages, an example of the former. What they share in common is the belief that human effort will have no effect upon the process, neither to hurry it up nor to prevent it. Daniel exhorts us to be true to the faith so that we might be among those who will profit by the coming of the Ancient of Days; but if we are not true to it the Kingdom will come nonetheless, despite us and to our eternal regret.

Although for apocalypticism creative advance and eternal norm are both primacies, the changing is under the control of the changeless, its instrument. The primacy of change makes the process leading to the realization of changelessness real, but the primacy of changelessness is what assures that it will happen. The creative advance is therefore washed free of significant contingency in order for it to fulfill its proper destiny. It must forsake being creative in order to be an advance that arrives at its ultimate destination, but it remains nonetheless an arena of real, relevant accomplishment, the place where ideality is made also actual.

But if a type-2 worldview is the host for this miscegenation, if type-4 normativeness is the import, then it is unlikely that a belief in the openness of the creative advance will be so easily abandoned. The contingency, plurality, novelty inherent in the notion of continual creation, perishing, and recreation will constrain the claim of ideality that its realization be necessary. The endpoint will be treated as a real possibility but its attainment not guaranteed. Type-4 normativeness will have transformed the ideal into an endpoint, no longer treating norms as only criteria by which to measure achievement as better or worse. But it will be an end hoped for although not assured, a prophecy but not a prediction.

This leads to adding a third primacy to the mix, one that takes the management of possibility as crucial to any goal of totalized accomplishment. For there is a legitimate way of seeing the world in which coordination is primary, in which the problem of divergent creative effort is thought to be the greatest challenge confronting societies and in which unification of that variety within a system is proposed as the best solution to that challenge. The practical value of system-building is that it prevents creativity from giving too much glory to the individual who is, after all, the sole source of any achievement. A system is a way to distribute the results of these individual achievements in a manner that benefits the whole society optimally. It is only fair and just that such distributive concerns be given their due, since it is the social totality that provides the conditions for individual achievement; the totality should therefore be the primary determinant of how that achievement ought to be used. The whole is more important than the parts in that it is the context that makes their existence and their enhanced realizations possible.

This third-level aspect dominates the type-3 worldview we have called "Aristotelian." If that strong version of the expositional level is now imported into a worldview dominated by the double primacy of apocalypticism, the result is revolutionary eschatology. Practical reason no longer serves the pragmatic purposes of individuals trying to prioritize their own varied interests or the political machinations of governments trying to balance the demands of varied, conflicting constituencies. Now practical reason is seen as serving ultimate reality, as being a proper servant of the ideal. For the ultimate ought surely to be realized in history if it is realizable. Within the perspective of revolutionary eschatology, the world of becoming and perishing is taken as capable of being transformed into the world of ultimates. So those possessed of the ability to effect this transition, to oganize human mind and muscle for the reshaping of history, have that task as their duty, their sacred vocation, their necessity.

Of such an amalgam of time-senses is a revolutionary ideology constructed, and those who believe such a witches' brew cannot but be expected to be its fanatical advocates. When the end of an action is the actualization of unqualified normativeness, all lesser ends – and all other ends are by definition thereby lesser – pale into insignificance. The management of the coming of the eschaton is the ultimate task of leadership, the bureaucratization of the Kingdom of God the highest expression of statecraft. It is a vocation marvelously appropriate to the "present progressive" perspective, indeed its ultimate expression.

It is not beyond the miscegenic capacities of human world-making to imagine introducing the last of the four typal primacies as well. Call to mind the first-level expositional perspective, the one concerned with the habits and familiarities of quotidian existence, the sense of commonality among individuals and between them and a past not so much known as felt, a past taken as the shrouded but ineluctable identity of one's culture and all that is important in the universe. Now permit this sensibility to slip into the eschatological mosaic in the form it would have under its primary type-1 interpretation. The result is twofold: First, ultimate norms are clothed with a penumbra of affective intensity that robs them of their critical reflexivity. Although remaining criteria for the judgement of beliefs, practices, and systems, they are no longer rationally perceived, no longer themselves tested at the bar of clarity and distinctness. They are believed blindly and not by reason of their capacity to provide the kind of rational justifications for belief that can withstand the continual assault of skepticism. And second, the yoking of affective belief and ultimate norms as coequal primacies yokes the traditional practices of a people with eternality. Utopia is then felt to be not only a future ideal but also a national destiny. Eschatology has reached its apotheosis in nationalistic and/or religious fanaticism: mandated by the very nature of things to turn the world upside down for God and country, *Gut und Blut*, destiny and dynasty.

Eschatology in its full realization is thus this terrible mistake, an illusory belief, an historical enormity. It is an error in every sense. [3] It binds typally distinct time-senses together incoherently, claiming simultaneous primacy for what can only be realized separately. [2] This blurred vision of things is disorienting, blinding effective action, turning the end of social order into something else than an instrument for commonweal, and as a consequence visiting death, degradation, unnecessary suffering, injustice on the human race. [1] By such horrors are a people cut off from the basic securities and orienting importance that give meaning to their lives, hope to their endeavors. [4] And so the consequences of eschatological belief and practice is the despair that signals a sense of having lost contact irretrievably with what is ultimately significant.

One of the tasks of philosophy, [3] at the ethnolevel where individual theorizing goes on as a proper cultural manifestation is to provide a critique of social enormity and illusion, so as thereby [2] to contribute to the healing of the fragmented sociality of one's community, this for the sake of [1] the better realization of everyone's happiness and [4] the reaffirmation of the ultimate value of the human enterprise as such.

V

[4]

Those who have remained attentive to the architectonic of this essay will have raised an eyebrow over a strategy that has been working down rather than up the divided line, and that has simply omitted a section relating to the noetic level. I have dealt with typology, development, and illusion, with time's structures, the pattern of historical change, and the pathology of the eschatological imagination. But where in this essay is the unification by means of normative assessment that I have been repeatedly claiming as one of the necessarily tetradic dimensions of type and typal exposition, ethneme and ethnemic exposition?

The answer lies in realizing what the fourth dimension of a Brumbaughian methodology is all about. An activity articulates a standpoint, from which other activities can be construed. So a member of a society, who is a constituent aspect of an ethnemic realization, acts in a context of other kinds of activities to which he or she relates. At the ethnolevel of theorizing, which is my standpoint in developing this essay, the other levels of activity – habit, invention, assessment – can be appreciated for their relevance and instrinsic worth. But this appreciation by definition is from the viewpoint of one who is theorizing. The other kinds of activity are therefore realities-for-theory; they appear as elements within a philosophic essay. They would appear differently were my standpoint more concrete, my purposes pragmatically inventive or directed toward routinized outcomes, or were my standpoint more abstract, my purposes assessive and normative.

Within this theoretizing standpoint, I can likewise perceive the place of my activity as contributing to the life of my society at this stage in its development. I can appreciate what it would be like to be theorizing at another historical moment rather than at this time when cultural coherence seems so much the victim of iconoclastic individualism, national divisiveness, and the balance of terror anarchy of international politics. I can also appreciate what it would be like to be theorizing in another culture, a contemporary of my own, or one long past, or one not yet arisen onto the stage of history. But my appreciating is always from this present standpoint, afflicted by its limitations and made potent by its virtues.

This situated theorizing of mine has proposed a fourfoldness to its task. One was to display a typology of the logically possible worldviews and their associated time-beliefs. This was the work of my first section. A further task was to develop a philosophy of history, a genetic analysis of the arising and perishing of worldviews. My second section sketched the crude outlines of such an endeavor. Another task was to show the ways by which worldviews can be imaginatively combined, pulled and pushed into shapes that have no realizable viability but which satisfy us as playful inventions by means of which we escape reality and through which our more practical imaginings are refreshed and stimulated. The third section of my essay illustrated this kind of theorizing by undertaking a critique of eschatological mythmaking.

The fourth of my theorizing tasks is normative. But this cannot be accomplished by crafting a fourth section to this essay. For normativeness at the level of philosophic prose-making is exhibited not by making still more prose. It is deployed in the choices I made, in my decision to write these particular words rather than others, my wish to use Brumbaugh's ideas to mentor my own, my puckish desire to construct my arguments in the same Chinese-box manner that characterizes the topic they articulate. That is, my fourth task is integrative of the other three, the creation of a whole which harmonizes its parts, gives them an integrity and an import they would not have separately. This dimension of essay-writing can be shown but it cannot be put onto paper, because to write down what I am doing would be [3] to categorize my efforts in some manner or [2] to tell the story of how they came about or [1] to convey my feelings about how important, interesting, satisfying the undertaking has been. But each of these efforts transmutes the act of unifying back into one of the elements to be unified.

Hence there cannot be a fourth part to this essay, despite the numeral '4' that appeared in brackets back a page or two. In the same way, the unity of [3] this completed theorizing essay with [2] the *kairos* and *chronos* of its writing, and with [1] the respect for Brumbaugh and the memories of his influence that motivated it, is no fourth thing in addition to the motivation, the theorizing, and the productive laboring. And yet that unity of my efforts exists as a single enterprise with its own distinctive virtues and vices, known through but not reducible to the perspectives by which it was constituted. It is this totality that I offer now in honor of Robert Brumbaugh.

NOTES

1. Robert S. Brumbaugh, *Unreality and Time* (Albany: SUNY Press, 1984), 11-13. I usually have this book in mind when I am making claims about Brumbaugh's views, but his general position is amply evidenced across all his writings and, for his students, remembered from every class.
2. Brumbaugh, chapter 6, concerns itself with Robert Hartman, *The Structure of Value* (Carbondale: SIU Press, 1967). I adapt Hartman's distinctions between systemic, extrinsic, and intrinsic value, and his notion of the extension of a value versus its definition. I apply these concepts to a typology of worldviews whereas Hartman utilized them in constructing an axiology: the science of value which he argues needs to replace all current philosophies of value.
3. Brumbaugh, 108. The matrix that is reproduced next appears on p. 111.
4. Please excuse the hasty dismissal of these additional four worldviews. A full justification is the task of another kind of paper. I simply want to assert the need to begin the typology with three paired criteria rather than two, even if my defense of the results of doing so is only promissory.

5. Thomas W. Overhold and J. Baird Callicott, *Clothed-In-Fur and Other Tales: An Introduction to an Ojibwa World View* (Lanham, MD: University Press of America, 1982). "Ethnometaphysics may be understood as a subdiscipline of philosophy (related to metaphysics as ethnohistory is to history) concerned with the exploration and analysis of the conceptual structures of different cultures" (p. xi).

6. Brumbaugh, 125: "There are exactly four types of philosophic system which recur throughout history .... All four system types have remained viable because all four work: each is confirmable."

7. Brumbaugh, 131.

8. Brumbaugh, 111. As is indicated in what follows, my schema combines math and theoretical science with applied science at level-3, in order to make room at level-4 for the sciences of normative measure, and it extends technology in the direction not of science but of craft.

9. This definition of a group or society by reference to what it is not finds classical expression in Henri Bergson, *The Two Sources of Morality and Religion*, trans. R. Ashley Audra and Cloudesley Brereton, with the assistance of W. Horsfall Carter (London: Macmillan, 1935); and, more recently, in Jean-Paul Sartre, *Critique of Dialectical Reason* (Atlantic Highlands, New Jersey: Humanities Press, 1976).

10. G.W.F. Hegel, *The Philosophy of History* (New York: Dover Publications, 1956). This straightforward interpretation is much disputed, however. For instance, Gillian Rose, *Hegel Contra Sociology* (New Jersey: Humanities Press, 1981).

11. Oswald Spengler, *The Decline of the West*, trans. C.F. Atkinson (London: n.p., 1932).

12. Arnold J. Toynbee, *A Study of History*, 12 vols. (Oxford: Oxford University Press, 1934-1961).

9

TIME, FREE WILL, AND BRUMBAUGH IN KANTIAN EPISTEMOLOGY

Manley Thompson

I

Whatever aspect of philosophy Professor Brumbaugh is discussing, he is almost sure sooner or later to be discussing aspects of time. At a metaphilosophical level, when he begins with the thesis "that there are exactly four types of philosophical systems which recur throughout history," he adds parenthetically three sentences later: "These are four aspects of time, each with its own appropriate logic, which match the four families of systems."[1] At a philosophical level, when he turns to the issue of ethical freedom versus scientific determinism, he begins with the difference that "scientific statements are verifiable and meaningful only with reference to past, ethical to present, 'tenses.'" His next sentence is: "'Aspect' might be a better word than tense here, since it is evident that scientists make predictions and ethicists discuss past decisions.'"[2]

In this paper I want to consider time in the context of Kantian epistemology and to contrast an aspect it has in this context with aspects Brumbaugh attributes to it. The aspect I will focus on is the role Kant assigns to time as a necessary formal condition of our knowledge of objective reality. This role is essential to Kant's argument that causal necessity holds universally for objects of possible experience, and it is just necessity that underlies the scientific determinism which stands in apparent opposition to ethical freedom in Kant's antinomy of determinism and free will. In remarks on this opposition, immediately preceding those quoted above, Brumbaugh notes that with the advance of the social sciences, a "legal psychology which talks about 'a corrupt will' will run the risk of being dismissed as an 'unscientific anachronism,' and jurisprudence will be replaced by sociology." He adds that "Kant had the correct diagnosis of this effect. Since science is possible only by presupposing unbroken and determined lines of cause and effect, a genuine incoherence of the phenomenal order cannot be imagined or observed. A free agent could never recognize himself in this mirror of the phenomenal order."[3] One may object that surely Kant did not hold that a genuine incoherence in the phenomenal order cannot be *imagined*, only that it cannot be observed. I will argue in defense of Brumbaugh's remark that when the role Kant assigns to time as a necessary formal condition of our knowledge of objective reality is taken into account and related to his view of the imagination, he would endorse the second clause in Brumbaugh's remark. I will make a few observations on how with this role assigned to time, we should understand Kant as holding that "science is possible only by presupposing unbroken and determined lines of cause and effect." I will urge that for this understanding we must turn finally to the regulative principles of reason Kant introduces in his Transcendental Dialectic. I will conclude with some remarks on how this understanding bears on Kant's resolution of the antinomy of determinism and free will and how his resolution contrasts with the one Brumbaugh favors. The arguments in Kant's Transcendental Analytic for causal necessity must be considered first, as without this necessity he has no basis from which to generate the antinomy. The direct arguments are those he gives in proving his Second Analogy of Experience, the principle that every change in an object of possible experience is the effect of a necessary antecedent condition.

II

Central to Kant's arguments for his Second Analogy[4] is his distinction between subjective and objective sequences of human perceptions. In his example, when we are observing a ship moving downstream, we perceive it successively at different positions along the steam. The order of our perceptions corresponds to the sucessive positions of the moving ship. We cannot observe it at a later position in its motion and then observe it at an earlier position because it is no longer observable at the earlier position when it has reached the later one. The order of our perceptions is therefore an objective sequence because it corresponds to the order in what we are observing. When, on the other hand, we are observing a house and look first at its roof and then at its basement, the sequence of our perceptions does not correspond to an order in what we are observing but rather to the order of our observations. We can observe its basement before its roof because the two coexist and either one can be observed before the other. The sequence of our perceptions in this case is subjective rather than objective.

Kant claims that if we accept this distinction between subjective and objective sequences of perceptions, we must understand the successive perceptions in an objective sequence as corresponding to a causal order in what is observed. I may look first at the roof of a house when I hear someone cry, "Look at that roof!" I may then subsequently look at the basement and regard the order of my perceptions as causally determined, as I may claim the person's cry caused me to look first at the roof. But in this case I do not regard the order of my perceptions as corresponding to a causal order in what I am observing, the house. I regard their order rather as corresponding to a causal order in my observations. The sequence of my perceptions is not made objective by the fact that I looked first at the roof, not because of my own free choice, but because I was caused to do so by reflex action in response to the person's cry. The sequence remains subjective because the causal order, whether the cause is free choice or reflex action, is an order in my observations and not in what I observe. If the cry had been "Look at that basement!" the order of my perceptions would probably have been reversed, but what I observed, the house, would remain unchanged. On the other hand, when I observe a ship moving downstream, my perceptions of the ship's positions relative to the banks of the steam correspond to an order causally determined by forces acting on the ship and are independent of any forces acting on me that determine where I look. If for any reason I look back at a place the ship has vacated, my perception is no longer in the sequence of perceptions that constitute my observation of the moving ship. The sequence of these perceptions is objective.

In claiming that we must understand the perceptions in an objective sequence as corresponding to a causal order in what is observed, Kant is not claiming that our observation is necessarily sufficient to determine what is the cause. Although we understand the ship's moving from A to B as causally necessitated, we do not regard its merely being at A as the cause of its moving to B. The cause is some force acting on the ship, such as the current of the stream or the wind in the ship's sails. In order to determine the cause we need to observe more than just successive positions of the ship as it moves downstream. With further observations we may or may not succeed in determining the cause. If we find that the current and the wind are too weak and that the ship is without a motor, we may be at a loss to determine fully the cause of its motion. We may entertain the hypothesis that some yet undetected force, perhaps some sort of cosmic ray, is acting on the ship, although this hypothesis is worthless unless we have observations besides those giving the successive positions of the ship that attest to the presence of such a force. But while our determination of the cause is thus always *a posteriori*, we know *a priori*, and therefore as a necessary truth, according to Kant, that the perceptions in an objective sequence correspond to a causal order in what is observed. We know it *a priori* because our knowledge in this case is simply knowledge of how we understand the order of our perceptions when we recognize their sequence as objective. To know that the order always corresponds to a causal order in what is observed is by no means the same as to know what, in any particular case, is the cause.

This claim to *a priori* knowledge seems open to the objection that it conflates a conceptual necessity determined by our understanding of the order of perceptions in an objective sequence and a causal necessity determined in what is observed. The objection has been stated forcefully by P.F. Strawson and I will begin with his statement. I will then urge that the Kantian reply to the objection depends on the role Kant assigns to time as a necessary formal condition of our knowledge of objective reality.

III

According to Strawson, Kant argues from (1) if I am perceiving an object changing its states (e.g. a moving ship changing its positions relative to the banks of a stream), then my perception of the object in an earlier state A precedes my perception of it in a later state B, to (2) the object is causally determined to pass from state A to state B. The argument, Strawson says, "proceeds by a *non sequitur* of numbing grossness," for it proceeds "by substituting one type of necessity for another."[5]

The necessity in (1) is the conceptual necessity of an analytic statement. (1) becomes analytic when perception is understood as entailing that a later cannot be perceived before an earlier change and qualifications are added to insure this entailment, e.g., that the perception is via a single sense modality (we might see the object in state B before we hear it in state A), that light from the object in state A is not deflected so as to reach the perceiver after light from it in state B, etc. With these qualifications and with perception understood as indicated, the consequent in (1) follows with analytic necessity from the antecedent. Unless we construe (1) in this way as analytic, we have no basis for proclaiming it necessarily true. But we cannot construe (2) in this way. In order to have a basis for proclaiming (2) necessarily true we must assume the causal principle that every change in an object is the necessary effect of an antecedent cause. Yet this principle is just what Kant's argument is supposed to prove and not assume. In arguing from (1) to (2) Kant substitutes in (1) causal necessity for conceptual or analytic necessity and indeed commits a *non sequitur* of numbing grossness.

The Kantian reply to this objection begins with the denial that (1) is an analytic statement. In the context of Kantian epistemology perception is not understood as entailing that an earlier cannot be perceived before a later change. After the proofs for his Analogies of Experience, Kant presents an explanation of what he calls "The Postulate of Empirical Thought in General." In the course of this explanation he notes that we can conceive of our having "a special ultimate mental power of intuiting the future" (*eine besondre Grundkraft unseres Gemüts, das Küngftige zum voraus anzuschauen* (A 222/B 270). For example, we can think of our being able to perceive changes located in time as we perceive points on a line representing time; so that we can perceive a later change before we look back along the line and perceive an earlier change.[6] Although this thought, Kant says, is "indeed free from contradiction," with it we "can make no claim to objective reality." If we made such a claim we would recognize no condition on our abilty to perceive objective reality except freedom from contradiction. We would ignore the epistemic condition the temporal form of our sensibility imposes on our ability to perceive objective reality. This epistemic condition on our sensibility, and not any logical constraint on our thought, determines that we cannot perceive a later before an earlier change. As fitted to Kant's argument, (1) is a synthetic *a priori* judgement proclaiming an epistemic condition on human perception of objective reality – synthetic because we can conceive of perception being otherwise and *a priori* because of the role Kant assigns to time as a necessary formal condition of our knowledge of objective reality.

When we reason that because we cannot perceive a later before an earlier change, therefore the order in an objective sequence of perceptions corresponds to a causal order in what we are observing, we are not substituting causal for conceptual necessity if we accept the epistemic role Kant assigns to time. With this role the necessity in our premise is not conceptual. Time does not place a condition on how we can think of our perceiving objective reality, but only on how we can actually perceive it. But now if the necessity in the premise is not conceptual, does it provide any basis for the conclusion that there is causal necessity in what we are observing? Kant's affirmative answer depends on his "Copernican revolution in philosophy," which proclaims that objects of the senses "must conform to the constitution of our faculty of intuition," i.e., our sensibility (B xvii). With this revolution, the reason we cannot perceive (have presented to us in intuition) a later before an earlier change is not that our perceptions must conform to the constitution of a changing object, but rather that since a perceived object must conform to the consitution of our faculty of intuition, all changes in the object must be perceived, in accord with the form of our intuition, successively in time. That we cannot perceive a later before we perceive an earlier change is then a basis for the conclusion that in the object a later cannot precede an earlier effect. The causal order of changes in the object must conform to the temporal order of our perceptions. The necessity of this conformity to the condition on our perceptions, and not anything we can discern in the object apart from this condition, is the *a priori* ground of causal necessity in the object. Kant's argument, then, is not a *non sequitur* given the role he assigns to time in his epistemology with his Copernican revolution.[7]

IV

Accepting this interpretation of Kant's argument, I want to return to Brumbaugh's remark that according to Kant "a genuine incoherence of the phenomenal order cannot be imagined or observed." I take it that the perception of a later before an earlier change would indeed be such an incoherence, and yet we have seen that according to Kant we can think of this incoherence without contradicting ourselves. But if we can think of it, why can't we imagine it? We can represent time, Kant says, only "under the image of a line" (B 156), and we therefore can represent a sequence of changes only by a sequence of points on the line, equating "is later than" with "is to the right of" or "is to the left of." But then surely we can imagine ourselves looking ahead along the line so that we perceive a later before an earlier change. Why aren't we then imagining a genuine incoherence in the phenomenal order?

Kant's reply, as I read him, has two parts. In the first place, a straight line does not represent time itself, but only an analogue of time. Although "we reason from the properties of this line to all the properties of time," there is the "exception, that while the parts of the line are simultaneous the parts of time are successive" (A 33/B 50). In perceiving successively points already marked on a line we are not perceiving changes occurring in time any more than we are when we perceive successively the roof and basement of a house. In both cases, the sequence of our perceptions is only subjective and not objective. We are not, then, imagining the perception of a later before an earlier change when we picture ourselves looking ahead along a time line. But we are, one may retort, imagining what it would be like to perceive a later before an earlier change. If this does not constitute imagining a genuine incoherence in the phenomenal order, what does?

The second part of Kant's reply is that we cannot imagine a genuine incoherence without freeing our imagination from the condition on our perception imposed by the temporal form of our intuition. But in imagining ourselves looking ahead along a time line we have not freed our imagination from this condition. We have not imagined what it would be like to perceive a later before an earlier change, but only what it is like to perceive changes represented by points marked on a line rather than the changes themselves. Although we can think without contradiction of our being able to perceive changes themselves in the way that we perceive their representations on a line, to entertain the thought is not to imagine what it would be like to perceive changes in this way. Our imagination is limited by the condition on our perception imposed by the temporal form of our intuition, and whatever conforms to this condition is not a genuine incoherence in the phenomenal order. We can think (conceive of) but not imagine a genuine incoherence. Such a thought has only the "logical form of a concept (of thought) in general" and is different from anything we can imagine because it "is completely lacking in content" (A 239/B 298).

Brumbaugh's full remark is equivalent to the conditional that if "science is possible only by presupposing unbroken and determined lines of cause and effect," then "a genuine incoherence in the phenomenal order cannot be imagined or observed." A fuller and more accurate statement would be that Kant holds the antecedent because of the role he assigns to time in his epistemology, while he holds the consequent because of the way he relates this role to our ability to imagine as distinct from our ability merely to conceive or think. If the consequent were that even the thought of a genuine incoherence is itself incoherent, Kant would have no ground for the resolution he offers for the antinomy of determinism and free will.

His resolution rests on the claim that we can think without contradiction of one and the same phenomenon as the effect of two
distinct kinds of causality, a causality of natural and a causality of
freedom (A 558/B 586). The crucial difference between the two is
that the latter is the causality of a cause to which we can assign no
beginning in time. Every natural phenomenon is related to other
natural phenomena in an unbroken and detemined line of cause and
effect. It begins at just the time it does because it is determined to
do so by its antecendent causes, and it in turn determines its effects
to begin just when they do. If the phenomenon, however, is a
human action we judge to be performed freely, we take its cause to
be a choice made freely by the agent and not another natural
phenomenon acting on the agent. As such a cause has no place in an
unbroken line of cause and effect, we cannot assign it a beginning in
time by taking it as the effect of an antecedent cause. Yet since it
has as its effect a natural phenomenon, a human action, this effect
must have a beginning in time; and we can assign it a beginning only
by placing it in an unbroken line of cause and effect. But we then
take one and the same phenomenon, a human action, to be both
determined and not determined by natural causes. We can resolve
the antinomy only if we can think coherently of this phenomenon as
the effect of two distinct kinds of causality.

The perception of an action that has no beginning in time is just
as much an incoherence in the phenomenal order as the perception
of a later before an earlier change. In both cases reference to
temporal order is given with a condition that makes nonsense of this
order. But if, as Kant holds, this order is simply a condition on our
perception imposed by the temporal form of our intuition, and if as
such it limits only what we can imagine as opposed to what we can
think, then we can resolve the antinomy. Every natural phenomenon,
according to Kant, has both an "empirical character (as a mode of
sense)" and "an intelligible character (as a mode of thought" (A
551/B 579). Since time as a form of our sensibility is a necessary
formal condition of our knowledge of objective reality, we can know
phenomena only in their empirical character and therefore only as
determined by natural causality. But we can think of them in their
intelligible character as effects of the causality of freedom, or as
Kant also calls it, "the causality of reason," which "in its intelligible
character, does not in producing an effect, *arise* or begin to be at a
certain time" (A 551/B 579). There is thus no reference to temporal
order when we think of phenomena as effects of free choice. We
never perceive the intelligible character, and in *thinking* a phenom-

enon solely with reference to its intelligible character we are not *imagining* an incoherence in the phenomenal order. With this distinction between empirical and intelligible character we resolve the antinomy of determinism and free will.

But this resolution is open to two related objections. In the first place, it seems to preclude our ever knowing freedom as an objective reality. If time is a necessary formal condition of our knowledge of objective reality, and if we abjure all reference to temporal order when we think of phenomena as effects of free choice, we likewise seem to abjure all claims to knowledge of freedom as an objective reality. Brumbaugh understands Kant as replying to this objection simply by distinguishing "levels of reality."[8] Although we can never know the reality of freedom at the phenomenal level, we can know it at the noumenal level as a product of our reason.

Yet if this is the whole of Kant's reply, his resolution of the antimony remains open to a second serious objection. If every natural phenomenon has both an empirical and an intelligible character, it has reality at both levels and is therefore at the noumenal level really an effect of the causality of freedom. But then, as Lewis Beck has put it, Kant's resolution "seems to justify the concept of freedom, if anywhere, then everywhere"; every natural phenomenon at the noumenal level is an effect of the causality of freedom, and this "is not what is meant by freedom in any interesting sense, because it is indiscriminately universal."[9] Beck goes on to quote a passage from the *Critique of Pure Reason* that indicates the sort of answer Kant has to this second objection.

> In lifeless, or merely animal nature, we find no grounds for thinking that any faculty is conditioned otherwise than in a merely sensible [mechanical, phenomenal] manner. Man, however, who knows all the rest of nature solely through the senses, knows himself also through pure apperception, and this indeed in acts and inner determinations which he cannot regard as impressions of the senses (A 546/B 574; the bracketed words are Beck's).

We thus have a knowledge of ourselves as rational agents that distinguishes human actions from other natural phenomena. Self-knowledge is the cornerstone of Kant's entire critical philosophy with its Copernican revolution. We cannot hold that the objects of our senses must conform to the constitution of our faculty of intuition if we cannot determine this constitution through a form of self-knowledge distinct from our knowledge of objects. Likewise in the moral sphere we cannot hold that human actions as distinct from other natural phenomena must conform to our thought of them in their intelligible character, if we cannot know this character through a form of self-knowledge distinct from our knowledge of other natural phenomena in their intelligible character. With this self-knowledge, the role of time as a necessary formal condition of our knowledge of objective reality is limited to the theoretical sphere. In the moral sphere, although we abjure reference to temporal order in our thought of human actions as effects of freedom,[10] we still have grounds for holding that in this thought we do not abjure reference to a necessary formal condition of moral reality. But then Kant's concept of freedom is not indiscriminately universal; it presupposes no claim to knowledge of noumenal reality except in the moral sphere.

Kant's resolution of the antinomy, then, involves considerably more than distinguishing levels of reality. Instead of looking for anything more in Kant, Brumbaugh turns to "the more satisfying explanation" that he believes emerges when we view the scientist and the ethicist under different "aspects" of time rather than levels of reality. I want to conclude with some remarks on the contrast between these two views of the antinomy.

V

In Brumbaugh's view the scientist and the ethicist consider events under different aspects of time. "It is not an accident, but is built into the logic of the situation, that the one finds only necessity in the future while the other claims to recognize freedom in the past." In predicting that an eclipse of the moon will occur at a certain time in the future, the scientist "is speaking from a standpoint still further future, thinking about the observations and data that will constitute the eclipse once it has become past." On the other hand, in discussing Socrates on trial, the ethicist "stands in the court with Socrates, in the aspect of a present moment where alternative options to be selected by a moral decision remain."[11]

From a Kantian perspective, a scientist in making a prediction presupposes more than merely that all natural phenomena occur in unbroken and determined lines of cause and effect. In accord with what we noted above in section II, to presuppose that the order of our perceptions in an objective sequence always corresponds to a causal order in what is observed is not the same as to presuppose that we can, in any particular case, know what is the cause. As scientific prediction rests on knowledge of particular causes, it is made with the presupposition not only that there are causes but also that at least some are knowable. Although a genuine incoherence in the phenomenal order can neither be imagined nor observed, it can, we have seen, be coherently thought. In his account of what he calls "regulative principles of reason," Kant pushes the thought of incoherence in another direction.

> If among the appearances which present themselves to us, there were so great a variety – I do not say in form, for in that respect the appearances might resemble one another [as they might still occur in a temporal order]; but in content, that is, in the manifoldness of the existing entities – that even the acutest human understanding could never by comparison of them detect the slightest similarity (a possibility which is quite conceivable), the logical law of genera would have no standing; we should not even have the concept of a genus, or indeed any other universal concept; and the understanding itself, which has to do solely with such concepts, would be non-existent (A 653-4/B 682-3).

Kant cannot counter the possibility of this incoherence with the claim of his Copernican revolution that objects of our senses must conform to the constitution of our faculty of intuition. This conformity determines only the form and not the content of our intuitions and does not affect the incoherence now in question. Even though we know *a priori* that appearances (natural phenomena) always occur under the form of unbroken and determined lines of cause and effect, when we make scientific predictions we must presuppose that appearances generally resemble each other in content sufficiently for us to group them into genera and species and to form particular causal laws in accord with the inductive principle that like causes have like effects. We must presuppose, in other words, what Kant calls "the systematic unity of nature." Although we have no ground for postulating this unity as "necessary, not only subjectively and logically, as method, but objectively also" (A 648/B 676), still, if we are to have a "sufficient criterion of empirical truth ... we have no option save to presuppose the systematic unity of nature as objectively valid and necessary" (A 651/B 679). But with this presupposition we have only a regulative principle of reason and not, as with

Kant's Second Analogy of Experience, a principle determining the formal constitution of experience (cf. A 664/B 692).

We thus cannot bring out fully the ultimate presuppositions of scientific predictions when we consider predictions only under an aspect of time, as we do when we stay only with the principle of Kant's Second Analogy. We must also consider predictions under an aspect of reason, as we do when we turn to the content as well as the form of experience. In this further consideration we are not concerned with an aspect of time. When we say that an effect of a certain sort requires a cause of a certain sort, we are not considering the causal relation under another aspect of time in addition to that which we express when we say that an effect cannot precede its cause. We are adding rationality to the temporality of the causal order, and our consideration is strictly atemporal. The claim with this addition is not that the objects of our senses must conform further to the constitution of our faculty of intuition, but that they must conform to the constitution of our faculty of reason. This additional claim has objective force as a regulative principle of reason determining the method of scientific inquiry and not as a principle determining the formal constitution of experience.

Regulative principles of reason in the theoretical sphere thus serve to counter the possibility of an incoherence in the phenomenal order that would keep us from knowing the causes of particular effects. A regulative principle does not proclaim that something is the case, but only that we must proceed as if it were. We must proceed in scientific inquiry as if nature were sufficiently uniform (like causes having like effects) to enable us to discover causes through inductive generalizations. The scientist in predicting a lunar eclipse assumes that antecdent conditions of past eclipses will resemble those of future eclipses and not merely that every eclipse is the necessary effect of some antecedent conditions.

In the practical or moral sphere, on the other hand, regulative principles of reason serve to counter the possibility, not of an incoherence in the phenomenal order, but of an incoherence in the thought of a causality of freedom as well as a causality of nature pertaining to one and the same object. While the behavioral scientist proceeds as if Socrates' actions were natural phenomena having causes in the phenomenal order that resemble the causes of like actions by other human subjects, the ethicist proceeds as if Socrates were a rational agent capable of initiating actions caused by free choice and not by antecedent phenomenal conditions. As Kant puts it succinctly, "in the case of practical principles, we have to proceed as if we had before us an object, not of the senses, but of the pure understanding" (A 685/B 713). The "as if" qualification removes incoherence from the thought that one and the same object is both determined and free. But the different regulative principles do not proclaim that the object is real at two distinct levels of reality. They proclaim only that in inquiry we have no option save to proceed as if we had the appropriate subject matter before us.

In dismissing Kant's resolution of the antinomy of determinism and freedom as based solely on a distinction in levels of reality and in turning to a resolution based on viewing scientist and ethicist under different aspects of time, Brumbaugh cannot account fully for the different presuppositions demanded by the two forms of inquiry. Although there are admittedly difficulties in the details of Kantian philosophy in working out a resolution based on regulative principles of reason,[12] it seems to me that any satisfactory resolution must take differences in subject matter, which are atemporal, as primary, rather than formal differences represented as different aspects of time. With different regulative principles it seems possible to accommodate differences in subject matter without dogmatic ontological principles proclaiming levels of reality.

"A cross-field logic," Brumbaugh suggests, "which takes account of differences in 'determinateness' may be able to give a perspicuous formal pattern that will be useful in diagnosis and inquiry."[13] He then presents a "class-calculus with tenses" that he believes comes close to achieving this purpose. Kant, in contrast, sees general logic as entirely without tenses. He rejects even the Aristotelian formulation of the principle of contradiction, that nothing can be and not be at the same time, in favor of the timeless formulation, "that no predicate contradictory of a thing can belong to it" (A 151-3/B 191-3). Temporal considerations enter only in epistemology or transcendental logic, which, in a transcendental analytic, purports to prove the principle that every natural phenomenon is the necessary effect of an antecedent condition, while in a transcendental dialectic it presents the consequent antinomy of determinism and free will and introduces regulative principles that make a resolution of the antinomy possible without ontological assumptions. If general logic in its articulation of the laws of thought were limited by temporal considerations, it might indeed be impossible not only to imagine or observe but even to think of a genuine incoherence in the phenomenal order, and a "cross-field logic" such as Brumbaugh envisions might be the only alternative to ontological assumptions for a resolution of the antinomy.

NOTES

1. R.S. Brumbaugh, "Systems, Tenses, and Choices," *Midwestern Journal of Philosophy*, (Spring, 1975): 9. Brumbaugh's views on types of philosophical systems and aspects of time are the subject of chapter 7 of his book, *Unreality and Time* (Albany, N.Y.: State University of New York Press, 1984).

2. R.S. Brumbaugh, "Logic and Time," *Review of Metaphysics*, 18(1965): 647-8. All subsequent page references for direct quotations from Brumbaugh are to this paper. As I am concerned throughout with Brumbaugh's interpretation of Kant, I quote only from this paper where he begins with a Kantian formulation of the problem of freedom versus determinism. I do not find a different interpretation of Kant suggested in his later works where he does not begin with a Kantian formulation of the problem.

3. Brumbaugh, "Logic and Time," 647.

4. The arguments I consider are in Kant, *Critique of Pure Reason*. trans. Norman Kemp Smith (London: 1929). All references to Kant are to this work. I follow the usual practice in giving references to the *Critique of Pure Reason*: A for the 1st ed. and B for the 2nd. The numbers are always page numbers in the respective editions. When only an A or only a B reference is given, the passage occurs only in that edition. The arguments I consider for the Second Analogy occur at A 191-3/B 236-8. When I depart from the Smith translation, I give the German in parentheses.

5. P.F. Strawson, *The Bounds of Sense* (London: Methuen, 1966), 137-8.

6. Kant does not give this example in the passage from which the quotation is taken, but simply contrasts intuiting the future with merely inferring it, as we have to do. Justification for introducing the example here emerges from further quotations I give below in section IV.

7. Cf. Lewis White Beck, *Essays on Kant and Hume*, (New Haven: Yale University Press, 1978), 147-53. Beck defends Kant against Strawson's criticism on the ground that the criticism is made from an ontological view that ignores the epistemic view that follows with Kant's Copernican revolution. But Beck does not relate the criticism to Strawson's claim that (1) is analytic.

8. Brumbaugh, "Logic and Time," 647.

9. Lewis White Beck, *A Commentary on Kant's Critique of Practical Reason* (Chicago: University of Chicago Press, 1960), 188-9.

10. This is not to say that our actions do not occur in a temporal order, but only that the free choices we make in deciding to act cannot be placed in a temporal order as necessary effects of antecedent causes.

11. Brumbaugh, "Logic and Time," 648.

12. Lewis Beck holds that such a resolution, which he is inclined to favor, "involves reading back into the Transcendental Analytic of the first *Critique* some of the conclusions of the Transcendental Dialectic. Specifically, it requires that the sharp distinction between constitutive category and regulative Idea be given up ... and that the Analogies of Experience ... be reinterpreted as regulative in the full sense of the Dialectic" (Beck, *Commentary*, 193). We would thus give up the sharp distinction I have emphasized between the causal principle derived from the role of time as a necessary formal condition of our knowledge of objective reality and the regulative principle that proclaims a systematic unity of nature. But if we blur the distinction between these two principles we cannot distinguish sharply between knowing *a priori* that every change has some cause and knowing *a priori*

that we can eventually discover its cause. We then leave Kant open to the criticism urged by Popper, that Kant's theory has "the unaviodable consequence that our quest for knowledge must necessarily succeed, which is clearly mistaken." (Karl R. Popper, *Conjectures and Refutations* (New York: Basic Books, 1962), 48.) I cannot argue the point here, but I do not think an appeal to regulative principles of reason in Kant's resolution of the antinomy necessitates an interpretation of the sort Beck proposes, which leaves Kant open to Popper's criticism.

13. Brumbaugh, "Logic and Time," 649; cf. Brumbaugh, *Unreality and Time*, chap 5.

10

SAINT AUGUSTINE AND CICERO'S DILEMMA

Brian Hendley

I

In 415 A.D., despite a heavy load of preaching, writing, and other ecclesiastical responsibilities, Augustine completed Book 5 of the *City of God*.[1] In it he returned to a topic he had dealt with before, most notably in his treatise *On Free Choice of the Will*,[2] the problem of reconciling God's foreknowledge with man's free will. In chapter 9 of Book 5 Augustine poses the problem in terms of what I shall call "Cicero's dilemma"; he then devotes the rest of chapters 9 and 10 to resolving it.

The dilemma is simply put: "if we choose foreknowledge of the future, freedom of the will is destroyed, and if we choose freedom of the will, foreknowledge of the future is excluded."[3] Cicero's solution was to deny foreknowledge in order to preserve free will. This is unacceptable to Augustine, who sees it as making men free by making them irreligious. He maintains that the Christian need have no fear in asserting both freedom and foreknowledge.

In this paper I shall summarize Augustine's formulation of the problem and his proposed solution. I begin with some preliminary remarks on foreknowledge, analyze Augustine's attempted solution of the problem, and end by indicating what I find wrong in his arguments and how I think he might have strengthened his case.

II

PRELIMINARY REMARKS ON FOREKNOWLEDGE

What does it mean to foreknow something? One interpretation would be that to foreknow is to know what will happen before it actually does. For example,[4] as I write this it is 4 P.M. on a sunny afternoon in July and I claim to know now that you will hurt your arm tonight. My claim cannot be corroborated now; its truth or falsity will be determined by what happens to you (and your arm) tonight. Suppose that you do hurt your arm tonight. Would you say that I had foreknown it, or rather that I had made an accurate prediction or a lucky guess? I would suspect that more than one corroborated claim would be necessary before anyone would grant that I really foreknew the future.

Perhaps what is lacking in the example is what Aristotle called knowledge of the reasoned fact, i.e., not merely knowing that such-and-such is the case, but knowing why, knowledge of the cause. Thus, my claim could be expanded to, "I know that you will hurt your arm tonight because you will play too much tennis." Notice that this is more than an admonition to the effect that *if* you play too much tennis tonight, you will hurt your arm. I claim to know now what will happen to you tonight and why. Again, suppose my claim is borne out; you do play too much tennis and hurt your arm. Am I entitled to say that I foreknew this?

There still may be other more plausible explanations of my corro-borated claim. I might know you and your habits quite well. You habitually play tennis on sunny evenings in July and there does not seem to be any reason to doubt that you will do so again tonight. A strong likelihood, yes, but this is far short of having knowledge of what will in fact happen. After the fact, I can explain what has happened to your arm ("too much tennis"); but does it make sense to say that I knew this before it happened? I submit that even granted an uncanny insight on my part into hard and fast habits on your part, we would still hesitate to say that I could know that you will hurt your arm tonight. Why?

For one thing, changeable creatures that we are, you might surprise us all and decide not to play tennis tonight after all. Or, less surprisingly, the weather might turn sour and you do not get a chance to play. You might play with your usual gusto, but suddenly come to your senses and stop before you hurt your arm. Your oppo-nent might be so good (or bad) that you do not get to play long or hard enough to hurt your arm. Then again your arm may have been sufficiently toughened by past matches that it does not sustain an injury. Or you might have finally purchased the racket of your dreams and thereby banished arm injuries forever. Obviously, I could go on listing reasons why you might not hurt your arm tonight. The point of the exercise is to show that there are too many circumstances for anyone, including yourself, to know now what will happen tonight.

It would follow from this that we can question the meaningfulness of any human claims to foreknowledge. According to our normal use of the word "knowledge," it is not something that someone can have before an event takes place. We may indeed be able to achieve a high degree of probability in our predictions or be reasonably certain of our explanations after the fact, but we cannot now know what will happen in the future. My example is meant to show that there are too many factors to take account of for such knowledge to be humanly possible.

This is not to take on the claims of soothsayers, diviners, mediums, fortune tellers, astrologers, and the like. Augustine himself makes some telling criticisms of them in the earlier chapters of Book 5. Religious prophets are a special case because they should more properly be evaluated as instances of human beings acting under divine influence and thus as pertinent to the question of what God can accomplish. The problem Augustine faces is that of reconciling God's foreknowledge with man's free will.

Divine Foreknowledge

Augustine seems to agree with my conclusion that human foreknowledge of the future does not make sense, but criticizes Cicero for striking out all foreknowledge of the future and thus denying the existence of God: "For it is a conspicuous act of madness both to agree that God exists and to deny his foreknowledge of the future" (*City*, 169). We Christians, he goes on to say, declare our belief in the existence of a supreme and true God who has a will, supreme power, and foreknowledge. We further declare that our acts of the will are free (*City*, 171).

The issue is thus joined by Augustine's declaration of Christian belief in God's foreknowledge and man's free will. It should be noted at the outset that the claim to foreknowledge under consideration differs in kind from my claim to know what will happen to you tonight. Here Augustine speaks of knowing all future events (*omnia futura*), which in turn implies knowing them in a determined order (*ordo rerum*) and knowing the order of preceeding efficient causes (*ordo causarum*). My example had to do with knowing one event and one of its causes. If that sort of knowledge before the event has been shown to be beyond human capabilities, surely Augustine's notion of foreknowledge can only be claimed for a divine being. This is why he criticizes Cicero for denying God's existence by denying foreknowledge.

The gist of my preliminary remarks was that claims to human foreknowledge make no sense. To say that "we sometimes foreknow the free decisions and actions of men" is really to mean that we can corroborate some of our claims about what will happen in the future. But this is not, without substantial further argument, identical to the claim that we knew an event before it took place. The formulation of the problem by Augustine in chapter 9 is in terms of a foreknowledge of all events and all their causes. It is this claim that brings out the full implications of Cicero's dilemma. If we grant such foreknowledge, then Cicero felt that "the whole basis of human life is overthrown: it is in vain that laws are made, that men employ reprimands and praise, denunciation and exhortation, and there is no justice in a system of rewards for the good and punishment for the bad" (*City*, 171). It was in order to avoid these sorts of disastrous consequences that Cicero denied divine foreknowledge. His dilemma results from being faced with two apparently incompatible choices: either all actions are foreknown by God and hence pre-determined, or they are not so foreknown because my actions are within my power and my will is free.

III

AUGUSTINE'S SOLUTION

Having presented us with such stark alternatives, Augustine proceeds in chapters 9 and 10 to resolve the dilemma. Rather than a single, clear-cut response, he provides us with a series of short, overlapping answers. I shall evaluate these under three separate headings, though it should be recognized that the answers are not mutually exclusive.

1. Christian Faith

One would expect the Bishop of Hippo to take a religious stand on this issue, and indeed Augustine tells us that the God-fearing mind accepts and supports foreknowledge and free will out of a feeling of religious loyalty (*fide pietatis, City*, 173). Whatever the outcome of the debates and disputes of the philosophers, Augustine reminds his fellow Christians that they can believe in God's foreknowledge, while having no fear that their acts of will are not free. He criticizes Cicero for his "rash assertions, blasphemous and irreligious as they may be," and contrasts them to the steadfastness with which "we Christians declare both that God knows all things before they happen *[Deum dicimus omnia scire antequam fiant]*, and that it is by our own free will that we act, whenever we feel and know that a thing is done by us of our own volition" (*City*, 174-5). He further instructs Christians "with faith and trust" (*fideliter et veraciter*) to assert the compatibility of foreknowledge and free will, since "the former is required for correct belief, the latter for right living. And there is no right living if there is no correct belief in God" (*City*, 187).

One could rightly charge Augustine here with begging the philosophical question by taking refuge in appeals to the Christian faith. He seems to admit that "we Christians" must believe that the dilemma is resolvable, even though we don't know how to resolve it. It is surely tempting for a Christian to beg off the question altogether and rely on God's having revealed to us that He has foreknowledge and that we have free will. It could be added, however, that this appeal to faith does not prevent Augustine from proposing other answers to the problem.

2. Freedom Because of Foreknowledge

Having made his appeal to faith, Augustine goes on to suggest that Cicero's dilemma can be resolved by a kind of merger of its supposedly incompatible parts. He argues that man must be free since God foreknows him to be. God's foreknowledge of future events entails His knowing the entire order of underlying causes. But our acts of will are part of this order of causes. Therefore, they are determined to be free since that's the way God foreknows them. Here is how Augustine puts it: "For in fact, our wills also are included in the pattern of causation *[in causarum ordine]* certainly known to God and embraced in his foreknowledge. For the wills of men are among the causes of the deeds of men, and so he who foresaw the causes of all things *[omnes rerum causas]* cannot have been ignorant of our wills among those causes, since he foresaw that these wills are the causes of our deeds" (*City*, 177).

Later in the chapter he asks rhetorically, "How, then, can the order of causes that is fixed in God's foreknowledge deprive us of all use of our will, when our wills play an important part in the order of causes itself?" (*City*, 181). How indeed, when it is the case that our wills have "just so much power as God chose to give them and also foresaw. Therefore, whatever power they have, they have it most assuredly. They themselves will in any case do what they are going to do, because he whose foreknowledge cannot be mistaken foresaw that they would have the power to do it" (*City*, 181). Consequently, it is because God knows all our acts of will that we sin when we sin: "For he whose foreknowledge cannot be mistaken foresaw that neither fate, nor fortune, nor anything else but man himself would sin. If he chooses not to sin, he certainly does not sin, and this choice not to sin was also foreseen by God" (*City*, 187).

This line of argument is more of a dissolution than a resolution of the dilemma. Augustine assumes that there is both foreknowledge and free will and then uses one to re-enforce the other. But what of their apparent incompatibility? How can God know now what I will freely choose to do in the future? If God does foreknow it, how can I be said to freely choose to do it? To define our acts of will as playing a part in the order of causes foreknown by God is not to establish that the will is free; our wills could just as well be following a predetermined pattern which necessarily will come to be as God foreknows it. To argue that we have free will because God foreknows our wills to be free is to bypass the issue of their apparent incompatibility that generated the dilemma in the first place

Perhaps this is not a second argument but merely a gloss on his appeal to the Christian faith. Once we declare our belief in the existence of a supremely powerful, foreknowing God, we need not fear for our freedom since He guarantees it. But we have already seen that the reasons for adopting this belief are not philosophically compelling. They merely serve to underscore the quandary that believers find themselves in. We can agree with Augustine that whatever power our wills have they have most assuredly; the question remains: how much power do they have? In a future already known and willed by God, what scope is left for man's free will? What part do our wills play in the order of causes? To arbitrarily state that they are free causes is not to provide a valid argument.

3. Freedom as Part of the Meaning of "Will"

Augustine tries another approach in chapter 10 when he distinguishes between two senses of necessity. The first refers to "what is not in our power, but accomplishes its end even against our will, for example, the necessity of death ...." It is necessary that each of us shall die. We do not will to die but we lack the power to prevent it. We shall die whether we will to or not.

Clearly, says Augustine, "our wills [*voluntates nostras*], by which we

live rightly or wrongly, are not under such necessity." We are subject
to certain constraints, some things are not in our power; but this
necessity does not apply to all that we do. Augustine insists that "we
do many things that we should not do if we were unwilling. To this
class of things belongs first of all the will itself. If we will, the will
exists; if not, it does not. For we should not will if we were
unwilling" (*si volumus, est, si nolumus, non est*; *non enim vellemus, si
nollemus*, (*City*, 182-3)).

The act of willing itself is held by Augustine to be a paradigm
case of necessity in the second sense, the sense in which "it is necessary for something to be as it is, or happen as it does." This is not a
necessity that takes away liberty or subjects us to what is not in our
power; rather it is a kind of conceptual necessity that follows from
the meaning of the term "will." We use this sense of necessity when
we say that "it is necessary for God to live forever." We do not mean
that something accomplishes its end against God's will, nor that He
is powerless to do or avoid doing something. We simply point to a
logical implication of the notion of His omnipotence. If God is omnipotent, He cannot die. "Not-being-able-to-die" is part of the meaning
of "omnipotence."

"The case is similar," says Augustine, "when we say that it is necessary, when we exercise will, to do so of our own free will" (*City*, 185).
To will means to do something that is within our power. Augustine
sees a conceptual link between our notions of "will" and "freedom."
Freedom is part of the meaning of "will" because to exercise the will
means to have things in our power. Just as being omnipotent entails
not-being-able-to-die, so too exercising the will implies having things
in our power or acting freely. To say that "God is omnipotent"
precludes saying that "God has just died"; similarly, saying "I will to
do or choose X" precludes saying that "it was not in my power to do
so." It is necessary (in the second sense of necessity) for the will to be
free because that is the way it happens to be. This fact is reflected in
our language. By definition, the will is free.

If Augustine is indeed making a linguistic claim about the will, he
must still face the charge that he has not shown that the acts of will
are really free and not eternally predetermined. We might use the
word "will" in a logically consistent and linguistically correct fashion
and yet not have resolved Cicero's dilemma. In exactly the same
way, we can spell out the logical and linguistic implications of the
notion of Divine omnipotence without thereby settling the issue of
whether there really is such an omnipotent being. All that Augustine
seems to have established is the fact that we certainly do talk and act

as if our wills were free. To say that "we wouldn't will at all if we were unwilling" is trivially true (i.e. to deny this is to claim that I will but I don't will, which seems contradictory). The question remains, when I will, do I freely will? How can I reconcile my acts of free will with God's eternal foreknowledge of them? Are we left with no philosophical answer to the dilemma? I would like to conclude this paper by briefly indicating some other approaches that Augustine might have taken.

IV

SOME OTHER APPROACHES TO THE PROBLEM

To begin with, although Augustine spends considerable effort in chapters 9 and 10 trying to defend man's free will, he does not critically examine the notion of "foreknowledge." This he takes simply to mean that "God knows all things before they happen" (*City*, 175). My preliminary remarks were meant to show that knowledge of things before they happen makes no sense on the human level. Various thinkers since Augustine have pointed out that to speak of Divine foreknowledge may also be misleading. God neither acts nor knows in time. He is eternal. His knowledge is not discursive; He knows all things as eternally present. There is no before and after in regard to God's knowledge. In other words, when we say that God "foreknows" the future, we are using a word with temporal connotations to refer to what is really a timeless knowing. God no more knows things before they happen than we do. It is only from man's point of view in time that God, who exists eternally, can be said to know now what will happen in the future.

Another way of putting the difficulty of making sense of the notion of Divine foreknowledge is to question the framework of the dilemma as Augustine presents it. As we have seen, foreknowledge for him means that there is a fixed order of future events and an underlying order of causes which is "determined for a foreknowing God" (*City*, 171). If all events and causes are already determined, then it seems that nothing is in our power and our wills are not free. But does it make sense to speak of a fixed order of events and causes in the future? Can we meaningfully speak of events and causes that have not yet happened? As I indicated earlier, the notions of "event" and "cause" can be used as part of a prediction (e.g. if you play too much tennis tonight, you will hurt your arm) or as expressing a certain degree of probability about the future (e.g. in all likelihood you will play too much tennis tonight and as a result hurt your arm). These are epistemological claims subject to verification. Augustine uses "cause" and "event" as ontological concepts which are meant to describe the structure of reality itself. He acknowledges that there is an order of causes and events, past, present, and future. Future causes and events take on an ontological status.

We might well balk at such a view of reality and insist that concepts like "cause" and "event" properly refer to elements of our past and present experience or to what we expect will occur based on such experience. These future expectations do not now refer to an existing reality. If Augustine has in mind the timeless reality wherein God dwells, then he should explain that the words "cause" and "event" are taking on a new meaning.

Another possible approach to the problem is to admit that free will and foreknowledge are incompatible but deny that this has irreligious consequences. This can be done by considering the logical implications of Divine omniscience in the same manner as Augustine himself has explained what is entailed by God's omnipotence. Just as omnipotence does not mean that God can do everything, indeed there are things like dying that by definition He cannot do, so too His omniscience does not mean that He can know everything but rather that He can know "anything it is not self-contradictory to say that any being could know."[5] Terrence Penelhum feels that "it is self-contradictory to say that any being could know ... what free actions another being will perform in the future. Hence even an omniscient being cannot know what actions free agents will do."[6]

Penelhum is pointing to the same kind of conceptual limitation built into the notion of omniscience that Augustine has admitted in regard to omnipotence. There is no limitation intended of God's power or knowledge; rather, we see the limits of our talking meaningfully about God. Just as it is self-contradictory to say that God has died, so, according to Penelhum, it makes no sense to say that God, or any other being for that matter, foreknows what I will freely choose to do. In creating free beings, God creates a sphere where such knowledge is a logical impossibility. Penelhum concludes that "foreknowledge and free will are indeed incompatible. What has to be abandoned in a logically coherent theism is foreknowledge of human actions, even on the part of God."[7] Rather than leading to a denial of God's existence, Penelhum sees the rejection of foreknowledge as a necessary part of a logically coherent theism.

Admittedly, such an approach would have seemed highly suspect to the Bishop of Hippo who was actively engaged in combatting heresies. And one might add that logical coherence is no guarantee of orthodoxy. Nonetheless, it seems to me that Penelhum's position avoids many of the pitfalls that Augustine gets into when he attempts to reconcile free will and foreknowledge. It is similar to Cicero's solution which Augustine refused to consider since he thought it "a conspicuous act of madness both to agree that God exists and to deny his foreknowledge" (*City*, 169). Penelhum's helpful suggestion is that once the full implications of Divine omniscience are understood, one can deny the possibility of foreknowledge without endangering God's power or knowledge. Ironically, Augustine is left with an unresolved dilemma because he ignores the very solution offered by Cicero.[8]

NOTES

1. Peter Brown, *Augustine of Hippo* (University of California Press,1969), 282.
2. Saint Augustine, *On Free Choice of the Will*, trans. A.S.Benjamin and L.H. Hackstaff (New York: Bobbs-Merrill, 1964).
3. Saint Augustine, *The City of God Against the Pagans*, Books 4-7, trans. William M.Green (London: Loeb Classical Library, 1963), 173. All subsequent Latin and English quotations from this book will be cited in the text as *City*.
4. For Augustine's own example of human foreknowledge, see *Confessions*, 11:18. This should be contrasted with his own strong statements about divine foreknowledge; cf., for example *City of God*, 22:2.
5. Terrence Penelhum, *Religion and Rationality* (New York: Random House, 1971), 396.
6. Penelhum, *Religion and Rationality*, 296.
7. Penelhum, *Religion and Rationality*, 298.
8. This is also a solution suggested by Robert Brumbaugh in his work on logic and time. Cf., for example, his observation that: "If it is inherently impossible for there to be omniscience as simultaneous knowledge of all history in full concrete detail, this may well be the key to the classical problem of pre-destination and free will." Robert S. Brumbaugh, *Whitehead, Process Philosophy, and Education* (Albany: SUNY Press, 1982), 59. In effect, I have been advocating a position similar to the "non-classical" view that Brunbaugh sees as an implication of process philosophy, i.e. the view that "since there are as yet no future facts, though God knows all that there is to be known, there are no future facts for Him to know" (122).

Part III: EDUCATION

11

EDUCATION AS A THEME OF PHILOSOPHY

Nathan Rotenstreich

I

Education is an activity whose essence is to some extent stressed in the term employed. It is an activity of leading, lifting up or instructing. The conjunction of an activity related to a person or to persons brings to prominence the unique and problematic character of education since it boils down to an activity of intervention in the human sphere. It is not related to circumstances at large to particular, that is to say individual, human beings. Unlike practice at large which is an intervention in circumstances, education as intervention relates to delineated human beings; but as delineated they are not isolated or left alone. The intervention qua education indicates that they are not left alone, but are open or perhaps even in need of intervention. In addition to that, as human beings, they are in a factual situation in terms of their very presence in the horizon of the reality or existence. From that aspect they are even dependent upon the reality in which they are finding themselves.

There is a nominal description of education as essentially elevating, or guiding the engaged human being to maturity, to that which goes by the German term *Mündigkeit*, sometimes translated "freedom from tutelage." It is obvious that the employment of this latter term may have different connotations, especially in a particular historical context, as for instance, the Enlightment. But our aim is to emphasize the position of self-control or one's ability to handle situations. In this sense the situation is one of distance between a person and the cicumstances in which he or she finds him or herself. Education is then an act of intervention in circumstances from which it is meant to free one, at least in part, to a position of – to put it negatively – an absence of full dependence upon the circumstances. Maturity or *Mündigkeit* indicates the relation to circumstances without a total immersion in them. This profile is already an indica-

tion of a sort of polarity which is inherent in the process of education and its tentative achievement, namely that the person needs
education in order to release him or herself from the continuous
impact of it or to come back to the term – from the continuous
intervention of it. Yet if in this sense education would be a tempo-
rary process, it is still sometimes suggested, and perhaps rightly so,
that the leading up by education by way of an intervention from
outside a person is meant to be replaced by a self-formation of the
person. Here again the polarity between the external intervention
and the internal shaping come to the fore.

II

It is appropriate to compare at this juncture the process of education
with the process of medical intervention in the body of a person,
since in both activities we encounter an intervention in the situation
of the individual or particular human being as a single person. But
the difference between the two modes of intervention becomes
prominent from two points of view. a) Medical intervention does not
accompany the person constantly. It is brought to prominence only
when there is a certain deficiency in the position or situation of the
singular organism, namely when there is a gap between the organism
as it is and that which the organism has to be – as what is called a
healthy organism. In this sense medical intervention is sporadic while
educational intervention is constant and accompanies the position not
only of the organism but of the person. b) Medical intervention is
aimed at the restitution of the organism, that is to say at the overcoming of the deficiency, present in it in order to reestablish the
functioning of the organism. As against this intervention, education
is meant to go beyond the situation of the person in order to lead it
to the development of its potentialities, and thus broadly speaking to
a situation of actualization of those potentialities. Thus education in
this sense is future-oriented, where the medical treatment is future-oriented by way of overcoming the inhibitions of the past.

III

This broad delineation of modes of activities leads us to a further step related to education, namely to the identification of those conditions which made the educational intervention not only an occurring fact but an essential one, that is to say the human being is unable to be one without the intermediary educational activity. Hence we could say that the very growth of the person qua human being is unattainable or not able to be present without the educational intervention. Two prominent examples show this dependence upon the educational activity in its direction meant to emancipate the human being from dependence. The examples at stake are the posture of the organism, namely the upright position, and speech. Both are achieved and not present from the very beginning of the existence of the individual human person. Both are activizations, or actualizations, of potentialities and become actual within the context of the environment. The activization of the linguistic capacity is a more prominent example because as an actualization it is also a confinement of the potentiality to the language of the environment which can be a lingo or a historical one.

The linguistic capacity is a universal one in the sense that the individual being is capable of speaking any language. Since the individual finds itself in a limited environment, the activization of its capacity is by the same token the absorption of the language of the environment. It might be an open question whether the same applies to the upright posture, namely, in a hypothetical sense: whether the organism left to itself, without any intervention of the environment, would develop out of itself in the direction of an upright posture.

In any case we may sum up this part of the direction of intervention by emphasizing that intervention in the human situation, as any intervention, is to change the given situation. But that change is one aiming at the development of that which is inherent in the individual and thus what is considered to be the normal condition of a human individual. But again this is one of those cases where normalcy and the normative condition coincide. Education is an instrument both towards normalcy and an embodiment of norm. Thus the educational activity is considered as justified both instrumentally and inherently. This is indeed one of those cases where the two directions of justification meet each other. But if this is so, then we are bound to raise an additional question, namely what is it that makes education a structural activity which contains more than one direction and – without being over harmonious – contains components which are justified from different angles, like normalcy and embodiment of norms?

This calls for an additional consideration which can be expressed as a conjunction between the vital need of the human being and its cognitive achievement. Human beings, as some trends in biology emphasize, are born unable to nourish themselves. They need the assistance of the environment and that assistance is both an intervention from the biological point of view and also from the social point of view. Biologically the human being cannot exist alone, and this vital character of its dependence is by the same token its dependence upon the societal aspect of reality, whether we attribute to that aspect an intrinsic position or not. Instrumentally the dependence is both biological and societal, since as a matter of fact, the assistance for the sake of the biological need comes about from the environment which is not identical with the existence of the species. Education, either deliberately or not, by activizing its own direction is anchored in the factual situation of the dependence upon the environment in its different dimensions directing the person to belonging to a social framework. Education makes explicit the factual situation and may turn it into a norm of human existence. That norm, unlike, for instance, the categorical imperative or benevolence, is anchored in a factual situation. Education wavers in this sense between dependence upon the environment in the factual sense and a possible deliberate engagement in it in the intentional sense. This duality within congruence may lead to an additional step in our attempt to identify the complexity of the educational activity in terms of the coincidence inherent in it when looked at from different perspectives.

IV

Education has been presented as an intervention. It is an intervention directed not only to human beings in their first stage but one carried out continuously from the outside, that is to say by parents or by those active in the environment. The passivity of the human being in its initial stage is the justification for the intervention. To put it differently, those who intervene represent the accumulated human wisdom leading to the conclusion and to the steps taken according to it; the human being cannot survive unless it is exposed to this intervention. In this sense the justification for the intervention is in the need or needs of the person-to-be exposed to it. The dependence upon intervention is its justification.

But the dependence has two directions – one in terms of the adjustment to the environment and the other in terms of the development of the self-activity of the human being to-be-educated. Nominally we can distinguish between these two directions; but factually the two, at least in the initial stage of education, coincide: one cannot be adjusted to the surrounding world for the sake of one's immediate need in terms of subsistence unless one develops a certain activity towards the surrounding world, an activity which is expressed in the first place in the response to that world. At the same time it has to be emphasized that education as an intervening activity is an instrumental one functioning for the sake of the human being to-be-educated and not for the sake of the intervening educator. Being an instrumental activity it opens, as a matter of fact, the door towards what can be described as self development which is both directed towards the environment as well as towards the activization of the agent to-be-educated. Because of that second aspect, the process of education may become what is called self-education, namely the self-activization of the agent or the actualization of its potentialities.

When we speak about interventions in the surrounding world, as for instance building a house, the building is a process. Yet as a process it has a visible end – both as a goal and as a point in time. Education as intervention is an on-going process and cannot be summed-up in an artifact. This is so because both directions, that is to say adjustment and development, are not summed up in products but are processes. Even when adjustment is not guided from the outside but becomes an internal component of the person at stake, it does not exhibit itself in a certain act or product. In this sense education presupposes the distance between the human being to-be-educated and the surroundings of its existence. Once there is a distance of this sort, there is no final act overcoming it. Only on-going acts meet the conditions and enable the person to be a master of them and at the same time different from them.

These components of education lead us to a conclusion as to the built-in conjunction to be found in the process of education and its aims. To employ at this juncture a philosophical terminology, we may say that education has its justification both in its instrumental position as well as in its intrinsic one. Instrumentally, education is justified by leading to the two ends which are two but coalesce, namely to adjustment and to development of the personality. But this instrumental position of education is meant to establish the position of the human person capable of activizing itself. That activization, whether it be called spontaneity or otherwise, represents the intrinsic position of the human being and therefore makes an activity aiming at the establishing of that position. The active person is both adjustable and adjusting, occupying the position of an agent as a semi-independent being.

There is one manifestation of the instrumental justification of education beyond the primary adjustment to the environment. We refer here to the functional aim of education, namely that the primary adjustment embodied in handling the nutritional needs of the person is replaced by a secondary adjustment which is expressed in being able to take care of the subsistence of the agent, not by receiving nutritional components directly, but for the sake of providing those components in terms of the grown up organism. The functional aspect of education is meant to safeguard the existence of the person in the direction of its encounter with the surrounding world. But at the same time there is no education in the functional sense, for instance in the direction of providing for the profession of the person, which does not depend, at least to some extent, upon the development of the capacities of the person. Concurrently there is no total congruence between the functional and the developmental components, since the person may have capacities and beyond above its functional needs and may mould itself towards a kind of co-existence between the functional capacities and the non-functional ones – as, to take a trivial example, one can function manually and be interested at the same time in music. There is a continuity from the adjustment in the primary sense to the functional direction of the activity of the person. Yet it is clear that on the level of function there is a sort of emancipation from immediate needs towards a broader horizon of the activities of the agent. In spite of the interaction between the functional or instrumental direction of the activities of the person and the developmental aspect for the sake of establishing the position of the person, the two directions have to be analytically distinguished. Moreover we cannot assume a pre-established harmony between those directions.

V

There is an additional conclusion which we have to reach from this attempt to draw out the phenomenological profile of education. We referred to education as a process; hence it is mandatory to distinguish between process and acts. There are, to be sure, acts of education as e.g. the teaching of elementary modes of behaviour. But that instruction is grounded in the on-going process, one performed first by the intervening agents and then performed by the agent itself. As a process, education presupposes a basic distinction, at least in the scope of human existence, between actuality and potentiality. This distinction is a fluid one because we do not point to a clear cut duality between actuality and potentiality. Every actual situation is, to use that play on words, at least potentially a potentiality and thus a point of departure towards a new actuality. Education embodied in acts and inherent in the process presupposes that distinction. Since acts come to an end and the process is on-going, the ingredients of the process turn the distinction into a more pointed one. Self-education presupposes that distinction even more prominently.

From the point of view of the perspective of justification, referred to before, we become aware that education is inherently a process which cannot be separated from the aspect of justification. Even when we take the view that acts of intervention are justified instrumentally or teleologically, since education involves human existence or human agents to-be, precisely because of that involvement the results of intervention cannot be indefinitely postponed. They have to be seen or tangible, in a sense, within the life span of the agent to-be. Since education refers to the developmental capacities, the justification in terms of the potentiality has to be equally, at least, taken into account when the achievement as such is understood as the actualization of the potentiality. A prominent aspect from this point of view is that aspect of education which Whitehead describes as the acquisiton of the art of the utilization of knowledge. Consequently he says that the only use of knowledge of the past is to equip us for the present and finally "there is only one subject matter of education and that is Life and its manifestations."[1] We may wonder whether this position is justified against the background of the rhythm of education and its built-in duality. The emphasis laid on the usefulness is only in a sense an enlargement of the aspect of adjustment present in education, since usefulness is a variation of the trend towards meeting the needs. If we take into account the justificaion of education in terms of development or activization of poten-

tialities, we cannot confine education to the direction towards usefulness. Again, usefulness is an application for the sake of the agent.
But – and knowledge is a case in point – the agent or the subject
faces a horizon of topics within which there may be topics which
perhaps generically are formulated by their usefulness. Once they
are formulated they can be detached or be taken from their original
place and have a position of their own. A Greek tragedy could serve
some cultic objectives; but once it is established, it gains an independent existence and can be seen as having an intrinsic position. Hence
there would be a correlation between the intrinsic aspect of the
development of the personality and the intrinsic component of the
topic to which the personality refers or to which it directs itself in
order to develop its capacities and not necessarily in order to take
advantage of that which it faces for its own needs – as usefulness
would imply.

If we take into account what Whitehead calls the rhythm of
education, we cannot come to a conclusion that education is one-di-
mensional. The attempt to identify the profile of education in order
to maintain both the descriptive aspect of the approach to it as well
as its axiological position leads us to some consequence of a broader
meaning, namely to that of the position of education in the scope of
philosophical concern.

VI

The process of education can be looked at as a paradigmatic facticity
of the human situation, representing not only that which is in the
process proper but also one anticipating the human position in
general. We come back to the two aspects of dependence and development. Dependence is an exhibition of the basic human finitude,
i.e., human beings are posited in situations and the necessity they
face is to come to grips with those. The trivial fact that human
beings do not create themselves places them in reality, though the
reality encountered primarily is not the reality at large but the
limited one of the situation or the circumstances. There is a two-fold
limitation inherent in the human situation, that due to the narrow
scope of circumstances and that which is due to the enlarged realm
and which goes by the term reality. To come to grips with reality is
imposed on human beings because of the situation as it is, yet this is
already to a certain extent an attitude of taking a stand vis-a-vis the
limiting circumstances. Even the receiver on the level of the

organism is not totally immersed in the circumstances. The receiver depends on them but it is he or she who is involved in the process. Hence it can be said that the adjustment to the circumstances contains in itself a certain ingredient of activity and therfore a certain degree of development. To be directed towards circumstances is to refer to them, and thus the duality of reality and approaching it comes to the fore in education in the primary sense of that term.

If finitude is one of the essential features of human reality, as for instance some trends of contemporary philosophy of existence emphasize it, then it has to be observed that the primary manifestation of finitude lies in dependence and not in the anticipation of the end in time exhibited in the anticipation of one's death. This is so since anticipation presupposes the directedness of consciousness or reflection towards the end in time which by definition lies in the future. Directedness toward the end presupposes the awareness of time, whereas limitation implies a dependence upon that which is and is not a reference towards that which is about to come. Hence, limitation in terms of dependence upon reality precedes the awareness of limitation in the direction of the reality to come. The paradigmatic position of education becomes manifest in this context from an additional point of view, namely that dependence does not amount to immersion in the realm of that which the human being to-be educated depends upon. The duality between the surroundings and the human being is the point of departure for the duality between necessity and the attitude towards it, though obviously the attitude already implies consciousness which is not yet explicit on the level of the first steps of education. To put it differently, the adjustment is dictated by the needs. These are a manifestation of necessity in terms of the position of the human being adjusting itself to reality and taking advantage of it. There is no adjustment without the developmental aspect which is implicit in the attitude and becomes explicit in the development of consciousness and thus of attitudes, knowledge, awareness etc.

Education is paradigmatic of the human situation because there are in it two built-in dimensions. The human person goes beyond itself, though the first steps of its going out are taken for the sake of its survival, and those that are imposed on it. But even adjustment presents the structure of a primary trans-personality – the human being cannot exist as a person confined to itself. It has to go out towards reality as a trans-personal realm in order to exist as a person. But here, too, the educational situation can be said to be microscopic, from the vantage of the human situation, because it presents within the primary stage of human existence the involvement between human beings and reality, which even instrumentally represents the trans-personal dimension. The more development goes on, the more the horizon of trans-personality becomes manifest or even open. Even the anticipation of death is trans-personal, though it applies to the person, because it anticipates the dimension of time which is beyond the present moment. But the trans-personal dimension can become manifest in the directedness of consciousness or knowledge towards nature or towards the universe at large and concurrently towards the trans-personal past, i.e., the historical one, the utopian future which lies beyond the personal dimension, and towards that which is in a sense present, like social existence or products of art, etc. The shift from the instrumental aspect to the intrinsic one, which we indicated before, becomes manifest in that context.

Let us mention here, precisely because we are in that situation, one empirical approach to education which is rather widely discussed in the contemporary era. The aspect of limitation is prominent in those discussions which point to the inhibitions imposed by circumstances on the development of the human being, for instance, the absence of incentives in the home of the child, poverty as characteristic of the circumstances, etc. The basic limitation inherent in dependence upon circumstances is presented and argued from the point of view of its impact on the development of the child, thus showing the excessive significance of the conditions which harm its development. On the other hand, just to give a full picture of the controversy at stake, those who stress development attempt to show that the capacities as such can develop and exposure to the circumstances should not be exaggerated beyond the primary relation between the child and its circumstances. It is not essential to take a stand on this controversy; what is meant by this presentation is to show that the profile of education as a structure and as a paradigm of the human position becomes apparent also in approaches to education – and we have to distinguish between approaches and the primary situation as such.

VII

We can move now to a second consideration related to the structure of education. In education we refer to individual human beings, and even further, to particular human beings. The particularity can become present both in the direction of adjustment as well as in the direction of development. But particularity cannot obliterate the primary fact that every human being is in need of education, and even the person's adjustment, let alone its development, cannot occur out of its own activity or resources. Education contains both response and initiative. But these directions or features are not characteristic of this or that individual human being. They are characteristic of the human species in general. The species can be considered as a sum total, but in the present context it is a whole becoming manifest in particulars. The human being to-be-educated in its primary stage cannot be seen as conceiving its involvement in the whole of the human species. But those participating in the process of intervention of education are aware of the fact that the particular human being at stake needs to be educated as any other particular human being is. The direction of development carries with it concurrently the awareness of the particularity or individuality of the person to-be-educated, more so when development turns towards self-development. Still both structural dimensions even when individually realized, both as materialized and as conceived, are characteristic of human beings in general. The individuality becomes an additional manifestation of the human position, but cannot replace the basic one related to human beings in general.

From this point of view, the individual existence is representative of the existence of the species. It carries in itself the point of departure or even the anchor for a moral evaluation of human beings. Since all human beings represent the species and all of them are in need of education, there emerges the correlation between the process of education and the implied human equality. In a sense we find in the encounter between adjustment and development the core of freedom; in another sense we find in the encounter between individuals and the species the core of equality. These two aspects are of a normative charater. We may come to realize that their normative position is somehow a continuation or an interpretation of that which is present in the factual situation which becomes manifest in the process of education.

We may conclude with a restatement of the position of education as an issue of philosophical consideration. We characterize education as an intervention. That intervention differs from the intervention in the surrounding world meant to establish an artifact like a bridge because the intervention considered now is one related to the various components of the human situation. Education has to be justified because of the inherent character of human beings even when they are exposed to intervention. This makes the activity of educational intervention an irreducible one and thus a basic datum, active as it is, of human existence. If we take philosophy to be an exploration of that which is basic, be it reality, ideas or presuppositions of knowledge, norms, etc., then education as an irreducible activity, one *sui generis*, is to be placed within the scope of basic data and thus within the scope of the themes of a philosophical exploration.

We have to distinguish between education in its basic structure and the impact of philosophy on goals of education according to the model of *paideuia*. That impact relates to systems. The present exposition of the position of education has been concerned with the fundamentals of education and not with what might be considered as shaping of education by way of ideals.

NOTES

1. A.N. Whitehead, "The Aims of Education" in *The Aims of Education And Other Essays* (New York: Mentor Books, 1949).

12

PHILOSOPHY BY CENTURIES: A DIRECTION IN TEACHING

George Kimball Plochmann

For since the sciences taken all together are identical with human wisdom, which always remains one and the same, however applied to different subjects, and suffers no more differentiation proceeding from them than the light of the sun experiences from the variety of the things which it illumines, there is no need for minds to be confined at all within limits.

- René Descartes, *Rules for the Direction of the Mind*, Rule 1

Nestled between undergraduate courses in philosophy, in which the student may be introduced to problems, or types, or even to the history, of philosophy, and graduate seminars which are conducted chiefly for doctoral candidates, there is a level of work which is open, as a rule, to both seniors and graduate students. The composition of the audience is likely to confuse the instructor, who privately is wishing he could teach a more carefully-selected group, but who, in trying to address old hands and relative neophytes alike, may easily be giving an authentic undergraduate course moderately well disguised by handing out extra bibliographies and by the absence of spot quizzes. By definition these hybrid courses should not merely repeat strictly undergraduate offerings, and by practice they are not supposed to be mere dilutions of fully advanced work. What, then, is left for them? What should be their subject matter, and how should it be imparted?

No single answer can be given, obviously, since institutions vary in their facilities and requirements as much as instructors vary in their interests and capabilities. Certainly a doctoral-level seminar should not be devoted to some conspectus of a philosopher's works; and in the hurly-burly of an undergraduate history course no more than two or three books can be sampled in the few days allotted to individual figures. ("If this is Tuesday, it must be Berkeley.") Consequently this intermediate course might well be the place for lectures and readings dealing comprehensively with the works of Plato, or Hobbes, or Wittgenstein, or whoever was to be examined in greater detail later on – or whoever happened to have no one at all to speak for him at the doctoral level. There are some alternatives to this plan, one of them being a course in the philosophy of science, which is a little too technical for most undergraduates but which does not require the specialized logic and mathematics needed for the seminars; or else a similar compromise in the theory of art. One could also attempt to provide a survey of some movement – the Phenomenologists, for instance, or the Cambridge Platonists, or philosophy in England between the World Wars, or the like. These are all suitable, but I should prefer to advocate instead a course which gives philosophy proportionately less than full attention but which places it in its historical setting by every means possible.

The limit for a semester course which one can deal with effectively, in most cases, is the span of a century, though in some cases more would be permissible, and in others, such as the 13th or 17th century, and certainly the 20th, half that period would be preferable. But for such centuries as the 3rd B.C., the 3rd A.D., the 4th or 5th, or 12th, 14th, 16th, a single intensive course could, if planned with care, be made to consider leading movements and figures relevant to the career of philosophy in that chosen period. Such a course requires a great deal of work in advance, even if taught by a team of specialists. My own feeling, as an outgrowth of both having participated for many years in an elaborate offering by a staff, and having tried many varieties of solo instruction, is that the latter is usually more satisfactory. This is by no means said in derogation of my excellent colleagues; but the advantages of being able to bring all aspects of a historical subject matter under the umbrella of a singular yet informal dialectic is virtually impossible in a committee. And these advantages far outweigh any difficulties that might be incurred when one person assumes responsibility not only for the general outlines but for the details as well. The time spent in long and frequent staff meetings can be better spent by one teacher in the library. He can interpret these to bring them into close connection with the writers who customarily figure in philosophic histories; and if he cannot, he might be happier minding more congenial scholarly tasks. The questions arising in the inquisitive student's mind are usually those bearing on the correlation of disciplines, and two experts, one in art and the other in philosophy , are likely to be as vague as one person, presumably a philosopher, who though he may fall short of detailed expert knowledge in fine art can still frame some categories by which he can deal with major figures and movements. If he does this, the student will have had the advantage of listening to a (perhaps tentative) theory of cultural history, and not to a medley of opinions which cancel each other out or, worse than this, overlook one another altogether. In the best instances, books can be edited, rewritten, re-apportioned; but verbal utterances delivered in a classroom cannot be recalled, and the frequently total disparities of opinion between instructors shows up later in muddled recollections of the subject matters and their synthesis.

I am not advocating any one theory by which to interpret a given century - there need be no concept of *Zeitgeist* setting in motion everything that happened in a certain century, no Spring-Summer analogies for clearing it up, no Challenge-and-Response theory riveting our attention upon specific historical forces. Indeed I incline to believe in a virtually infinite complexity in historical trends, a complexity so great that to find any single principle animating a given epoch is beyond our best hopes. (This does not contradict the earlier assertion that we require a unifying dialectic for the teacher-historian; the dialectic itself can be complex, and can well include chance and misdirection as co-operative keys to interpretation. I am only saying that such categories as these two, in the hands of one teacher, would run into bewildering collision with a doctrine, maintained by another man, that propounded linear historical necessity or else what Joyce called "a commodius vicus of recirculation.") Nor do I think that a numerically "exact" designation of a time-limit is any more unassailable than is a cultural manifestation such as we find in Hegel's conception; merely because of the complexity just now referred to, we cannot fall back upon arbitrary time-spans or geographic stretches. The 19th century probably began in 1789 and ended in 1914, and western Europe sometimes includes Spain or Hungary, and sometimes does not. Allowances can be made, however, for this in the planning, and it would be poor teaching indeed that failed to lead inquiry back to earlier movements in part determinative of conditions in the century at hand or forward to its effects upon what came after. Plato makes Socrates say that the good dialectician cuts at the natural joints, and this seems patently to hold true of the historian as well.

So much for the sort of theory intended to illuminate the chosen subjects and the years during which they are made to show themselves. In passing to the breadth of its application, let me say that I find most anthologies and histories of philosophy setting rather narrow limits to the field. Philosophers are ranked apart as a special class and represented as being influenced almost entirely by their study of other philosophers, and then described as effective only in changing the attitudes of some few followers, in respect of a handful of explicit doctrines. This view holds true, on occasion; doubtless many of the lesser figures of the 10th century were provincial, if only because they had so few books available, and travel was perilous. But with most of the major personages in the history of thought the situation has been far different. They have had interests, accomplishments, and connections, through reading or friendships, far wider than their writings in metaphysics or ethics or whatever might lead us to suppose, and moreover they have as a rule been sensitive to the events of their times – occasionally, as with Augustine or Thomas or Leibniz, they have become important actors in them. No philosopher has lived in an atmosphere so rarefied that he did not suffer or profit from economic changes, or from the accessions of rulers or the elections of presidents. This was true even of the medieval saints, many of whom found themselves in serious conflict (or else benign agreement) with active princes, popes, and lesser dignitaries. Nor is it proper to neglect the important experiences of a philosopher when estimating the validity of his thinking. When Kant remarks on form and color in art, it would seem needful not only to know that he had read some previous critics, but to know also, as least in general way, what sorts of paintings he had actually seen, or whether he had been privileged to talk to some artists. When Schopenhauer has something to say about the functions of music, then the student should form some idea of his own of the sort of music the philosopher had in mind, for his remarks are sound enough for the Classical period, but would clash with the principles of Palestrina and his predecessors and would be falsified if applied to virtually anyone after Gustav Mahler. In the same way, the remarks of Descartes on mathematics are not cut from the same cloth as those of Hume. This is owing partly to wide differences in the competences of the two men, but also to changes in styles of mathematical thinking that had taken place in the almost exactly one hundred years elapsing between the *Discourse on Method* and the *Treatise of Human Nature*.

My reader has by now earned the right to a statement of some principles to help justify this inclusion of what most treatments of philosophic analysis and even philosophic history quite evidently hold to be irrelevant. Three criticisms can be made chiefly of the epistemic underpinnings of this pedagogic structure. It may be that instead of according proper attention to the warranties and consecutants of philosophical reasoning we are dribbling out farfetched conjugations of ideas simply because we hope to convince by the sheer weight of fuller contexts; it may be that instead of establishing the integrity of philosophy as a discipline we are reducing it to a mere outcropping of the more fundamental bedrock of economic and political movements; and it may be that instead of the liberal inquiry in which we should be jointly engaged we are encouraging our pupils to hold no truths at all and letting them founder in a wash of skeptical ideas of which every one is relative to every other, there being no firmer standard of truth than there is in ordinary day-to-day opinion. We should take these three objections seriously, if for no reason but that a course such as I am proposing is one of the most difficult to give, and the hours spent upon its planning and execution should be better occupied with other sorts of philosophic activity if the objections turn out to be sound.

By way of some answers, my first point is that I maintain that teaching and learning are carried on primarily through propositions in a measure entire of themselves, that is, that they stand or fall with reference to what they say and not with reference to a lengthy sequence of somewhat similar or (as in Hegel) contradicting propositions. Still, in a secondary sense, these same propositions become ever easier to understand and they grow ever richer in association, if not in explicit meaning, as their connections become more numerous and more definite. The connections in a course in intellectual history can be with other words, or images (as of places or persons or even buildings and dramatic circumstances), or other statements intended to be taken as true. One truth does not alter another, but illuminates it, cuts off wrongheaded interpretations of it, by means of the logical contrasts it forms, or its analogies, or the divisions whereby it separates out germane from ingermane aspects of a universal term, or by generalizations in which two specifically different ideas are brought under one head.

Here we must take into account the paradox that the departmental system, which has done such great service in making colleges and universities manageable, has also been the instrument by which they have become fractionated so that not the faculties but the knowledge imparted by the faculties has become unmanageable. It is especially lamentable that the rage for analysis so prominent in philosophical circles during most of this century has had a similarly partitive effect upon the practice of philosophy itself, tending to divide the analysis from the subject matters and the practical concerns that could have a direct bearing, for good or ill, upon our lives. The tendency in what is called philosophical analysis has been to treat each proposition as an entirely unique entity, cut off from its fellows in consectutive discourse; and to endeavor to find a proposition's meaning not from connections that the original author may have allowed his reader to see, but from the intrinsic grammar of the words themselves. All too often it happens that the clarifying of one proposition by this method makes havoc of its neighbors, so that we begin to ask whether the author could make sense at all, or, more broadly, whether *any* author similarly equipped and motivated to philosophize, could do any better.

I am trying to keep to a narrow line between the assumption that each word has its fixed meanings, its fixed rules for use, which render attention to a broader context unnecessary and distracting, and the opposite assumption that there is a vague whole of discourse or even of existence without whose grasp it becomes impossible to bring out the proper exegesis of any statement. To repeat: a proposition is ordinarily true or false in its own terms, but its connection with appropriate reinforcing statements in a science or a system, or its opposition to contrasting statements, is needed for the individual mind to understand the original proposition. Ultimately, the interpreter must accept all the help he is afforded in a text, together with collateral materials drawn from letters, diaries, attacks, defenses, and together with the myriad of historical events that may suggest why the author has said what he has said. For this reason the interpreter sensitive to the cultural milieu as well as to the syntax and semantics of terms is likely to produce a more coherent, rational reading than one attuned to grammar and logic alone.

To the second point. I shall readily concede that the primary and proper nature of philosophy is in its own interpretive function – it interprets a world, and if the philosophy is in any way true, it should be so irrespective of the tides of human fortune that by power of association lead up to the statement of doctrine. On the other hand, the mere fact that it is, as William of Ockham would say, a fabrication, a product made through intellectual effort, and that it can have social and political consequences mild or severe – this fact makes philosophy and the propositions which carry its prospective truths a part of these very historical tides which philosophy seeks to transcend. But the assertion that philosophic ideas do not spring up in historical and cultural vacant lots should not lead us to suppose that such ideas can be altogether reduced to the social, economic, and artistic environment of the particular thinkers we may be studying. The teacher, in other words, has scarcely discharged his whole responsibility when he has detailed this environment. For historians of culture this might be deemed sufficient, but the teacher of philosophy has the duty to be philosophical, that is, to be able to extract proper meanings from the terms used, to weigh the relations of contrariety, independence, etc., and thereby estimate the possibility of truth and falsity in propositions, and finally the validity of the arguments supporting assertions and denials. The teacher of the course I am proposing, no less than any other teacher of philosophy, must above all be capable of drawing generalizations from particulars, and of adducing instances of generalizations. He must not forget his role in the encouraging of a back-and-forth movement between the universal and the individual, a role which if adequately rehearsed will prevent him both from losing himself in broad and perchance tautologous commonplaces and also from losing himself in historical particularities insufficiently related to each other. Consequently the philosophical historian, despite the fact that knowledge of social and other circumstances might have suggested to the thinkers of a period certain principles or conclusions, still would need all his skills in reading to discover from the works exactly what their writers intended. The plight of the English labor force suggested to Marx some of his leading ideas (though it did not to countless other men), yet an exegetical art is required before we can confidently say just what was suggested, how Marx connected his ideas, and why he argued as he did and not otherwise. All this comes from internal study of the text, of course, and none of it can be directly – I had almost said naively – made a part of the accumulation of historical data. In a course on the 16th century, to take one example, Philosophy is not merely a special instance or even manifestation of economic and social facts; ideally all aspects of the century should be treated with great care, thoughtfully, with original distinctions regarding cultural history emerging from the study of Machiavelli and the Mannerists alike. That is a counsel of perfection, of course, and short of it the best to be done is to expend most of the interpretive effort upon some of the philosophers, a little less upon Marlowe and Shakespeare, and perhaps even less upon the social data and economic and political trends of the time. It is a matter of proportioning, because teaching is a species of rhetoric too, in which the claims of the subject matter (which are paramount) must be weighed against those of teacher and student as well.

Now for the third objection, which has to do not with the subject matter but with what takes place in the head of the student. Knowledge is exact (when we attain it!), and, as Aristotle remarks, the belief which one entertains when one has grasped demonstrative knowledge is and must be unshakeable; yet it seems to me that dogmatism is a trait so untoward in its effects that the successful teacher must forego some of the privileges of communicating "sure and pure truths" and instead promote a spirit of liberal inquiry in the early stages of philosophic study, at the same time outlining an orderly dialectical selection and arrangement of his materials. It is hardly certain that a tight little system, his own or something borrowed from the tradition, a system in which all the analogies come out even and truth is traced directly to a single root principle, is the most adequate way to grasp reality or to suggest prudent courses of action. On the other side, it is hardly to be supposed that a program merely calling into question all truths except the requirement that we leave everything an open question, is a better alternative to a dogmatic theory. If left to themselves, most discerning readers would, I believe, prefer an open system, steering between the rock and the whirlpool. It would be a system of historical explanation boasting sufficient flexibility to permit some diversity in its applications, employing several methods, one being supervenient when occasion demands upon the others, that is, when special problems of the diverse subject matters demand it. (For example, we may consider the struggles of the Church and the various states in the 13th and 14th centuries from a theological and political point of view, using methods appropriate to these disciplines; but such a procedure will not adequately explain the causes and effects of the Black Death, for which new considerations must be brought into play.)

We have had open systems, I believe, in the dialogues of Plato that both entrap and liberate us, in the great (though probably mangled) treatises of Aristotle, in some of the elegant summas of the 13th century, in the promisory notes of Leibniz and Peirce, in works by Kant, Hegel, Whitehead, and a few others. But the overt abandonment of the time-tried and time-sanctified philosophical mission which these men carried out using their several means, the mission to see the whole world, though not necessarily the world-whole, is a misfortune resulting in the overspecialization and provincialism plaguing more and more divisions of the university. Philosophy should, I think, provide a remedy for this, not merely aggravate the disease.

Let each instructor find a unifying principle for him or herself, if need be, for wholeness and unity take many forms and are exemplified in many degrees. A single philosopher-historian might easily locate unifying concepts wherewith to explain movements in the 15th century different from these which he or she used to interpret the 19th, for example; or a different way of explaining the reason for trends in 17th century painting from what would best account for the relations between the Impressionists, Post-Impressionists, and Expressionists; or again, differences between the character of the history of science at any time and the history of disciplines traditionally held to be philosophical. I am therefore not asking for a single principle of synoptic inclusiveness that we know we shall never reach. I am asking only that when we study philosophy we practice a little of what has been preached until the last few decades – that we use it, precisely because it can distinguish analytically between diverse types of wholeness, diverse kinds of cause. In so doing, philosophy would again become enriched, more than it will by feeding endlessly upon propositions uttered in the rarefied atmosphere of professional debate. The later Middle Ages encouraged men to make themselves ridiculous by arguing over the most fragile and obscure matters having little to do with life as they lived it, with real desire and love and devotion to beautiful things. (How many of the later theologians wrote appreciatively of the wonderful churches and cloisters that gave them house and comfort?) It may be, though I have not yet conceded the point, that the age of philosophic systems, open or closed, is forever past, and that we have embraced the extreme of systemless inquiry, never to relinquish it. Medieval inquiry was parodied by Rabelais and his point-of-the-pin jig that can be placed by the side of Bradley's more recent complaint about a bloodless ballet of categories. Philosophy still more recent is rather self – parodied by the questions centering round the grammar involved in saying that I can feel my own toothache and that you cannot. Even if the systems are gone, and there will never be another Whitehead, this scarcely means that the wholeness of view which men such as he once taught must be abandoned in historical study as well, and that because we should erect no system of our own we should also fragment our history of culture. The "depth grammar" of toothaches may be trivial indeed; but a discerning interpreter of the 20th century could do much to relate such stressful bickerings to the history of science, the arts, and much more in our time, turning the debates once again into fascinating data.

When any discipline loses track of its alliances and cross-references, it turns inward. If we require that philosophy be totally self-nourishing and self-pleasuring, it will soon bore and then disgust the brightest newcomers among our students. If we insist upon some circumscribed, finite system of thought, we will alienate the freer spirits. If we reduce philosophy to a mere set of methods to be wrought upon other sciences, it will lapse into tedious disputation. Philosophy has a set of methods, but it also has a variable set of subject matters – whatever is presented to it for reflection, in fact. If we can inform our students of the places that philosophy might occupy, its manifold tasks, and its subjective but far-reaching effects, we will have done something to overcome the partiality and particu-larism of modern-day teaching, and replaced it not with some cloudy and ill-demonstrated totality but with a fresh appreciation of ways in which details fit into a rich and ever-changing whole.

But you will not need to explain this assertion to a student who has already immersed him or herself, even if briefly, in 17th century thought.

13

WHITEHEAD: TEACHER OF TEACHERS

Nathaniel Lawrence

"Get hold of the big ideas and put them to work." This is one of those simple and shining epigrams from Whitehead which I find irresistible. I shall make three uses of it in this paper. One of them is already under way. Getting hold of the big ideas is itself a big idea, and I intend to put it to work. A second way of using it is as an example of Whiteheadean mottoes in general. They have a common characteristic, that they may inspire different applications, some of which may be quite incompatible. I'll return to that point shortly. The third use is that this educational motto, emphasizing big ideas, is almost an invitation to put educational philosophy in its metaphysical setting, for – whatever else you may say of metaphysics – it is full of big ideas.

My effort in this paper is to get hold of a few big ideas and put them to work. Secondly, the epigram is an example of a whole family of Whiteheadean utterances whose meaning can be construed so variously that no clear educational policy is indicated, even though much that is valuable in teaching and in curriculum planning can be inspired and defended by them.

There is only a superficial paradox in the fact that provocative epigrams can suffer diverse interpretation. Religious sayings also, even ones that don't come from oracles, have the same property. Nonetheless, although I'm a good American and the pluralism of William James runs richly in my veins, I dislike the suggestion that our educational preferences are merely matters of taste. So let's take an example.

Suppose that I decide to teach Plato's *Republic* as the ideal introduction to beginning philosophy students. It's full of big ideas. But why not start with logic? Aren't the rules of sound reasoning pretty big? Or suppose I choose ethical issues of current interest, like abortion and reverse discrimination. Aren't murder or the charge of murder and the relation between law and society big enough for you? There are fine contemporary anthologies on these subjects, full of ardent reasoning. Or, finally, how about the environment? That's pretty big, too. We might even go whole hog and invite St. Thomas and Heidegger in to tell us about the ultimate environment: Being. There's a big idea – Being itself. But how big an idea do you want to get hold of and why?

Now that does involve taste, prior preference, and a lot of other things. The fact that other things function in the choosing means that a personal decision need not be regarded as merely subjective, even if it originates in a subject, namely, the teacher. Nor is it arbitrary, though it may be free in the sense that the chooser is the primary agent, and hence is primarily responsible for the outcome. One is reminded of Harry Truman's famous desk motto, "The buck stops here." Truman knew the price of freedom.

So what is regarded as big is usually partly a matter of personal decision, but it does not need to be private or whimsical. It should have the authenticity which comes from personal commitment. Wholly objective standards for universally reliable big ideas are hard to come by, and again, hard to apply. The personal element not only may, but must be decisive. Let us turn to the decider, then, the teacher himself. Here Whitehead gives us a well-engineered jolt. The "chief aim of a university professor," says Whitehead, should be "to exhibit himself in his own true character, – that is, as an ignorant man thinking ...."[1]

It will be useful to look at this epigram slowly. The "chief aim of the university professor" should be "to exhibit himself," etc. One feels uneasy about this opening: exhibit himself as what? Entertainer? Good Guy? Polymath? Deep Thinker? Wise? All of that is wiped away by what actually follows – "in his own true character." No pose, then, no care for even the preformed ideal that, say, the new freshman may have of the philosophy professor as terribly profound, a stange soul, burdened with a further sight than most men, and so on. Just the opposite: "... exhibit himself in his own true character." And what is that? "... an ignorant man thinking." Too cute. Socrates did it long ago and fooled nobody. Socrates feigned ignorance, but felt sure enough of his life principles to bet his life on them, even when it cost him his life. Indeed he could simply have resorted to bribery, stealth, and flight, and still saved his life. Moreover, that was Socrates. Who wants an ignorant college professor? There's plenty of ignorance around, cheaper to buy than the collegiate kind.

There are two closely related things Whitehead could mean, and I suspect he meant both. One might say that once one gains certain information and even certain wisdom, it is no longer of lively interest, and we must turn to newer horizons. Or he might mean that what started out to be an end, in the search for orderly knowledge and understanding, has not been devalued, but has lapsed instead into value as a means, a kind of use value, no longer intrinsic but extrinsic. I like the latter notion better, partly because it smacks of John Dewey's instrumentalism, but even more because that notion of the instrinsic which becomes extrinsic is Whitehead's own language in speaking of an actual occasion, and because it suggests that education is a process in the strongest sense of process, not the finite process of canning peaches, but more like the continuous process of an expanding evolution or maybe even an expanding universe.

The process is indicated in the final word, "thinking." "An ignorant man thinking." Doing something. For thinking there is always the indispensible requirement of ignorance. If you run out of ignorance, you lose the initiative for thought. And if you've stopped thinking, how do you expect the student to be drawn to thinking, or even to know much about how it's done? So we should keep a large supply of the sense of ignorance on hand. Many a college teacher quits before he retires. "Thinking" means staying on the move, fearing complacency, which is the image of death. The college professor is surely not in this respect basically different from other teachers. He ought to be an exemplar.

The idea that education is a process is by now a little trite. What is much less recognized by student and teacher alike is that if that is so, its ultimate monitor and guide, between classes, through summers and beyond formal schooling, must be the student herself or himself. The energy of the process must originate internally. In the essay, "The Rhythm of Education,"[2] Whitehead spells out three phases of the process: (1) the initial excitement of novelty, where the immediate surface appeal of the new data, the new idea, the shining fact, draw the enthusiasm of the student to themselves. This is the stage of Romance. (2) The mastery of technical detail, the attention to accuracy, order, precision, and completeness. This he calls the phase of Discipline. This is where rote and memory have their roles, and it is in amplification of this theme that Whitehead speaks of self discipline. (3) Finally, there is the phase of Generalization, where the understanding gained is applied over larger areas than those from which it began. This is a kind of transcendence which carries with it a new excitement and the adventure of discovery. It becomes a romantic phase of its own.

Familiar also is the conviction that the self-educational posture must be incarnated in the teacher, with no false impersonation or trivial disguise. There is an old saw that attitudes are not taught but caught. But neither of these ideas carries an authority from a wide metaphysical scheme. After all, Heraclitus saw the world as unending process and did so with obscure mystical fervor, while the author of *Ecclesiastes* saw it so also, but with cynical fatigue and something like melancholy. Moreover, although the task of the teacher as role model has a new name, it is as old as the scholastic process itself. Neither education as process nor the teacher as exemplar is the fundamental idea.

The basic idea that underlies both Whitehead's theory of education and his metaphysics is the idea of value. With this notion we come to the third use of the "getting hold of the big ideas" principle, namely, go to the place where the big ideas grow. Not every big idea lies nestled in a nice metaphysics, of course. "Love your enemies" or "All motivation is orientated toward either sex or death," are big ideas. There are plenty of big ideas that have no explicit metaphysics for a matrix, and some may have no metaphysics at all. Socrates, for example, seems to have scorned cosmology, if we are to believe the *Apology*; and I guess he would have thought that metaphysics was barren, if not worse. Nevertheless, for Whitehead metaphysics was a mature passion and the outcome of a lifetime of reflection. It emerges in the wake of a philosophy of science, an earlier mathematical logic, and some splendid, forthright lectures on education, to say nothing of a fascination with intellectual and cultural history. The themes of the educational lectures are not merely intimations of metaphysical conceptions; they are also workshops for ideas that ultimately break through the limitations of their educational intent. For example, Whitehead's early philosophy explicitly avoided metaphysics. It insisted on the isolation of mind from nature, the limitation of mentality, and, finally, the role of the mind as comprehending nature, yet not interactive with her. This is all changed, or at the very least markedly revised, by the time the metaphysics appears. The ferment lies in the readily accessible educational writings. The humane vocabulary of "mental," "feeling," "prehension," "experience," "grasping," "satisfaction," "inheritance," to name only a few, are necessary for his later philosophy. Each identifies an important educational concept. Largely wanting in the early philosophy of science, they emerge with technical meanings in the metaphysics.

So the meaning of the educational theory is illuminated by the metaphysics, but also the converse is the case: the metaphysics is illuminated by the educational theory. The two cohere in a very special way. At the beginning of *Process and Reality* Whitehead develops the idea of "coherence" as a technical concept. Ideas, he says "cohere" when "what is indefinable in one such notion cannot be abstracted from its relevance to the other notions."[3] This is exactly the case with educational theory and metaphysics. For example, if I may anticipate, the complex relations between freedom and creativity ultimately reduce to fundamental indefinables, if they are not such indefinables to begin with. Yet we can understand them better by examining how they are related, in the educational process in particular, and in the world process in general. "It is the ideal of speculative philosophy," says Whitehead, "that its fundamental notions shall not seem capable of abstraction from each other."[4] Clearly, for Whitehead, the same mutuality between the macrocosmic world process and the microcosmic educational process holds.

Nowhere is this reciprocity more evident than in the notion of value. "Value," says Whitehead in *Science and the Modern World*, "is the word I use for the intrinsic reality of an event."[5] Out of context this seems to be another piece of hyperbole like the remark about a university professor being an ignorant man. "Intrinsic" we think of as being an honorific term, as though value were the primary reality. Indeed the context is very large. Fifteen pages later, and in another chapter, Whitehead finally distinguishes between intrinsic reality and extrinsic reality, showing them as reciprocally requiring one another and complementary in their function also. The coherence of intrinsic and extrinsic reality is a big idea in Whitehead's metaphysics, but let us shelve this analysis for the moment and look at its forbear in an educational essay on freedom and discipline.

Whitehead is talking about the double function of the teacher. "It is for him [the teacher] to elicit the enthusiasm by resonance," says Whitehead, "from his own personality, and to create the environment of a larger knowledge and a firmer purpose .... The ultimate motive power, alike in science, in morality, and in religion, is the sense of value, the sense of importance."[6] Again I ask your indulgence in a scholastic inventory. Consider "... resonance from his own personality." So the subjective, personal element in the teacher ought to generate enthusiasm. I hope most of you bridle, even bristle, at this interpretation. The teacher as entertainer – interesting, a little risqué perhaps, but lively and above all exciting – is somewhere between boring and annoying. However, that is not quite what Whitehead said. He said "elicit." It is a precious word; it goes back to Plato and even further to Socrates, who thought of himself as spiritual midwife. The midwife can help at birth, but can neither bear nor inseminate from her own resources. Whitehead says nothing about creating enthusiasm. Indeed, what is elicited is to be regarded as already there, awaiting release. But that's only the first phase. It is, in fact, a special case of the first burst of creativity in the birth of an actual occasion. Beyond that burst comes the teacher's creative role, "... to create the environment of a larger knowledge and a firmer purpose." Again we may gloss over graceful prose too quickly. Whitehead did not say "generate (or provide) knowledge," nor did he say "provide the student with a firmer purpose." Even here the subjective element is not to be trampled. "The ultimate motive power ... is the sense of value ...." Whitehead then continues the quotation we've been considering to say that this sense of value "takes the various forms of wonder, of curiosity, of reverence, or worship, of tumultuous desire for merging personality in something beyond itself."[7] Elsewhere he says, "Cursed be the dullard who destroys the sense of wonder," and of religion he says that it is what we do with our solitude. The emphasis on internal relations is unmistakable.

I have deliberately withheld the sentence which precedes the whole sustained passage I've just been analyzing. I think that Whitehead put it in the wrong place. Here is what he says: "What I am now insisting is that the principle of progress is from within: the discovery is made by ourselves, the discipline is self-discipline, and the fruition is the outcome of our own initiative."[8] That's the model for any actual occasion which first becomes something for its own sake, which has intrinsic reality, and whose internal relations by definition are only indirectly relevant to the outside world. Relevance to the outside world is the business of a larger process supervening on the microprocesses; Whitehead speaks here, in an educational essay, of larger knowledge and firmer purposes. These have to do with the interiority of an enduring object, rather than a constituent least event. They are internal to the enduring object, but external to its minimal parts, which perish and become immortal. But now think of the scope of the last phrase also: "... a tumultuous desire for merging personality in something beyond itself."

To my ear "tumultuous desire for merging personality in something beyond itself" applies very well to the discovery of love and its spiritual and physical desires. There is an implicit warning, in what Whitehead says, that there must be a personality to bring to this desire, something of a self to offer as much as a self which wishes to receive. The "tumultuous desire," however, applies just as well to the exciting and deepening of personal energies that sponsor the plunge into a profession. The implied educational warning is the same: First let there be something of a person to perfect in that merging, whether it be through commitment to another person or through commitment to a profession. There is always the presupposition of interiority, of an entity's first becoming for its own sake, intrinsically, before it can relate and grow, through extrinsic relations, and thereby become intrinsic to the enlarged entity, the enduring object.

Both in the actual occasion and in the larger organism with its basic task of endurance, there is a primal urge. Whitehead speaks of this as the "underlying energy of realization" and again the "underlying eternal energy."[9] Later, in *Religion in the Making*,[10] he calls it "creativity" and indicates that the creativity outruns the individuated creatures. Each individual event is thus the outcome of a limitation, as Whitehead puts it. "Realization therefore is in itself the attainment of value. But there is no such thing as mere value. Value is the outcome of limitation."[11] And again, "The organism is a unit of emergent value, ... emerging for its own sake"[12]

Thus the parallel between the educational theory and the metaphysical synthesis is very close. As we have seen, he calls the creativity the "motive power," a "principle or progress from within," and says that we know it as the sense of value, which requires self-discipline. Metaphysically generalized, the self-discipline is, of course, internal limitation, the selection and harmonizing of aspects of eternal objects.

I must confess that I have always been just a shade uncomfortable with this way of handling the value-fact dichotomy. I feel about it much as I do about the traditional forms of the doctrine of evolution, namely, that although it leaves something to be desired, it is incomparably better than the alternatives. So I shall be Whitehead's advocate in order to speak with a single voice: Whitehead's views are quasi-neo-platonic: to be is, in at least limited degree, to be of value. Realization is in itself the attainment of value. It is perilously close to a generalization of, "To be is to be good," and then, of course, all those problems about Leibniz and Voltaire and the best of all possible worlds loom up. But there is a thin, tough difference in Whitehead's formulation. Realization is the attainment of value. Value is not a status nor is it a property. It is the outcome of a process. Real value is actual value, something that has happened to bring together in one finite embodiment the boundless creativity and the topless hierarchy of possible values, namely, the realm of eternal objects. The something and the happening are identical, and the entity which they are has a factual side and an axiological side.

Merely in existing, however briefly, the event has value status. Just these aspects of certain eternal objects hve been brought together in one harmonious unity by something resembling purposive choice. Whitehead puts it this way: "The organism is a unit of emergent value, a real fusion of the characters of eternal objects, emerging for its own sake."[13] He then goes on to say, "Thus, in process of analyzing the character of nature in itself, we find that the emergence of organisms depends on a selective activity which is akin to purpose."[14] What Whitehead is pointing out is that the characters of eternal objects, which elsewhere he calls "aspects," are not wholly different from the bricks, mortar, and wood that are of value to a wall, *in order for it to be a wall*. A larger inclusion, like the wall's being of constitutent use to a building, would be like the smaller event included in a larger enduring object. The obvious differences are that the wall is static and has an external telos, while events are dynamic and temporal and have an internal telos.

Now I should like to ask you to consider a question that I find rarely raised in Whiteheadean commentary. We are all attracted to some extent by the claim that value and fact lie together at the heart of reality, and that dealing with the one without the other is likely to be futile. We generalize the notion of purpose by stripping it of conscious reflection and intent, so that it can extend to telic explanations which efficient causation is inadequate to handle. But specifically what leads Whitehead to this decision? Usually we debate the acceptability of his theory. It will be of some use to consider how he comes to this view himself. The discussion will have to be a little technical.

Whitehead was dissatisfied with the evolutionary theory of the time. It was 1924. Physical theory was being ruffled by the apparent conflict between quantum theory and relativity theory. Among other things, quantum theory seemed to demand discrete units of energy, while relativity theory required continuous propagation. If coherence is the test for what science shall dominate the other sciences, physics seemed to have lost standing. Whitehead was openly undertaking to extend the biological metaphor to a general metaphysics, which would provide a joint basis for both relativity theory and quantum theory. The sucess of that venture is dated, but two things are still important. (1) Making biology the dominant science was a bold invention. After all, organic matter is only a restricted case of physical matter. (2) It was even more bold, considering that the rather unspeculative biological theory of the time, somewhat intimidated – one might say – by the stern command from physics to be precise, had problems of its own.

For a half century, says Whitehead, there have been "unsuccessful attempts to impress biological notions" on seventeenth-century materialism;[15] but there is an unsolved problem: if we are only given "configurations of matter with locomotion in space as assigned by physical laws," how can we account for living organisms?[16] Something has to be added to raw matter as such.

Speaking for Whitehead rather than from him, there are really two problems. One is that an individual organism, with its cooperating and functionally interrelated parts, can't be described in the language of physics without omitting a great deal. The second problem is that the evolution of life itself is a wholly incomprehensible idea to physics, which is unprepared to deal with novel unities and their incorporation into increasingly complex forms. Yet this is what evolutionary theory begins with.

Let us pursue this dilemma a bit further, since it bears, I believe, on Whitehead's theory of education and also depends upon it. The first difficulty can be stated simply. In an organism, the description of its parts can only be completed by reference to what they are for. Indeed, properly to know the part is to know how it functions in the continuing life of the whole organism. Whitehead puts it this way, in general terms: "... the sheer statement of what things are, may contain elements explanatory of why things are."[17] The rule he proposes is a must for living things. His tentative "may contain elements, etc.," tells us in effect that he is preparing to extend the conceptual apparatus of biology, language and all, to all levels of existence. And why not? Physics is too narrow to be stretched to biology. Why not take the rich language of biology, closer to our own experience in any case, and see if it can be modified for simpler configurations of matter, to show the entities and laws of physical sciences as minimal or limited cases of biological relations?

In that case the least moment in the life of even an electron is a simple organism, almost devoid of the incorporation of novelty which we associate with life, new therefore not in its internal pattern, but only in the new time which it exhibits by contrast with its antecedents. The conceptual problem of the emergence of living from non-living, the problem, as Whitehead put it, of how we can account for living organisms arising from mere matter in motion, can be answered in terms of evolutionary development. Evolution thus antedates what we would normally call "life." Life is the result of evolution first, and then itself evolves. This is not word magic, the mere switching of one term for another. The stock doctrine of evolution of the time held to a genetic repetition of type with random variation producing new genetic forms, most of which were either internally dysgenic or externally unsuited for the struggle for survival. On this view, a handful of survivors would be genetically sound, superior specimens, armed, armored, or more amorous than their predecessors. They would then pull ahead in the competition for food, space, etc. Evolution itself is thus like the sturgeon, prodigiously pouring out millions of eggs, so that a few might mature to continue the act of reproduction. But this panorama gives us only a partial explanation of evolution itself. It accounts not at all for the fact that the current of evolution, with some eddies, has constantly been toward more and more complex forms of life, with more and higher life functions supervening on the older ones. In a purely physical system any occurrence should be predictable from the prior states of matter. But what is there at one level of evolution to predict what the next will be? For that matter, value as measured by the traditional test of survival can be trivial. There are rocks in Greenland that are now thought to be upwards of three billion years old. What does the survival of the fittest mean, save tautologously that those who survive demonstate it? Over against this stands what Whitehead calls "the problem of evolution ... the development of enduring harmonies of enduring shapes of value which merge into higher attainments of things beyond themselves."[18]

The ultimate result for Whitehead is that the release of "value," "mentality," and the like, from their narrow confinement to human affairs alone, and of "organisms" and "feeling" from their application to living beings only, opens the way to a better understanding of the continuity of life in the present world and through the depths of time. Ultimately he will install the idea of mentality at the very foundation of the actual occasion, but this does not happen in *Science and the Modern World*. *Religion in the Making*, and *Symbolism*[19] are still to come. However, there is one other vision that Whitehead has here, at the very inception of the philosophy of organism; it is of the nature of evolution itself. He speaks of the theory of "organic mechanism" as requiring not only an "evolution of enduring pattern," but an "evolution of the laws of nature" themselves[20] and finally even of "wider evolution beyond nature itself." It is not too much to say that Whitehead here has himself given a fine demonstration of how ultimately generalization, which the philosophy of organism certainly is, introduces a new stage of Romance, of excitement in the encounter with novelty. It was a Romance he never submitted to the stiffening treatment of Discipline in his own later thought.

There are other aspects of this new vision and of how and why Whitehead undertook his critique of physical science. There is, for example, the depth of his religious interest and curiosity which arose from his family training, breaking through in the middle and late period; but we are concerned with the interrelation between his educational views and the birth of the new metaphysics.

In education, too, he found the element of value at the root of all teaching. The debate, provoked by the studies of Dewey and others, as to whether or not public schools should teach values, could never have seriously detained him. He would have held that there is nothing to teach but value. We always teach value at least implicitly, for example by imposing the standards for what facts to include and what not. A fact having no value thereby has nothing to recommend it to either teacher or student. But what Whitehead is at pains to apply in a very homely way is the idea that the reality of values is solidly embedded in what is physical. Before his first work on the philosophy of science appeared, Whitehead gives us a view of nature which is not at all the object of mathematical analysis. He says, "... nature can be kept at bay by no pitchfork; so in English education, being expelled from the classroom, she returned with a cap and bells in the form of all-conquering athleticism." Now this was the nature which reappeared in the Lowell lectures, composed of events whose intrinsic reality is value, which is the proper domain of the mental aspect of reality. It is also the same theme that Whitehead pronounces in a comment to William Ernest Hocking: "The simplest notion of the Real," he writes, "... is History. And what is the prime character of History? Compulsion – symbolized by the traffic cop – No, this is still too intellectual – *being tackled at Rugby, there is the Real*. Nobody who hasn't been knocked down has the slightest notion of what the Real is ...." And Whitehead goes on to say that how you take the real is an act of "self-creation" and that freedom "transforms the situation," as against mere "organic reaction."[21]

In between nature as not to be held at bay by a pitchfork and as revealed in History and delivered by knock-down jolts, Whitehead had written that nature is closed to mind and that nothing can be added to our understanding of nature by saying that there is a mind knowing it. But this is nature systematized, brought to order and quieted for observation, not nature encountered and lived.

I do not wish further to visit the field of battle on Whitehead's development. It is a small and ancient little skirmish of no widespead interest at its best. My point is that before *Science and the Modern*

World, there was a healthy respect for nature as the field of value embodied physically in what happens to you, and in some sense responsive to mind. When one stops to think about being kicked in the shins, it puts a strong and simple interpretation on "feeling" as a synonym for "prehension." The humanistic feature of the early educational writings becomes synthesized in *Science and the Modern World*, with the otherwise formal philosophy of science in a way that leads on to a new metaphysics of nature. The reason we turn to the larger context of Whitehead's educational views is that these metaphysical views are funded by and grow out of an earlier preoccupation with educational theory. The metaphysics adapts to the educational views. It provides context and overview for notions that are derivative from ideas first expressed in popular talks about education. Moreover, the power of Whitehead's persuasion has a momentum which far outdistances his systematic achievements. A decade after *Process and Reality*, in the last six lectures at Wellesley, the earlier theme in the educational writings appears repeatedly. For example, Whitehead says, "... the notion of worth is not to be construed in a purely eulogistic sense. It is the sense of existence for its own sake, of existence which is its own justification, of existence with its own character."[22] Four years earlier at Chicago he said, "Newton's methodology for physics was an overwhelming success. But the forces which he introduced left Nature without meaning or value .... a dead nature can give no reasons. All ultimate reasons are in terms of aim [*sic*] at value. A dead nature aims at nothing. It is the essence of life that it exists for its own sake, as the intrinsic reaping of value."[23]

It is almost impossible, however, to emphasize too strongly the influence of the theory of evolution on Whitehead's philosophy, both for its questions and for its examples. In retrospect, it seems almost inevitable that his revised view of nature would be dominated by it. In 1917 he writes in an essay called "Technical Education and Its Relation to Science and Literature," that there is a "reciprocal influence between brain activity and material creative activity .... It is a moot point whether the human hand created the human brain or the brain created the hand."[24] Either side of this issue would have been widely regarded as speculative only sixty years before. And in "The Rhythmic Claims of Freedom and Discipline," published the year before *Science and the Modern World*, he specifically links the teacher's role in education to the Darwinian view of nature. The teacher, as evoker of enthusiasm and provider of a wider environment of knowledge and purpose, "... is there to avoid the waste, which in the lower stages of existence is nature's way of evolution."[25] Natural evolution may, it seems, teach us much, but we are not to imitate it too slavishly. The evolution of man, we might add, is a matter of human responsibility and of human purpose. And it is to this end, in the same essay, that Whitehead bears down on the subject of the sense of value, the sense of beauty, and aesthetic education. The sense of value, he says, "imposes on life incredible labours, and apart from it life sinks back into the passivity of its lower types."[26] In the metaphysics the first phase of actualization arises as the creativity of something coming to be for its sake. This corresponds to the phase of Romance in education. But if the individual occasion is to become something even for itself, many factors have to be adjusted to one another. And if its value is to endure, it must do so in a larger and more continuous enduring object. For both of these demands the rule of Discipline or limitation applies. As in the world process, so in the educational process. There must be not only the aesthetic delight of encounter but also "the aesthetic sense of realized perfection." Whitehead goes on to ask "whether in our modern education we emphasize sufficiently the function of art," and he closes his essay with as gloomy a finish as any I can think of in his writings. We "practically shut out art from the masses of the population." He worries about "maimed" "aesthetic emotions," and wonders if an aesthetic education, sophisticated and integrated to education as a whole, wouldn't "lend some force" to the somewhat more stern appeal of the values (favored by clergymen, prophets, and statesmen) "of the love of God, the inexorableness of duty and the call of patriotism."

These two last points strike me strongly: (1) the primacy of the study of living things and (2) the need for education of the emotions beyond the level of the obvious.

(1) If we take Whitehead seriously – and I do – it would seem that the most important science to study would be biology. By definition it is closer to the life we live. Moreover, the perils of biological ignorance seem to stretch from idiocy in the use of drugs to aesthetic and physiological ruin of the matrix of nature, the nature in which we are embedded and from which we have evolved. There is some hope that the current flurry of attention to our relations with the environment has a chance of getting past the fad phase, engined as it is by self-interest. Whitehead's theme is deeper than these considerations, yet capable of funding them as they need funding. The very conceptual structure and the nature of the inquiry into nature provides a richer and more revealing way of regarding the world. It

was Whitehead's personal triumph that the trained mathematician and theoretical physicist turned organicist could say of logic, against the lure of precision in the exact sciences, that the "exactness is a fake." It was his last public utterance.

(2) The education of the emotions is in a sadder, or at least more primitive, state. The faintly prophetic tone of Whitehead's observation about England seems well borne out in the United States. The Romance of immediacy we know well. The reaching out of emotions to the rest of the world of value under discipline and the upward reach toward more sophiscated feelings have never been regarded as essential parts of education. They are treated as optional decor. We forget that the transformation of immediate and simple aesthetic appeal into mature aesthetic reponse must accompany other kinds of growth.

I am reminded of Walter's theme in *Die Meistersinger*. It is a charming bit of nothing until it receives the discipline it so badly needs. Then it becomes the Prize Song. I also remember my grudging acceptance and dislike of the rote of learning the multiplication tables, until one morning a great light broke over me, and I saw the whole thing: a vast panorama of multiplication tables as condensed and rapid addition, with subtraction and division thrown in for good measure. It was a Generalization, growing out of discipline, and it plunged me into a Romance with mathematics that lasted halfway through college. It was then that I learned another lesson, that not all limitations are self-imposed. In particular, I discovered that I was not a member of the subspecies *Homo sapiens mathematicus*, but, rather, a lightly talented relative.

The trouble is that feeling comes first and we forget that it will continue to be there throughout the whole educational process, no matter how we separate value from fact for curricular neatness, or for information and skill in teaching toward professional expertise. I have yet to hear of a high school that insists on the basic and needful character of an education in sculpture, painting, dance, music and so on. The latter two, dance and music, are commonly taken over by pop entertainment exclusively, and the child's total resources and possibilities may be preempted in that way. It is simply silly to see some source of evil here, even given the rock riots and Saturday night fever. What is poor is that lack of depth and variety of emotional expression. Since there is virtually no element of deliberate and exacting devotion, of transport, of melancholy, or of ennobling inspiration, life itself is not represented in the pop aesthetic forms, so that dance and music become violent alternatives, capsules of relief from a hard world that enable you to go back and hang on to an indifferent and soulless existence. The aesthetic element here belongs to a separate fantasy of chaotic lighting and unearthly sound; it is incapable of integration to the normal existence. Divorced from that existence, it is at best a medication. It is all immediacy, renewable through the day by quick fixes from tape, radio, and so on. It is only a small step from these abstract immediacies to those of success, professional prominence, and the acquisition of possessions. We still have not learned from the counter-culture revolt of the sixties and the echoes of that revolt in the seventies, that emotional development is a part of total development. If the appropriate phases of valuation, emotion, and feeling are absent from the educational growth of students, it will be undertaken in other ways, as a matter of need. Primitive values are universally appealing, in the absence of training, and they will be universally espoused, if no others are to be found. These values will guarantee the development of only primitive emotions and the expression of primitive feelings. No amount of intellectual development barren of aesthetic fulfillment can rectify the imbalance. No technical knowledge and no professional skill can replace the loss.

Human evolution has passed out of the hands of physical nature, beyond bone structure and physiological intricacy. It now relies on conscious human purpose, namely, on education. As teachers, do we have ourselves the aesthetic sensitivity and the breadth of recognition of our place in nature to do well what no other profession does at all?

NOTES

This paper was presented by the late professor Nathaniel Lawrence of Williams College at the Conference on Whitehead and Education held at Claremont, California, October 9-11, 1980. It is published here for the first time with the kind permission of Mary Lawrence.

1. A.N. Whitehead, *The Aims of Education and Other Essays* (New York: Macmillian, 1929; reprint, New York: Mentor Books, 1949), 46. In all cases where a book has appeared in a reprint all subsequent page citations are to the reprint.
2. Whitehead, *Aims of Education*, 26-38.
3. A.N. Whitehead, *Process and Reality* (New York: Macmillian, 1929; reprint, New York: Harper Torchbooks, 1960), 5.
4. Whitehead, *Process and Reality*, 5.
5. A.N. Whitehead, *Science and the Modern World* (New York: Macmillian, 1925; reprint, New York: Mentor Books, 1948), 89.
6. Whitehead, *Aims of Education*, 49.
7. Whitehead, *Aims of Education*, 49.

8. Whitehead, *Aims of Education*, 49.
9. Whitehead, *Science and the Modern World*, 99.
10. A.N. Whitehead, *Religion in the Making* (New York: Macmillian, 1926; reprint, New York: Meridian Books, 1960).
11. Whitehead, *Science and the Modern World*, 89.
12. Whitehead, *Science and the Modern World*, 101.
13. Whitehead, *Science and the Modern World*, 101
14. Whitehead, *Science and the Modern World*, 101.
15. Whitehead, *Science and the Modern World*, 43.
16. Whitehead, *Science and the Modern World*, 43.
17. Whitehead, *Science and the Modern World*, 88.
18. Whitehead, *Science and the Modern World*, 89
19. A.N. Whitehead, *Symbolism: Its Meaning and Effect* (New York: Macmillian, 1929; reprint, New York: Capricorn Books, 1959).
20. Whitehead, *Science and the Modern World*, 101.
21. William Ernest Hockling, "Whitehead as I Knew Him," *Journal of Philosophy*, (14 September 1961): 512.
22. A.N. Whitehead, *Modes of Thought* (New York: Macmillian, 1938; reprint G.P. Putnam's Sons: Capricon Books, 1958), 149.
23. Whitehead, *Modes of Thought*, 183-184.
24. Whitehead, *Aims of Education*, 58.
25. Whitehead, *Aims of Education*, 49.
26. Whitehead, *Aims of Education*, 49.

Part IV: HISTORY OF PHILOSOPHY

14

MAPPING FRIENDSHIP

Philip Bashor

I

Friendship as a philosophical theme, prominent in classical literature, neglected but never abandoned since, shows signs of revival. It represents thought about a socially significant phenomenon indispensable to personal welfare, understanding of which is challenging in itself and in relation to other factors, susceptible to conceptual confusion. In this essay I suggest the use of Brumbaugh's cosmographic analogy to clarify theory on the subject. But let me first venture a preliminary survey of the terrain, noting some landmark literature from pre-Socratic times to our own, before attempting cartographic projection.

In my own article[1] I contrasted the results of Aristotelian and Platonic method, the one rather sharply focussed on a special relation (really, a trait of character) of unique value and satisfaction among adults of standing, the other more broadly open toward a fundamental value in various fields of application. For Plato we run into its all-important but problematic relation to *eros*, seeing something in *philia* not irrelevant to the latter but not identical with it. For Aristotle its many problems are practical ones, which the mature man of prudence, distinguishing what is required in it from marital, filial, economic, and political obligations, needs to learn to handle well. What is the secret of those justly famous sections of *Nicomachaen Ethics*? Not only that he distinguishes friendships of rational soul from those of pleasure and utility, but also, I argue, that Aristotle's definiton of the former – a mutual wishing well to one another under certain circumstances – expresses clearly and relevantly, if not explicitly, each of the four dimensions of adequate causal explanation. Platonic literature, on the other hand, seems to have viewed attribution of friendship as more of a generalization over all sorts of relations, presupposing form underlying and constituting the truth of it, giving priority to knowledge (itself systematically ambiguous) and the means of attaining it. These canonical sources need to be supplemented by reference to other ancient thinkers to obtain a more well-rounded view.

Taking as samples of extreme opinion, there is Empedocles, for whom friendship is constitutive and strong, and Democritus, for whom it is ephemeral and weak.[2] For the former, Love (*philia*) or Adhesive Love (*philotes*) is, along with hate, one of the twin original universal causes of nature: necessary, self-evident, constant, uncreated and eternal ("never shall infinite Time be emptied of these two"), explicative of all unities (combinations), value-laden and of persons as well ("through her they think friendly thoughts and perform harmonious actions, calling her Joy and Aphrodite"). For Democritus it is equally obvious that there is no presence of friendship, or its analog, in nature itself or in natural explanation. Like similar values and qualities it is a frail phenomenon in the imagination of men, noting of it in the *Fragments* only that concord is necessary for war (likely a practical defense measure rather than a Heraclitean paradox) and that mutual cooperation is for sale (rich lending to the poor).

Preserving contrast, but in far more subtle, complicated, and ample ways, official Stoic and Epicurean discussions are classic (in Hastings,[3] Harnack is quoted as saying "the history of the Greek schools of philosophy is at the same time the history of friendship," suggesting another contrast, with Edwards' *Encyclopedia of Philosophy*, containing no mention of it). While Epicurus retains the notion of friendship as a rare, if not unique, quality of human experience, he goes far beyond his Democritean ancestry to encourage and to extoll its value ("of means of happiness by far the most important," Principle Doctrine #27). This must be primarily because of its purity (from pain), its freedom (of choice, following swerve doctrine), its utility (against preventable natural and social ills), and strikingly, its unique ability to provide acceptable agreement of opinion. That we might go so far as willingly to die for a friend threatens the system's consistency, otherwise grounded in self-interest, but provides for response in the direction of Hume's later powerful premising of a natural sympathy. Value of friendship also threatens consistency of the Stoic moral system whose typical norm of self-sufficiency (of the wise and virtuous) would seem to make true personal friendship unnecessary and impossible. Yet Mind (reason) *is* universal, pervading life, making such concrete relationships as family, state, fortune, and friendship acceptable when they are in accord with Nature. I thus see (in a long history with many sources) a converging tendency around this theme: Stoic austerity moderated to allow concrete values due to the universality of the cosmological premise; Epicurean utility moderated to allow expansion of values due to beginnings of its freedom-and-sympathy elements.[4]

Cicero,[5] certainly – his essay rivaling that of Aristotle for top honors from classic sources – occupied the strong middle ground, rejecting "fine distinctions of little advantage" from the schools. He thus defends the known reality of a superlatively prized relationship against Stoic theoretical autarchy and emphasizes in it the non-reducible moral requirement of virtue in the context of divinity and constitutionality against Epicurean theoretical expediency. If politics be the art, science, or practice of social power, Cicero, more protected by aristocratic and less exposed to democratic assumptions about it than we are, knows from experience how poignantly friendship is indispensable to it and at greatest peril from it, as do we. Consisting of "the harmony of opinion on all things human and divine, with goodwill and mutual affection" (VI, assuming practical limits), it is not of weak "need" but "is generous and noble." Consistency under stress (military and political) is obtained by its entailing nothing dishonorable. In fact its highest value lies precisely in constancy and stability (reaching even to a kind of immortality, XXVII), potential for which is "easily perceived," he declares smoothly, by taking "due care" when young (XXV), in a world presumably dominated by fickle fortune, vulgarity, and deception. Rather ominously, though, in view of the late Roman reputation for pederastic vice, he makes no distinction between friendship realization and that of sexual passion (influenced by a common Latin root?).

But Montaigne,[6] rather more wise and warm (from our point of view), also classically oriented, but Christian, does. Hypothesizing a possible ideal marriage of both body and soul, he neither sees nor expects any within a thoroughly class-constituted society. Rather, contrasting sharply with the sexual, friendship when true (not merely of companionship or duty), is fully of the mind and affection, an inexplicable unity of soul, not at all ethereal, but rare.

Emerson's great essay[7] (for those few able and willing to give it the patience it demands) postulates soul as a metaphysical component, not merely a literary device, thereby taking on a problem which Montaigne ignores: that of cause. With a mastery of image and metaphor, the Stoic tension of virtue and practicality, the Epicurean tension of self-interest and goodwill, the Ciceronian tension of power and peace, the Montaignean tension of affection and love, if not theoretically resolved is at least effectively self-contained. "Self," both agency and awareness, undeniable, intangible, irreplaceable, invaluable-also often insatiable and insecure? – is the key. Emerson admits anyone and everyone (selectively) into friendship (at least when undistorted by racial, national, or economic alienation), whether reciprocated in consciousness or not, especially those contributing, for a time, to the self-development of each other, pressing on to its inner purpose: to know the very essence of life ("the nut itself"). Yet he finds high communion with only a few capable of complete truthfulness (holding nothing back) and tenderness (excluding nothing), whether in conversation or in letters, their differences a function of a deep identity. It is finally only in and of himself, unseparated from what is whole ("the essence of friendship is entireness").

Earlier, over in Koenigsberg, producing a line of thought which lends in the Emersonian direction while critically restraining himself from going all the way with it, Kant[8] teaches university youth – all too prone to romantic excesses – a doctrine of friendship, useful and inspiring, if rather more prosaically articulated. Although the principle involved presses on (as we know) to universal and all-inclusive goodwill, realistically there are limits: "he who is a friend to everyone has no particular friend," reminding his auditors that "friendship is not of heaven but of earth." Using different terminology from Aristotle for a similar distinction, true friendship is one of sentiment or disposition (of feeling), rather than of physical need or "taste," its psychological value being that of self-disclosure (completeness of which is, however, unwise), its moral value being that of self-correction (aptness of which may be questionable). Friendship is the practical means for partially overcoming the conflict between self-love and love of humanity, through "generous reciprocity of love." I note especially, as fundamental for the mapping analogy of my own essay, Kant's rather blunt assertion of its a priori character, giving warning as well: "Friendship is an idea, because it is not derived from experience. Empirical examples of friendship are extremely defective," adding "in ethics, however, it is a very necessary idea."

Let me pause here, suggesting that the reader draw his own examples from the rich storehouse of western (and eastern) literature, with reflection and responses appropriate to them. I ask whether strong evidence is not thus available that "friendship" remains an open, vital, philosophical inquiry of distinctive logical interest and social importance, needing clarification? Or perhaps the special sciences in our day have pre-empted this theme also, along with so much else?

A recent bibliography provides convenient references. Barkas[9] cites 603 published items, 67 unpublished ones, gives 23 organizations on this subject of emerging interest, useful in marriage studies, family, socialization, role, and life cycle. She characterizes the subject as one of a voluntary, caring relationship, based neither on kinship nor legality, of "dyadic" relations and "network" connections, sharing common interests, feelings, experiences, and memories, on different levels of intimacy. Friendship is presumed to represent a basic social need (or several of them), reinforcing self-esteem, affecting health and intellect, requiring identifiable skills. Different patterns and problems emerge under different conditions, especially for life cycle and gender, also for workplace and recreation. Types identified include inalienable friends, best friends, fast friends, close casual friends, and expedient friends. An inverse relation between romantic connection and friendship network has been reported. Various sources note such factors as: symbolic interaction, exchange relations, private negotiations, self-disclosure and self-validation, homophily (probably heterophily as well, not mentioned), degrees of institutionalization, situational determinants, affective tone. Bigelow notes three stages of development in friendship leading up to the internal-psychological; Selman five, leading up to the autonomous-interdependency stage. An earlier bibliography on the psychological literature[10] was not available to me. Concerning the effects of industrialization, scarcely to be underestimated, Horn writes, "urban friendships, while harder to make, may be more intimate, more highly valued, or more emotionally intense than relationships in nonurban settings, precisely because they are juxtaposed with so many impersonal contacts."

By such information, much of it powerfully to the point, it is easy to be overwhelmed. Does that indicate that social science method and results are eliminative of philosophical treatments such as are found in classical works? My own feeling is to the contrary. Precisely what is apparent here is the need for orientation, for more far-seeing and systematic interpretation, sensitive to alternative evaluation, by means of which closer critical examination of and application to individual cases and particular claims can also be made effective. Before turning to a cosmographic hypothesis to this lead effect, let me briefly mention a few more recent whole works directly pertinent to friendship theory.

Addressed to the populace at large of a somewhat de-traditionalized industrialized society, postulating an initial condition of "perfect strangers" (highly susceptible to many forms of ill-health), Duck[11] uses incisive points of psychological observation to facilitate the process of coming to close personal relationship ("becoming friends") signified by the degree of physical intimacy involved (regardless of sex), writing his work in an aggressively realistic or activistic manner, quite opposite to that of Emerson's concern for quality of consciousness (or "soul"). "Friendship is skill,"[12] Duck says, the "for life" in his title not designating the fidelity of a conventional marriage vow but rather the degree of sucess, possibly quantitative, in attaining this end of shared physical intimacy, for which verbal exchange is but a preliminary means. At least equally realistic but more dispassionately so, sociologist Bell[13] treats friendship as a relatively enduring and warm personal relation with broad, general behavioral repertoire, exhibiting cultural factors of equality, voluntariness, and openness to private negotiations, with implicit (not stated) rights and duties, a value in itself not merely instrumental to other values. It exhibits psychological qualities of self-definition, trust, self-disclosure, acquired naturalness, testability, and wide acceptability of behavior (within limits). Symptomatically, Duck cites an average of 5.6 "close" friends; Bell a norm of only 2-3 "best" friends. The latter also examines its role in socialization of children and emotional support during adolescence, its tension within marriage and its special significance for non-married, its natural decline in old age.

Theological literature has recently produced two outstanding studies to which we should also give attention. Meilaender[14] proposes to face frankly and fairly the tension between the undeniable necessity and value of friendship and the absolute and uncompromising demands of Christian love. (Attention to the latter has been widely cited as cause for decline of attention to the former in ethical literature.) This tension is evident in five ways: preferential vs. universal, reciprocal vs. unreciprocated, changeable vs. constant, civic vs. transcendent, and leisured vs. vocational or service-oriented. Each of these is explored in detail, citing relevant thought from Augustine, Aelred of Rievaulx, Martin Luther, John Calvin, Jonathan Edwards, Jeremy Taylor, Soren Kierkegaard, Joesph Butler, and Reinhold Niebuhr. Offhand, one might think that the tension can be resolved by simply attributing friendship to man and *agape* to God; but the "confusion" of the two seems too much built into the whole project of theological ethics and the system from which it springs, going back to elements of original Christianity (see also Hastings for detail on biblical friendship), to expect its elimination.

Doubtless much conflict is due to unnecessary exaggerations, for example of a Romantic-Rousseauist notion of society and both puritan and secularized notions of work, perhaps also earlier monastic-medieval premature otherworldliness and, for Meilaender himself, I might add, over-reliance on an Aristotelian definition of what friendship is. In the end no theoretical reconciliation comes to view. For Meilaender the answer is thus one of practical wisdom under God's providence and grace (what he calls *ambulando*), best expressed in the Anselmian paradox between divine disposition (of the moral task) and divine distribution (of the moral resource). "The tension between particular and universal love is 'solved' only as it is lived out in a life understood as pilgrimage toward the God who gives both the friend and the neighbor" so that "if in the course of that sojourn friendship with its delights may often constitute a pleasant resting place, we ought never to mistake it for home."[15]

Also, C.S. Lewis earlier published a well-known work,[16] wise as any other source we have mentioned. In it Friendship – somehat restrictedly interpreted as close companionship based on a common interest – figures as one of the four loves, Affection – undefined, closest to animal response, e.g., for what is familiar and domestic – is another, and Eros is a third – also restrictedly interpreted, as that complete absorption in another person of the opposite sex called "being in love," i.e., romantic love. These "natural" loves (because, I presume, they are spontaneous to the human condition) are contrasted to a fourth: the non-natural love for the unlovable called Charity, both a reality in God and an image in man, the nature of which is taken to include many ramifications of giving, receiving, needing, and appreciating, Lewis thus importantly avoiding oversimplications of some of the more conventional literature. No denying the blending and overlapping of these four loves, he admits, signaled by the very different uses of the kiss at different times for each of them. But, aside from the confusing possibility of self-love being an important, distinctive mode, it is puzzling to the philosopher (as also to the scholar, writer, artist) who lives by means of values of the mind, that love of ideas, love of truth, beauty, knowledge – presupposed in his definition of friendship – is not separately identified. I suppose, however, that he is talking about inter-personal love, seeing degrees of sincere self-forgetfulness (overcoming of negative self-centeredness) in natural affections, in companionship relations, and in passionate-romantic attachments, all evidencing a transcendent origin, without an explicit connection to which, in and by means of *caritas*, none are trustworthy and sufficient.

Let me attempt just one more précis. Lawrence Blum[17] exemplifies what close analysis in contemporary moral philosophy can achieve. Not dealing with friendship per se, but using an Aristotelian point of view on the subject, he queries its effect on moral theory. Dividing the phenomenon for this purpose between its personal aspects (liking, affection, trust, approval) and its altruistic aspects ("substantial concern for the good of the friend for his own sake, and a disposition to act to foster that good, simply because the other is one's friend,"[18] he sucessfully defends the distinctive moral value and rightness of preferential relations so entailed against conventional use of Kantian criteria of impartiality, universalizability, disinterested motivation. Blum's results rest heavily on the genuineness of altruistic emotions (compassion, concern, sympathy, operating at different levels and in different degress, connected with distinctive traits, responses, and attitudes) which he defends against both a rationalistic bias against and an egoistic dismissal of them.

Or, are our various writers on "friendship," whether seeming to agree or not, talking about the same thing? Doubts readily arise, and should arise, as to whether in using the same word, more or less, they are addressing the same subject and/or referring to the same object. But, apart from closest analysis of each thinker's whole mode of speech, plus my own sure knowledge of all that is relevant to the case, how am I to decide? Better reasonably to lay some initial trust in communicative powers (necessary in any case) that different accounts expressing sincere concern and intelligent thought are at least touching upon some common but complex phenomenon, showing different degress of adequacy for different purposes (so Brumbaugh approaches the far deeper issue of time).

II

In graduate school I was most impressed by Brumbaugh's fourfold comprehensive cosography, and have remained so since. I understand these divisions to represent decisions concerning what is most real and true, especially with respect to time and form. On the one hand there is the Platonic mode, emphasizing integral eternal forms, a unified timeless eternity of being above and within the field of flux and things. On the other hand there is an Aristotelian mode, emphasizing plural real forms of things, unchanging components complexly constituting things in change. In contrast, there is also a processive mode, not really maturing until more recent philosophy, giving continuous time full play, with things and forms conceived as temporal functions of or moments within it. And, an atomic approach postulating disconnected multiplicity everywhere, of which things are mere combinations coming to be and passing away, often ignoring form and purpose. Thus, in abbreviated matrix:

	One:	Many:
Being: (rest)	Platonic	Aristotelian
Becoming: (motion)	processive	atomic

Using McKeon,[19] some systems show these differences more with regard to things (classical realism), some with regard to thoughts (modern subjectivism), and some more with regard to words (contemporary language theory). Surprisingly accurate and illuminating understanding of prominent varieties of philosophical thought are thus obtained.

Stalknecht and Brumbaugh's *Compass of Philosophy*[20] is the central work on the issue, moving from root metaphor (the machine, the specimen, the diagram, the work of art) to deeply rooted metaphysics and critical methodology (organized systems of philosophy), through all phases of intellectual activity and pattern of interpretation in between (models for engineering, biological science, mathematics, and art). Brumbaugh's "Preface to Cosmography,"[21] explaining clear transformations and confused superimpositions, introduces the project, included in most of his major work since. *Philosophical Themes in Modern Education*[22] identifies types of learning (as form recognition, as information storage and retrieval, as habit and accumulated experience, and as aesthetic insight). Typology distinguishes time as a logically reversible series of successive moments, as natural stages of organic growth, as field subject to graphic display, and as degrees of irreversible directional intensity, in *Unreality and Time*.[23] Less openly, the classification is nevertheless implicit throughout *Whitehead, Process Philosophy, and Education*,[24] for example, in teaching as laying stress on student motivation, on aptness of curricular organization, on efficiency of skill acquisition, and on providing a creative sense of shared presence.

Note how Brumbaugh attempts to include his own position fairly, along with others, an intention calling for moves of such delicacy of subjectivity and objectivity of self and other as readily to be thought impossible. Yet there is no proof that delicate combinations of subjectivity and objectivity of judgment are impossible; there is overwhelming evidence that it does occur, and there is good reason to believe that the very meaning of philosophy depends upon it.

Note also these points: (a) by including one's own, the picture is not merely a number of abstractly theoretical, indifferent possibilities; (b) by including others it is not merely a rhetorical expression of one's own; (c) simple or direct opposition is included, but alternatives are not limited to it, as in polemics; (d) one's own is not represented merely as a rational balance between two irrational extremes; and (e) theory is not limited to a rather long list (five or more), a set, a sequence, with no ordered relation, or which, if somewhat sound, is logically reducible to simpler terms. Rather, the cosmographic analogy expresses to me a combination of self-affirmation, opposition, balancing, and openness, both well-ordered and non-dogmatic, generalized over experience, fruitful for future use, respectful of recognized values in ordinary experience, science, philosophy, and art.

And, I note as negative evidence for this approach, not mentioned by its author: "evil" might come from the machine factor of life (determinisms), "confusion" might come from the aesthetic or artistic factor (in process); "irrelevance" from the abstract diagrammatic factor; and "pedantry" from the excessively recurring specimen factor. If, against inveterate skepticism, there is evil, confusion, irrelevance, and pedantry, there are presumably factors from which they spring, to which they refer.

But how is friendship, or the theory of it, to be mapped out using cosmographic anaolgy? Here is a suggested line of interpretation, without attempting full development of it, nor full application to cases in question.

In Platonic perspective, friendship might appear as an ideal harmony of relations, perfectly fulfilled only in the realm of intelligible form itself (coincident with value). It is imperfectly exhibited in what we see of the similarities and differences in various regions of attention, the likes and the unlikes, in personal strivings and social relations, in meaningful communications partially succeeding, often failing. For synoptic reason, however, an inner harmony dominates, at least implicitly, the motions within the whole, however much (to spirit and appetite) conflicts, contradictions, frustrations assert themselves from time to time in various ways.

In Aristotelian perspective, keeping metaphor under firm control, friendship clearly belongs to a very special kind of experience, that of close cooperative relations between persons of mental and moral good health (virtue) and mutual goodwill, under relatively definable conditions which are wisely to be cultivated as far as possible, and wisely to be terminated when necessary. True, something comparable can obtain among healthy animals at play, in useful agreements at work, and on occasions of state ceremony in well-organized societies. But these have other names properly designating different functions and natures.

Processive thought sees friendship as relation and continuity, similar to Platonic thought, but more realistically, not so dominated by unity, completeness, and form. There are open networks, webs, nexūs of occasions, of different degrees and types, never for a moment really just the same, changing, we trust, creatively. We find friendships of experience (meaningful personal relations) in natural process, in the adventurous evolution of culture (with its tensions and surprises), and in the challenging freedom and inventiveness of ongoing intellectual dialogue for which, ultimately, boredom alone is death.

Finally, in atomic thought, friendship first appears as something impossible, or at least as incidental and irrelevant. It may also appear as a puzzlement, a momentary enjoyment, even as an occasional rare and happy success in the midst of the real difficulties and drives of life. It is intellectually significant in providing a degree of intersubjective confirmation within a justified general skepticism about knowing the way things really are. Not an original distinctive phenomenon or fact in itself, friendship might be attributed to observations of certain relatively tight connections or bonds, some of them dyadic, which, however, have a disturbing tendency to disappear upon closer inspection. Dispositions for such,or belief in them, can provide an interesting subject for causal, predictive, or logical inquiry. Above all, "friendship" is the kind of word which calls for more analysis.

Summarizing:
Platonic: fundamental, universal, integrative harmonic
Aristotelian: high interpersonal bond of virtue
Processive: open networks for creative realization and re-interpretation
Atomic: fortunate agreements; subject for analysis

This is not to deny a possible unity within or behind such difference in theoretical approach, nor to deny intermediates, mixtures, blends, nor distinction between ideal types and actual cases. I would call this approach a mapping of friendship, using coordinates from the compass of cosmography to obtain useful orientation to reflective thought about and intentional practice in the matter. Pending further argument, earlier references might then be placed as follows:

Platonic: Emerson, perhaps Montaigne and Lewis
Aristotelian: Cicero, Kant, Bell, Meilaender, Bloom
Processive: Empedocles, Stoic, parts from Barkas
Atomic: Democritus, Epicurus (Hume), Duck

In conclusion let me turn two questions against the project as presented so far. Brumbaugh, undoubtedly Platonist, collaborates creatively first with Stallknecht, then with Lawrence, both oriented to Whitehead, epitome of mature processive metaphysics. Also, in one of his most recent works, Brumbaugh designates Whitehead as a Platonist and identifies himself with the need for more concrete procedure and vision in education against exaggerated abstractionism of the traditional liberal arts, springing from Plato. Is not something awry? Should not friendships – and these scholarly, philosophical, closely collaborative relationships based upon common values as well as, likely, personal affection, mutual respect and goodwill, are indisputable examples of such – keep to their own corners, each to each? Cross-classificatory friendships, apparently, often occur; we should all be able to think of examples, perhaps of ones which might have occurred but did not, or should occur but have not. Does not this fact of cross-boundary close connections undermine the validity, or reduce the significance, of the cosmographic approach, at least on this subject?

Also, in a similar vein, is not friendship too personal, too spontaneous and warm in its very essence, too much rightly unpredictable and inexplicable to be submitted to the coldly detached "mapping" analogy at all? "Do not figure friendship but open yourself to it, and enjoy it," seems good advice. Is there not discomfort, maybe outright contradiction, in the very notion of a mapping of friendship?

Overlapping facts, possible conflict in essence, are appropriate warnings, I think, against taking cosmographic analogy too far, or in the wrong way. In addition to distinctions usefully drawn, there is unity, there is mystery, there is overriding interest; nor is the philosophic enterprise limited to the formation of set schools, the defense of types. Calling now upon navigational analogy for a conclusion: trustworthy orientation through great waters, often deceptively calm, sometimes turbulent, stormy, treacherous, potentially deadly – otherwise irresistably appealing, enlarging, immensely fruitful and productive, of beauty and of peace – is essential to the human quest, for which good mapping is invaluable, showing us new and deeper dimensions beyond those with which we are familiar. But friendship, in theme and thought, seems to touch upon additional needs and values than just learning where the various possibilities are situated.

NOTES

1. Philip S. Bashor, "Plato and Aristole on Friendship," *Journal of Value Inquiry*, 11(1968): 269-280.
2. Kathleen Freeman, *Ancilla to the Pre-Socratic Philosophers* (Oxford: Basil Blackwell, 1952).
3. James Hastings, ed. *Encyclopedia of Religion and Ethics* (Edinburgh: T. & T. Clark, 1924).
4. Cf. Whitney J. Oates, ed. *The Stoic and Epicurean Philosophers* (New York: Random House, 1940)
5. Marcus Tullius Cicero, *Essay on Friendship (Laelius De Amicitia*, trans. A.F. Inglis (New York: Platt and Peck, 1908).
6. Michel de Montaigne, *The Essays of Montaigne*, trans. G.R. Ives, vol. 1 (Cambridge, Mass.: Harvard University Press, 1925).
7. Ralph Waldo Emerson, *Essays of Ralph Waldo Emerson* (Garden City, New York: Blue Ribbon Books, 1941).
8. Immanuel Kant, *Lectures on Ethics*, trans. Louis Infield (London: Methuen, 1930).
9. J.L. Barkas, *Friendship: A Selected, Annotated Bibliography* (New York: Garland Publishing Company, 1985).
10. Georg V. Coelho, *Psychological Newsletter*, 10(1959).
11. Steve Duck, *Friends for Life: The Psychology of Close Relationships* (New York: St. Martin's Press, 1983).
12. Steve Duck, *Friends for Life*, 30.
13. Robert R. Bell, *Worlds of Friendship* (Beverly Hills, California: Sage Publications, 1981).
14. Gilbert Meilaender, *Friendship: A Study in Theological Ethics* (University of Notre Dame Press, 1981).
15. Meilaender, *Friendship*, 102, 106.
16. C.S. Lewis, *The Four Loves* (New York: Harcourt Brace Jovanovich, 1960)
17. Lawrence A. Blum, *Friendship, Altruism and Morality* (London: Routledge and Kegan Paul, 1980).
18. Blum, *Friendship, Altruism and Morality*, 43.
19. Richard McKeon, *Freedom and History* (New York: Noonday Press, 1952)
20. Newton R. Stallknecht and Robert S. Brumbaugh, *The Compass of Philosophy: An Essay in Intellectual Orientation* (New York: Longmans, Green, and Co., 1954).
21. Robert S. Brumbaugh, "Preface to Cosmography," *Review of Metaphysics*, 7(1953): 53-63.

22. Robert S. Brumbaugh and Nathaniel M. Lawrence, *Philosophical Themes in Modern Education* (Boston: Houghton Mifflin Company, 1973).
23. Robert S. Brumbaugh, *Unreality and Time* (Albany: SUNY Press, 1984).
24. Robert S. Brumbaugh, *Whitehead, Process Philosophy, and Education* (Albany: SUNY Press, 1982).

15

ALBERTUS MAGNUS AS COMMENTATOR ON ARISTOTLE'S PHYSICS

Helen S. Lang

After Aristotle's works were recovered in the Latin West in the early 13th century, they formed the subject of a variety of different types of commentaries. Ostensibly, the commentary as a form is a secondary source focused on the texts and arguments of Aristotle. But, they are far from neutral re-statements of Aristotle by disinterested scholars. In fact, medieval commentaries present a range of philosophic possibilities from Neoplatonic interpretations of Aristotle to the development of a theory of impetus. In this paper, I shall consider Albertus Magnus' commentary on the *Physics*, focusing on the argument of *Physics* VIII.4, everything moved is moved by another. After briefly considering Aristotle's argument which forms the subject of the commentary, I shall turn to Albert's commentary itself, arguing that it possesses its own logical structure – it consists of four tractates and four theses – as well its own philosophic commitments – Albert's concepts of motion and movers derive from Neoplatonic sources. Albert's commentary at once transforms Aristotle's *Physics* in its formal structure, in its logic and in its concepts. In short, the commentary is on Aristotle's *Physics*, but the physics of the commentary is Albert's own.

Aristotle announces the problem of *Physics* VIII in the opening lines: does motion begin and will it someday end, or is it not a kind of life to all naturally constituted things.[1] Motion, he answers, must be eternal and he offers a proof of this thesis based on his definition of motion as the actualization of the potential *qua* potential by something actual (*Physics* VIII.1.251a 8ff.).

Physics VIII.2, raises and briefly answers three objections to the argument that motion must be eternal. But Aristotle says, these answers need to be made clearer (*Physics* VIII.2253a 2,6,21). The first two objections collapse into a single question: how can the cosmos be constituted so that some things never move, some things always move (making motion in things eternal) and some things both move and rest? (*Physics* VIII.3.253a 22-24) The answer to this question occupies *Physics* VIII.4-6. Everything moved is moved by another; the series cannot go on to infinity; therefore, there must be a first mover which is unmoved (*Physics* VIII.4.256a 2, V.256a 3-20, V.258b 9). Because it is unmoved, it produces an unceasing and unvarying motion in the first moved, which in turn moves everything else; everything else, being moved by something itself moving, exhibits the greatest variety of motion, including motions that start and stop (*Physics* VIII.6.260a 2-11). Thus, by exhibiting the construction of the cosmos, the argument answers the question how it can be that some things never move, some always move and some both move and rest, thereby confirming that motion in things must be eternal.

The remaining objection from chapter 2 occupies *Physics* VIII.7-10 and may be briefly mentioned. If motion in things is eternal, there must be some motion capable of moving forever, without starting or stopping (*Physics* VIII.7.260a 21-23). Aristotle argues that this motion must be circular locomotion and, in fact, is the motion of the outermost sphere of the heavens (*Physics* VIII.9.265a 14-15, X.267b 5-8).[2] The characteristics of the first motion require a mover which is partless, immaterial and without magnitude (*Physics* VIII.10.267b 25).

The main point which I wish to make about these arguments is that, although a first mover appears in both, a proof of a first mover is not their object; their object is to support further the thesis that motion in things is eternal by resolving the most serious objections raised against it.[3] Thus for Aristotle, *Physics* VIII presents one, and only one, thesis, namely the eternity of motion; and it is presented in the language of potency and actuality, the concepts which for Aristotle define motion.

We turn now to *Physics* VIII.4. Its ultimate purpose is to show why motion is eternal by exhibiting the construction of the cosmos. Its immediate purpose is to show that "everything moved is moved by another." Aristotle divides motion, movers and moved things into four exclusive and exhaustive categories, i.e. natural and violent, animate and inanimate. The purpose of the argument is to show that there is a mover for each category. When Aristotle identifies, or thinks that he identifies, a mover for each category, he closes the argument, and chapter, asserting "everything moved is moved by another" *Physics* VIII.4.256a 2).

Aristotle starts with the most obvious case in which a mover is required, violent motion, and works to the least obvious case, natural inanimate motion, the motion of the elements such as fire and earth. When the elements go to their respective natural places, fire goes up and earth down, their motion is both natural and inanimate (*Physics* VIII.4.255a 7). What moves them? As potential the elements must be moved by something actual and the problem of identifying the mover of the elements is the problem of identifying the actuality of their natural potency.[4] Fire is potentially up, earth down; their respective natural place is actually "up" and actually "down." In the absence of external hindrance, potency is always actualized by its respective actuality. If nothing intervenes, natural place always moves its respective element, earth goes down and fire up. (I may add parenthetically that the Byzantine commentators, Philoponus, Simplicius, and Themistius, all identify natural place as the mover and actuality of the elements.)[5]

We may note, as it will be important for Albert, that on Aristotle's view, potency is by definition nothing other than incomplete actuality, so that on contact with act potency cannot fail to be actualized. Hence, no further cause connecting potency and act is required. Aristotle's definition of motion is in this sense fully teleological and so too in turn is both the problem of elemental motion and its solution. An identification of actuality, i.e. a mover, constitutes a complete explanation of motion as actualization of potential *qua* potential.

Let us turn to Albert's commentary on *Physics* VIII. It is divided into four tractates – a form which may originate with Avicennia and Neoplatonism – and these tractates are further sub-divided into chapters and digressions. The chapters deal directly with the arguments of Aristotle, as Albert construes them; the digressions treat either historical or theological issues. Here we find one mark of medieval readings of Aristotle's *Physics*: problems having no theological implications for Aristotle – he does not possess a theology of creation – for his commentators bear an immediate unavoidable theological significance which must be addressed. The theological problem of *Physics* VIII, of course, is Aristotle's argument that motion must be eternal. *Genesis* declares that in the beginning God created the heavens and the earth. The two claims must be somehow reconciled.

The formal structure of Albert's commentary – tractates sub-divided into chapters and digression – provides the first clue to his resolution of the apparent conflict between *Physics* VIII and *Genesis*. Tractate 1, which considers *Physics* VIII.1-2, i.e. Aristotle's opening formal proof of motion's eternity, consists of seven chapters and eight digressions. Thus, digressions form more than half the tractate and all but one are theological. Seven chapters represent Aristotle, seven digressions representing theology. These digressions settle the question of motion's eternity vis-a-vis God's creation, so that the primacy of God's causality and creation are firmly established. Aristotle's argument that motion is eternal does not contradict the truth given in the words "in the beginning God created the heavens and the earth." According to Albert, the eternity of time is an eternity of a never-ending succession of parts, while God's eternity is of an entirely different and prior order – God is immutably eternal.

The force of these digressions appears at the end of Tractate 1. Five successive digressions close the tractate; but in closing the tractate, they also close Aristotle's arguments in Physics VIII.1-2. By introducing a distinction between the immutable eternity of God and the successive eternity of motion – a distinction not found in Aristotle – these digressions guarantee the superiority of God to motion and subordinate the world to God. Furthermore, the digressions finalize a subordination of physics to theology, eternal motion to creation, by separating Albert's concluding substantive chapter on Physics VIII.2 and the opening of Tractate 2, which takes up Physics VIII.3. In short, digressions complete the argument about motion's eternity (and creation) and separate Physics VIII.1-2 from the remainder of Physics VIII.

For Aristotle Physics VIII.3-6 and VIII.7-10 are subordinated to Physics VIII.1-2 because by solving objections to the thesis that motion must be eternal, they provide further indirect proofs of that thesis. When Albert closes the argument for motion's eternity at the end of Tractate 1, he in effect emancipates these arguments from their subordination to the problem of motion's eternity. On his reading, they must possess theses of their own.

In fact, according to Albert, Physics VIII presents not one thesis, but four identified by the titles of the four tractates: (1) concerning the eternity of motion (Physics VIII.1-2), (2) an investigation of the properties of motion according to the consideration of a first mover (Physics VIII.3-6), (3) concerning a perpetual motion according to nature so that a first mover may be known (Physics VIII.7-9) and, finally (4) concerning the characteristics of a first mover (Physics VIII.10). Here we see the relation between the tractate structure of Albert's commentary and its content. For Albert, the four tactates of his commentary divide Physics VIII along its logical lines, as he construes them; and each tractate presents the thesis at stake in its section of Physics VIII. The structure of the four tractates and the logic of the four theses are indistinguishable. And they present the *Physics* VIII of Albert's commentary.

In his four tractates, with their four theses, Albert faces a problem all his own. Aristotle subordinates all subsequent arguments of *Physics* VIII to the single initial thesis of motion's eternity. Because Albert construes *Physics* VIII as presenting four theses, he faces the problem of relating them to one another. And he does relate them: the four theses from *Physics* VIIII enter into a progressive hierarchy from the lowest reality, i.e. successive (and eternal) motion in things, to the highest reality available within physics, spiritual self-moving motion, the first cause of motion.

In this hierarchy, we find both Albert's conception of physics as a science and, for him, the purpose of *Physics* VIII as an argument. For Albert, physics and *Physics* VIII start from the lowest level of reality, physical things exhibiting motion, and work toward the highest level of reality – and the cause of motion, i.e. soul defined as self-moving motion. In this sense, the commentary derives not only its tractate structure from Avicenna and his Neoplatonism, but also its concepts. The progressive order of the four theses formed by the four tractates unite with a Neoplatonic conception of reality tiered into layers of ascending degrees of self-identity. Not only the structure of the four tractates and the corresponding logic of four theses, but also Albert's conception of physics as a science are embraced by the unity of the commentary as an enterprise.

Although space does not allow a full consideration of this point, I would like to suggest that this point holds true generally of medieval commentaries on Aristotle. Their structure, logic, and concepts unite to produce the Aristotle of the commentary. So, for example, Thomas' commentary is structured around *lectiones* and proceeds by ordering earlier arguments to later ones so that *Physics* VIII becomes a proof of a first mover whom Thomas identifies as God, while Buridan treats *Physics* VIII in a set of *questiones* which allows great freedom relative to the text and his treatment of *Physics* VIII in part develops a theory of impetus.

In Albert's restructuring of *Physics* VIII, what becomes of the problem of elemental motion and the identification of its mover? This argument becomes a strikingly Neoplatonic account of motion and movers, whose ultimate origins lie in Plato's arguments in the *Phaedrus* and *Laws* 10.[6]

Briefly summarized, Albert arranges Aristotle's four categories of motion into an ascending hierarchy. The lowest motion is violent motion, both animate and inanimate; here a mover is obvious.[7] Next in the hierarchy is natural animate motion, when it is physical. This motion must be distinguished from the natural animate motion, which is spiritual and which, according to Albert, is discussed in *Physics* VIII.6. There we reach the highest kind of natural animate motion, the spiritual self-identical motion of soul (*Physica* VIII.2.5.3). In *Physics* VIII.4, we have the lower form of natural animate motion, the motion produced by soul when by its presence within body, it moves body (*Physica* VIII.2.3.567b). Albert replaces Aristotle's definition of motion in things as the actualization of the potential *qua* potential with a Neoplatonic definition of physical motion as the by-product in body of the presence of soul.

After physical motion as the by-product of soul in body, the elements, natural inanimate motion, are next in the hierarchy of motions. How does Albert account for fire going up and earth down? Albert's account of elemental motion requires, and returns to, his theology as established in the digressions of Tractate 1. When God created the world, he made matter receptive to form by placing in matter receptive principles called inchoate form or, alternately, passive potency (*Physica* VIII.1.13.549b-550a, VIII.2.4.570a). This principle is not itself matter – matter is unknowable and drops out of Albert's account – but, like Neoplatonic seminal reason, is a rational principle which by its presence in matter enables matter to receive form (*Physica* VIII.1.13.549b-550, VIII.2.4.570a). Furthermore, when God created the world, according to Albert, he not only related form and passive potency by making passive potency receptive to form, he also oriented form once it is present in passive potency toward operation (*Physica* VIII.1.13.551a, VIII.2.4.571b-572a).

This account of potency contrasts sharply with Aristotle's account. For Aristotle, potency is not inchoate form, but rather is associated with matter, which as matter "desires" form (*Physics* I.9.192a 22-24). By definition potency, for Aristotle, cannot fail to be actualized on contact with actuality and hence there is no need for a cause connecting potency to act – the role of God for Albert.

Albert uses passive potency and the orientation of form to operation to reinterpret Aristotle's entire account of elemental motion. The generator of the element, Albert says, gives receptive passive potency first form which passive potency waits to receive. Thus the generator, which brings form to waiting potency, is the mover of the element required by the argument, i.e. "everything moved is moved by another." Aristotle never mentions the generator as the mover of the elements; instead, Albert's mover resembles not the actuality of

Aristotle, but the God of the *Timaeus* who gives form to matter (*Timaeus* 30b-c). If nothing impedes, then the ordering, given by God, of first form, e.g. the form of fire, immediately leads it to operation, e.g. fire goes up.

Aristotle's argument identifies a mover for each of the four categories of motion, working from the most obvious case to the most difficult. The identification of natural place as the actuality and hence the mover of the elements solves the immediate problem of elemental motion, so that Aristotle may conclude that "everything moved is moved by another" within the resolution of the objection to the thesis of motion's eternity.

Albert closes the argument for motion's eternity at the end of Tractate 1. This argument in Tractate 2 functions within an inductive proof of the cause of motion, ultimately soul itself defined as self-moving motion. Within this inductive proof, Aristotle's four categories of motion become a hierarchy of ascending levels of reality leading to this cause. Within this hierarchy, the problem of elemental motion is the problem represented by this level of reality and it is solved not by natural place but by Albert's account of the generator of the elements plus the ordering by God of form to operation.

Several conclusions follow for Albert's commentary on *Physics* VIII. (1) Conceptually Albert's account of elemental motion derives from Platonic and Neoplatonic sources. Concepts such as passive potency and the radical unintelligibility of matter are superimposed onto Aristotle's argument. In some sense, Aristotle's argument lends itself to a Neoplatonic interpretation because of shared terminology such as potency and form and because both Plato and Aristotle argue that "everything moved is moved by another." But for Aristotle, this proposition ultimately involves an unmoved mover, while for Plato it ultimately involves a self-moved mover, in fact self-moving soul. Their *cosmoi* are constucted accordingly. Albert clearly sides with Plato.

(2) In reading *Physics* VIII, Albert introduces theology into the *Physics*. He reforms Aristotle's argument using Neoplatonic concepts in the service of his own theological commitments. In this sense, however Neoplatonic Albert's construal of *Physics* VIII, it nevertheless constitutes an original argument and an original moment in the history of philosophy.

This point brings us to the broader issues of Albert's argument. It is, after all, a commentary on *Physics* VIII. But as a commentary, it does not so much follow Aristotle's arguments as dominate them;

and this gives us the key not only to Albert's commentary, but to the medieval commentary as a philosophic genre. We reach here our final conclusions.

(3) The structure of Albert's commentary becomes the structure of *Physics* VIII. That is, the commentary consists of four tactates with four theses. Read through Albert's commentary, *Physics* VIII too breaks into four theses. As formal elements in the construal of *Physics* VIII, the chapters and digressions of the commentary make their contributions to the closure of the argument concerning motion's eternity and a new beginning in another, the investigation of motion according to its cause. In this sense, Albert does not follow Aristotle's arguments but reforms them according to his own conceptions and problems.

(4) Here we reach our final point concerning Albert's commentary: its unity as philosophy. I have already suggested the main features of this unity. The tractate structure, the progressive ordering of the four theses, and the concepts at work within this structure indicate a strong intellectual vision – that of a Neoplatonist. Again, the formal role of Albert's digressions in Tractate 1: they establish the superior eternity and causality of God and the superior truth of *Genesis* to natural causality and Aristotle's *Physics*; this theology in turn provides the necessary conditions for the account of elemental motion in Tractate 2. The unity of Albert's commentary is very much the unity of a theological commitment which establishes the grounds within which physics or philosophy must operate. And if this ground too has its ultimate origins in Plato, as it most assuredly does, it nevertheless has been entirely reformed into a Christian theological framework and reading of Aristotle's *Physics*.

Here we possess the unity of Albert's commentary on *Physics* VIII. No element of it falls outside the bounds defined by Albert's own theological and philosophic commitments. Hence, we have in Albert the unity and originality of the commentary as a philosophic genre: Albert gives us both a commentary on Aristotle's *Physics* and the *Physics* of his commentary. And, I would suggest, he is but a case study for the medieval commentaries as a genre.

NOTES

1. Aristotle, *Physics* VIII.1.250b 13-14. References to Aristotle are to the Oxford Classical Text.
2. On construing the Greek text of this passage, cf. H. Lang, "Aristotle's Immaterial Mover and the Problem of Location in *Physics* VIII," *Review of Metaphysics* 35(December 1981): 321-335.
3. Cf. H. Lang, "Why Fire Goes Up: An Elementary Problem in Aristotle's *Physics*" *Review of Metaphysics* 38(September 1984): 69-106.
4. For the following argument, cf. *Physics* VIII.4.
5. Cf. Lang, "Why Fire Goes Up," 100-101.
6. Plato, *Phaedrus* 245C 5ff; *Laws* X.894B 5ff. References to Plato are to the Oxford Classical Text.
7. Albert, *Physica* 8, tr. 2. c. 3 (ed. Borgnet 3: 567b). All references to Albert are to the edition of Borgnet, B. Alberti Magni, *Opera Omnia* (revision of 21 folio volumes published by Pierre Jammy, OP, Lyons, 1651, (Paris: Vives 1890-99). Indicated by volume, followed by page and column a or b when necessary.

16

DESCARTES IN MEDITATION AND METHOD

Berel Lang

Something, if all by itself, may rightfully appear very imperfect; but if it is seen in its role as a part in the universe, it is most perfect.

Descartes, Fourth Meditation

I

Before Descartes decided on the "Discourse on the Method for Rightly Conducting the Reason and Seeking for Truth in the Sciences" as a title, he had alluded to that work more simply as the "History of My Mind *l'esprit*" – and the structure of the *Discourse* was indeed to remain that of an historical narrative in which the authorial "I" recounts a sequence of experience and thought leading to the formulation of a method and the conclusions that followed from it. Descartes employs a conventional grammatical form in this narrative: the first-person singular, simple past tense; and the evident reason for his choice of this means of representation, as unlikely philosophically as it is common for story-telling, is that the "analytic" method that the *Discourse* is a discourse on has itself the form of autobiographical narrative. It follows, according to Descrates, the historical – and to that extent the logical – progress of thought. In this context, thinking moves, moment by moment, from cause to effect, just as do individual moments of the perception of events and the direction they give to experience as a whole. Thus, the autobiographical narrative of the *Discourse* both recounts Descartes' discovery of a method and affords a view of that method at work. Although it might be argued that there is no significance in this doubling effect, that a method can be proposed without at the same time being used in the description – so, for example, that the *Discourse* could as well have been written as a treatise: third person, present tense, passive voice – Descartes himself tells us that for his method, there is good reason why the connection between description and act should be exhibited – practised – in his text. It had not been his intention, he writes to Mersenne (27 February 1637) explaining his choice of "Discourse" rather than "Treatise" in the title, to "teach" the method: the method is a "practice rather than a theory."[1]

The discussion here will later speak more systematically about Descartes' conception of the analytic method, in particular as that method determines the constuction – the art – of the *Meditations*; but for the moment, reference to the latter work is only foreshadowed by reference to a second, less obvious reason for Descartes' allusion to the first-person singular, past tense in the *Discourse*. This is the fact that as this grammatical structure is applied to the history of the person who is speaking (in particular, to his thoughts or his feelings), it also serves to block or at least to defer objections or interruptions with which a reader might otherwise break into the sequence of narration. If I say that yesterday I thought that I could fly, I am not inviting judgement either of the present claim that I can fly or of the assertion that yesterday I could indeed fly. I am reporting, ordinarily as part of another and longer story, a thought that I had yesterday – and at least this much, that I had the thought yesterday, would ordinarily pass without question since I am a privileged if not the only only possible chronicler of my own thinking. Even the listener or reader who regarded such a claim as a symptom that unwarranted diagnosis would be implying acknowledgement of the report itself as true. (If the report as a whole were regarded as a symptom, there would be no place within the context or perhaps outside it either for any discussion of truth, however long deferred.)

To be sure, any such narrative sequence may evoke substantive reservations or questions on the part of the reader. And certainly, in the history he recounts in the *Discourse*, Descartes proposes as "ideas" that he had had, assertions that are not self-evidently true and that would, moreover, be contested if they had to stand on their own, detached from the contextual claims that they "truly" had been thought. Moreover, partly by omission – since he never suggests that the conclusions he arrives at in the course of this intellectual history had been subsequently (from the later vantage point from which Descartes-the-writer writes) displayed – and by commission, as he often states or implies for his conclusions in the *Discourse* that they disclosed themselves as true not only when he first came on them but that they continue to do so at the time of writing, Descartes opens the *Discourse* to objections directed beyond the incontestability of claims of past first-person experience at the contingency of present claims of knowledge or truth for which there is no first-person privilege. Even with respect to the latter, however, the narrative structure within which all of his assertions appear requires the sympathetic and even only the prudent reader to read to the end of the narration, in order to see if at any later time, within the narrative past or from the vantage point from which as writer he "now" looks back on it, Descartes might have reconsidered what he had earlier reported as his thoughts at the time. The reader, in other words, is impelled by the form of the work to reserve judgement until he sees how the narrative "comes out." This prescription is not, of course, for an indefinite deferral. Short of trumpeting like Protagoras that he, Descartes, is the measure of all things and not only of his own thoughts, a doctrine with which the *Discourse* itself is finally sharply at odds, the autobiographical narrative of the *Discourse* would have the effect only of deferring objections and counterarguments, of urging that judgement be reserved until, as he would in the reading of other "fables" (one of Descartes' own designations in the *Discourse* (Part 1)), the reader joins the narration in the actual present that they – the narration brought to conclusion, the reader at the end of his reading – eventually reach in common and at the same time. Then, the reader is in a position to judge, to affirm or to deny and certainly, in any event, to question.

An issue that the *Discourse* leaves over is whether this feature of deferral in the text is anything more than an incidental consequence of Descartes' evident impulse for dramatization – self-dramatization at that (he might, after all, have been using philosophy itself incidentally, as a means of writing about himself); whether, more pointedly, philosophical significance is to be attached to it, or if, as may seem likely at first glance, it makes no more than a rhetorical or ornamental (a "literary") difference in the presentation of an otherwise quite "normal" philosophical system. This question moves us abruptly away from the *Discourse* to the text of the *Meditations*. For there, even with the shift in narrative time from the historical past used by Descartes in the *Discourse* to the virtual present he uses in the *Meditations*, we find that the objections to the assertions of metaphysical truth in the latter are deliberately and explicitly deferred – to be formally acknowledged only as a later and distinct supplement to the text. Even without Descartes' many references to his plans for the organization of the *Meditations* and his several instructions to Mersenne about how the Objections and Replies are to be arranged there, we might infer from their proportions alone – they are six times longer than the *Meditations* themselves, often repetitive – that Descartes had a specific purpose in mind, both in deciding to solict and to include them at all, and then in placing them as he did, complete and separated from the body of the *Meditations* itself.

I shall be considering various aspects of this purpose in a later section of this paper; but one side of the question of why Descartes would gather the objections in one place (whatever the place) rather than have them interspersed topically in the text, has to do with his reason for soliciting and publishing responses to the *Meditations* at all – and reference to the latter point is relevant here. One element of that rationale was clearly prudential and strategic – Descartes' concern to insulate his writings and himself from religious and social criticism or possible persecution. He had, we know, withheld publication of *Le Monde* when he learned of Galileo's trial in 1633; and even the *Discourse* and the scientific essays which it prefaced, purged of references to the issue of whether it was the sun or the earth that moved, had stirred critical reactions that Descartes was anxious to avoid in response to what he took to be the more radical character of the *Meditations*. One means of avoiding unpredictable and possibly dangerous criticism was to anticipate it by authoritative approval. Thus,

The less [the ignorant contradiction-mongers] understand it, the more eloquent they will be unless they are restrained by the authority of a number of learned people .... If you agree, I would dedicate it to all the masters of the Sorbonne, asking them to be my protectors in God's cause. For I must confess that the quibbles of Father Bourdin have made me determine to fortify myself henceforth with the authority of others, as far as I can .... (Letter to Mersenne, 30 September 1640)

For this purpose, moreover, to have all the objections gathered in one place, associated with their respective respondents (the latter being known even if they were not explicitly named) would allow readers to see that the objections, however rigorous, did not carry with them condemnation. The very absence of condemnation from comments offered by eminences of the learned and clerical world would in fact be a protective hedge; so, even objections might serve as an *imprimatur*.

But this, admittedly, is no intrinsic reason for the deferral of the objections. A more immediate concern would be for such intrinsic reasons if they exist – and as Descartes, it turns out, himself provides them. He suggests, for one thing, that the objections to the *Meditations* need to be formulated (published and then read together with his replies) as following the order of the *Meditations* themselves, since then the order of the objections would, whatever their merits or defects, correspond to the order in which the assertions they were questioning had been made. This insistence at once underscores and begs the question of what in the links that determine the sequence of the *Meditations* is so important for the reader's understanding. We find the answer to that question, I shall be proposing, by a process of detection that relates Descartes' own explicit testimony about the need to defer readers' objections to the *Meditations* to his conception of the method "practised" there. This conjunction leads in turn to a conception of the meditation as a medium of philosophical expression. The evidence that bears on this line of argument includes many central themes of Cartesian metaphysics that have often been discussed independently and quite aside from their occurrence in the *Meditations* – and I shall be suggesting that such dissociation is tendentious, that it has in fact distorted what such accounts then conclude to be Descartes' "position" in the *Meditations*. The latter objection, moreover is not only a comment about the importance of taking seriously the more general contexts in which allegedly limited philosophical arguments appear. For beyond this, Descartes' wish to defer objections reflects what he takes to be the unusual connections established in the sequence of argument in the *Meditations*. It is the requirements made by those connections – historical, logical, metaphysical – that lead Descartes to what otherwise might be seen as purely a formal or aesthetic matter: his continuing and serious reflection on what meditation – the practice, the literary genre, and finally, the character of his *Meditations* – is.

A direction is given to this line of interpretation in a striking statement written by Descartes to Mersenne (24 December 1640): "I do not think that it would be useful, or even possible, to insert into my meditations the answers to the objections that may be made to them. That would interupt the flow and even destroy the force of my arguments." The claim that the "interruption" of the meditations in order to respond to (and by implication, before that to have stated) certain objections might "destroy" the force of his arguments must be startling to most modern readers. If the claim were true, of course, it undoubtedly would be a good reason (for Descartes, at least) for hoping to defer such objections. But how could it be true if we are here addressing the Descartes of "clear and distinct" ideas, those building blocks of knowledge which, attached to one another, constitute, on most interpretations, what Descartes takes to be the whole of the philosophical – and real – world? Would not the very notion of a distinct idea argue against a claim for the "flow" of an argument that could even be disturbed, let alone "destroyed" by the interruption of objections? The answer to these questions and to others that branch out from them, is rooted in the connection between Descartes' conception and practice of method in the *Meditations* and the philosophical genre of the meditation that Descartes in part inherits, in part creates. Viewed from one perspective, that connection is close, virtually reducible: the principles that characterize philosophical method and philosophical style respectively merge. From a second perspective, Descartes' interest in method and his concern with the dispositions of philosophical genre and style are not only distinct but at odds with each other, almost contradictory, since method is to be held quite apart from the ornamental or aesthetic boundaries of genre and style. These two perspectives are not only alternate ways of reading Descartes, imposed by readers who themselves have special interests in one or the other of them. They are, I shall be arguing, conflicting impulses in Descartes himself who was also, we recognize, a dominant influence in the history of the traditions of interpretation that now find themselves interpreting him. We shall then be considering these two versions of what amounts to another Cartesian dualism, lesser known than the mind-body dualism, but, for the same Descartes who would at once affirm and attempt to overcome the mind-body distinction, hardly less fundamental or compelling. We might well suspect, in fact, that the two dualisms – method/style, body/mind – are related, first conceptually, and then in the task they leave over. For on Descartes' own account of the central dualism of body and mind, he acknowledges that there must be some way of fitting the two pieces together again. We may hope, then, for the equivalent of a pineal gland as a mediating point for Descartes between style and method.

II

We learn about Descartes' method in the *Meditations* from what he says about it as well as from his practice in that text. Probably the most definitive reference that Descartes makes to that method appears in his Reply to the Second Set of Objections:

> Analysis shows the true way by which a thing was methodically discovered and derived, as it were [to] effect from cause, so that if the reader care to follow it and give sufficient attention to everything, he understands the matter no less perfectly and makes it as much his own as if he had himself discovered it. But it contains nothing to incite belief in an inattentive or hostile reader; for if the very least thing brought forward escapes his notice, the necessity of the conclusions is lost .... Synthesis contrariwise employs an opposite procedure, one in which the search goes as it were from effect to cause .... It does indeed clearly demonstrate its conclusion; and it employs a long series of definitions, postulates, axioms, theorems and problems, so that if one of the conclusions that follow is denied, it may at once be shown to be contained in what has gone before. Thus the reader, however hostile and obstinate, is compelled to render his assent. Yet this method is not so satisfactory ....[2]

This well-known comparison between the method of analysis and the method of synthesis has a number of surprises for the modern reader, beginning with the contrast between the "inattentive or hostile" reader and the reader who "cares" and who gives "sufficient attention." The synthetic method that will "compel" the former reader might be expected to emerge as the more inclusive and adequate of these two alternatives, on the assumption that an argument that can convince hostile readers would *a fortiori* serve for sympathetic readers. By contrast, the analytic method which persuades only readers who are not hostile might well be judged to have limited force, even to be tendentious as it assumes a disposition in the reader to go along with the sequence of argument rather than to test it. Descartes himself anticipates the latter charge – that critics might claim that it was "unfair of me to want to have the truth of my contentions admitted before they have been fully scrutinized ..." (Reply to the Second Set of Objections). Nonetheless, it is in this direction that he turns, following and defending the analytic method as the stronger of the two alternatives for what he has meant to say and do in the *Meditations*.[3]

What is it, then, in the practice of the "hostile or inattentive" reader and the synthetic method that the reader who "cares" and the analytic method he follows avoids? In the statements by Descartes quoted above, the principal discrepancy between the two seems to be only that for the former, the sequence of argument would open itself to interruption by objections. This is, it might be argued, hardly an extraordinary occurrence, and it would in any event be an unlikely basis for the selection of something so fundamental as a philosophical method. But that characteristic would matter, indeed it would be crucial, if the connectives in the sequence of argument were not only logical but actual, if the steps in the sequence corresponded to a development of history or experience and not only to a process of logical inference: for here the interruption by objections would be isolating a part of the sequence and testing that part by itself, when it was the development of the sequence – the progression of autobiographical fact that had led the writer up to the present from which he writes and that was to lead beyond it – that was being "asserted."

This is, in fact, the basis on which Descartes' preference for the method of analysis turns. If – as the synthetic method presupposes – an argument were arranged not temporally but logically or spatially, if the conclusions of the argument were derived from a set of "definitions, axioms, postulates" that served collectively as premises, then any of the possible conclusions as determined only by the constraints of logic might be inferred or tested at any time. The order of such discussion would thus be constrained only by the "order of topics" – that is, the order of whatever at a particular time, on an atemporal grid of what was logically possible, most interested the writer. His arguments, then, would be "disjoined," and understandably so – since he would be in a position to "say as much about one difficulty as about another" (Letter to Mersenne, 24 December 1640). But the structure of the *Meditations*, we are to understand, is not of this kind. In it, the sequence of argument does not begin or continue as the interest of a reader (or before him, the writer) may be stirred, constrained only by logic, but where he can actually begin and continue. It is the possibility of argument itself (and finally also, of the arguer) that is tested there. Thus the order of proof is inseparable from the determination of its force: to break the sequence by isolating one of its steps, even by anticipating or skipping ahead, is to confuse and then unavoidably to distort the line of argument – its connectives – which Descartes alleges to be essential to the determination of the argument in each of its moments. The interruption of meditation is thus only incidentally a psychological phenomenon; disruption of the sequence affects the substance and not only the representation of the argument. Thus when Descartes calls for patience from his readers, when he quarrels with readers who do not take ample time to formulate their objections to the *Meditations*, there is more here than only an author's plea for a conscientious reading. The character of the argument is alleged to require not only time taken with each step, but the deferral of judgement (if not quite the "two or three years" that Descartes suggests that likely objections should take) until the place of each step is identified within the whole.

The reasons for the latter requirement appear in the difference between what we would now speak of as the "hypothetico-deductive" method (of synthesis) and the analytic method.[4] The former will not do – would never do, on Descartes' account – for establishing a foundation of knowledge just because of its starting point in hypothetical premises: definitions, axioms, postulates. We could, setting out from such premises, be certain that what follows from them indeed follows from them, and this could be assessed at each step of inference; but the truth of such conclusions would be tested only so far as the premises also had been tested – and this cannot be assured by the synthetiic method itself. For Descartes, as James Collins writes, in the synthetic method we are "held captive in a skeptical suspension of assent to the truth of its principles and their inferred consequences."[5]

An important issue that was, in Descartes' view, decided by the difference between the two methods appears in the dispute that Descartes himself entered about the logical standing of the *Cogito*. "Was not that statement an abbreviated syllogism (enthymeme) with the major premise suppressed?" – the question was directed at the *Cogito* almost immediately on its appearance and has been repeated frequently since. And Descartes' own response is explicit: that the *Cogito* is not the question-begging syllogism it would be if the concluding "sum" were held to follow from the addition of a major premise (that "all thinking things exist") to the explicit minor premise, "I think." Quite the contrary, in fact: we would never know that "All thinking things exist" except as we began with the knowledge that "*I* think, therefore I exist." "For it is certain," Descartes writes specifically about the *Cogito* in the Reply to the Second Set of Objections, "that in order to discover the truth we should always start with particular notions, in order to arrive at general conceptions subsequently ...." (cf. also the Letter to Clerselier, 12 January 1646, where Descartes directs much the same reply to Gassendi's similar objection.) To be sure, Descartes' dissent here does not resolve the question of what the logical status of the *Cogito* is. But if we can safely assume that Descartes knew that the syllogism "All thinking things exist; I think: therefore I exist" was a valid argument, then his rejection of that formula as a rendering of the *Cogito* strongly suggests that in his view the *Cogito* achieved something more than only logical or "synthetic" validity.

One such alternative basis for the analytic method, as has already been suggested, is that provided by the actual order of events, in the correspondence it articulates between the "virtual" time within the sequence of argument and the "real" time or history outside it. The plausibility of such a basis for the analytic method is underscored as we recall that in the *Meditations* it is the possibility of knowledge as such that is being tested. What is first at issue in the *Meditations*, in fact, is not so much the question of where the Cartesian meditator can begin to rely on claims of knowledge, but where the beginning of the meditator himself is. This same issue of origins, moreover, remains an issue in the successive stages of Descartes' argument; it is never detachable from them, and in fact it constantly forces a relation among the later stages themselves. This is not to say, of course, that parts of the sequence of argument (including the *Cogito* itself) could not be separated and assessed by themselves, out of context, but only that to do this would turn into a question of logical inference a sequence of assertions in which it is the actual world (including a place for the thinker of that world) that is being constituted.

To be sure, according to Descartes, this actual world discloses itself to the act of meditation, not, as might be expected from his emphasis in this connection on the historical process, to the senses. The hard work that Descartes associates with the process of meditation (which turns out to be an identical labor for the reader and the writer) above all requires a disengagement from the senses. Interruptions in the sequence of meditation would be most likely to come, in fact, from critics who had failed this process of disengagement, who were not themselves meditating at all: "The majority of objections [to the *Meditations*] would be drawn from perceptible things, whereas my arguments get their force from the withdrawl of thought from objects of sense" (Letter to Mersenne, 24 December 1640).

Descartes may seem to move too quickly here in his assumption

that the critic who interrupts the process of his (Descartes') meditation must be at cross-purposes with that process; and indeed he
might be claiming (circularly) that someone who broke into the
sequence of argument would by that fact be known not to have been
meditating, to be oblivious to the force of the sequence. But he
might mean, more subtly, that objections likely to be obtruded
would oppose particular moments or items of evidence to what, in
the line of his own argument, was intended to be not a number of
particular claims, each of them one among a number of possibilities,
but a cumulative sequence of steps that were not only logically
consistent but also, beyond that, actual – made actual in the process
of meditation. There is no avoiding the sequence in the act of
thinking about thinking. Objections or counterarguments
(themselves, after all, a "genre" of discourse) characteristically allege
a conflict between the objector's evidence (drawn from any possible
source) and individual claims that have been abstracted from the
original sequence of argument. It is this two-fold process of abstraction that Descartes is contesting. (A less likely counter-argument
would be directed against the whole of the original context – an
objection that in the case of the *Meditations* would challenge the existence of the meditator as well as the content of his meditations.)

Descartes' emphasis on the intensity of concentration required for
meditation, the need for disengagement on the part of the meditator
from the occasional and contingent moments that comprise sensible
experience if he is to have access to the continuities and necessity of
the analytic method, is an important clue in any attempt to understand Descartes' settling on the meditation as an important – in a
strict sense, the most important – genre of philosophical discourse.
More needs to be said yet about the way in which the Cartesian
meditation is shaped to take account of the continuities and the
actual process of the analytic method – but that aspect of the meditation, too, is linked to its denial of a role in meditation to the senses.
It should be lost on no one that one of the two intentions announced
for the *Meditations* in Descartes' full title – to demonstrate the
"distinction of the soul from the body" – is thus also held by him to
be a condition for the practice of meditation. The soul must be itself
– and by itself – if meditation, or the proof of the soul's existence, is
to be possible.

III

The disengagement from the senses and its corollary in the process of systematic doubt of which the senses are the first and principal object do not by themselves account for Descartes' conception of the meditation either as practice or as a literary genre. What is missing from them is the feature of temporality or sequence that turns out to be crucial in Descartes' preference for the analytic over the synthetic method. The requirement of disengagement might, in fact, seem to be at odds with this other feature. Numerous traditions of writing and teaching on the art of meditation both prior and subsequent to Descartes have viewed the withdrawl from the senses as a means of eliminating or minimizing the effects of the temporal character of experience; and the literary traditions in which Descartes most immediately places himself seem also to deny the requirement (or even a capacity) of sequentiality as a feature of the meditation. Montaigne is often acknowledged to have been the creator of the genre of the personal essay to which the *Meditations* is in a variety of ways indebted (he is also, on other grounds, an important figure in the Cartesian background, if only for giving a point to the suggestion that Descartes was as much interested in attacking skepticism as he was in dislodging scholastic dogmatism.[6] "All that is certain is that nothing is certain," Montaigne had had inscribed on a beam in his study – certain grist, in any event, for the Cartesian mill. Descartes writes, as though in direct response, in the Second Rule: "He who doubts of many things is not more learned than he who has never thought about them.") But the "I" encountered by the reader in Montaigne's *Essays*, even in the varied settings through which Montaigne leads it, is nonetheless static, a constant that relates past events in its thought and experience to a present time from which it looks back, and that appears then not so much as an "outcome" or consequence of the past as a distributor of equity, balancing and reconstituting the pieces of that past.

Descartes also drew, more explicitly, on the work of the Stoics for whom the meditation was also at once a literary genre and a mode of action. But here again, in Seneca whom Descartes cites with some frequency, or in Epictetus and Marcus Aurelius, the internal structure of the practice or the genre of the meditation is not sequential or cumulative. It is a notable feature in the meditative writings of these authors (for example, in Marcus Aurelius' *To Himself* or in Epictetus' *Manual*) that a reader can break into the text at almost any point and still be affected by the impulse for detachment that animates the writing as a whole or when it is read in sequence. This is entirely understandable, since if the Stoics as writers wished to sustain *apathia* and detachment in the reader, it would be inconsistent for them to require the reader to subordinate himself to anyone else, even to the writer or his prescription for a series of inferences. The meditation as a genre implies a freedom on the part of the reader to act on what the writer is placing before him, a freedom equal to that of the writer when he affirms or denies. Only so is it possible truly to comprehend the clear and distinct ideas of knowledge: the compulsion that the latter carry with them thus presupposes the prior freedom of the understanding.[7] (Almost always the evocation of freedom in the meditation is the more pointed because it discloses the past as a history of bondage. Descartes' disengagement from the senses that would previously have misled him is a lesser but consistent version of Epictetus' emancipation from slavery.)

The literary genre that most nearly anticipates the feature of temporarity added by Descartes to the feature of disengagement or freedom characteristic of the traditional meditation is in fact not the meditation at all but the autobiography. That genre[8] is built around the category of authorial sequentiality according to which the events of a life are traced from within the life itself – thus from a beginning to the later point from which the autobiographer, at the time of writing, looks back at the steps in that sequence. To be sure, some autobiographies turn out to be mere chronicles, no more "inward" or reflective backwards than biographies; furthermore, in those as well as in other autobiographies, the emphasis on chronological sequence may be so strong as to preclude any sense of the disengagement that I have suggested might link the genre of autobiography with the meditation. But Descartes is not only deliberate in his choice of the meditation as a genre; he also contrives the genre, making certain that it does his work – and it is in this light that we may understand the conjunction of disengagement and sequentiality not otherwise characteristic of the autobiography or the meditation by themselves.

This is not to say that there were no precedents to the *Meditations*. Just as Descartes, at the suggestion of his correspondent who had noticed the similarity, goes to the library in Leiden to read (so far as anyone knows, for the first time) Augustine's version of the *Cogito* in *De Trinitate*, so he might also have looked back to Augustine's *Confessions* as anticipating the elements of which he would constitute his own *Meditations*.[9] Even this great precedent, however, often cited for its unusual joining of a spiritual history with the self-awareness of the mind writing the history, does not quite meet Descartes' requirements, since Augustine's account of his development does not claim the logical force that Descartes ascribes to the development in his narrative. Augustine undoubtedly conceives the movement in his *Confessions* as a form of ascension, but the autobiographical progression of the *Meditations* has a stronger necessity to it than whatever it is that internally connects an historical sequence reported only as it occurs or even as it might have been willed (Descartes' autobiographical "I" is also an impersonal "I", meant to denote a prospective reader as well as the writer; this is another basis for the same conclusion).[10] The same difference pertains, though with slightly different emphasis, between the *Meditations*, on the one hand, and Bonaventure's *Journey of the Mind into God* and Loyola's *Spiritual Exercises*, on the other – works sometimes cited as predecessors. In both the latter, the stages of development (Bonaventure's six "steps," Loyola's four weeks), although internally related, are as a whole contingent. It is at least possible that any given stage might be reached without reference to the prior ones, and the stages are, furthermore, meant progressively to exclude certain thoughts rather than, as in Descartes' work, to achieve necessity by having thought everything, what can be doubted and what cannot.[11] (Derrida is surely correct in arguing against Foucault that madness, too, is taken by Descartes to be well within the domain of thinking.)[12]

Although there is no evidence that Descartes thought of himself as altering the literary genre of the meditation, he was clearly aware that the feature of sequentiality, of the cumulative and uninterrupted development of argument on which he insists in the *Meditations*, imposed a strain on the direct confrontation between mind and idea that the act of meditation had characteristically represented. Only so, it would seem, is it possible to understand the lengths that Descartes goes to in arguing that the *Meditations*, read in sequence yet achieves the force of clear and distinct ideas viewed directly by the meditator; only so, I shall be suggesting, can we understand the escape from the charge of circularity – that Descartes believes he has assured himself – a charge that was directed against the *Meditations* virtually from the date of its composition. In this way, moreover, Descartes' conception of the *genre* of the meditation founds for his reader the substantive purpose of his thinking in the *Meditations*. It is difficult, in fact, to separate those two aspects of his work – and the objection that since (on the argument here) Descartes deliberately shaped the genre as a vehicle for his method, there should be nothing surprising in the discovery that they came to fit each other, argues as much for the claims of an intrinsic or necessary connection beyond the actual one as it does against it. Descartes turned to the meditation with certain general expectations of the medium itself, and when we add to those general expectations the specific methodological implications he finds there, we recognize in Descartes, however unexpectedly, an important contributor, both in practice and in theory, to the "poetics" of philosophical discourse.[13]

For Descartes, moreover, the role of the meditation is related quite specifically to a number of the substantive issues of the *Meditations* which are more usually viewed as standing quite apart from the form or genre of that work. One group of the issues turns on the function that Descartes ascribes to memory – a function required at once in the mind of a knower or, more immediately, in the mind of Descartes' reader. The importance of this function becomes evident as we recognize that it is only by the role assigned to memory that Descartes hopes to escape the charge of circularity directed against him, a charge that would, if demonstrated, be serious for any philosophical argument and fatal for a purportedly "foundationalist" theory of knowledge.

The alleged "Cartesian Circle" has been given a variety of formulations which in common turn on the relation between the *Cogito* and the proof of God's existence, and specifically on three steps in that relation. (1) The relation starts in the apparent contradiction between claims that, on the one hand, the proof of the *Cogito* is indubitable, and, on the other hand, that only with proof for the existence of a God who is not a deceiver does the possibility of certainty or of true knowledge arise. (2) The contradiction in these two claims (and then the circularity that follows when they are joined – that certainty is required in the "proof" of God's existence in order that certainty, as sanctioned by God's existence, should be possible) gives way as (3) the contradiction is shown to be only an apparent contradiction. We shall see that it is in the last of these steps that the genre of the meditation appears as an almost necessary medium for the sequence of argument that Descartes asserts and then defends in the *Meditations*.

More fully elaborated, these three steps take the following form: the *Cogito*, Descartes alleges at the beginning of the Third Meditation, serves as a standard for all other truth: "Thus I now seem to be able to posit as a general rule that what I very clearly and distinctly perceive is true." But shortly after that passage, Descartes also interjects: "... I ought at the first opportunity to inquire if there is a God, and if there is, whether or not he can be a deceiver. If I am ignorant of these matters, I do not think I can be certain of anything else." Descartes goes on then to prove the existence of God – and the "circle" thus emerges. The premises in the proof of God's existence must be true and are judged so because they are seen clearly and distinctly (this includes the *Cogito* argument itself and then the criterion of truth based on it); but their (and all other) truth depends on the proof of God's existence and its corollary that God is not a deceiver. Thus, God must be known to exist in order to be known to exist.

Descartes thus seems to make his way from an apparent contradiction into the menace of circularity – and in order to avoid either of those pitfalls, he must somehow, it seems, establish a distinction between the force of clear and distinct ideas seen as such and the role of God as a guarantor of certainty.[14] A possible basis for such a distinction might be found in differences between the specific kinds or types of ideas that the two criteria (respectively) validate, and this is in fact the strategy that Descartes follows. On the one hand, certain clear and distinct ideas can be known in the present; on the other hand, certain clear and distinct ideas (sometimes linked to or incorporating the others) can be known only through memory and its guarantor, God (who is also, then, the guarantor of meditation and the *Meditations*).

I have mentioned before that Descartes alludes on a number of occasions to the demands made by the practice of meditation, and to the difficulty of retaining the ideas meditated "before" the mind; so he acknowledges to Chanut (1 February 1647) that even his own mind "is easily tired by them, and the ... presence of sensible objects does not allow me to dwell on such thoughts for long." Such difficulty could only be compounded when the act of meditation had not one idea or object before it was sequential, when the meditator was obliged to keep before him a complex series of steps – like that, for example, in the *Meditations*. Descartes himself suggests that there are limits to what meditation by itself, without memory, can accomplish – in other words, to what the mind can at a moment encompass as a clear and distinct idea. To be sure, there are numerous examples of ideas that can be seen clearly and distinctly in the present; the sequence of "cogito ergo sum" may be the most forceful but is only one of them.[15] But what else, how much else of the extended argument in the *Meditations* as a whole – a sequence that we have seen Descartes insist must be viewed as a whole – can be encompassed in a single, compresent view?

A key text that addresses this question appears in the *Conversation with Burman*, as Burman directly confronts Descartes with the charge of circularity – arguing that the axioms in the proof of God's existence (in the Third Meditation) require a guarantee, by way of the validity of clear and distinct ideas, which only God himself is supposedly qualified to provide. Descartes' denial of the charge of circularity in this context is unequivocal: "He [the author of the *Meditations*; Descartes refers to himself in the third person as suggested in the record of the conversation by Burman himself] knows that he is not deceived with regard to [the individual axioms][16] since he is actually paying attention to them .... Since our thought is able to grasp more than one item in this way ... it is clear that we are able to grasp the proof of God's existence in its entirety. As long as we are engaged in this process, we are certain that we are not being deceived, and every difficulty is thus removed."[17]

Descartes does not claim here that the proof of God's existence is the most extended proof that can be established on its own, by "actually paying attention" to it and without the presupposition of God's existence. It seems unlikely in fact that he would place a specific limit on the extent of ideas that can be grasped clearly and distinctly in a single viewing, although it is evident that he recognized both that there is such a limit and that its existence makes special demands, when the limit is exceeded, on the structure of the meditation. The response to Burman cited, in any event, corroborates other statements, principally in the Reply to the Second Set of Objections, from which we may infer, first, that some valid claims to knowledge do not presuppose God's existence (thus, an escape in principle from the charge of circularity), and second, that God's existence does serve as a guarantee of knowledge at least in those contexts where it is a memory of clear and distinct ideas on which the claims of knowledge depend. In the latter role, memory both establishes the possibility of a complex sequence of meditations and disarms the charge of redundancy against Descartes' use of God as a guarantor of knowledge. It is in connection with the latter claim in particular that we see the relation between Descartes' escape from the Cartesian circle and the generic features of the Cartesian meditation.

Exactly how God's existence serves as guarantor for ideas not seen (at the time) clearly and distinctly has been a matter of dispute. (The issue of God's existence as a guarantor of knowledge must at any rate be distinguished from the question of God's role as the guarantor, through the act of creation, of existence. Even the latter role, including God's power to have made everything different from what it is, does not explain how the knowledge of God's existence serves man as an epistemological guarantee for certain of his clear and distinct ideas.) Cottingham, who focuses on this issue in the Introduction to his edition of the *Conversation with Burman*, argues that the guarantee provided by God's existence is directed against "the essential *disconnectedness* that would be a feature of knowledge without God" (xxxi), and thus that God's existence establishes the "possibility" that memory does not deceive us as we now recall having had a particular clear and distinct idea. But this account does not seem commensurate with the force that Descartes ascribes to God's existence as a guarantee, since Cottingham seems to establish at most only the possibility of knowledge, not, for any particular case (let alone for all such cases taken together) of the alledged memory of a clear and distict idea, the status of that possible knowledge as actual. And if God's veracity does not accomplish the latter purpose, the meditator-reader would, for a progressively larger part of the *Meditations*, be left not with certainty and knowledge, but only with the fallible memory of what might be certain and known: where, still, would certainty come from?

A similar objection applies to Ian Hacking's interpretation according to which God's existence and then his veracity are needed for reassurance in those cases when we remember having been certain of an idea but also believe (because the proof is not immediately before us) that we might have been "wrongly convinced."[18] Here again: if – against Descartes' position – the original certainty of clear and distinct ideas carried over to our memory of them, then God's veracity would not be required any more than it was needed to certify the original clarity and distinctness. If the original certainty does not carry over to memory, then (on Hacking's account) God's veracity could be appealed to for certifying any memory of certainty, those which were in fact mistaken in their remembered claims of certainty as well as those which were correct. And Descartes nowhere claims the infallibilty of memory as such for any object or kind. If he did, there would hardly be a need for God in the role of guarantor.

An important consideration to be noted here is that Descartes is not, in the context of this discussion of the charge of circularity, assigning a role to memory in general, even the memory of the person for whose particular references to memory God's existence may serve as a guarantee. Descartes explicitly states this at the same point in the *Conversation with Burman* where he rejects the charges of circularity: "I have nothing to say on the subject of memory. Everyone should test himself to see whether he is good at remembering. If he has any doubts, then he should make use of written notes and so forth to help him" (p. 5). If we are to reconcile this bland denial with the explcit references Descartes does make to the role (and our need) of God as guarantor of memory (an odd inversion of this need is Descartes' appeal in the First Meditation to the hypothesis of the "evil genius": without keeping the possibility of the evil genius in mind, Descartes might forget to doubt the "longstanding opinions [that] keep coming back again and again"), and if we are to avoid the defects in the attempts cited above to explain what God is a guarantor of, we must, it seems, distinguish among (1) the function of memory in general (here we can take Descartes at his own explicit word), (2) the memory of a kind of object or force that would itself guarantee memory (in which case God's role as guarantor would be redundant) – and lastly, (3) certain quite specific sequences of memory, one of which is represented by the line of argument in the *Meditations*. For although it is true that Descartes speaks of God as the guarantor of clear and distinct ideas that are not at the time directly apprehended, the context in which that response appears pertains to the claim of certainty on behalf of clear and distinct ideas made in the *Meditations*. And although it is true that in the *Meditations* Descartes makes claims that he also asserted elsewhere, in texts organized quite differently, there is one thing distinctive about his formulation of those truths in the *Meditations*, and that is precisely the order in which they are asserted and related there, including, of course, his claim to have doubted everything that could be doubted. If memory is not guaranteed either as a function of clear and distinct ideas as such, or as it responds to a kind of clear and distinct idea, then it must be the arrangement or order of the ideas (including their purpose) to which the guarantee is related. It is just such an order that we have seen Descartes stress, time and again, as he plans the writing and the reading of the *Meditations*. That order is related to the requirements for meditation as such. Descartes implies that one cannot meditate simply about anything one chooses, whenever one wants to. And is it so unreasonable to hold that there could be no meditation at all if the existence of the meditator remained in question? – or that proof of that existence would entail other quite specific commitments as well? The order of the *Meditations*, in any event, is both evident and regarded by Descartes as necessary – an order that can only be sustained, it seems, as God guarantees the memory by means of which a view of the whole and the judgment of it as certain is possible. The clear and distinct ideas of the *Meditations* form both a necessary and actual sequence. This feature should itself be evident at any point in the *Meditations* (the question can be raised and answered at any moment in the sequence of how or why the "I" reaches that point); and thus if one of them is placed in doubt, they are all in doubt. The proof of God's existence – more specifically, the proof of his veracity – provides assurance that they could not all be in doubt (which would now be the case if any one of them was in doubt) and thus that the sequence is indeed a sequence of proof. Single ideas or even, up to a point, complex arguments, can be perceived clearly and distinctly without proof of the support of God's existence. God's veracity is required when the more complex meditative sequence appears, the elements of which constitute a whole but require the function of memory for knowledge of that whole. God is thus guarantor of the practice, and then of the genre, of the meditation. It is not too strong to claim, moreover, that He serves in this role because the power of clear and distinct ideas is limited so far as concerns the capacity of their human knower to hold them before the mind. Consider the analogy of a runner on a track: on the first lap, the runner counts "one," seeing "clearly and distinctly" that he has just set out. By the eighth or ninth lap (probably earlier), he can no longer distinguish in memory among the laps he has run – but the number he counts depends on each of the numbers (and laps) before. He must somehow then know clearly and distinctly in the present – the ninth lap – that he has known with the same force in the past although he does not directly know that past; otherwise the only number of laps he could count would be the small number that he could keep before his mind.

Would this contention not revive a claim that has already been criticized: God as the guarantor of any clear and distinct ideas that memory (which we know to be fallible) might allege and look back to? And again, if this were the case, either God's role would be redundant, or all (and certainly any particular) memory could be claimed as infallible. But it is not just any idea that God is guarantor of; it is the possibility that all such ideas in the meditative sequence might turn out to be false that Descartes guards against – the possibility, in other words, that knowledge is impossible. It is the possibility of meditation itself, after all, of establishing a ground of certainty for the self of the meditator, that is at once tested and asserted in the *Meditations*, and so – circularly but not viciously so – the process of meditation, as it assumes the possibility of such certainty, would be dependent, in Descartes' account, on the remembered (and guaranteed) conclusions of the *Meditations*.

It is significant, in this connection, that Descartes refers so often to the role of the conclusions of the *Meditations*, encouraging readers to rely on them rather than to keep repeating the process of meditation by which the readers would have first reached those conclusions – but always with the stipulation that the "conclusions" of meditation should not be mistaken for the process itself. So he reassures Elizabeth (28 June 1643): "I think the best thing is to content oneself with keeping in one's memory and one's belief the conclusions which one has once drawn from [meditation] and then employ the rest of one's study time to thoughts in which the intellect cooperates with the imagination and senses." Again, in the *Conversation with Burman*: "You should not devote so much effort to the *Meditations* and to metaphysical questions .... It is sufficient to have grasped them once in a general way and then to remember the conclusions."[19] There is some irony in the fact that precisely because of the distinctive character of the Cartesian meditation – the close bond between its temporal and its logical character – the meditator (and so for Descartes, also the reader of his *Meditations*) is obliged to take them either all or nothing: they do not come in pieces. Even the apparent conclusions, understood properly, are mnemonic devices for recalling the process of meditation. Thus, in the non-meditative (and greater) part of the life of a Cartesian meditator, it is memory and habit that recall the force of the meditations, although, of course, without substituting for it. But this is possible only because of memory's role, based on God's warrant, in the act of meditation itself.

IV

The genre of the meditation is for Descartes, then, intended both to provide a literary means and to solve an epistemological problem: to show how the force of "clear and distinct" ideas perceived directly and in the present can be maintained over the course of a sequence of ideas that would not be clear and distinct if the sequence, with its long and complex detail, were viewed apart from its content and in a context other than that of meditation. Finally, (or at least so I have been claiming) these two functions of the meditation – the genre and the practice – are hardly distinguishable. Descartes believes, in fact, that the reader who accepts the invitation to meditate with him, that is to read him, will also be committed to the steps and then the conclusions of that process of meditation. Descartes insists again and again on the practice of his work as meditation – not as thinking (as that applies to all mental activity) and not even as demonstration or argument. In the Reply to the Second Set of Objections, he writes, "Hence ... I rightly require singular attention on the part of my readers and have especially selected the style of writing which I thought would best secure it .... My writing took the form of meditations rather than that of philosophical disputations so that I might by this very fact testify that I had no dealings except with those who will not shrink from joining me in giving the matter attentive care and meditation." Or again, in a remark to Silhon (Letter, May, 1637): "But as for intelligent people like yourself, Sir, if they take the trouble not only to read but to meditate in order the things I say I meditated ... I trust that they will come to the same conclusions as I did."

To be sure, there is no possibility of demonstrating that the genre of meditation conceived by Descartes was (or remains) unique in its capacity as a medium for the kind of argument that Descartes placed in it; but it is clear that alternate philosophical genres available to Descartes were rejected by him on at least that ground. The philosophical treatise, for example, as Descartes himself suggests, involves a logical and atemporal structure; it requires the commitment of narrator or reader only to the implications of its premises – but in no necessary order and with no attachment at all to the premises. This objection applies as well, in a slightly variant form, to the geometric method (Descartes takes the trouble in his Reply to the Second Set of Objections to show that he could have used this method had it – contrary to the fact – served his purpose: "I append here something [!] in the synthetic style that may I hope be somewhat to my reader's profit"). The Platonic dialogue (I have not found any comment by Descartes on the dialogue as such in its role as a philosophical genre)[20] if not simply a vehicle for skepticism, is a means of deferring the determination and certainty that Descartes believed to be always present and accessible in the meditation. And the objections and responses characteristic of the "summa" as a genre would have provided a means differing only slightly from the series of objections and replies that Descartes included, but only as an appendage, in his own *Meditations*.

It might be objected that the claims thus implied for the relation between style and method in the *Meditations* do not demonstrate either that the form of the Cartesian meditation is intrinsically (much less, exclusively) tied to method or that the meditation as a genre is unique in its capacity for philosophical expression. But again, it is difficult to know how much such claims could be argued except as Croce, for example, asserts on *a priori* grounds a unique relation not only between the kinds of form and content but between any particular instance of that conjunction. On the other hand, the likely objection that what Descartes "says" or "argues" in the *Meditations* could just as well have been said or argued by other means has itself to be treated with suspicion as *a priori* or stipulative. For that apparently modest appeal to common sense typically begs an important question in its formulation of what Descartes "says" or "argues" – terms which themselves are almost invariably embedded in a quite specific conception of knowledge. The basic assumption in the latter conception regards philosophical discourse as a propositional structure that is a function as a sequence or whole of the properties of its paths, namely, the independent – and independently verifiable – propositions. But on the account given here of Descartes' intentions in the *Meditations*, precisely that conception of saying or philosophical assertion is a central point of dispute. The genre of the meditation, like the act of meditation, turns out to be a doing as well as a saying, and the doing is in fact broader than saying, much broader if saying is regarded only as putting together a string of independent propositions. The difficulty of demonstrating that the meditation is a necessary means for Descartes' project, in fact, cuts two ways. For if it is not a necessary or exclusive means, we may hope to identify other possible ones; but none, in fact, seemed evident to Descartes, and if we take seriously the requirements that Descartes set himself, it could well be argued that none seems more evident now, in later philosophical practice. (This does not mean, of course, that the alleged requirements are themselves beyond dispute.)

Even if objections persist to the claim for an intrinsic and necessary connection between method and style in the *Meditations*, moreover, the fact (as it happens) of a connection between them is clear and distinct. Descartes was concerned in the *Meditations* to establish what was said there first in his own life and then in the life of the reader who was thus to be no mere observer but an agent in the same process. The medium of expression was frankly intended to make an unusual provision for the second party in the standard contract between writer and reader – not only the "implied" reader that all texts provide for but an active participant whose role was to be identical with that of the implied author: reader, in effect, becomes writer; to read a meditation with understanding of what meditation is, is to meditate. ("He understands the matter no less perfectly and makes it as much his own as if he had himself discovered it" [Reply to Second Set of Objections].) The genre of the Cartesian meditation, moreover, clearly is intended to match its form to that of the objects or issues at stake. If the possibility of radical doubt is truly to be tested, then the possibility of reconstruction must be available in the same medium once that skepticism is breached; both possibilities must carry conviction if either one does – and thus the genre of writing, in its claims on the act of meditation and the uses of memory, at once threatens the existence of the writer and provides a means for that existence which averts the threat.

It is also, then, the genre of the Cartesian meditation that is at issue – being asserted and tested – in the *Meditations*. To be sure, the *Meditations* has as its subject the "demonstrations" that Descartes maintains in them, the existence of God and the distinction between mind and body. It also has as its subject the method that Descartes in his earlier *Discourse* had named and that in the *Meditations* he even more fully displays and acts on. But in addition to these, Descartes has before him, and so also places before – or in – his reader, the practice of meditation, the role of the meditator, and the method and art of the *Meditations* as his subjects. As Descartes himself, the "I" meditating, is every place present in the *Meditations*, so too is the act of writing.

NOTES

I am indebted for comments on this essay that I have tried to take into account to Helen S. Lang, Richard Lee, William Sacksteder and Forrest Williams.

1. Except where otherwise indicated, references here to the correspondence are taken from *Descartes: Philosophical Letters*, trans. and ed. Anthony Kenny (Oxford: Clarendon Press, 1970).
2. Except where otherwise indicated, the text of Descartes cited is that edited by Elizabeth S. Haldane and G.R.T. Ross (Cambridge: Cambridge University Press, 1970).
3. Descartes uses "analytic" and "synthetic" in the context cited here in a different (although related) sense from both the then standard usage of the terms and his own usage elsewhere (which is close to that of the standard usage, e.g., in the *Regulae*). In that standard usage, "analysis" refers to breaking down the objects or elements of an argument to their least knowable parts, "synthesis," to the process by which those least parts are put together. (See for a discussion of the standard distinction, P.A. Schouls, *The Imposition of Method* (Oxford: The Clarendon Press, 1980), Chap. 1). The emphasis in the Reply, as cited here, is on the difference between the respective orders of argument in the two methods, corresponding to their development in experience, a difference between them that seems a distinctively Cartesian addition to the standard notion.
4. Descartes' objections to the synthetic method apply equally to the syllogistic form

of demonstration of the Schoolmen and to the *modus geometricus* which he took as the more serious rival to his own method. Although for both of these, the premises need not be hypothetical – i.e., that they may independently be known to be true – there is no requirement of this within the method itself.

5. James Collins, *Interpreting Modern Philosophy* (Princeton: Princeton University Press, 1971), 65.

6. Cf. on this topic A. Koyre, *Entretions sur Descartes* (New York: Brentano's, 1944), 33.

7. Although it also seems at odds with the radical freedom that Sartre finds and approves in Descartes. See the volume on Descartes in *Les Classiques de la liberte*, with Sartre's Introduction (Genevre-Paris: Trois Collines, 1946).

8. As Momigliano points out (*The Development of Greek Biography* [Cambridge, Mass.: Harvard University Press, 1971]), the genre was not named until the 19th century and before then had always been a marginal follower of biography – itself, from its origins in the Greeks until the 19th century, a problematic genre.

9. Cf. E. Gilson, *Etudes sur le role de la pensee medievale dans la fonction du systeme cartesien* (Paris: 1930), 193.

10. Cf. D. Judovitz, "Autobiographical Discourse and Critical Praxis in Descartes," *Philosophy and Literature*, 5(1981): 102-3.

11. L.J. Beck (*The Metaphysics of Descartes* [Oxford: Oxford University Press, 1965], 31) notes also that retreats at La Fleche, Descartes' school, were organized on the basis of Loyola's exercises, suggesting a likely influence on the structure of the *Meditations*. But again, it is the structural frame at most for which Descartes is thus indebted, not for the content or the activity of meditation. Like any exercises, Loyola's are preparations for something else, a set of instructions; one could hardly be said to have done Loyola's exercises by having read his book in the way that one could have meditated by reading Descartes. Again, in contrast to Descartes' *Meditations*, the *Spirtual Exercises* constantly invite the use of the senses and the imagination. So, e.g., the Fifth Exercise of the First Week requires the reader "to see with the eyes of the imagination those great fires [of Hell], and the souls as it were in bodies of fire." For an account that claims a closer likeness in these works to Descartes, see A. Rorty, "Experiments in Philosophical Genre: Descartes' Meditations" *Critical Inquiry*, 9(1983).

12. J. Derrida, "Cogito and the History of Madness," in *Writing and Difference*, trans. A. Bass (Chicago: University of Chicago Press, 1978).

13. For a more systematic account of the question of a "poetics" of philosophical discourse, see B. Lang, *Philosophy and the Art of Writing* (Lewisburg, Pa.: Buckness University Press, 1983), Chaps. 1 and 2.

14. In the Third Meditation, Descartes seems to subordinate the claim of clear and distinct ideas to the power of God. Without knowing that God is not a deceiver, he writes "I do not see that I can ever be certain of anything." It is not altogether a satisfactory solution, but the likeliest means of judging the apparent contradiction between this statement and others in which clear and distinct ideas are alleged to provide knowledge not guaranteed by knowledge of God's existence would seem to be by attending to the passages in which Descartes is actually responding to charges of contradiction.

15. See on this point Hartman and Schwartz, "Translators' Introduction," to Kant's *Logic* (Indianapolis and New York: Bobbs-Merrill, 1974), lx-lxv.

16. Descartes, in Burman's account of his reply uses the term "axiom" in this context, evidently without believing that doing so would take him back to the synthetic method. The alternate explanation that Schouls gives *The Imposition of Method*, p.

17 – that the analytic method includes the synthetic method – seems to me groundless. Descartes himself, in the Reply to the fourth Set of Objections, makes room for "provisional" assumptions in the analytic method.

17. *Conversation with Burman*, trans. and ed. J. Cottingham (Oxford: Clarendon Press, 1976), 6-7.

18. I. Hacking, "Proof and Eternal Truths," in S. Gaukroger, ed. *Descartes* (London: Harvester, 1980), 173.

19. J.L. Beck would explain such statements in terms of Descartes' wariness of the censor *The Metaphysics of Descartes*, p. 4. This may well be a side of Descartes' concern here, but it seems unlikely to have been the whole of it. His concern with the issue, in any event, goes back to the *Regulae* (cf. Rule 8), written before Galileo's trial and the other encounters with public reaction that were later to contribute to Descartes' wariness.

20. In specific references to Plato, Descartes ignores the generic role of the dialogue altogether (cf. Rule III in the *Regulae* where he addresses as one the "arguments" of Plato and Aristotle. Of his own dialogue (*The Search after Truth*), Descartes writes in his prefatory comments that it is meant to make the arguments he advances "equally useful to all men." But in the fragment of his dialogue that survives, Descartes' purpose, through his spokesman, Eudoxus, is discursive and didactic in a way that places it closer to the form of the treatise than to the dialogue.

17

KIERKEGAARD AND THE NECESSITY OF FORGERY

Josiah Thompson

I

For some time the philosopher has been associated with direct discourse. He is not expected to present his readers with puzzles to be solved or with codes to be deciphered. He is expected to lecture to his audience, to tell them as directly and clearly as possible what he has in mind. This is not to say that what the philosopher says is easy to understand. On the contrary, the inherent abstractness and difficulty of his ideas may make them extremely hard to understand. But he is expected to do what he can to ease his reader's burden; he is certainly not expected to hide what he is saying.

With Kierkegaard, however, everything changes. From the first line of any of his philosophical works one recognizes that one is not dealing with a philosopher in proper *persona*. Instead, one is dealing with an author who is constantly hiding, ducking, disappearing; never speaking directly, but only posing riddles, trapping us in conundrums, laying down false trails and then laughing when we take the bait. In short, we recognize that Kierkegaard is hiding from us. He could have published standard philosophical essays under his own name but he did not. Rather, he decided to create a whole "marionette theater" of different pseudonyms while himself remaining offstage. Why? I want to answer that question by paying special attention to his major pseudonymous work, *Either/Or*, and to the special problem posed by its ambiguous authorship.

II

There is first of all the blunt fact that Kierkegaard's authorship of *Either/Or* was hidden. He once remarked, "In one sense, I began my authorship with a forgery"[1] – and forgery is not too strong a word for characterizing the intricate ruses he employed to conceal his authorship of *Either/Or*. He had a friend, Jens Giødwad (editor of *Faedrelandet*) make all the arrangements with the printer and the bookseller. When, in spite of these precautions, whispers began circulating alleging Kierkegaard's at-least-partial authorship, his first inclination was to continue the ruse through a public exchange of letters between himself and the pseudonymous "editor" of *Either/Or*, Victor Eremita. "I ask Victor Eremita to give up his pseudonymity so that I again can live in peace," wrote Kierkegaard in the draft of a letter to *Berlingske Tidende*, going on to do Victor the favor of drafting his reply. "As I myself," wrote Victor, "do not know whom the esteemed authors of (*Either/Or*) are, I clearly cannot know with certainty that you are not one of them." "I must say, however," he added icily, "that I find it unlikely since your obvious passion would not tempt anyone to credit you with the required patience." Perhaps from a conviction that a denial of authorship could only associate him more with the book, neither of these letters was sent to the press.[2]

What was sent was a brief article under the anonym "A.F. ..." entitled, "Who is the author *Either/Or*?"[3] After surveying both the "outward" and the "inward" indices of authorship, after summarizing various hypotheses that had been brought forward – is it the work of two authors? of three authors? of fifty authors? Is it the work of an old man? a young man? a licentious man? an upright man? a married man? a bachelor? – after summarizing all these speculations, A.F. ... concludes it is a good thing the author's identity is hidden since the reader "must now have only to do with the work without being distracted by his personality."

A similar line is taken by Victor Eremita in explaining why he titled the work *Either/Or*. According to him, the "historical result" only distracts the reader from considering the conflict of the two views: "When the book is read, then A and B are forgotten, only their views confront one another, and await no finite decision in particular personalities."[4] Both A.F. ... and Victor seem to be saying that the historical identity of the author should remain unimportant to the reader, or, as Johannes Climacus will put it in the *Postscript*: "A communication in the form of a possibility compels the recipient to face the problem of existing in it."[5] On this view, the question "Who is the author of *Either/Or?*" is fit only for the literary gossip columns. The reader addressed by *Either/Or* will swiftly put it aside in confronting the two life-possibilities put forth in the papers of A and B.

But might this view be false? Might it be only another move in a complex dialectic of deception? Kierkegaard went to great pains to make his reader ask the question, "Who is the author of *Either/Or?*" No reader could be expected to glance at the title page –

EITHER - OR
A Life-Fragment
Published
by
Victor Eremita

First Part
Containing the Papers of A

– without being teased by the question of the author's identity. Even less could a reader finish the book's preface without very much wanting to know who was behind this complex literary *jeu d'esprit*. Far from being an easily disposable triviality, this question may have the power of leading us to the very center of *Either/Or*. It could be the bait Kierkegaard has laid along our path. In his sense of the term, *Either/Or* may very well be a "forgery"; but if so, it may be a "forgery" whose final lesson is that human life itself is "forgery." To grasp this austere conclusion it is first necessary to take the bait; we encounter it in Victor Eremita's preface.

III

Eremita begins his preface with a query about doubt: "It has perhaps sometimes occurred to you, dear reader, to doubt a bit the correctness of the well-known philosophic maxim that the outward is the inward, the inward the outward" (*E/O* 1.3). Has the reader, for example, ever cherished a secret which appeared too precious to share with another? Or has the reader ever come into contact with anyone where something of the kind was suspected? Or perhaps neither, and yet still the reader might be no stranger to this doubt which "comes and goes," which "flits across your mind ... like a passing shadow" (E/O 1.3).

Soon it becomes clear that all this talk about doubting the co-incidence of inner and outer is only a circuitous way of leading up to an explanation of how the papers constituting the book were discovered. For the mode of their discovery, it turns out, only confirms Eremita's conviction that the outward is hardly ever the inward. He had found them in an old, but recently purchased, desk. Anxious not to miss the post-stage and having found his wallet empty of cash, he had turned to the money-drawer in the desk. Alas, it was jammed. A hatchet was fetched, but a sharp blow to the desk failed to dislodge the recalcitrant drawer. Instead, a secret panel was jarred open revealing the papers. "In my heart I begged the desk for forgiveness," writes Eremita, "while my mind found its doubt strengthed that the outward is not the inward" (E/O 1.6).

The papers themselves confirmed Eremita's doubt, for both, in their own ways, evidenced a discrepancy between the writer's outward appearance and his inner reality. The one set – designated by Eremita "the papers of A" – were written on vellum paper in quarto size with wide margins. The handwriting was elegant and, now and then, careless. Their content was various – essays on assorted aesthetic topics, short aphorisms in a lyric style, finally a long narrative called "Diary of the Seducer." They all made evident a contradiction between A's witty, ironic, often carefree exterior, and an interior life clouded by boredom and despair. "His external life," Eremita points out, "had been in complete contradiction to his inner life" (E/O 1.4). Not quite the same can be said of B, the writer of the other set of papers. Except for a final sermon, allegedly written by a Jutland priest and friend of B, these are all in the form of long letters jotted down on a legal pad in the clear, somewhat spreading hand of what might be a business man. From their content Eremita is able to infer that they were in fact written to A by a civil magistrate named Wilhelm. Here according to Eremita, the distinction between inward and outward is not so profound inasmuch as B only "concealed a more significant inwardness under a somewhat commonplace exterior" (E/O 1.4).

Up to this point everything is straightforward; we have no reason to question Eremita's narrative. He even tells us in great detail how he went about his editing chores, arranging B's papers in terms of their logical order while letting chance determine the order of A's. "I have added a translation of the Greek quotations scattered through the essays which is taken from one of the better German translations" (E/O 1.8), he adds. All is straightforward until we come to Eremita's discussion of the last of *A*'s papers, "Diary of the Seducer." Here for the first time we begin to suspect that Eremita may have put his own principle to work in offering us an outward account of the papers of *A* and *B* that does not match their inner reality.

For *A* himself had written a short preface to the "Diary of the Seducer" wherein he explained in Eremita-like fashion how it had come into his possession. Once again a desk is central. *A* had been a guest in the Seducer's apartment when he noticed that "contrary to his custom" (*E/O* 1.299) the Seducer had left his desk unlocked, exposing a number of loose papers together with a tastefully bound book in a broad quarto. On the front of the book was posted a vignette of white paper on which the Seducer – really a young man named Johannes – had written "Commentarius perpetuus No. 4." This strange title was too much for *A*'s curious nature and he ended up snitching both the book and the loose papers. Examining the materials later, he was able to discern that the book was simply a diary wherein Johannes the Seducer related in detail his seduction of a girl named Cordelia. The loose papers consisted of brief sketches of erotic situations together with outlines for letters. But the story does not end here, for *A* quickly realized he was acquainted with the Cordelia of the "Diary." From her he was able to secure some of the letters that had been sent both by and to Johannes during their love affair. Although these letters were in all cases undated, *A* was able to infer their dates through a close study of the "Diary" which here and there hinted at the motives for the letters. All this material carefully copied by *A*'s hand and ordered by his mind came to form what he called "my manuscript" (*E/O* 1.306). It is this "manuscript" on which Victor Eremita comments in his preface to *Either/Or*.

"The last of *A*'s papers," observes Eremita, "is a story entitled, 'Diary of the Seducer'" (*E/O* 1.9). But *A* did not present it to us as a story! *A* told us it was the real chronicle of a seduction which he had stolen. Eremita continues: "Here we meet with new difficulties, since *A* does not acknowledge himself as author, but only as editor. This is an old trick of the novelist, and I should not object to it, did it not make my position so complicated, as one author seems to be encased in another, like the nesting parts of a Chinese puzzle box. Here is not the place to explain in greater detail the reasons for my opinion. I shall only note that the dominant mood in *A*'s preface in a manner betrays the poet .... [Furthermore] the idea of the Seducer is suggested in the essay on the 'Immediate Erotic' as well as in [the essay called] 'Shadowgraphs' ..." (*E/O* 1.9).

Eremita leaves the question of authorship ambiguous, never exposing "the reasons for my opinion." But if his suspicions are borne out, if the *persona* of editor is only "an old trick of the novelist," then we have been taken in by *A*. Johannes the Seducer may very well not be a separate person, but only a *persona* of *A*. Asked whether the Seducer is one of the authors of *Either/Or*, we would have to reply: "We suspect not."

Nor does the charade end here. In the same paragraph Eremita professes a trifle too forcefully his distance from both *A* and the Seducer ("I who have simply nothing to do with this narrative, I who am twice removed from the original author..." (*E/O* 1.9), while four pages later gently tickling our suspicion that he himself might be playing the game earlier ascribed to *A*. "During my constant occupation with the papers," he writes, "it dawned upon me that they might be looked at from a new point of view, by considering all of them as the work of one man. I know very well everything that can be urged against this view, that it is unhistorical, improbable, unreasonable that one man should be the author of both parts, although the reader might easily be tempted to play on words, that he who says *A* must also say *B*. However, I have not yet been able to relinquish the idea" (*E/O* 1.13). Of course, if we accept Eremita's earlier story that he found the papers of *A* and *B* in a desk and that the handwriting, paper, and content of the two sets of papers were quite different, then the hypothesis of single authorship is of course "unhistorical" and "improbable." But it is only Eremita's word that guarantees their "historical" character, and we must not forget that likewise it was only *A*'s (now suspect) word that earlier guaranteed the "historical" character of the Seducer's diary. Might it be that Eremita has been playing with us all along, actually demonstrating his principle that the inward is not the outward by offering us allegedly real authors who are in reality only his imagined creations? Might it be that like the Seducer (and possibly too like the Jutland priest) both *A* and *B* will have to be scratched from our list of possible authors of *Either/Or?*

Eremita continues his explanation of why he has been unable "to relinquish the idea" that one man was the author of both parts:

Let us imagine a man who had lived through both of these phases or had thought upon both. *A*'s papers contain a number of attempts to formulate an aesthetic philosophy of life .... *B*'s papers contain an ethical view of life. As I let this thought sink into my soul, it became clear to me that I might make use of it in choosing a title. The one I have selected (that is, *Either/Or*) precisely expresses this (*E/O* 1.13).

The title *Either/Or* expresses the perspective of a single author who "either had lived through both of these phases or who had thought upon both." Yet who could that single author be but Victor Eremita?

Now we can see how important was Victor's initial "doubt" about the coincidence of inward and outward. His whole preface has turned out to be a parable illustrating the validity of this doubt. Outwardly, he has offered us a fully detailed historical account of the provenance of the papers. Yet at the same time he has subtly, ironically undermined that account, nudging us again and again to suspect something different. Outwardly, like Kierkegaard's anonymous letter writer A.F. ..., he has cautioned us against troubling ourselves with the question of authorship. Yet at the same time his detailed preface has fired our interest in that question; it is that question, indeed, which has been the central concern of the preface. It has been the bait which has lured us deep into a troubling landscape where finally it has become impossible to distinguish the real from the unreal, person from *persona*.

We have encounterd what – in a literary-critical sense – has been called the problem of "the unreliable narrator,"[6] and we have encountered this problem in a complicated skein. On the most tenuous imaginative level we encountered it in *A*'s preface to the "Diary of the Seducer." From the Seducer's point of view his diary is a straightforward chronicle of his affair with Cordelia. But again and again *A* undermines the perspective of the Seducer, suggesting to the reader that as narrator the Seducer is not to be trusted. "With a keenly developed talent for discovering the interesting in life," *A* remarks, "he constantly reproduced the experience more or less poetically. His diary is therefore neither historically exact nor simply fiction, not indicative but subjunctive" (*E/O* 1.300). As we have seen, this skein of untrustworthiness must be unraveled further. Eremita's remarks about *A* make us distrust *A*'s narrative as to how the diary came to be found. Finally, Eremita's words undermine his own position as a trustworthy narrator, bringing into question the very existence of the Seducer, *A*, Judge Wilhelm, and even the Jutland priest. The perspective of *A* is not the perspective of the Seducer; nor is it the perspective of Judge Wilhelm, the Jutland priest, or even Victor Eremita himself. In important respects they all conflict. But due to the ambiguity of authorship we are permitted no single perspective from which to resolve the conflict; we are given no ground we can call real. If we ask for the real author of *Either/Or*, Kierkegaard presents us with a pseudonym, the hermetic Victor, who immediately splits into other pseudonyms: the aesthete, equally inclined to refer us to yet another pseudonym, and the civil magistrate, Wilhelm, who may or may not be the Jutland priest. Instead of a person we constantly encounter only a *persona*, whose interior world, once entered, is found to be in motion, spinning off fantastically into yet another *persona*. Nowhere can we find solid ground on which to stand, a single perspective we can call real; everywhere we encounter only ambiguity.

IV

Yet it is not simply from "outside" (so to speak) that the pseudonyms of *Either/Or* appear ambiguous. It is not simply that as readers we are left in the dark as to who the speakers of *Either/Or* really are. For they too are troubled and confused as to who they are. Victor, the aesthete, the Judge – in the end all three appear as fundamentally double-minded, as beyond the outlooks ascribed to them, as incapable, finally, of achieving a single, sharply-etched, identity.

This is especially apparent with respect to the aesthete. On the surface he is witty, ironic, even carefree. "To be a perfect man is after all the highest human ideal," he writes at one point, "Now I have got corns, which ought to help some" (*E/O* 1.27). At another point philosophy and philosophers come into the cross-hairs of his sarcasm: "What the philosopohers say about Reality is often as disappointing as a sign you see in a shop window which reads: PRESSING DONE HERE. If you brought your clothes to be pressed, you would be fooled; for only the sign is for sale" (*E/O* 1.31). Yet behind the wit and irony one senses a deep and constant melancholy. In the same section from which the two citations above were taken he writes, "I feel the way a chessman must when the opponent says of it: that piece cannot be moved" (*E/O* 1.21). Or again: "I do not care for anything. I do not care to ride, for the exercise is too violent. I do not care to walk, walking is too strenuous. I do not care to lie down, for I should either have to remain lying, and I do not care to do that, or I should have to get up again, and I do not care to do that. *Summa Summarum*: I do not care at all" (*E/O* 1.20). At times the aesthete may appear enthusiastic about this or that project, but the enthusiasm (as the Judge points out) "is always a falsehood" (*E/O* 2.208). "You are constantly hovering above yourself," cautions the

Judge, "but the fine sublimate into which you are volatilized is the nullity of despair, and beneath you you behold a multiplicity of subjects for learning, information, study and observation" (*E/O* 2.203).

The aesthete evidences this "hovering" quality in many ways. In one particularly haunting passage he pictures himself as inhabiting "a feudal castle ... lost in the clouds." "From this abode," he writes, "I dart down into the world of reality to seize my prey; but I do not remain down there, I bear my quarry aloft to my stronghold. My booty is a picture I weave into the tapestries of my palace. There I live as one dead. I immerse everything I have experienced in a baptism of forgetfulness unto an eternal remembrance. Everything temporal and contingent is forgotten and erased. Then I sit like an old man, grey-haired and thoughtful, and explain picture after picture in a voice as soft as a whisper; and at my side a child sits and listens, although he remembers everything before I tell it" (*E/O* 1.41). The aesthete's consciousness has become big enough to encompass both the "old man" who spins the web of story and also the child who "remembers everything before I tell it." A similar split becomes apparent in a witty and spirited essay entitled, "The Rotation Method." In it the aesthete offers a kind of handbook for holding at bay "the nothingness which pervades reality" (*E/O* 1.87), that is, boredom. According to him, one should eschew friendship, marriage, and all permanent relationships. One should use the arbitrary to amuse oneself; one might, for example, go to see just the middle of a play, or read only the last third of a book. Insted of listening to what a lecturer might be saying, one might closely follow the descent of a droplet of sweat from his brow to the tip of his nose. But soon we come to realize that the writing of the essay itself is only a project of amusement on his part, an attempt to outwit boredom. The essay itself – as well as each of the stratagems depicted in it – is only an attempt at self-trickery. But since he is the source of the trickery he also remains beyond it, unable to be taken in by it. This sense of the aesthete's consciousness as fundamentally duplicitous, of it composing itself in some ineradicable way beyond itself, is grasped clearly by the Judge. "Your thought has hurried on ahead," he notes, "you have seen through the vanity of all things, but you have got no further. Occasionally you plunge into pleasure, and every instant you are devoting yourself to it you make the discovery in your consciousness that it is vanity. So you are constantly beyond yourself, that is, in despair" (*E/O* 2.199).

The Danish term for despair, *Fortvivlelse*, signifies more than its

English counterpart, since it bears within it the morpheme *tvi* for "two," signaling the doubling of consciousness (*Tvivl* in Danish means "doubt"; *Tvivlesyg* "scepticism"; *Tvetydighed* "ambiguity"). Hence to speak of the aesthete as "in despair" is to ascribe to him a doubled consciousness, not unlike the "double-mindedness" (*Tyvesyndethed*) later described in *Purity of Heart*. The aesthete may appear to persevere in one project or another, but every moment he is beyond it, recognizing its nullity, recognizing in fact the nullity of all aesthetic projects, the failure of his life. This latter recognition is communicated ironically through his preface to the Seducer's Diary, a preface which ends with this comment on the Seducer:

> He did not belong to reality, and yet he had much to do with it .... He was not unequal to the weight of reality; he was not too weak to bear it, not at all, he was too strong; but this strength was really a sickness (*E/O* 1.302).

As readers of Eremita's original preface, we already know (or at least suspect) that the aesthete is really describing himself, that in pointing out the Seducer's "sickness" he is really remarking on his own. Once again the "Chinese puzzle-box" structure of the book has proved important, revealing this time the interior duplicity of the aesthete's life, the fact that he cannot help but live beyond himself.

At first glance, Judge Wilhelm, author of the papers of *B*, appears to be the polar opposite of the aesthete. Husband, father, and man of affairs, firmly anchored in the world through a permanent commitment to his chosen profession, he would seem to be the very antithesis of the melancholic and mercurial aesthete. Whereas the aesthete wrote mannered and ironic essays, the Judge writes straightforward letters; his tone of earnest admonition could not be farther from the aesthete's antic indirectness. All this at first glance; then we look a bit closer at these 70,000 word so-called "letters." True, the Judge begins each with an epistolary greeting – "My Friend" – but even he is aware that the letter form is forced and artificial. The aim of these lines, he points out at the beginning, "is to make still one more attempt to force into the form of a letter the copious inquiry which is remitted to you herewith" (*E/O* 2.5). Only a few pages later the pretense is given up with the Judge's admission that "I am compelled to call what I am here writing a little inquiry, although at first I thought only of a big letter" (*E/O* 2.29). So what we have is a treatise or inquiry masquerading as a letter. But the masquerade is even more complicated, since, as the Judge points out on the first page, he is writing on large sheets of foolscap in ruled columns, paper which might give the impression this was some kind of official document. Once again, through a pattern that has become repetitive, we are prompted to question whether the outward is the inward, the manifest the concealed.

All the more reason, then, to question the Judge's motives in writing these admonitory letters to his "young friend," the aesthete. Even on a manifest level there are clues that the Judge is adopting a *persona* in these letters. His very act in writing them – the way he writes them – is unsuited to his chosen role as ethical exemplar. "Perhaps in my letters," he speculates, "I might even succeed here and there in being eloquent, though this is a gift to which I make no claim and which my profession in life does not require of me" (*E/O* 2.9). Several hundred pages later he observes even more interestingly: "Here I will bring my theorizing to an end. I feel keenly that I am not suited to this part, nor do I desire to be, but I should be completely satisfied if I might be regarded as a fairly practical fellow" (*E/O* 2.270). Why the "theorizing?" Why the writing of 70,000 word treatises on marriage and the ethical life? The Judge makes no secret of his desire to save his "young friend" from the perdition of aesthetic despair. But is this the only – or even the principal – reason for these "letters"?

The letters themselves have such an odd character: jumbled, fragmentary, sometimes dialectical and pompous, they often seem to double back on themselves. Judge Wilhelm criticizes the aesthete for living in imagination but often invites the aesthete to accompany him on imaginative excursions: "Imagine a little peasant girl on Christmas Eve," he suggests, "Imagine a young man .... Imagine the Emperor Nero" (*E/O* 2.45, 65, 192). He criticizes the romantic bias of the aesthete's life, yet now and then reveals a similar bias in his own life (*E/O* 2.21, 181). Even more to the point, his relation to his "young friend" seems extraordinarily complex. The ending of the second letter with its assertion of secrecy – "I will never talk to you about it. That you receive such a letter remains a secret .... I can well love you at a distance even though we often see one another" (*E/O* 2.338) – this ending communicates nothing so much as the tone of a clandestine affair. There is condescension in the Judge's relation to A, but there is also a kind of preoccupation. He is repelled by A, but also fascinated, even obsessed, by him. "I sometimes feel with a certain indignation," he tells A, "that you infect me, that I am letting myself be carried away ... into the same aesthetic-intellectual intoxication in which you live? With you, therefore, I have a certain feeling of insecurity ..." (*E/O* 2.17). In actual fact, then, the Judge is not nearly so confident about the adequacy of the ethical life as he may have seemed. These letters are in effect an *apologia pro vita sua*, a defense of the Judge's bourgeois life against the laughter of the young aesthete. More than a defense, they are also an idealization of that life.

Consider, for example, the closing pages of *Either/Or* where the Judge describes his own life as bourgeois. He allows that now and then he too comes to "subside into himself," permitting a "melancholy" to gain ascendency over him. But swiftly the presence of his wife resuscitates him. "I take part in everything she undertakes," he observes, "and it ends with my being again reconciled with time, finding that time acquires significance for me, that the instant moves swiftly" (*E/O* 2.312). He goes on to relate how he returns from work to the beautiful tones of his wife's lullabye, how he enters to "hear the cry of the little one" which to his ear "is not inharmonious" (*E/O* 2.329). There is a peace here, a feeling of time passing happily, of a harmony between individual and world, that is quite touching. Touching – but when we stop to consider – also false to the core.

For this is not Judge Wilhelm's own life, but an image of the bourgeois life as idyll that he is imagining. Even his supposed "descriptions" of his wife are poetic fancy, for we never meet her directly but encounter only his refraction of her into the ideal wife, the eternal feminine with her exemplary "comprehension of finiteness" (*E/O* 2.316). As we consider the Judge's letters as a whole, we come to recognize his fundamental volatility. They do not portray a man anchored in the concrete through action, but rather paint the features of an extravagant bourgeois who has substituted a romance of the commonplace for the aesthete's diary of seduction. His mind is filled with visions of a life that has become lively through self-choice, of a wife whose sole function is to cure his melancholy with her cheerful innocence, and finally of a lonely religiosity that takes shape in the alleged sermon of a nameless Jutland priest. Much as the "Diary of the Seducer" closes *Either/Or*, Volume 1 by pointing beyond the aesthete's fancies, so this sermon ends Volume 2 by pointing beyond the Judge's bourgeois idyll.

The title of the alleged sermon is "The Edification Implied in the Thought that as Against God We are always in the Wrong." Its lesson is the disastrous effect of trying to calculate one's own moral worth, an attempt that leads inevitably to self-doubt and ultimately to despair. Using one of the Judge's favorite expressions the Jutland priest asks, "One does what one can? ... Was it not for this reason your dread was so painful ... that the more earnestly you desired to act, ... so much the more dreadful became the duplicity in which you found yourself, wondering whether you had done what you could ..." (*E/O* 2.347). But the Judge had proposed to vanquish "dread" and "duplicity" through his notion of ethical choice. In a preface to the alleged sermon – supposedly a gift the Judge is sending along to his "young friend" as moral instruction – he hints that in sending it he means to acknowledge the failure of the ethical life. "Take it," he implores his young friend, "I have read it and thought of myself – read it then and think of yourself" (*E/O* 2.342).

It is important to hold in mind the alleged character of the sermon. Ostensibly it is in the handwriting of the Jutland priest who wrote it, but Victor Eremita makes no mention of any such third hand-writing in his account of the manuscripts. If Judge Wilhelm is really its author (just as we believe *A* to be the author of the "Diary of the Seducer"), then clearly it shows a move on his part beyond the standpoint announced in the earlier two letters. Adopting this premise (which like all ascriptions of identity in *Either/Or* must remain open to question) it becomes apparent how the two volumes are similarly structured. Each volume finally reveals its pseudonymous author as beyond the position ascribed to him. Neither the Judge nor the aesthete should be identified with the view each is supposed to represent. Their own outlooks are inherently ambiguous; the Judge is only ambiguously an ethical man, the aesthete only ambiguously an aesthete. And when we turn to the position of the putative author of the whole book, Victor Eremita, ambiguity is only compounded. For where does Victor stand? We have only his covert hint – "let us imagine a man who had lived through both of these phases" – that he is somehow beyond both viewpoints.

In this way, then, it is not simply from "outside" – from the reader's standpoint – that the speakers of *Either/Or* have ambiguous identities. For we see now that from "inside" they betray a similar ambiguity, a fundamental incapacity to identify themselves with the view they supposedly exemplify. Beyond themselves in some ineradicable way, they can be what they are only in the mode of not being it. Their lives awash in ambiguity they fade from view leaving us only with a series of perplexing questions. Is the Jutland priest really Judge Wilhelm? Is the Seducer really the aesthete *A*? Or are all these figures only various *personae* of Victor Eremita? We cannot know the answers to any of these questions, since the book provides no answers. It provides only a fictional landscape where strategem is coiled within deception, where perspectives shift and collide leaving the reader no firm ground for judgement, where all clear seeing is impossible, where the most one is granted is a face half-seen in a mirror or a shape disappearing around a corner.

V

The pattern exemplified in *Either/Or* is reflected in the other pseudonymous works. For here too we encounter characters separated from the life-views they espouse or describe. While the Judge and the aesthete were beyond the views they represented, in the remaining work we encounter pseudonyms fascinated by life-views they can imagine but not live. Think now of Johannes de Silentio who can imagine the faith of an Abraham but cannot live it. Or of Constantine Constantius who can imagine the thunderstorm of "repetition" but who cannot himself receive it. Or of Frater Taciturnus who only through a "thought experiment" can entertain the possibility of a life that lies beyond him. Or finally of Johannes Climacus, who, although unable to make the movements of faith, can conceptually construct the ladder (Latin: *climacis*) leading to it. It is true that many of these pseudonyms entertain visions of an existence became preternaturally dense, of a life made truly lively, of a humanity passionately fulfilled. But what commentators forget in offering us this vision of existence as Kierkegaard's, is the distance the pseudonyms insist upon between themselves and their visions. Johannes de Silentio does not exist as a knight of faith, nor Climacus as a subjective thinker; they insist upon the contrary. From the standpoint of the individual pseudonym his existence is neither thick nor substantial nor opaque, but infinitely porous, ventilated by dreams, fancies, hopes, fears, taunted by such myriad possibilities that often he becomes fantastic even to himself.

Thus witness the appearance of pseudonyms like those in *Either/Or* whose trustworthiness, even whose existence, vanishes with the scratch of a pen. For just as in *Either/Or* A called into question the veracity of the seducer – and Eremita his very existence – so in later books we observe whole pseudonyms disappearing in the twinkling of an eye. After tempting the reader into taking seriously the identity of the "young man" in *Repetition*, Constantine Constantius suddenly admits it is all a joke – the "young man" is really his imaginary creation. Likewise in *Stages on Life's Way*: after describing in florid detail how he found Quidam's diary at the bottom of a lake,

Frater Taciturnus finally admits that he made up not only the diary but Quidam himself. The question – Whom are we to believe? – is not just a question for the reader of *Either/Or*, but a question for the reader of any of the pseudonyms. Take, for example, the *Postscript*. In that book are we to believe Johnanes Climacus, and if so, when? When he tells us the book is an innocent amusement, or when he tells us it is an earnest attempt to protect Christianity from the depradations of speculative philosophy? When he describes in tones of moving solemnity the suffering of the subjective thinker, or when he slyly exclaims, before revoking the whole book, "Why this sounds almost like earnestness!"

The world of the pseudonyms is really the world of *Either/Or* writ large, a world where we never encounter Kierkegaard speaking directly, but only posing riddles, trapping us in conundrums, laying down false trails and then laughing when we take the bait. It was a sense for this world that prompted John Updike to insist that "duplicity was the very engine of Kierkegaard's thought," that he was a "man in love with duplicity and irony and all double-edged things."[7] I believe Updike is right but that he fails to go far enough. For it is not simply that Kierkegaard favored "duplicity," but rather that he saw the human condition as inherently duplicitous. "The possibility of doubt," wrote Kierkegaard's pseudonym Johannes Climacus, "then lies in consciousness, whose very essence is a kind of contradiction or opposition. It is produced by, and itself produces, a sort of duplicity."[8] Somewhat later, Anti-Climacus makes a parallel point in *The Sickness Unto Death*. After pointing to the centrality of fantasy in the human psyche – that "it is not one faculty on a par with others, but is the faculty of faculties" – he goes on to identify it with the self:

Fantasy is the reflection of the process of infinitizing .... The self is reflection, and fantasy is reflection, it is the counterfeit presentation of the self which is the self's possibility.[9]

If this equation stands, its consequences are devastating. For it follows necessarily that we cannot escape illusion about ourselves. To use Climacus' words, "we are in a half-obscurity about our own condition" (*Sickness*, 181) not in any accidental way, but in an essential way. For none of our possibilities are really ours, all are counterfeit images, fabrications that we are beyond in the very act of reaching towards them.

The argument, I believe, runs something like this: Try to level with yourself. Try to discover who you really are and what you truly want. You say in your heart of hearts you are only a simple man who wants to be happy. Alright, try it. You'll soon discover that you're searching for an imaginary self which never was nor ever could be. You try to catch hold of immediate life and swiftly immediacy vanishes. Or try something else. You say you really are an ethical man and that what you want is just to live a life of duty. Try it. But don't forget to ask yourself what founds this life, ultimately, but your choice of it. And don't pay too close attention to the guilt which soon stalks your footsteps and makes the ideal of duty recede before you. Or say that you want to be a religious man. Once again faith recedes as quickly as you near it, always slipping just out of your grasp, always subject to the doubt that it is only "bad faith." Any possibility you choose you will recognize sooner or later to be *not* you; nor do you have the opportunity of not choosing since not choosing is itself a chosen possibility. Except for the single escape clause hinted at by Anti-Climacus – the grounding of the self "transparently in the Power that constituted it" (*Sickness*, 147, 162) – any attempt to realize self-identity is doomed to failure. Although Kierkegaard may not always have been clear on this point, I think the outcome of his thinking is to define human experience as nothing more or less than the activity of duplicity.

If this view be accepted, then it becomes clear why the authorship of *Either/Or* in particular and the pseudonymous works in general have been wrapped in such "Chinese puzzle-box" ambiguity. If human identities are by their very nature ambiguous, if we are who we are only through a kind of self-impersonation – that is, by being always distant from ourselves – then it is clear that the device of pseudonymity has become itself a parable of the human condition. When the aesthete impersonates the Seducer, when the Judge imper-sonates the Jutland priest, or finally when Victor Eremita imperso-nates all of them, their masquerade only illustrates the self-imperso-nation of our own lives. It was an awareness of this sort which made Kierkegaard complain in his journal: "Each time I wish to say some-thing there is another who says it at the very same moment. It is as if I were always thinking double, as if my other self were always somehow ahead of me" (1A.333).

As we remarked at the outset, the most obvious consequence of the device of pseudonymity is to leave the identity of the author ambiguous. This ambiguity must be seen to have meaning on a variety of levels.

On the most straightforward, literary level it simply poses the problem of the unreliable narrator. In trying to answer the question, "Who is the author of *Either/Or*?" we necessarily must ask the question, "Who is telling the truth in *Either/Or*?" But this latter question – like the former – has no answer. In trying to answer it we as readers become more and more perplexed; we finally recognize with a vengeance the point Climacus later argues in the *Postscript* – that all "historical results" are the products of belief but not knowledge. Like the speakers of many of the pseudonymous works we seem to have been caught up in a puzzle with no solution. On this literary level, ambiguity of authorship has performed the function of inducing in the mind of the reader the state of mind exemplified in the book. In this way *Either/Or* becomes something more than a mere description of "double-mindedness" no matter how vivid; rather it becomes a device for showing the reader his own "double-mindedness."

On a philosophical level it performs a more general function, for here the claim embedded in the authorial stance is simply that there is no such thing as a privileged perspective. In capsule form, this is really the claim Kierkegaard wants to prosecute through his pseudonym Johannes Climacus in the *Postscript*. According to Climacus, the speculative philosopher claimed such a perspective for himself; he claimed to see *sub speciae aeternitatis* and the right to proclaim the results of that seeing directly. This notion, suggests Climacus, is a classic case of philosophical *hubris*. Such a privileged and eternal standpoint may indeed exist, but it exists for God and not for the speculative philosopher. For the rest of us – we must be prepared to live in a world where no one can see the truth clearly, and hence where no one has the right to proclaim it directly, unambiguously. Although the lectorial stance of the speculative philosopher required it, there is no privileged perspective available from which the truth may be discerned. In *Either/Or* we are denied the solid footing we require in order to judge between the utterances of the speakers, to distinguish the veridical from the chimerical. Inferentially, this is the lesson of all the pseudonyms: the privileged perspective is absent. To make the same point in another way: by writing pseudonymously Kierkegaard is simply showing us – not telling us – that God does not speak!

Finally, however, Kierkegaard is a religious writer, and it is on a religious plane that the device of pseudonymity and its consequence – ambiguity of authorship – gather their richest meaning. As we have seen, the ambiguity we encounter in trying to disentangle the speakers of *Either/Or* is not accidental but essential. Our inability to find out who they really are is echoed by their own inability to find out who they really are. They – like us – are imposters, shot through with volatility. Their minds – like ours – are inflamed with visions, tantalized by hopes, overfull with theories they can never validate, doubts they can never assuage, feelings they can never comprehend. Like us, they never succeed in becoming integral, never overcome a fundamental volatility and duplicity. Kierkegaard, I believe, means for us to grasp this volatility and duplicity as the limit of our condition, a limit through which – darkly, ambiguously – the presence of God might be suspected. For it is the single, often repeated refrain of Kierkegaard's negative theology that God appears to man only at the limit. Within the frame of that theological vision man can see God only fleetingly – out of the corner of his eye, so to speak – as he encounters his own unsurpassable limits. I mean to suggest that in *Either/Or* we have been given a taste of those limits in the ambiguity of conscious life which is the book's ambience. Ambiguity – I can hear Kierkegaard saying – is the very abode of the religious man. He must learn to live there and not flee from it, for it is only there that God's absent presence may be discerned. And here our argument comes full circle. For Kierkegaard once characterized God in the following terms, terms we might think equally applicable to the real author of *Either/Or*: "No anonymous author can more cunningly conceal himself, no practitioner of the maieutic art can more carefully withdraw himself, ... than God. He is in creation, and present everywhere in it, but directly He is not there" (*CUP* 218).

Kierkegaard knew that literature and philosophy – like human lives – must be fabrications. We fabricate our lives just as artists and thinkers fabricate their works. It is not just *Either/Or* which is a "forgery." Nor, on a larger scale, is it literature and philosophy which are fraudulent. Rather it is man himself who is finally duplicitous, man himself who secretes illusion from his very pores yet cannot stop yearning for the replacement of illusion by a reality so unknown it can only be called divine.

NOTES

1. *Søren Kierkegaards Papirer.* Second Edition. Edited by P.A. Heiberg, V. Kuhr, and E. Torsting. In 20 Volumes (Copenhagen: Gyldendal, 1909-48), 9, Section A, Item 171. Successive *Papirer* references will appear in parentheses in the text: e.g. (9.A.171).
2. The drafts of both letters appear in Volume 4 of the *Papirer* 4.B.19-20.
3. This article appeared in the Feb. 27, 1843 issue of *Faedrelandet.* It is reprinted in

Søren Kierkegaards Samlede Vaerker, First Edition, (Copenhagen: Gyldendal, 1901-06), 13.407-410.

4. Søren Kierkegaard, *Either/Or*, Vol. I (Princeton: Princeton University Press, 1971), 1.14. Successive references to *Either/Or* will appear in parentheses in the text: e.g. (*E/O* 1.14). I have checked this translation against the original and where necessary have changed the wording of excerpts to more accurately reflect Kierkegaard's Danish.

5. Søren Kierkegaard, *Concluding Unscientific Postscript* (Princeton: Princeton University Press, 1944), 320. Successive references to the *Postscript* will appear in parentheses in the text: e.g. (*CUP* 320).

6. Wayne Booth, *The Rhetoric of Fiction* (Chicago: The University of Chicago Press, 1961), 158-159, 295.

7. John Updike, "The Fork," *The New Yorker* (Feb. 26, 1966), 134.

8. Søren Kierkegaard, *Johannes Climacus or, De Omnibus Dubitandum Est* (Stanford: Stanford University Press, 1958), 149. I have changed the translation to agree more precisely with the Danish text.

9. Søren Kierkegaard, *Sickness Unto Death* (Princeton: Princeton University Press, 1968), 163-164. Once again I have adjusted the translation to more accurately reflect the meaning of the Danish text. Successive references to *Sickness Unto Death* will appear in parentheses in the text: e.g. (*Sickness*, 163-164).

Part V: BIBLIOGRAPHY OF THE WRITINGS OF ROBERT S. BRUMBAUGH

ROBERT S. BRUMBAUGH - BIBLIOGRAPHY

Books:

1950   with Newton P. Stallknecht. *The Spirit of Western Philosophy.* New York: Longmans, Green.

1954   with Newton P. Stallknecht. *The Compass of Philosophy.* New York: Longmans, Green. Reprinted New York, 1974.

1954   *Plato's Mathematical Imagination.* Bloomington, Indiana: Indiana University Publications, Vol. 29. Reprinted New York, 1968.

1961   *Plato on the One.* New Haven: Yale University Press. Reprinted New York, 1972.

1962   *Plato for the Modern Age.* New York: Crowell Collier. Reprinted Westport, 1979.

1962   edited with Rulon S. Wells. *Plato Manuscripts: A Catalogue of Microfilms in the Plato Microfilm Project, Yale University Library,* Parts 1, 2, 3. New Haven: Yale University Library.

1963   with Nathaniel Lawrence. *Philosophers on Education.* Boston: Houghton Mifflin.

1964   *The Philosophers of Greece.* New York: Crowell. Reprinted London: Allen and Unwin, 1966, and Albany: SUNY Press, 1969.

1965   *Ancient Greek Gadgets and Machines.* New York: Crowell. Reprinted 1968.

1968   edited with Rulon S. Wells. *The Plato Manuscripts: A New Index,* New Haven: Yale University Press.

1969   Editor. *The Impact of the Six Great Trials.* New York: Crowell.

1973   with Nathaniel Lawrence. *Philosophical Themes in Modern Education.* Boston: Houghton Mifflin. Reprinted 1985.

1978   *The Most Mysterious Manuscript: The Voynich 'Roger Bacon' Cipher Manuscript.* Carbondale, Illinois: SIU Press

1982   *Whitehead, Process Philosophy, and Education.* Albany: SUNY Press.

1984   *Unreality and Time.* Albany: SUNY Press.

Monograph:

1982   *History and an Interpretation of the Text of Plato's Parmenides.*
        Philosophy Research Activities, 8, Microfiche.

Articles:

1947   "Broad and Narrow Context Techniques of Literary Criti-
        cism." *English Journal* 293-299.
1948   "Note on the Numbers in Plato's Critias." *Classical Philology*
        40-42.
1949   "Note on Plato, *Republic* IX., 587D." *Classical Philology*
        197-199.
1949   "Early Greek Theories of Sex Determination." *Journal of
        Heredity* 40: 49-50.
1951   "An Aristotelian Defense of 'Non-Aristotelian' Logics."
        Journal of Philosophy 48: 582-585.
1951   Review of R.P. McKeon's *Democracy in a World of Tensions.*
        In *Indiana Law Journal* 592-595.
1951   "Teaching Plato's *Republic* VIII and IX." *Classical Journal*
        46: 343-348.
1951   "Colors of the Hemispheres in Plato's Myth of Er (*Republic*
        616E)." *Classical Philology* 46: 173-176.
1951   "The Genetic Theories of Empedocles." *Journal of Heredity*
        42: 301-303.
1952   "Plato's Divided Line." *Review of Metaphysics* 5: 529-534.
1952   "Plato Studies as Contemporary Philosophy." *Review of
        Metaphysics* 6: 315-324.
1952   "Genetic Theory in the Pythagorean School." *Journal of
        Heredity* 43: 86-88.
1952   "On Recent Translations." *Yearbook of Comparative and
        General Literature* 1: 1-2.
1953   "Preface to Cosmography." *Review of Metaphysics* 7: 53-63.
1953   "Logic and Longitude: The Syllogism, East and West."
        Proceedings of the 28th Indian Philosophical Congress 143-147.
1954   "Plato's *Republic* 616E: The Final 'Law of Nines'." *Classical
        Philology* 49: 33-34.
1954   "Duty Between Nations and Their Citizens." *Report of the
        UNESCO Indian Philosophical Congress* 27-30.
1954   Review of R.B. Levinson's *In Defense of Plato.* In *Classical
        Philology* 49: 105-106.

1954 "Plato's Genetic Theory." *Journal of Heredity* 45: 191-195.

1954 "Aristotle's Outline of the Problems of First Philosophy." *Review of Metaphysics* 7: 511-521.

1954 "Some Recent Works on Aristotle." *Review of Metaphysics* 7: 602-612.

1954 "Plato's 'Parmenides': A Report on New Source Material." *Review of Metaphysics* 8: 200-203.

1954 Review of R.P. McKeon's *Freedom and History*. In *Journal of Philosophy* 51: 531-533.

1955 Review of P. Merlan's *From Platonism to Neo-Platonism*. In *Philosophical Review* 64: 318-319.

1955 "Aristotle as a Mathematician." *Review of Metaphysics* 8: 379-393.

1958 "Plato's *Cratylus*: The Order of Etymologies." *Review of Metaphysics* 11: 502-510.

1958 "Aphilosophical First Philosophy." *Proceedings of the 11th International Philosophical Congress* 11 (Venice): 48-58.

1959 "Plato's *Parmenides* and Positive Metaphysics." *Review of Metaphysics* 13: 271-277.

1959 with Nathanial Lawrence. "Aristotle's Philosophy of Education," *Educational Theory* 9: 1-15.

1960 with Rulon S. Wells. "The Plato Microfilm Project," *Yale Library Gazette* 1-4.

1960 "A Latin Translation of Plato's *Parmenides*." *Review of Metaphysics* 14: 91-109.

1961 "Science, Science Fiction, and Fiction." *Yale Scientific Magazine* 22-29.

1961 "Kinds of Time: An Excursion in First Philosophy." In *Experience, Existence and the Good*, edited by I.C. Lieb, 119-125. Carbondale: SIU Press.

1961 "Plato and the History of Science." *Studium Generale* 9: 520-527.

1961 "Logical and Mathematical Symbolism in the Plato Scholia." *Journal of the Warburg Institute* 24: 45-58.

1961 "Platonic Possibility: Eternal Objects and the Myth of Er." *Actas Segundo Cong. Extraord. Interamericano de Filosofia*. Costa Rica. 347-351.

1961 "Papyrus Hibeh 184: An Early Footnote to Plato." *Actas Segundo Cong. Extraord. Interamericano de Filosofia* 351-355.

1961 "Justice and Jurisprudence: A Socratic Dialogue on Martin v. Donlin." *Connecticut Bar Journal* 127-134. Reprinted in *Insurance Counsel Journal* 1962: 116-120.

1962   "Plato" and "Proclus" for 1962 revision of *Encyclopedia Americana*.

1964   with Col. Paul H. Sherrick. "Pneuma and the Earth in Space," *Studium Generale* 17: 263-266.

1964   Foreword to L. Versenyi's *Socratic Humanism*. New Haven: Yale University Press.

1965   "A Reply to Charles F.S. Virtue's Review of 'Philosophers on Education'." In *Studies in the Philosophy of Education* 4: 83-85.

1965   "Logic and Time." *Review of Metaphysics* 18: 649-656.

1965   "Whitehead as a Philosopher of Education: Abstraction, Action, Satisfaction." *Educational Theory* 15: 277-281.

1965   "Logical and Mathematical Symbolism in the Plato Scholia, II: A Thousand Years of Diffusion and Redesign." *Journal of the Warburg Institute* 28: 1-13.

1965   "Gadgets and Greek Philosophy." *Greek Heritage Magazine* 38-45.

1965   "Greek Gadgetry." *Helicon* (Literary Magazine of Saybrook College, Yale University) 1-13.

1966   "Applied Metaphysics: Truth and Passing Time." *Review of Metaphysics* 19: 647-666.

1966   "Whitehead's Educational Theory: Two Supplementary Notes to *The Aims of Education*." *Educational Theory* 16: 210-215.

1966   Review of I.M. Crombie's *An Examination of Plato's Doctrines* Vol. 2, "Plato on Knowledge and Reality." In *The Modern Schoolman* 43: 274-277.

1966   Review of L. Taran's *Parmenides*. In *International Philosophical Quarterly* 6: 496-499.

1967   "Kinds of Time: An Excursion in First Philosophy." In *Experience, Existence, and the Good: Essays in Honor of Paul Weiss*, 119-126. Carbondale: SIU Press.

1967   "A New Interpretation of Plato's *Republic*." *Journal of Philosophy* 64: 661-670.

1967   "Plato at Skidmore." *Politeia* (Skidmore College Literary Magazine) 5-13.

1967   Review of Gilbert Ryle's *Plato's Progress*. In *Journal of Value Inquiry* 1: 271-274.

1968   "Letter to a Selective Conscientious Objector." *Yale Alumni Magazine* 34-35.

1968   "Protection from One's Self, a Socratic Dialogue on Maycock v. Martin." *Connecticut Bar Journal* 34-35.

1968 "Three Lectures: Applied Philosophy, Education, Location." Two Orde Wingate Lectures and one Hebrew University Philosophical Society Lecture. In Hebrew translation, *IYYUN* Vol. 19. English summaries, *IYYUN.*, 19: 262-264.

1968 "Logical and Mathematical Symbolism in the Plato Scholia, III." *Journal of the Warburg Institute* 31: 1-11.

1968 Review of C.J. Glacken's *Traces on the Rhodian Shore.* In *ISIS* 332-333.

1970 Review of C. Bigger's *Participation.* In *Journal of Value Inquiry* 4.

1970 "Plato's Philosophy of Education: The *Meno* Experiment and the *Republic* Curriculum." *Educational Theory* 20: 207-228.

1970 "Applied Metaphysics and Social Unrest." *Metaphilosophy* 1: 66-70.

1970 "Plato's Atlantis." *Yale Alumni Magazine* 22-28.

1970 "From Time to Time." *Yale Reports* #571.

1970 "The Divided Line and the Direction of Inquiry." *Philosophical Forum* 2: 172-199.

1971 Review of A. Wyller's *Der Spate Platon.* In *Classical World* 64: 160.

1971 "Cosmography." *Review of Metaphysics* 25: 333-347.

1972 "Scientific Apparatus Onstage in 423 B.C." *Yale Classical Studies* 22: 215-221.

1972 "Changes of Value Order and Choices in Time." In *Value and Valuation*, edited by John W. Davis, 49-63. Knoxville: University of Tennessee Press.

1972 "The Text of Plato's *Parmenides.*" *Review of Metaphysics* 140-148.

1973 "Education and Reality: Two Revolutions." *Thought* 48: 5-18.

1973 "Cosomography: The Problem of Modern Systems." *Review of Metaphysics* 26: 511-521.

1973 "Formal Value Theory: Transfinite Ordinal Numbers and Relatively Practical Choices." *Journal of Human Relations* Vol. 21.

1974 "Botany and the 'Roger Bacon' Manuscript Once More." *Speculum* 49: 546-548.

1975 "Systems, Tenses, and Choices." *Midwestern Journal of Philosophy* (Spring): 9-13.

1975 "A Response to Professor Plochmann." *Midwestern Journal of Philosophy* (Spring): 14-16.

1975   "The Solution of the Voynich 'Roger Bacon' Cipher." *Yale Library Gazette* 347-355.

1975   Abstract of "Plato's *Meno* as Form and as Content of Secondary School Courses in Philosophy." *High School Philosophy Newsletter* 3: i, 3 ff.

1975   "Plato's *Meno* as Form and as Content of Secondary School Courses in Philosophy." *Teaching Philosophy* 1: 107-115.

1975   Comments on "Plato's *Meno* as Form and as Content of Secondary School Courses in Philosophy." *Teaching Philosophy* 1: 116-125.

1975   "The Knossos Game Board." *American Journal of Archaeology* 79: 135-137.

1976   "Notes on the History of Plato's Text: With the *Parmenides* as a Case Study." *Paideia* 67-78.

1976   "The Voynich 'Roger Bacon' Cipher Manuscript: Deciphered Maps of Stars." *Journal of the Warburg Institute* 39: 139-150.

1976   "Plato's Relation to the Arts and Crafts." In *Facets of Plato's Philosophy*, edited by W. Werkmeister, 40-52. *Phronesis*, Supplementary Volume 2.

1977   "The Puzzle of the Copyist of Yale's Olympiodorus Manuscript." *Studia Codicologica.* edited by the Berlin Academy, 113-115.

1977   "Robert Hartman's Formal Axiology: An Extension." *Journal of Value Inquiry* 11: 259-263.

1978   "The Unity of Aristotle's *Metaphysics*." *Midwest Journal of Philosophy* 6 (Spring): 1-12.

1978   "Of Man, Animals, and Morals: A Brief History." In *On the Fifth Day*, edited by R.K. Morris and M.W. Fox, 6-26. Washington, D.C.: Acropolis Press

1978   "Notes on Art, Aesthetics, and Form." *Par Rapport* 1: 23-25.

1978   "Metaphysical Presuppositions and the Study of Time." In the *Proceedings* of the International Conference for the Study of Time, edited by Fraser and Lawrence, Vol. III, 1-21. New York: Springer Verlag.

1979   "Space: Neither Void Nor Plenum." *Process Studies* 7:3 161-172.

1979   "Causes and Revolutions in Aristotle's Political Theory." *Paideia* Special Aristotle Issue (Winter).

1980   "Time Passes: Platonic Variations." *Review of Metaphysics*

33: 711-726.

1980 with Jessica Schwartz. "Pythagoras and Beans: A Medical Explanation." *The Classical World* 73: 421-423.

1980 "Criticism in Philosophy: Aristotle's Literary Form." In *Philosophical Style*, edited by Berel Lang, 294-310. Chicago: Nelson Hall.

1980 Review of N. White's *A Companion to Plato's Republic*. In *Teaching Philosophy* 3: 233-234.

1980 "Teaching Plato's *Republic* VIII and IX." Revised Reprint from *Classical Journal* 46 (1951): 343-348. *Teaching Philosophy* 3: 331-337.

1980 "The Purposes of Plato's *Parmenides*." *Ancient Philosophy* 1: 39-48.

1980 Notes on "A Day in Court," "The Lead Rule," "The Names of Poseidon's Sons and the Historicity of Atlantis," and "A Cautionary Note About the Plato Ms. Venice T." *Ancient Philosophy* 1: 81-85.

1981 "A Classical Invention in Modern Incarnation: The Geometric *Psykter*." *Ancient Philosophy* 1: 179.

1982 Review of J. Owens' *Aristotle*. In *Classical World* 15: 377-378.

1982 Review of G. Lloyd's *Magic, Reason and Experience*. In *Classical World* 76: 169-170.

1982 "Cantor's Sets and Proclus' Wholes." In *The Structure of Being*, edited by B. Harris, 104-113. Albany: SUNY Press.

1983 "Doctrine and Dramatic Dates of Plato's Dialogues." In *Essays in Ancient Greek Philosophy*, Vol. 2, edited by Anton and Preus, 174-185. Albany: SUNY Press.

1983 "Note on Systematic Mispunctuation of Plato Mss. of the B Family." *Ancient Philosophy* 3: 89-90.

1983 "Diction and Dialectic: The Language of Plato's Stranger from Elea." In *Language and Thought in Early Greek Philosophy*, edited by K. Robb, 266-276. La Salle, Illinois: Monist Library of Philosophy.

1984 Review of R. Neville's *Reconstruction of Thinking*. In *Philosophy and Rhetoric* 17: 182-184.

1984 Review of J.T. Fraser's *The Genesis and Evolution of Time*. In *Review of Metaphysics* 38: 121-122.

1984 Editor. A.N. Whitehead, "Discussion Upon Fundamental Principles of Education, (1919)." *Process Studies* 14: 41-43.

1984 "The Mathematical Imagery of Plato, *Republic* X." *Teaching Philosophy* 7: 223-228.

1984   Review of Charles Hartshorne's *Insights and Oversights of Great Thinkers: An Evaluation of Western Philosophy.* In *Ancient Philosophy* 4: 253-254.

1985   Review of B.A.F. Hubbard and E.S. Karnofsky's *Plato's Gorgias: A Socratic Commentary.* In *Thinking* 68.

1985   Review of Sal Restivo's *The Social Relations of Physics, Mysticism, and Mathematics.* In *Review of Metaphysics* 38: 682-683.

1985   with Rulon Wells. "Yale's Plato Project." *Diotima* 13: 19-28.

1986   "If Aristotle had become head of the Academy... " *Energeia*, Etudes Aristoteliciennes Offertus A Mgr. Antonio Jannone, 102-116. Paris: Librairie Philosopique J. Vrin.

1986   Introduction to Brian Hendley's *Dewey, Russell, Whitehead: Philosophers as Educators.* Carbondale, Illinois: SIU Press.

1987   "Plato's Ideal Curriculum and Contemporary Philosophy of Education." *Educational Theory* 37: 169-177.